MEMORIAL EDITION

WITH PREFACE AND ADDITIONS

Southern Belle

By MARY CRAIG SINCLAIR

with a Foreword by Upton Sinclair

© 1957 BY MARY CRAIG SINCLAIR
© 1962 BY UPTON SINCLAIR

LIBRARY OF CONGRESS CATALOG CARD NUMBER 62-13777

SINCLAIR PRESS

LITHOGRAPHED IN THE UNITED STATES OF AMERICA
BY TYLER PRINTING COMPANY, PHOENIX, ARIZONA

CONTENTS

IN MEMORIAM

My beloved wife, wise, kind and lovely human soul, who guided my life for forty eight years, went to her rest at the age of seventy eight.

She had written and published this book of memoirs. The choice of title was mine.

This Memorial Edition has been prepared for free distribution to public libraries of cities and towns; libraries of universities, high schools and hospitals — anywhere over the world where people may be free to read the book. A copy will be sent, as long as copies are available, postpaid, to libraries which ask for it.

UPTON SINCLAIR

January, 1962

SINCLAIR PRESS, P.O. BOX 2503, PHOENIX, ARIZONA, U.S.A.

FOREWORD

THIS IS THE STORY of a Southern belle, told by a real one. There may be those who will smile at this statement, thinking that all the charm and romance the term implies were just the imaginings of weavers of fiction. But there were many Southern belles and many men fell in love with them. Many men loved the one who lives in this book, and there was one true "first love." There were other suitors, midnight serenades, dancing on the lawn in the moonlight and a real wildcat escaping from its chains and taking part in the revelry.

My Southern belle remembers tenderly those dear dead days in that romantic "Old South." It was truly romantic, as she will prove to you; there was so much that was beautiful about it that it was easy to forget that there were old ex-slaves in the kitchen and in the cabins in the lane—still happy to serve their "white folks" in freedom. But this Southern belle was never complacent about those old black people in their ignorance and helplessness. She was not happy about many things in that beloved South. She troubled her elders with questions—her uncles, who owned great cotton plantations, and her father, the judge, who was called the richest planter in his part of the Mississippi Delta and had handled the estate of Jefferson Davis and of Davis' widow.

This Southern belle came North to Yankeeland to a finishing school just across Fifth Avenue from one of the Vanderbilt palaces. Several years later she came to New York again, seeking a publisher for a manuscript she had written about the sad fate of Winnie Davis, known to all the South as "the Daughter of the Confederacy." This time the daughter of Mississippi met many strange people, never known or imagined by the old South: the "intellectuals," the standard-bearers of causes, the crusaders for the "disinherited of the earth." She met figures of the literary world, all new and amazing: Clayton Hamilton, Walter Lippmann, Sinclair Lewis, Max Eastman,

Floyd Dell and Art Young. The California poet George Sterling fell on his knees before her and called her "a star in alabaster." He vowed to write her a sonnet a day for a hundred days and did so; the book of collected poems, *Sonnets to Craig*, is in the libraries.

Mary Craig Kimbrough, whose Southern mother had commissioned her to investigate the lineage of her titled English ancestors, was to find herself one evening seated across the dinner table from a cultivated colored gentleman. As the wife of a crusader, she was to find herself taking part in a public demonstration on lower Broadway devised to tell Mr. John D. Rockefeller, Jr. how *not* to run his Colorado coal mines. In short, this Southern belle gave up the moonlight and magnolias, the balls and the beaux, the luxury and the peace of mind for a new sort of adventure, in a world where there was poverty, danger, and distress of mind.

She undertook to be the helpmeet of a man who had set out to help in the ending of poverty and war in the world. It took Craig to Britain, Holland, Germany and France, to New York and California, with a Mississippi sojourn on the way. It required many crusades in which he bankrupted himself and her as well. It required a year-long entanglement in a bitter political campaign. She helped him to write and publish three million books and pamphlets, flowing into every country in the world. She built and guarded three storerooms to house his eight tons of literary papers and the thousand translations of a crusading author's works into some sixty languages.

In the course of her story you will meet many of the famous personalities of our time: Albert Einstein, George Bernard Shaw, Bertrand Russell, Blasco Ibañez, H. L. Mencken, Theodore Dreiser, Thomas Mann, Van Wyck Brooks, Henry Ford, Luther Burbank, Theodore Roosevelt, William McDougall, William Fox, Charlie Chaplin, Douglas Fairbanks, Sergei Eisenstein and many others. And most important of all, you will meet Craig, the loveliest woman I have ever known.

—Upton Sinclair

Monrovia, California
September, 1957

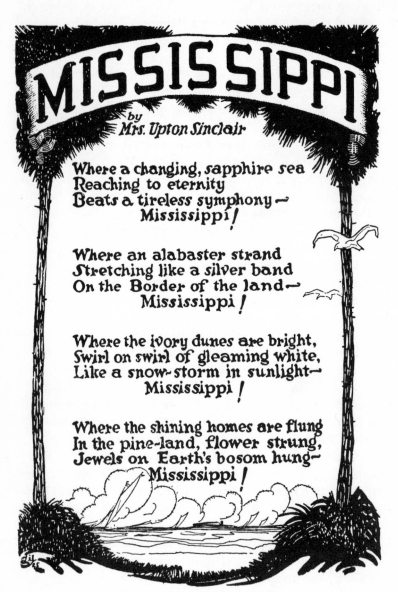

MISSISSIPPI

by
Mrs. Upton Sinclair

Where a changing, sapphire sea
Reaching to eternity
Beats a tireless symphony—
    Mississippi!

Where an alabaster strand
Stretching like a silver band
On the Border of the land—
    Mississippi!

Where the ivory dunes are bright,
Swirl on swirl of gleaming white,
Like a snow-storm in sunlight—
    Mississippi!

Where the shining homes are flung
In the pine-land, flower strung,
Jewels on Earth's bosom hung—
    Mississippi!

1. WHEN THE WORLD WAS YOUNG

I WAS BORN in the midst of vast cotton plantations. It was from them that my father's wealth came, and in our winter home in Greenwood, Mississippi, I spent more than half of each year of my childhood.

The owners of the plantations had inherited them. After the Civil War devastated the land, and set free their slaves, they had gone down the Mississippi to New Orleans, or up to St. Louis, and borrowed money from the banks to restock and re-equip their places and recoup their fortunes. The ex-slaves had been put back to work in the cottonfields, and so by the time I was born, things were about as they had been during the days of slavery.

These proud white people thought they were the lords of creation, and no "damyankees" could make them change their minds or their ways. Pleasure was the chief concern of their lives, and they sought it and had it, just as their parents had done in the old days. The Negroes also were a pleasure-loving people, not far in their minds from the jungles of Africa where their ancestors had lived.

My father, a hard-working judge, banker, and plantation owner, used to look at them and deplore the "natural defect in the blood of the Negro" which made him shiftless and averse to responsibility. There were people who thought that God had ordained this, and it was fortunate for the cotton planter, who could not have labored to raise his own crops in a sun that was as hot as Africa's. And it was fortunate for Mama too, for how could she have lived with so many babies, and so many parties to give, if there had not been Negro mammies and housegirls and cooks?

Aunt Catherine was a fixture in our kitchen long before I arrived on earth. She had been a slave, and though slavery had been abolished many years earlier, it had made no difference in Catherine's status as she knew it; she still "belonged," and

1

nothing on earth could have separated her from the family whose social prestige she shared. "Us colored peoples wuz happier then," I heard her say many times. "Us colored peoples had no 'sponsibility. De white folks had dat. An' dat's what I doan like about freedom, I doan want no 'sponsibility."

Among their former masters these black people had enough to eat, enough to wear, and roofs over their heads. The white planter furnished these because he could not afford not to; and the blacks had that thing precious to them, security.

Once one of the shopkeepers' wives in the town made an effort to seduce Catherine away from the family, and she came home and told Mama about it. "You know what dat white ooman done—she 'vited me in an' tole me to set down in her parlor! I wouldn't work for *no* white ooman what told me to set down in her parlor."

There were at least half a dozen ex-slaves of the family, both men and women, who lived in the cabins of our lane, and did a little work only when they felt like it. All of them had food from our house or from the plantation, and if they became sick, a doctor was called by the white folks. We were taught to treat these elderly blacks with the respect due to their age; without exception they were called "aunts" and "uncles." Catherine would say to one of my brothers, "Doan you give me no sass, boy. If you give me sass, I'll tell yo' mammy." And she never had to.

From infancy on I was used to black arms holding white children, and to black caresses. I never had anything from the black people but love. I heard their stories of slavery days, and learned much about the Civil War from them. Today in memory I plainly hear the voice of white-haired "Uncle" Henry telling a child how he was "the bodyguard" of my real Uncle William Morgan all through "de War"—there was only one war in the mind and speech of any Southerner, white or black, in those days. "I done carry him off de battlefiel' when he got shot," Uncle Henry would say; "wid dese yere arms I carried him, an' he tell you I save his life."

One night a fight broke out among our black people who

Our winter home was in Greenwood, Mississippi (*above*) and we spent our summers at Ashton Hall on the Mississippi Sound.

Half a dozen ex-slaves lived in the cabins of our lane and did a little work on the plantation when they felt like it. Uncle Jim, a field hand, never came into the "big house" in his life.

Portrait of Papa, hanging in Greenwood Courthouse, painted by Hunter's wife, Sally.

Mama, who always prided herself on the "blue blood" of her family.

were attending a dance in a cabin beside our woods. My father seized the empty shotgun which was always in the hall closet; he rushed off into the darkness, and my mother seized his loaded rifle and followed, ordering me to stay in the house. She was going to protect my six-foot-two father!

Unnecessary, because on the plantation, Papa's will was the law. These were "his" Negroes, and he would not shoot them because he knew they would obey him, and he needed their labor in the cotton fields. He waded among them, wielding the shotgun as a club and shouting to them to "get out." He was a powerful man, and they ran in a drove, scattering as they reached their homes. And then there was the task of binding up the wounds, which were made by razors, folded back, so that cuts were not deep but were long and bloody. Trusted house servants were sent to do this work. There was no doctor for ten or twenty miles, and if the foreman and the plantation manager happened not to be at hand, the plantation owner had to go with the servants to look after "his own."

This was in the Delta district of Mississippi, where we had our winter home, on the banks of the deep and dangerous Yazoo River—the Indian name means "river of death." My father became a judge, and after that he had to deal with other men's Negroes as well as his own.

Every year, at the approach of hot weather, Mama would move us from Greenwood to Ashton Hall, our summer home on the Mississippi Sound between Gulfport and Biloxi. The old house was set well back from the beach road in the midst of wide-spreading liveoak trees. It was spacious, and hospitable-looking, with wide galleries, roofed, and with banisters on all sides. It was built by slaves before the Civil War, out of hand-sawn lumber brought from Florida by schooners, and Papa was proud of the fact that it was still as "sound as a dollar" because nothing but well-cured lumber had gone into it.

Back of it was another ancient structure, a two-story building in which were the large kitchen and upstairs the servants' rooms. The kitchen was separate from the "big house" so that no odors from the enormous meals of sea foods prepared in it could reach the noses of the white folks.

The "big house" was always packed with guests, and the servants were busy during the daylight hours preparing elaborate meals, mainly of sea food, for this company. The menservants sat on wooden benches under the great oak trees, cracking the crab claws, peeling the shrimp, opening the oyster shells, and cutting up the okra, onions and bell peppers which went into the famed crab-gumbo of the Gulf Coast.

Back of the kitchen was an enormous arbor of scuppernong grapes, the vines so old that no one knew whether they were antebellum like the houses. We did know that these grapes made delicious wine, and that in some bygone day they had been used for this purpose. Mama was not the kind of homemaker who bothered with supervising canning or bottling—she was too busy with her children and guests. There was every kind of excellent wine to be bought in nearby New Orleans.

The world was young because we were young. The freshness of the dawn lasted through all hours of the day, for we were seeing and feeling only the joy of being alive on an earth which had no diseases, no perils, no sorrows; at least we did not know there were such things. When the west wind became too strong, it brought to us swarms of mosquitoes from the Louisiana marshes. We were uncomfortable when these insects bit us, and we slapped at them and anointed ourselves with oil of citronella and ran to shelter behind gauze wire and mosquito netting. But we did not dream that these pests, which came only occasionally, brought in their stings the germs of malaria, and sometimes of the deadly yellow fever.

We felt that we were immortal, that all things were immortal, and that Papa and Mama were all-powerful. These two would always know how to heal our sicknesses and disperse our sorrows. We were entirely safe and secure from all harm forever. This is the glory of childhood.

Papa never came to the coast until September, except for weekends. He had to stay in the hot and dangerous Delta until after the late sessions of court. When he came to play for a happy month with his precious family, he went to the beach every morning to see the seine pulled by the Negro menservants. This was a daily event of great excitement, and everyone except Mama gathered on the beach to see the contents of the net when it was dragged up on the white, dry sands. My tall, dignified father never left his room in the morning until he was fully dressed in one of his clean blue-and-white-striped seersucker suits. And Mama never returned to the beach after the morning swim; she did not want to spoil her peaches-and-cream complexion with sunburn. But the rest of us still wore our bathing suits and were barefooted when the seine was pulled.

This net was perhaps 50 feet long, with weights at the bottom; two Negroes would wade out for some distance, one following in the other's footsteps, and then the front man would turn and wade to right or left, and when the net was parallel to the beach each would haul his end to the shore. The treasures which came out of that subtropical water outshone those which Aladdin found in his magical cave. Jewels are dead things, but here for the delight of a brood of healthy children was life abounding—leaping, wriggling, quivering, kicking. There were shrimp, crabs and a dozen kinds of fish, striped or banded or spotted, black or white or red or brown; fishes flat, or long and thin, or puffed up like balloons; fishes that croaked, fishes that flopped about madly and had to be grabbed before they got back into the water.

Now and then there would be a thrilling novelty, mysterious, perhaps dangerous: a horseshoe crab, for example, fairly round and flat, with a long tail and spikes on it—and could it sting you? We were never sure. We knew that the salt-water catfish, with their black needles sticking out, could give poisonous stabs.

Dink, our lively fox terrier, would rush in barking to challenge an energetic crab, and rush away again yelping. Some of the crabs were formidable, with powerful claws eight inches long, always upraised for battle; they would scuttle this way and that, trying to get back into the water. They had a disconcerting way of darting to one side or the other, and Dink could never learn this trick.

Out of two or three haulings of the seine would come buckets

full of shrimp, and of crabs and fish—more than the family
could consume at its largest, when there were several children,
and the servants, and many guests. The surplus was dumped
into a big pot in the back yard and boiled for the caretaker's
chickens, and we ate the chickens he raised for us.

We had a wharf, extending far out into the water, and
also we had what was called the "oyster pier" about a mile
from the shore; almost every winter the storms damaged these
wooden structures, and sometimes swept them away entirely.
Mr. Bebb, the caretaker, wrote us when this happened and
Papa had them replaced before we came to the coast. There
were big lumber schooners out on the Sound, heavily loaded,
and now and then they were caught in severe storms and had
to dump part of their cargo; whatever was washed onto our
beach went into rebuilding wharf and pier. The beach was
ours, and also the water, or so we thought, and no one ever disputed the claim. Ours also was the oyster bed, a mile out; Papa
had "planted" it, and he would order a schoonerload of oysters
to replenish it now and then. All summer long we would row
or sail to the "pier" and a colored boy would "tong up" oysters
and open them for us to eat on the spot.

A good part of the day we children wore bathing suits. A
boy's suit came to his knees, but girls wore bloomers which
came to their ankles, not for beauty but for modesty. At low
tide we splashed about and had water "fights"; at high tide we
swam and floated, and so learned to take care of ourselves. One
scene is forever impressed on my mind: several of the little ones
were in the water when there was a warning shout—the black
fin of a shark was cutting the water nearby. We splashed wildly
to the beach, and one of my little brothers, Hunter, clambered
up a slimy post which had been left in the water from a previous year's pier. There he clung until a rescue boat took him off;
he was cut by barnacles, but not by sharks.

The wharf had a bathhouse with a covered porch around it,
from which we children could fish and catch crabs. Farther out
on the wharf was a sort of summerhouse, and if the mosquitoes
were bad we would have pallets carried out to this place and

sleep there. These swarms of mosquitoes came only when there was a high west wind, but when they did come, no gauze wire, no sort of netting could keep them out of the house.

My brothers had a sailboat as soon as they were old enough to sail it, and I had a rowboat. Mama didn't like me to row, because she said it would make my hands large, and that was not aristocratic; but somehow I managed to wheedle this privilege, and at dawn would row out toward the pier and watch the sunrise. I could never tire of that silent glory; the sun half out of the water, the clouds painted with a dozen shades I could not name, and these reflected on the water below. I would greet Papa being rowed out by a Negro boy to the oyster pier to fish. This boy always came with him, and carried his basket of shrimp for bait; he would bait Papa's hook and take off the fish as Papa caught them. Large ones could be caught from this pier, and here my harassed father got his rest from the cares and problems of plantation life and the courtroom.

Oh, how kind and patient he was—and how I loved him! That I should ever do anything to displease him was wholly beyond the possibility of my thinking. I was taught to believe in God, and this was easy for me, for I knew He must be like Papa.

The summer homes of a dozen wealthy New Orleans families, and of Mississippians, several of them members of our family, were strung along the water's edge all the way from Mississippi City to Beauvoir, the Jefferson Davis home; the total distance was five or six miles. These antebellum homes were set in the midst of ancient liveoak trees, and back of them for miles inland were virginal pine forests, with here and there, scattered several miles apart, a few cheap, unpainted board shacks in which lived the people Mrs. Jefferson Davis called "the clayeaters," wretchedly poor, ignorant, and with the deformities of in-breeding. One family had some children who had six toes on a foot, another had six fingers on a hand, and all of them had complexions the color of the clay which they ate to satisfy their starved bodies. It was discovered many years later that all of them had hookworm.

Those of us who were God's more fortunate children, in that
we had money and fine homes, were afraid of these poor people
because of their dreadful looks, manners, and ignorance, and
we never went near them. But a few miles back of the homes of
the rich was a beautiful deep bay, in which Papa liked to fish
for sheepshead. In order to reach this choice fishing ground, it
was necessary to pass several of the squalid shacks of the clayeaters, and we saw, as we drove past, the meagerness of their
home-raised food supply. They planted no vegetable gardens,
raised no poultry nor livestock. They had a few fig trees and
watermelon patches. They traded watermelons and figs for a
scant supply of cheap clothing at the small country store near
them, run for the benefit of the fishing parties on Back Bay.

Papa always came back happy and exultant from one of these
jaunts into the interior, for the sheepshead were abundant, and
he displayed the baskets of black-banded fish. When he fished
from our pier on the Sound he caught speckled trout and other
fish for broiling, also a delicious little panfish called a croaker
because it made a strange noise after it was pulled from the
water. On rare occasions he caught red snapper and another
kind of red fish, and pompano, an especially fine-tasting fish.

Mr. Bebb, a wizened little Welshman, was what is called
"a character." He was there alone for all the winter months and
was pledged never to leave the place for a single hour. The
tramps from the North swarmed to this warm coast in winter,
and not merely would they break in and loot a house but set
fire to it—this had happened in the past to several of the beach
homes. Mr. Bebb was provided with a shotgun, which he never
fired; the sight of it and the snarls of his dogs were enough.

We had cows, but he called them his, for he took care of
them, winter and summer. Our grounds extended back from
the beach about a mile; first when you went back was "the
brake," a stretch of swampy forest. There were little pools of
stagnant water here, and in them lived the water moccasins.
You could not walk more than a few yards without seeing one,
or maybe several, each in his watery bed, watching you, no

doubt, but his eyes never moving. The cows killed them with their sharp hooves, but the population did not seem to diminish, and we children were never allowed to go there.

Beyond the brake was a wide meadow, incredibly bright and green, and here the cows pastured undisturbed. Beyond that was the "pineywoods," extending for miles. We owned a stretch of this woodland and Mr. Bebb felled trees, cut them into logs, and split them for firewood for Aunt Catherine's kitchen range and for the laundry pots outside. The little Welshman looked frail but was wiry, and shirked no task.

When Mr. Bebb's cows had "carves"—that is what he called them—he raised them "by hand," and could never be induced to send one to the butcher. His "by hand" way of feeding them was his own invention; he would bunch his fingers, dip them into a milk pail, and then hold them for the "carf" to suck. He never came into the house except when the grown-up members of the family were away. Then he would ask permission of the older children and would come in and seat himself at the piano and play what he considered music.

It was on the beach road a mile or so from Ashton Hall that we got Jimmie. We children had a pony cart and one day some of my small brothers went on a drive. There were stretches of beach frontage on which were no buildings at all, and in one of these empty spaces my brothers saw a tiny Negro boy sitting on a log, weeping loudly. They stopped and asked what was the matter, and he said, "Mah mammy done kill mah pappy and mah pappy done kill mah mammy an' Ah's *hongry*." His name was Jimmie, and if he had a last name he didn't know it.

The boys bought some food and gave the little fellow a meal on the drive home. His tears dried quickly and he began to sing in a loud but melodious voice. This delighted my brothers, and they encouraged him to go through his repertoire. It was not a long one, and only a few words of each song were intelligible, but Jimmie did not bother about that. He liked music, and not words, so he just made sounds which resembled the words, and carried them well on the tunes of the popular songs to which he had attached them. His favorite was one to which he had got the first words correctly: "You lakka me, an' Ah lakka you, an' we lakka bofe de same—."

Papa had an investigation made among the people of the pine woods, but could find no report of a Negro couple being killed or of a missing child. The child made himself a member of the family, and was the liveliest of all the youngsters, half-servant and half-pet. A born comedian, he would show the whites of his eyes and his gleaming white teeth, and dance and sing whenever asked to. He soon learned the family ways and made himself into a great convenience. It would be "Jimmie, run upstairs and bring my book," or "Jimmie, run tell Adam to harness the horses."

In the middle of a hot afternoon he would say to the children, "Doan you want some ice cream?"—and of course they did. Jimmie would go to Adam, one of the houseboys, and say, "The chillun wants some ice cream." Adam would prepare the mixture, and Jimmie would crack the ice and put in the coarse salt and sit and turn the handle of the freezer for half an hour. Then he would have his share along with the others.

Jimmie played with and at the same time helped to care for the younger children; he learned quickly what was forbidden them, and kept them out of danger. My little brother Duke didn't learn to walk for a year after he should have, because he rode everywhere on Jimmie's back; it was called "toting," and Jimmie loved to be useful! He had his pallet in the nursery and slept on the floor—in winter in front of the fireplace, with his head to the fire.

Jimmie grew into a big sturdy boy very fast, and somehow, just by watching, he learned to drive the first family automobile, a thing called a "White Steamer." So he became the family chauffeur. Mama wanted to make a preacher of him, and offered to send him to a Negro college, but Jimmie's inclinations were not that way. The day came when he went off to Detroit, on his own, and the last we heard about him was a letter begging for help; he was in jail—as he phrased it, "on account of an automobile tire."

The "Old South" of my childhood was an enchanted land. Surely there is now no place in our country that so swarms with life, of field and forest and water! In the Delta, around our winter home, the blackberry patches grew to the size of cottages. The rabbits that hid inside them would not run out when the Negro women and children picked the berries but would merely shift their positions. We would go into the woods for persimmons and for nuts, and they were so plentiful that we would take two "spring wagons"—so called, I suppose, because they had springs, which the heavy cotton wagons probably didn't. One wagon would be to carry the children, and the other to bring back the forest treasures. There were enormous trees, and the ever-present Negro boys would clamber up and shake their branches. There were pecans, hickory nuts, and another variety we called "scalybark"—I do not find it in the dictionary. A trusted colored man would be sent along with a shotgun and would have no trouble killing a dozen fat squirrels.

I did not look at these slaughtered wild things and did not want them killed. But for a while my oldest brother, Orman, two years younger than myself, was the only one big enough to play with me, and I had to do what he wanted; he was aggressive and dominating, made so on purpose, for that was the way for a Mississippian to be. He must not be afraid of anything in this dangerous world.

When Orman was a big enough boy Papa taught him all about guns, and I sat in on the lessons and later had my own gun. When Orman went hunting, I went along, and once Orman came back and told with great glee how I had shot at a lark and killed a rabbit! But I wept when I saw a bird I had shot fluttering on the ground with a broken wing. "Never again!" I declared, and that was my last hunting trip.

I learned all about horses, because there were always a number in the pasture, including Old Mabel, a carriage horse who had earned an old-age pension, and which we rode when we were not more than three or four years old. There were young and lively horses, and later on I learned to do what the boys did: run beside one, seize him by the mane, and leap onto his bare back. I rode sidesaddle—only there was no saddle and no stirrup in the pasture.

Because there was no one else to play with, I played with the boys, and took the punishments. Marbles, for example; there was a game called "knucks," and if you lost, which I usually did, I would put my clenched fist on the ground and the boys would shoot marbles at it. This hurt a lot, but I never made a sound. That was what Orman would have done; I never heard him cry, and never a sound when he was hurt. When he was told to go and sit in the corner until he would promise to be good, he would sit there all day, or at least until Mama found an excuse to get him out. He would be good, but he wouldn't be *made* to say so!

I was good, too, but for a different reason—because I couldn't imagine doing what my parents disapproved. My training was to be quiet and "ladylike"; so when I climbed into our big apple tree and got stuck, I just sat there until I was discovered.

There was a pear tree in our orchard on which grew huge winter pears; they would be handled as if they were jewels, each wrapped in paper and put away in the attic to ripen. Bunches of bananas would come from New Orleans and be hung in the attic, and barrels of Northern apples and Florida oranges would be stored in the basement. These came by steamboats on the Yazoo River. There was a bend in the river just beyond our house, and just before a boat came around this bend it would blow its deep, hoarse whistle, and the Negroes in the garden or the orchard would stop work and exclaim, "Dah she comes!" They would lean on their tools while she approached, with a swooshing of her great hulk cutting the water, like the skirts of a huge woman approaching.

Mama liked expensive foods best. Papa teased her and said it was because she considered it proof of her aristocracy. The steamboats brought anchovies, caviar, guava jelly, and other imported articles. They were ordered for her by a Jewish grocer who had, Papa said, the brightest mind in Leflore County. Papa would sit in front of the shop and discuss world affairs with him for an hour at a time. Then he would come home and say, "I never cease to wonder at the minds of these people. They had a great literature thousands of years ago."

That literature was what Mama's church called the "Old Bible," and which, it taught, had been replaced by the New Testament. But even so, Papa would read a passage from it every evening to all the family, including the servants. There were some things in it of which Mama disapproved; such as, for example, the instruction to "be fruitful, and multiply, and replenish the earth." Mama was doing her full duty in that respect, but she did not approve of talking about it. She would say severely, "You may skip that, Mr. Kimbrough." That was how she always addressed him, and he addressed her as "Miss Mary Hunter." This was a custom in the South.

Mama was born a Southworth and christened Mary Hunter, for her mother. The name Southworth meant much in Mississippi, and, as I later discovered, in Massachusetts. This consciousness of high origin produced in my darling mother a sense of ineffable superiority, lifting her and her brood above most temptations of the flesh and all weaknesses of the spirit. "No child of mine could ever have an oily skin, or a pimple, because they have 'blue blood' in their veins," she would say. "No daughter of mine could ever be 'fast,' no son could ever be a coward or a cheat—there is a family tradition."

How she managed to combine this hauteur with the most devout Christian humility may puzzle some, but it didn't Mama. She was perfectly certain that she had a limited number of equals in the entire state; yet in the little Delta town of Greenwood she established a church for the then poverty-stricken denomination called "Campbellite." She provided for its itinerant preachers, and every Sunday sent her carriage to gather up the town tinker and the sempstress and other humble ones to bring them to the service.

My mother was left an orphan and her family plantation was ruined in the Civil War. She was raised by her Aunt Sallie Morgan of the revolutionary Virginia family, from which came some of Mama's great pride. Aunt Sallie, then a spinster, put her beautiful niece in a convent in Kentucky to be educated by the careful nuns. But Mama, with a highly emotional nature, elected to become a nun herself. When word of this reached the family an uncle came quickly and snatched her away, and took her back to the church of her parents. She was made into an Episcopalian; but when she married Papa, she became a "Christian," or what others called "Campbellite." Mama retained fragments of the rituals and creeds of all three of these denominations and taught them to us, without a sense of their incongruity.

When Aunt Sallie looked about for a proper husband upon whom to bestow her treasure, she selected a graduate lawyer from the University of Virginia, a man of fine looks and high character, who possessed the calm and level-headed qualities which Mama's emotional nature needed. He was a Mississippian, and his plantation also had been ruined during the Civil War and had grown up into brush. He had lived on crackers and cheese while establishing his law practice, having told his mother the day he returned from Virginia with his law diploma in his pocket: "I won't accept another dime from you." Mary Hunter Southworth did not love him, but she admired him, and married him because she was persuaded to. Mama never regretted the step. Papa adored her and she was the incentive which made him struggle tirelessly to give her everything that money could buy.

In the course of time, this devoted mother bore ten children, yet found time for many things other than homemaking. She loved horses, and drove wild ones. She traveled, and attended conventions of the United Daughters of the Confederacy. Once in New Orleans, she met Madame Schumann-Heinck—and that was an adventure to tell her friends about year after year. The great diva gazed at her in rapture, exclaiming, "Oh, you beauty, *du schoenste!* You should be on the stage! What do you do?" Mama said, "I have a large family of children." The stout, exuberant German mother demanded, "But you have a voice? You must have!" Mama explained that she had been educated in a convent, where the nuns had given her good musical training. "You will sing for me!" declared the

diva, and took Mama into one of the parlors of the hotel. Her
accompanist struck some chords, and Mama sang Schubert's
"Ave Maria." When she finished, Schumann-Heinck caught her
in her arms and wept, saying that not to use that glorious voice
for art was a crime. But Mama had not been thinking about
art as she sang; the feeling she had put into the song was religious—the Catholic part of her worshiping the Blessed Virgin.

From adventures such as this she would come home to her
children, and if she ever repined or dreamed of grand opera we
never knew it. No mother could have been more tender and
conscientious, and if the children took advantage of this it was
nothing new in human history. She taught us to walk slowly
and to be quiet in the house; she sent us outside to romp in the
big grounds around it, and the children of the neighbors were
encouraged to join us. Never for a minute were we out of
Mama's mind. If a silence fell outside she would become uneasy
and send a servant to see what we were doing.

However lenient Mama might be, our father was a different
matter. We obeyed him, and did not argue. I was a shy little
girl, and often had to be persuaded to come out and have my
long red-gold hair and my big brown eyes displayed to company. There was one dreaded old gentleman who would insist
on taking me on his knee, where I would have to turn my head
to avoid his horrid whiskers; the moment I heard he was coming, I was up and away. That of course was unacceptable behavior, and when Papa came home and heard that I had run
away from Cousin Anselm again, he performed his usual elaborate ritual. Leading me out into the garden, taking out his
pocketknife and cutting a switch off a peach tree, and slowly
trimming off the leaves and twigs, he would say solemnly, "This
is going to hurt me more than it hurts you."

But he never touched me. Instead, he would say, "Now, am I
going to have to do this? Or will you promise never again to
run away from company?" Of course I promised, and then my
wonderful father would take my hand in his and stroll among
the fruit trees and berry vines, picking a peach for me, or a
couple of juicy plums. All of us adored him, but none of us

ever realized that he never fulfilled his role of executioner. And
so we dared not disobey him.

Mama had got a good education from the nuns in the
graces and the arts. She could play the piano, and sing wonderfully. But she was as weak on spelling as I was on arithmetic;
when she made out a grocery list, she wrote "shugga" and when
it was a laundry list she wrote "pance." But she had decided
that I was "bright" and she had determined long ago to develop
my mind. She employed governesses, who lived in the house
and grabbed me whenever they were able. Also I had teachers
who came to the house: piano teacher, voice teacher, elocution
teacher, and one who taught me the skirt dance. Every morning
I stood in the bathroom while Papa was shaving, and recited
the multiplication table to him. From both Papa and Mama I
learned ethics and etiquette; I absorbed these unconsciously by
observing the expression of distaste on my mother's usually
smiling face when some improper behavior or person was referred to. It was a stern code, and we were supposed to be born
with it.

And then, whenever there was a moment's leisure, Mama
would say, "Now, sit down and read." Papa, who read whenever
he could, provided me with the books: first, those appropriate
to children—*Tom Sawyer* and *Huckleberry Finn, Pilgrim's
Progress,* Lamb's *Tales from Shakespeare, Gulliver's Travels,
The Swiss Family Robinson.* Later, I had a set of Washington
Irving in blue cloth with gold lettering. Then Stevenson and
George Eliot, and then Sir Walter Scott, Thackeray, and other
favorites of my father.

Summer was supposed to be playtime, but the demon of culture pursued me even to Ashton Hall. A professor of piano
from New Orleans had come to the coast to rest and didn't
want pupils, but Mama persuaded him, and twice a week he
hitched up his horse and buggy and came to teach me Brahm's
Hungarian dances.

When I was thirteen, it was decided that I was to matriculate
at the Mississippi State College for Women. The problem was
grammar, about which I had been taught nothing; I obeyed

most of the rules without knowing them, but that was not enough. Mama undertook to teach me, and got the required textbook, the arrangement being that she was to study each day's lesson to "refresh" herself, and then teach it to me; but when the hour arrived, Mama had been too busy or had forgotten, so we would puzzle out the lesson together. The age for matriculation in the college was 14, but Papa was certain that I had reached that age mentally. He traveled with me to the town of Columbus and in the president's private office the situation was explained. Dr. Frazer, the president, gave me an "examination" there and then. By good luck I was able to answer all his questions correctly, and he told Papa I had passed.

There were a couple of weeks before the opening, and I went home and thought it over and did not like it. The day for departure found me in a very unhappy state of mind, for I had never been away from home before, except for visits to relatives and friends. But now for three long months I would not see my beloved Papa and Mama—not until Christmas! It was a night train, and there in our front hall stood the liveryman with the two-horse carriage to take me to the depot (so we called it). It was raining hard outside; and there was I, shedding buckets of tears. The man waited patiently, watching the clock, and finally said it was my last chance to catch the train. Papa said sternly, "Remember, my daughter, you are no longer a baby."

On board the train, I wept myself to sleep; but at the college I met a lot of other girls and in two or three days I was busy and no longer homesick.

I attended that college for three years, and Mama's high opinion of my intellect took another upward leap; I made a record which caused a woman teacher to come rushing to my room in excitement. There were some two hundred girls in the school every year, and I was the first girl ever enrolled who had got a grade of 100 in the course called English!

The Gardner School for Young Ladies was situated on Fifth Avenue, New York, in the most highly strategic location to attract girls from other parts of the country; it was directly across the street from one of the Vanderbilt homes. The letter

accompanying the school catalogue explicitly stated that at
school receptions the young ladies had opportunities to meet
the millionaires of the world's richest city. I am sure that Mama
did not want me to make a "catch" among these Yankee millionaires, but she did want me to know how to handle myself
in the great career she envisioned for me. So I set out from
Greenwood to New York by way of Atlanta, the first long journey I had ever made alone.

The school was located exactly where the catalogue said it
was: in the midst of the homes of multimillionaires. The fashionable Episcopal church, St. Thomas's, was a few blocks away,
and we were marched there every Sunday morning for worship.

It was the palace of Cornelius Vanderbilt IV which faced
us directly. It had heavy curtains at all the windows, and
so did our school. It was strictly against the rules to peer out,
but this rule was not strictly obeyed. It was not difficult to open
a tiny crack between curtains in order to peek out; and such
wonderful sights were to be seen! Alfred Gwynne Vanderbilt,
driving his tallyho coach with several matched and magnifi-
cently decorated horses, and horns blowing like Gabriel's
chariot coming down from heaven—surely it was part of the
"finishing" of girls from the country to have at least a glimpse
of such a sight. On the walks which we took every afternoon we
more than once saw a small boy and a girl escorted from one of
those mansions, and we wondered what the life of such fairy-
tale children might be. Years later, this same boy became my
friend.

Mrs. Gardner was a majestic lady who always dressed in
black satin, and sat in state. She had a barouche driven by a
coachman who turned out to be her husband, Dr. Gardner! He
was a quiet, solemn man who kept very carefully out of the way
of the young ladies. Every evening he would walk over to Sixth
Avenue and come back with a little brown paper bag. When
schoolgirl curiosity could no longer be borne, one of us managed to brush against him as he ascended the stairs and knock
the package from his hand. It contained a five-cent apple pie,

purchased on that forbidden street of delicatessens, saloons, pawnshops and the Elevated.

Every afternoon Mrs. Gardner took one of her "young ladies" to drive with her; this was supposed to be a great honor. She did not take long to honor me, and on the way she talked with embarrassing directness. The substance of her communication was that I had the gracious manners of a true lady; I was serene, my voice was low, I deferred to my elders, and while I spoke frankly, I never said anything to wound anyone's feelings. Southern young ladies had these characteristics, and for that reason she always made it a point to have several in her school. Most of her pupils came from the West, being daughters of lumber barons and cattle kings and copper magnates and such *nouveaux riches*. "Their manners are apt to be crude," said my preceptress, "and their voices too loud and nasal."

It seemed that I was never to break any rules, or in any way descend from a fictitious throne, so as to set an example for the Westerners who were delicately given to understand that they were to imitate me even in those idioms of speech which I had acquired from my Negro mammies. Mrs. Gardner told me also that she was sure I would be diligent in my studies and have a good chance to be valedictorian of the graduating class. I was not a little awed by the dual responsibility, and fearful that I might have to walk a straighter line than I wanted to.

I studied my textbooks some, and the people about me more, for I was always interested in psychology. But I did win the valedictory, probably because my classmates studied even less than I did. The teachers were conscientious maiden ladies, and two or three rather pathetic-looking foreign professors; some of the girls—always called young ladies—made fun of these foreign gentlemen. My fellow pupils were as new and strange to me as the professors, representing parts of America about which I knew nothing. There was one Jewish girl among them, and for her Mrs. Gardner apologized delicately, explaining that she was very, very rich; her family owned a great department store in Baltimore. As my roommate at the Mississippi State College for Women had been Jewish I saw no reason for the apology.

We had three excellent meals every day, and the cold climate, new to me, stimulated my appetite; I did full justice to those meals, even though I had to get over a prejudice against Yankee cooking—especially against the habit of pouring hot sauces over cake and serving it as dessert. I grew to my full height of five feet, seven inches, and left the school weighing more than a young girl should. But as several of the other girls weighed much more, I felt quite "svelte," as Mrs. Jefferson Davis described me.

Every morning before breakfast, and again in the late afternoon we were taken for a walk, always up the Avenue and into Central Park. We were a parade to be looked at by others on their strolls—a long line of pretty young things walking two by two, with one teacher walking by the first pair and another teacher by the last pair, keeping a sharp eye on all the other pairs, to make sure there was no impropriety, no "nods and becks and wreathèd smiles." There was plenty of opportunity, for well-dressed young men did not fail to stare at us, and sometimes to grin, which caused us to giggle. In the park we played about for a bit, ran instead of walking, and tossed a few snowballs at one another; then we formed into line again and marched back to school.

On Saturday afternoons we were free to see the city, with any chosen teacher for a chaperone—to go shopping, have an ice-cream soda at Huyler's and buy quaint Oriental objects at Vantine's; or we could go to a matinée. But I had a duty call to pay on these afternoons, on Mrs. Jefferson Davis.

The Davis family played an important part in my life. Their home was on the Mississippi coast, about half a mile from Ashton Hall by the white shell road. The ex-President of the Confederacy had spent the last years of his life there, writing his story, *The Rise and Fall of the Confederate Government.* He was a sad and broken man, after defeat in war and long confinement in prison. Mrs. Davis, the former Varina Howell, gave him devoted care, even acting as his amanuensis while he, almost blind, wrote that enormous two-volume work. With them at Beauvoir was their daughter Winnie, known as the "Daughter of the Confederacy." She tried to be a source of happiness

As Mary Craig Kimbrough, the eldest daughter, I grew up in the midst of the vast cotton plantations of the Delta. This was my graduation photograph (1900), by Aime Dupont, Fifth Ave., New York.

Ashton Hall, our summer home on the Mississippi Coast. From a watercolor painted in 1897 by Papa's mother, Charlotte Gray Kimbrough.

to her suffering father, but became an added sorrow to him; for here he made the dreadful decision that she must not marry the Yankee who had won her heart.

The Davis house, Beauvoir, was similar to Ashton Hall, but the Davis family was poor and too proud to accept any sort of help. My great-uncle, William Morgan, whose place was next-door, declared that they were starving, and he would pack a basket of food and personally carry it over at night and leave it on the porch, tap on the door, and then steal away. Next night he would come back and get the empty basket. When a storm damaged the house he had it repaired.

Papa was Mrs. Davis's attorney. She owned a plantation, "Brierfield," and he tried his best to sell it advantageously for her; but a change in the Mississippi River had turned it into an island, and of course during the Civil War it had grown up with brush. Being neighbors, we saw them often; I was told that at the age of three I had sat on Mr. Davis's knee, but I do not remember it. Some time after his death Mrs. Davis moved to New York, as she had been invited by Joseph Pulitzer to write articles for his New York *World*.

There she was, when I was a schoolgirl at the Gardner School, living in a small apartment hotel with an Irish maid. It was a family duty to call on her, and cheer her up. Her older daughter lived in the far-off West with an invalid husband, and Winnie had died under very sad circumstances.

The old *grande dame* had become quite stout and was crippled, living painfully with her memories. She had written Mama sadly, "The dear old leisurely days are over," meaning that she was earning her own living, which she had certainly never been trained to do. She had been very high and had fallen with the Confederacy. I had been taught to pay her homage, and I did; but after I had answered all her questions about my "dear Mother" and her "dear Chancellor," my father, there was not much else that we knew to talk about; and I am ashamed to say I made excuses and got away, for there was a great city out there, with matinées, concerts and a myriad of sights. My grandmother once remarked, "We have to be old to realize how little we mean to the young."

2. FIRST LOVE

It was June, the loveliest month of the year. The trees and shrubs and grassy fields were green and tender. The train rolled slowly to a stop by the long wooden platform of the small-town depot, and I hurried out from the sleeping coach to the vestibule, where the conductor stood gravely waiting to help me down the steps. I was only 17 and my heart was beating fast with happy excitement. Oh, how marvelous to be at home again—and with my diploma in my handbag!

"Hello, Sister!" a boyish voice called out, and there at the foot of the steps stood my young brother, Orman, with his hand outstretched to help me down. "I'm fourteen," he announced, proudly, before I had time to say a word. "Mama says I don't have to wear short pants any more, not *ever* again! How do you like my uniform?"

I kissed his cheek and patted his Confederate gray back. "It's beautiful," I declared, "and how do you like my new dress? It's the newest shade of blue, and such lovely soft silk. Feel it!"

We were at the carriage now and I stepped in and sat down in the front seat. He climbed in beside me and picked up the reins. The Negro boy who was standing by the horses' heads stepped aside, but before Orman said "Get up," a young man on the back seat of the carriage spoke suddenly. "Wait," he said, firmly, "I want to drive. You sit back here, Orman." My adolescent brother, conscious now of his oversight in not introducing me to the guest in our carriage, stammered an apology and hopped out.

"Don't mention it," said the guest, taking his place on the front seat with only a brief smile at me. But I had time to observe that he had mischievous brown eyes, and what Mama would call "well-chiseled features." Now it was I who said "Wait." I wanted to sit on the back seat, and jumped out on my side without an explanation, or anyone to help me.

After I had got into the back seat beside Orman, the new driver lifted the reins and gently tapped the two bays. "Get up," he said, and we were off.

Since Orman had not introduced me, even after being reminded, I thought this must be someone I was not supposed to mee'. Maybe he was a client of my lawyer father. Maybe he was only one of the cotton buyers who came to town in and out of season, and had got into our carriage because he wanted to meet a pretty girl. I was pretty, of course. All young creatures are; and I took compliments from men as a matter of course—it was the custom of the country.

But whatever plausible or implausible reason I gave myself for getting into the back seat, the real reason was not clear to me for a long time afterwards; I only knew I had felt an impulse to remove myself from close contact with a sudden and mysterious danger.

As the horses trotted briskly along the dusty road out of town to the plantation road, along the swiftly-flowing river, I was thrilled anew at being home again. Everything seemed wonderful, the familiar old stream, deep and treacherous, the weeping-willow trees on its banks, dipping their rich green branches into the water on either side, and the plantation wagons we passed, bringing the laughing, sweating black men to town to load the wagons with supplies for the plantation commissary—bright-colored calico and unbleached "domestic" (muslin) for the Negro women, blue jeans for the Negro men, cornmeal, salty fat bacon, canned "oyst-yers," sardines, snuff, "chawin' tebacker," and so on for all the field hands. I loved everything we passed. It was a part of "home," and that was an enchanted word to me.

But while the young cadet just back from the Kentucky Military Academy showed off to his big sister, telling me in his high-low ever-cracking voice, of the sprinting race he had won and the honors on the football field, I stole glances at the man who sat in front.

I liked everything I could see, the way his hair was cut, its light brown color, and the shape of his head. I could not see his face because he sat there motionless and silent, making up his mind—as I learned later—that something tremendous and world-shaking had happened to him!

Since that day, I have heard many discussions of "first love" and almost as many different opinions. Some call it "romantic," and others, not so romantic, call it "puppy" love. It has been called enchantment by some, and insanity by others. Whatever it is, it is a deep, overpowering experience that does something profound and often dangerous to all who experience it.

I think that the wealthy and more or less sophisticated young college graduate in the front seat had no doubt had romantic experiences at least as numerous as his years in a university town. Many mothers took their daughters on visits to attend the balls and cotillions which in those days were part of the social life of a small college town such as Oxford, Mississippi. But as for me, I had had not even one love affair! I had been far too closely chaperoned for anything of the sort. And so I was wholly unprepared for what came into my life as a result of this brief encounter.

When we arrived at home and drove under the *porte-cochère,* there stood my darling, beautiful mother, in a rose-colored dress, so girlish herself that when we traveled together she was often thought to be my sister. I forgot the young stranger entirely, hopped out of the carriage, ran to Mama and embraced her with happy tears. She had tears in her eyes too, but did not overlook her unexpected guest.

"Come in, Jerome," she called to him; and he called back, "Tell 'Uncle Luke' to catch another chicken for my dinner. I'll be here at six o'clock, and I'm a permanent boarder from now on." After a smile at me he walked quickly away.

It was the most delightful smile I had ever seen on anyone's face—gay, impudent, and very, very sweet, or at least so I thought, and felt the blood come and go in my cheeks as I stood there, blushing but unwilling even to ask who he was. I knew now, however, that he would never have been so self-assured if he had not known that my careful and proper mother considered him socially acceptable, someone with whom she could be informal.

The house servants standing back of Mama on the big porch now took possession of me. "Lawdy, honey," cried Aunt Catherine, giving me a hug. "You sho' is pretty! Ain't she, Alberta?" Aunt Catherine had a fairly light complexion but Alberta was coal-black, and so were most of the other servants who stood beaming at me. "She sho' *is* pretty," said one. "But her hair is goldener than her mama's hair." "It sho' is gold color," agreed "Aunt Ellen," the laundress. "Jes' the color of her ma's weddin' ring."

Jerome Winston came to dinner, in a white linen summer suit which seemed to increase his height; he made himself thoroughly at home. He told me later that his pride had been so hurt by the rebuff I had given him in transferring to the back seat, that it took all the time of the drive for him to make up his mind what to do. I had the same proud nature, and I understood.

On this first evening, however, everyone could see that he was bent upon becoming a member of the family. He tousled my younger sister's golden hair when she was passing near him, and when she stopped and gave him a stern look, he laughed at her and did it again. My young brother Morgan giggled, and Sallie, the indignant would-be young lady, marched haughtily from the room. He led Mama into conversation about her new church, and asked solemnly if he could join the congregation and teach a Sunday school class. He finally got Papa into the conversation by calling the Old Testament "great poetry."

After dinner, the Negro man who called himself the "Kimbrough butler" answered the telephone and brought word to Mama that Mr. Barry wanted to drop in for an evening visit. Our high-handed visitor spoke up at once: "Now look, Judge. Don't you think the time has come to tell Mr. Barry, and all the other candidates, that this is *my* girl?"

Mama quietly told George to tell Mr. Barry that we would be happy to see him, and then to Mr. Winston she declared, "Mr. Barry said just what you did, you know, when *he* saw the photograph."

"What photograph?" I asked, quickly.

"The one of you when you graduated," said Mama, innocently. "You see, Daughter," she went on, "your father got the
mail at the post-office that morning and carried it with him to
the bank. While he was opening it in his office there, Jerome
came in and saw your photograph and—well, Mr. Barry came in
soon after—and said the same thing."

Papa's eyes twinkled as he added, "But Mr. Barry said more
than that—he said, 'If I were not so old, I would say that is my
girl.' "

So I had my chance to snub my too self-assured admirer
again. "Well, it doesn't really matter," I said, indifferently, "because I'm going to bed early, and catch up on sleep. No one got
any rest last night in the sleeping car."

But Jerome Winston was more than my match. He was
slender and lithe, and he made a quick change from his chair
to my sofa, just as George opened the door and ushered in Mr.
Barry. "As I was remarking before Mr. Barry came in," he said
to me, in tones intended for Mr. Barry's ears, "no one, not even
my good and dear friend, Mr. Barry, could fail to see that you
have fallen in love, young lady, and it's love at first sight."
Then to Mr. Barry he announced, cheerfully, "Craig just told
me that what I asked for on our drive this morning is now
mine. I asked for her hand, and I'm sure you'll be the first of
my friends to congratulate me."

"You're certainly a magnificent actor, Jerry," remarked Mr.
Barry, dryly. Then to me, "Child, I came by to welcome you
home, and to tell you how all of us love you for making your
dear father and mother so proud. I'm sure you could not realize
how much they wanted you to win that valedictory." He drew
up a chair and sat down in front of me, and gave me a long,
searching look. Then he said, "Your mother didn't have your
shining gold hair, but those lovely, dancing brown eyes are
hers, and those dimples." Then he took Jerome Winston's hand
and laid it on mine. "You are a well-matched couple," he said.
"I hope she will not spurn you as her mother spurned me, when
we were as young as you."

The old house had not changed since I last saw it, but the furniture had. Mama had sent her antique rosewood sofas and chairs to New Orleans and they had come home "done over" in white brocade adorned with pink rosebuds. Those in the big front hall were done in olive-green panne-velvet and looked lovely with the cream-colored French velvet draperies. Some of the testers of the "four-poster" mahogany beds upstairs had been re-covered with colored silks, and some of the interior walls of the house had been frescoed by a Swiss painter whose prices, Papa said, had kept him from buying a "little piece of land" he had coveted for the past four or five years. The Marechal Niel rose vine by the west gallery was a dream of pale gold blooms, and bowlfuls of them were in every room in the house.

However, we were leaving all of this in a few days for the usual summer at Ashton Hall. I loved the beach, and always wanted to go there as soon as the hot weather came to the Delta. But now, for reasons I did not want to admit even to myself, I asked Mama if we had to go so soon.

I think she understood better than I did, for she answered cheerfully, "Oh, you will be a young lady there as well as here. Remember, you are no longer a schoolgirl. We'll have room at Ashton Hall for *your* friends this year; we can make out a list, and invite whomever you please. The Dulaney girls are young ladies now, and there is Mary Pillow."

"But," I protested, "I've got used to having some men friends, Mama. We had a reception every Friday night at the school. The brothers of the girls came, from Harvard, Yale, Cornell, and all over. You don't want me to be an old maid, do you?"

Mama laughed. "How old do you think you are?" she asked.

The next afternoon a Negro boy arrived with a long cardboard box which bore the name of a florist in Memphis. Opening it was a ceremony which Aunt Catherine, Alberta, Jimmie, my younger sister Sallie, and Mama all shared with me. We knew it contained flowers, but what kind?

"Why, Sister," cried little Sallie, her eyes dancing, "they are American Beauties! And just look at the length of the stems!

They must have cost,—I can't imagine how much they must have cost!" She picked up the tiny envelope which lay inside, and handed it to me. My hand trembled as I drew out the card and saw what was written on it: "To my girl, forever, and forever yours, Jerry."

"He is very impertinent," Mama said. But she could not hide her pleasure.

However, she had no idea of letting me be monopolized. When George answered the doorbell at dinnertime, he found not only young Mr. Jerome Winston standing outside, but three other "young gem-mens." There were Shelby Steele, son of a business friend of Papa's and Charlie Nichols, a cousin, and John Hemingway, a young man I had never heard of before. All of them had come for dinner!

After George had taken their hats and coats, he hurried back to the kitchen to help Aunt Catherine get the first course ready for the table. She was in a bad humor, and I heard her giving George a scolding in tones loud enough to call down Mama's wrath on her poor old head. She had more than any cook could do on such short notice, and I decided to see if I couldn't help. But Aunt Catherine raised her voice higher than ever and ordered me to "git out-a" her kitchen.

This brought Jerome to join in the racket. "Let us stay and help you, Aunt Catherine," he wheedled. "This is the first dinner-party my girl and I ever gave."

The harried old servant stood still, and took a good look at the brash young man. Suddenly all the worry and haste fell from her, and she turned slowly and began to lay out the oyster plates. "You *sho* is got jedgment, young gem'man, whoever you is," she said, in a calm, friendly voice. "Now please, sah, git out'a heah and lemme git dinner fo' de white folks."

Jerome Winston evidently understood the power of suggestion. I was becoming used to the idea that I was "his girl."

Two of my young lady cousins had come in while I was in the kitchen, and one of them had gone to the piano and begun to play "Hiawatha," the Indian love song which was then the rage. Jerry began to sing the words, and quickly put his arms around me and waltzed me into the drawing room. Everyone joined in the singing, "You are my *own*, my *sweet—*." We waltzed on, and I forgot there was anyone else in the room—or indeed, in the whole world—but this lithe and audacious young man whose eyes were smiling into mine.

The spell was broken by a blond stranger with pale blue eyes. He stepped to Jerry's side and tapped him on the shoulder, the ballroom signal to change partners, and I waltzed away with the stranger.

"I don't know you," I told him. "You will have to tell me your name."

"You never will know me," he said. "I'm an unknown. But it doesn't matter—I know *you*. And I'm here because I am Sir Galahad. Or maybe I'm just Don Quixote—but whoever I am, I intend to rescue a maiden! A certain tall, dark-eyed man thinks that he can walk off with the prettiest girl that ever wandered out of heaven into this vale of tears. Do you like poetry?" he ended, abruptly.

"No," I said. "But I want to know why the tall dark-eyed man should not walk off with the maiden."

"Because you are *my* girl," he answered, calmly.

Jerry was waiting for us; as we came around the room, he stepped out and tapped Sir Galahad on the shoulder. He was not smiling and his face was pale. As we moved out of earshot of his rival, he muttered: "The nerve of him! Your mother says she did not invite him, and neither did the Judge."

The music stopped, and so did we. But Jerry did not take his arm from around my waist. Instead, he steered me firmly toward the door which led to the west gallery. I held back, and reminded him that I was the hostess and must stay with my guests. But he answered, "They seem to be having a very good time without you," and continued to move me firmly through the door. I looked back into the room and saw that my guests were grouped around the piano, and my girl cousins were seating themselves to play a duet. All of them were talking, and paying no attention to us. I let Jerry guide me into the darkness of the gallery. Then both his arms were around me and he had kissed me.

"I thought you were just trying to get me away from that gentleman," I stammered, completely surprised, and at a loss as to what I should say. I knew I should be indignant, but I was not; I was happy, happier than I had ever been before in my life.

It was the first kiss. No sweetheart had ever dared such a liberty before, and it seemed to me to be something so overwhelmingly wonderful that it would have been ridiculous to pretend indignation. Jerry drew me to him and kissed me again. "That one means that you are going to marry me," he said. "Now send all the other men away. You are no longer free."

At dinner, the American Beauty roses covered the center of the table. Mr. Hemingway fastened his pale blue eyes intently on them and declared portentously: "You may think they are magnificent, but wait and see!"

Jerry scowled at his rival, and I began to worry about his temper, and his self-assurance. Did he really feel that he owned me? And would he make a scene with the other man before the evening was over? If so, I must say something that would bring him to his senses. I waited until there was a momentary lull in conversation. Then I leaned forward pointedly and spoke to the uninvited guest: "Yesterday when I invited you to come to dinner, Mr. Hemingway, I thought you would let people know that you *liked* me! But you didn't even ask Mama to seat you by me at the table. I feel snubbed!"

I didn't dare to look at Jerry, and the silence of the others at the table seemed frozen. It was a brazen overture but John Hemingway was not a man to be startled. He replied instantly, "Why, my darling young lady, how could I know that an invitation from you to dinner implied your infatuation?" He turned to Mama and coolly asked, "Is it too late, dear lady, to place me where I belong?"

Mama had been vexed because I had gone off to the gallery with Jerry, and now she stepped quickly into the opening.

"It isn't too late, Mr. Hemingway," she said, sweetly. "I'm sure Mr. Winston won't mind changing places with you."

Mr. Winston replied "Not at all," and rose from his chair. He bowed elaborately to the table and said, "Good night." Then he turned and faced the enemy. "And as for you, sir, wait and see." And he was gone. My heart sank to a bottomless abyss.

Papa's chair at the table had remained vacant. He had been called to a neighboring town on business, and evidently had been detained. I was glad of this, for he would have been shocked. Mama was delighted. She liked pranks, and she was glad I had put Mr. Jerome Winston in his place. She was quite sure he would like me better for it.

But I was sure he was gone forever, and my heart was sick with remorse. Why on earth had I done this cruel thing! Of course no one except Mr. Hemingway, not even Mama, knew that I had not invited this pallid stranger to dine with us; but even so, I had hurt the man who loved me, and as I now thought, the only man I could ever love.

But the deed was done, and I must pretend to be unconcerned. In this, Mr. Hemingway gave me valiant support. Whatever kind of queer fish anyone else might think John Hemingway to be, from now on my opinion of him was high. He was strange-looking, with pale, yellowish hair, of a lighter shade than his slightly tanned complexion, and a small, sickly mustache matching his hair. His eyes were a shade of light blue, so lusterless that no one would ever guess what a quick, humorous mind looked out from them. He had seen instantly what I was doing, had jumped into the game with relish, and the next day would follow up with a surprise attack.

After dinner Mama invited the same young people to drop in the following afternoon for an eggnog, and my cousins had asked if they could bring two or three other friends with them. There must be no slowing down of entertainments and good times, and the way to do this was to keep "open house." Everyone at the dinner party would feel free to bring someone else.

Mama had decided to grant my request and postpone our departure for Ashton Hall.

Early the next afternoon, she told me to put on my pink mousseline de soie dress with medallions of dark pink and gold roses stitched on it. It was my most becoming one, she said, and Dr. Firmin Bondurant was coming down from Oxford to see Papa, and would stay overnight with us as there was no night train he could conveniently take back. Mama was lovely herself in a new buff-colored taffeta dress, and I saw that she was setting *my* cap for the scholarly bachelor. This was a preliminary to next year's commencement ball at the University of Mississippi.

Aunt Catherine's kitchen was in turmoil, with so many eggs to be carefully broken, separated and beaten up, and so many bowls of cream being whipped. Papa kept the door to his liquor cabinet locked because George was developing a craving for strong drink. Papa would come home to pour it into the mixture at the right time, and to ladle up the eggnog. June was a strange time of year for eggnog, but Mama's recipe called for more whipped cream than eggs, and this turned the concoction into something more like syllabub; also, it required much less alcohol. It was just something to give the young people an excuse to get together.

But I did not expect to have any fun. The only person I wanted to see would not come!

The guests began to arrive, and soon it was clear that Aunt Catherine had been right when she had estimated that there would be twice as many as Mama had invited. They soon overflowed onto the galleries; and there in the glory of my pink mousseline, I tried to be as gay and carefree as Mama.

While Papa was stirring the eggnog I heard him talking to someone whose voice was familiar, but I could not believe that it was Jerry. I hurried back to the dining room, and there once more was the man whose mere presence lifted me into a state of breathless happiness.

"What—," I began, but he did not let me finish. "What it adds up to," he said, "is that the Judge and I are doing very well, thank you. Don't neglect your Prince Charming."

Papa said, "Tut, tut, young man. You can't get very far with a proud girl like this by acting brashly. She is literal, like her mother. She will take you at your word."

And so, Jerry went back with me to the gallery. He elected now to be debonair and started a romp with my little sister Sallie around my chair. I saw that he was trying to seem unaware of what had happened the night before, and I thought he was wonderfully game. So I was sorry for him. He was as proud as I was, and I knew that nothing but a deep love for me had caused him to swallow his pride and come back *so soon*. I caught Sallie and drew her down on the arm of my chair, with the result that Jerry came and kissed both of us.

A spring wagon drove in at the front gate and stopped by the gallery and Mr. Hemingway jumped out, followed by a large Negro man. In the wagon was a whole dogwood tree in full bloom, and they lifted it out and held it upright on the front steps.

"I told you to wait and see!" said Sir Galahad, triumphantly. It was his answer to long-stemmed American Beauty roses.

Jerry was the first to laugh. He helped the two men bring the tree up the steps, and set it between two of the fluted columns of the gallery. Then the two came in to share an eggnog toast "to the queen of *all* hearts."

Shelby Steele was an extremely tall, lanky fellow, who looked like an aristocratic Englishman without his monocle. When he went calling in the afternoons, dressed in his Prince Albert coat and striped trousers, he carried a cane, and was so British-looking that long before my return from school, my grandmother had named him the Duke of Bedford.

Now this Duke emerged from among the other afternoon guests, and said that he had an announcement to make: it was summer now, and soon everyone would be leaving the Delta for the mountains, or the coast, and before they went, the young men of the town wanted to honor the young ladies with a grand ball. It would be on the twentieth of June in the new brick store owned by the Stein brothers, enterprising merchants who had offered the as-yet-unopened store for the occasion, rent-free. It was a large building, with plenty of room for an impressive grand march.

Amid oohing and other exclamations of delight from the girls, the dating began. Shelby had already made sure of his date with Mary Pillow, a gorgeous blonde who had been my childhood playmate. He now came over to me and said that the young men of the town had voted for him to be master of ceremonies, and that, since I was to be the first debutante of the next season, he wanted me to lead the grand march. (He might have added a second reason, that his father and mine were close associates in business.) He said, furthermore, that he wanted me to choose my own partner for that grand march!

Immediately there began an Alphonse and Gaston pantomime between John Hemingway and Jerry Winston, each pretending that he would give way, but each really trying to step in front of the other. While they were executing this maneuver in front of me my handsome bachelor Uncle Lewis came through the front door, and I got up quickly and went to him. He was very proud of his pretty nieces, of whom there were several, and liked to go to balls and dance with them. He was not a very good dancer, but now I invited him to lead the grand march.

My Uncle Lewis was a fine criminal lawyer with an unhappy past. He had loved an exquisitely beautiful girl, who loved him. But she had a married sister who made her husband jealous by her open and continuing interest in other men. In Mississippi society, this was a disgraceful way for a woman to behave; she was considered "fast," and therefore the blood of her family was "tainted," not fit to mingle with ours. Uncle Lewis, however able a lawyer, knew no more about heredity than did the others of his family. He believed in the wall of pride which the Southworths had built around themselves for generations past, and one of the foundation stones of that wall was the freedom of blood from tuberculosis, insanity, venereal disease, and "fast women." I don't know whether he and the lovely girl whose heart was broken by the hardness of this wall ever came to any spoken understanding on the subject, but their marriage never came about.

Now my uncle stayed on at the eggnog party on the pretext that he had come to discuss a pending lawsuit with Papa. He was a teetotaler, so George brought him some whipped cream and cake.

The next day a Negro man came to the house with a note for me from Shelby Steele, also a gift—a wildcat chained inside a strong wooden box. The note read, "This cat will eat all knights but me. I have entered the lists."

I ordered the Negro to take the fiercely snarling animal away, but Mama countermanded the order. "No girl ever before had such a novel pet," she declared, and had George help the man fasten its chain to one of the columns on the west gallery. "Everyone who comes into the drawing room will be delighted to peek out the window at that terrifying creature!"

It had such a ferocious temper that no one dared go on the gallery that day. The man who had brought it said that no one should get close to it—the way to feed it was to throw some raw beef at it. For the next two days we fed it according to instructions, and each time it greeted the bearer of the food with a terrifying leap forward and frightful snarls. It showed no signs of becoming tame.

In our little town of Greenwood there was a Negro band, a part of every Delta town, to furnish the music for the endless balls and parties the white people gave. It had no resemblance to a jazz band but was really an excellent orchestra, with banjos, mandolins, guitars, violins, a horn and a bass fiddle, all played by dignified, genuinely gifted musicians who had melody and rhythm in their souls. They had no training whatever, but they had a natural gift. All they had to do was hear a tune, whether a popular waltz or a church hymn, and they could play it on one or more instruments.

Now the band was to play for me, and I was to lead a grand march, at a ball given partly in my honor! I could hardly bear to wait for that enchanted evening.

Two or three days after the eggnog party, after the household was sound asleep one night, there arrived silently on our lawn a group of young white gentlemen. With them was the town band, which seated itself quietly on the front steps and began to play a "cakewalk," then the popular fad of the music halls.

I was being serenaded, and I jumped out of bed, enraptured, and sped to the window. In the moonlit garden the almost ghostly figures of the assembled beaux were prancing through a quadrille, no one calling the figures, no one making a sound. This was romance—this was love, moonlight, magnolias, and music, all in one thrilling hour. I recognized each of the dancers, and each was to me a splendid knight in armor, tilting on the field of chivalry for my favor. Latham Ray was too stout, and so was Joe Ellington; Shelby Steele was too thin, and Jerry, my true hero-knight, was too small, opposite the mighty Duke of Bedford. But none of this really mattered—all of them were handsome, and all soul-stirring to my happy young heart!

The music had dropped lower when suddenly a diabolical snarling and yowling rent the air, and a ball of claws, fiery eyes and gray fur leaped around the gallery toward the musicians, then bounded off to one side towards the dancers. The scene changed to one of electrified human figures, some going over fences, some catching coattails on pickets, some disappearing under garden benches. The Negroes, having left their instruments behind, were running in a long stream down the big road toward town.

The ball of fur and claws had changed its course and was following the galloping Duke of Bedford into the back yard, apparently intending to eat him first. But the Duke won the race and stumbled in through the back door of the kitchen, leaving the door open but shouting to the family to close all doors and windows. He raced to the side door of the drawing room and peered out, as if expecting his pet to return there. Then, hearing a yowl from upstairs, he started there, presumably to rescue the family. But halfway up, he saw the fiery eyes glaring at him from above, and he went down as nearly flat as his surplus length would allow, while the creature bounded over him and out into the back yard again. It paused just long enough to tear into shreds a flock of fine white ducks which had camped there for the night. Then it disappeared in the direction of the woods.

By the time the serenaders had returned for their uncompleted quadrille, Mama and little sister Sallie had got out the customary wine and cake. Jerry then borrowed the cake knife and again tapped Shelby on the shoulder. This time his words were, "I dub thee Duke of Bedlam."

This affair ended the era of knighthood; there were no more competitive exploits. Jerry and I became formally engaged, and all through the following day he was announcing it on the main street of the little town.

So now my mother and his mother took charge of our future. The first thing was the matter of the début party which Mama had planned for me. Mrs. Winston thought it would be silly to go ahead with the event. What could be the purpose of a début for a girl who was already engaged?

"But," argued Mama, ominously, " 'there's many a slip 'twixt the cup and the lip'." And if such a slip should occur, what would the future hold for me? If I ended up as an old maid, at least it must not be because I was deprived of a début party!

Mrs. Winston saw no reason whatever why there should be any slip 'twixt the cup and the lip, and no good reason for the long engagement Mama insisted on. Her son was of a proud and jealous temperament; he was deeply in love, but he might object to having to compete with other men for the attentions of his fiancée. This might cause friction and lead to great unhappiness.

But Mama had set her heart on both a long engagement and a début party. She wanted the latter event to take place on her wedding anniversary, which was in November, and she had already got out her wedding gown from a chest in the attic, and was having it altered to fit. Also, Papa's wedding suit had been sent to a cleaner who was working on some mothholes it had accumulated.

"You can save these costumes to wear at Sallie's début," argued Mrs. Winston.

"But you see," argued Mama, "Tiffany is engraving the invitations right now. And besides—"

Mrs. Winston broke in: "Change the wording and make them wedding invitations! Do the same about your wedding clothes—wear them at your daughter's marriage, on the date of your own!"

Mama found this an interesting idea. It would certainly be most romantic—the same clothes, *and* on the anniversary of her own wedding! So the two began to plan the wedding. Of course, only the bride could wear white. But there was the matter of the costumes of the bridesmaids. Jerry's sister was an angel in pale blue. Since she was to be matron-of-honor, this left only pink for the bridesmaids, *of course*.

"I don't think it is necessarily a matter of *course*," said Mama, coldly. "My choice has always been pale green. It is so lovely with Mary Craig's red-gold hair and brown eyes."

"But *she* will wear white!" argued Mrs. Winston.

Mama went back to the matter of the début party. Her mind was no more to be changed than Tiffany's engraving plate. Positively the event was to take place, and the flowers, the wines, even the catering were ordered. But after all the expenditure of mental and financial energy, a cruel and inexorable fate stepped in. It was discovered that within a month or so after the chosen date Mama was going to have another baby!

I thought about Jerry and about almost nothing else. He had slipped into my life as simply and naturally as the glory of the sunlight on my garden of roses, giving it new color, new fragrance, new beauty. There seemed to be a glow of warmth emanating from his presence, and when he would turn suddenly toward me and gaze into my face, everything in the world disappeared from my consciousness but this all-encompassing person.

He was slim and walked swiftly, always with his chin up, and a slight smile lurking. He was a rich man's son, and indulged his taste for elegantly tailored clothes. He liked my expensive clothes, too, and especially the heavy brocaded satin

ballgowns in pale colors which my Aunt Shel Southworth presented to me. He agreed with her that they made me more
"queenly," and he liked to enter a ballroom with a queen.

The days sped by, filled with the indescribable happiness of
merely seeing him, or expecting to see him shortly. There was
to be no début party, but the ball in Mr. Stein's big new store
building was only a few days off. Mama had put in a rush
order for my ball gown, of spangled white tulle, and Jerry had
ordered his favorite red roses for me to carry in the grand
march. Uncle Lewis had told him that I liked pink roses better,
and that he, Uncle Lewis, had ordered these. But Jerry had
gambled on my giving preference to a fiancé over a mere uncle.
I could present the pink roses to one of the numerous middle-
aged chaperones who would take part in the grand march.

On the night of the ball, Mr. Stein's new drygoods
store was a dream of fairyland. The front of the building was
wide open, as the glass display windows had not yet been installed. Across the road from it flowed the deep, dark river—
but not so deep in summer time, and not dark tonight because
it gleamed with the reflections of the ballroom lights. For two
days wagonloads of evergreens had come in from the woods,
and a half-dozen Negroes inside the store had swiftly tied the
palmetto "fans" and other shrubs into bouquets. These were
laid, with stems against the wall, inside the empty shelves which
were deep and held them in position. Between the bouquets
of greenery were tubs of cut flowers—cape jasmine blooms,
roses, honeysuckle, magnolias. The finished effect was of walls
completely covered with tapestries of beautiful flowers. Overhead, festoons of white and baby blue tarletan hung and drifted
like clouds on a summer sky.

The merchant had prepared an up-to-date brick building,
with all conveniences, including two dressing rooms at the rear
end. The one for his lady clerks had a long mirror in it so
that these prim widows or old-maid sisters of Civil War veterans in straitened circumstances could make sure that no petti-
coat was too long and no blouse in disorder at the waistline.

There was ample width for a dance floor, as the counters

had not been installed, and now along one side was a row of chairs brought in for the occasion. The chaperones would occupy these, as well as any unfortunate young ladies who turned out to be wallflowers. The famed chivalry of Southern gentlemen just could not be stretched to the point of dancing with a girl who had no charm, or who got her feet in the way to be stepped on, or moved about so heavily that it took too much strength to whirl her.

Uncle Lewis and I arrived late, because he had discovered at the last minute that his evening clothes had grown too small. My brother Orman had been sent scurrying over town to borrow a suit from some married friend who was not going to the ball. But no one was worried about our lateness—it was a characteristic of all Southerners, only some were later than others.

But Jerry was not late; he was waiting for us on the sidewalk outside, determined to enter the ballroom with "his girl." He didn't mind if Uncle Lewis went along with us—any elderly relative might do that. I was carrying the pink roses, and Uncle Lewis carried the American Beauties!

We entered the building, Jerry on one side of me, and my uncle on the other. Then, in his usual quick manner, Jerry stopped and reached over and took the red roses from Uncle Lewis, and the pink roses from me. He handed the pink roses to my dignified uncle and exclaimed, "Craig says she wants you to present these to Mrs. Steele over there with the chaperones. She thinks you should take them to her." Mrs. Steele was sitting nearby, and at once began to smile and exclaim, "Oh, no! They are *too* lovely for *me!*"

My poor, dear uncle was too gallant to do anything but walk over and present the lady with the bouquet. Of course I could not lead a grand march without an armful of roses, so I had to accept those Jerry was holding out to me.

It was late, and the band started to play a Sousa march. As we walked down the floor, other couples fell in behind us. Uncle Lewis marched with his usual dignity, and with a stern face. He had been shocked by Jerry's sleight-of-hand, and it would take him a few minutes to recover his party spirit. Jerry was walking at my other side, looking innocently happy, and I was smiling, too, because I didn't want anyone to think there was anything amiss. But soon I recovered from my surprise, and said to him, firmly, "Now, Jerry, I've had enough of this. It is absurd, and you must go away!"

His answer was to call out loudly, "When we reach the end of the hall, all ladies will turn to the left, all gentlemen to the right, and march back, single file, to the front of the room." There was nothing else to do but follow instructions; I turned to the left, and Uncle Lewis to the right. And so I was marching back to the front of the room, along with Jerry, at the head of the line of ladies, while Uncle Lewis led the line of gentlemen.

Uncle Lewis had now recovered his savoir faire, and was really amused. He called out, jokingly, "Salute your partners." But Jerry took him at his word and halted the line by stepping in front of me and bowing low, then, dropping to one knee, he caught one of my hands and kissed it. "No need to flash those dimples at me," he said, "for I'm already yours, my beauty!" This turned the grand march into a romp; some couples began to dance a two-step, others tried to organize a quadrille, and Uncle Lewis, in his best orator's voice, called to the band leader to give us a schottische. I went quickly to him and we skipped off, side by side, executing his favorite dance. When Jerry came and tapped him on the shoulder, I held on tightly, and declared, "Oh, no, not *this* time! Goodbye, Mr. Winston. Glad to have met you."

Everything had to be polite; so Jerry bowed, smiled, and went off "cakewalking." He extracted a large green palmetto fan from a shelf, and cakewalked around several couples, fanning himself, and them, until he reached the front of the store —and then the sidewalk outside.

He did not come back, and of course I was indignant, for I was now left with no dancing partner. When the band stopped playing, Uncle Lewis took me to a chair and seated himself beside me. During the ensuing intermission, Shelby Steele and

several other young men joined us, and I accepted Shelby's
request to give him the next dance.

It was a waltz. When Shelby and I were halfway around
the room someone tapped him on the shoulder, but before he
made the parting bow, he asked, "Is Jerry coming back?"

"I hope not," I answered, coldly.

"I'll forgive him," laughed Shelby, "even if you won't. It's
giving the rest of us a break."

The other young men were no less gallant, and I managed
to have a good time in spite of a gnawing worry. It was beginning to be an old story, this matter of Jerry's possessiveness.
But deep in my heart I loved him for it and was distressed because I had sent him away.

As the following day passed with no word from him,
my concern became acute. But I was too proud to send word
to him. I did write a note, but I tore it up, and went on hoping that a boy would come with one from him. I went downstairs before dinner and had George take the pink roses from
the table, replacing them with some red ones from the garden.
But Jerry did not drop in for dinner. The evening hours
dragged on, and still he did not come.

At about eleven o'clock, being in my room, I heard someone
step up on the porch, and knock softly on the front door.
Because of the lateness of the hour he had not rung the bell,
I thought, and so I ran down to open the door myself. There
he stood, looking very pale, and very solemn.

"I could not stay away," he said. "I wanted to see you, even
if you refused to speak to me."

I bit my lip, trying to be calm enough to answer coldly, for
he had not said why he wanted to see me; maybe he wanted
only to apologize and then leave forever. I said, indifferently,
"No apology can make me understand. You had no right to be
rude to Uncle Lewis. If you think I am your *property*, you are
mistaken."

"May I come in?" he asked, humbly. "I won't stay long. That
is, no longer than necessary to give you my excuse."

"Yes," was all I could say. Then as he stepped toward me,

I put my arms around his neck, and began to cry happily on his shoulder.

A moment later, I told him to go and come back tomorrow, because Mama was not feeling well, and I did not want to risk waking her. He said, "I have a good excuse for what I did," and kissed me again quickly, and was gone.

The next morning, when I went in to tell Mama what had happened, she was sitting up in bed, drinking her morning coffee and looking as fresh and lovely as when she was my age. Aunt Catherine stood leaning against one of the big posts at the foot of the bed, getting menu instructions for the day. After Mama had told her to have George include some anchovies when he ordered the groceries, the shrewd old Negress turned to me with a grin and said, "I'll cook de squabs de way Mr. Jerry tole me to, jes' so you'll git use teh havin' things *his* way. Dat young man sho' ain't gwinna stan' fo' nothin' else in *his* house, Miss Ma'y Craig. Jes' watch what Ah say, chile."

After she had gone I told Mama about Jerry's late call, that he had said he had a good excuse. She raised her eyebrows, then proceeded to tell me that we were to take the evening train for the coast.

"You are to go on ahead, Daughter, with Alberta and your older brothers, and I will leave with the smaller children tomorrow morning. In this way, you and Alberta can get things ready for the younger ones before they arrive. I am going to take Lou as cook this year, as the work there is too heavy for Catherine. But Catherine will come with me, too. There will be work enough for all of the servants this summer, because you will have so much company."

"Oh, Mama," I protested, "I do want to see Jerry tonight. It is *so* important—his excuse, I mean. I do not want to go on being engaged to a man I do not understand."

But Mama was determined that I must take the evening train. She reminded me that she had stayed here in this dangerous Delta later in the hot season than ever before, and on my account. Now that the ball was over, I must consider the welfare of my young brothers and sisters. Suppose one of them should catch malaria—how would I feel?

So that evening we set out for the coast, Alberta, my older brothers and I. Always hitherto we had gone in one troupe, and what a show it was! The railroad men called it "the Kimbrough circus." They all knew us, for one of my uncles was attorney for one of the roads on which we traveled. There was in that troupe one stately lady, and a varying number of little ones, perhaps a baby in arms. Sometimes there was a white governess, and always there were half a dozen black servants—the nurses being permitted to travel in the car with the white folks, provided the lady said she had need of them. There was a pet bird in a cage, and a pet kitten in a box, and in the baggage car there was Dink, our terrier, who had to be fed and given water, for the cars were all hot. In the fall when we returned home there would be also one seagull and one pelican. There were lunch boxes and bottles, and bags and bundles beyond count. It was necessary to change trains twice, and there were poor connections, and hours of waiting between trains, so the whole circus had to be piled into a bus and taken to a hotel. Mama's motto in public was "Be quiet and dignified," so the Kimbrough circus was not noisy.

Mama, Jimmie, Aunt Catherine, Lou with her small black daughter, and my little brothers and sisters arrived next day. Two Negro men were driving through the pine woods in a wagon loaded with household goods to replace those which had rusted or mildewed during the winter. Two horses hauled this wagon through three hundred miles of sand, and behind it followed a pony for our cart, which stayed under the high front gallery of Ashton Hall all winter.

I soon found that the new cook was to furnish me with a literary occupation. Lou was a woman from the plantation who did not like to leave her "man" to run wild with other women in her absence. She felt that she must keep in close touch with him by sending him a letter twice a week, and I was to be her amanuensis.

I assumed that he was her legal husband because she spoke

of him as "my ole man." But my brother Orman asked Lou
the name of her child, and she replied, "Edna Lee Laura Liza
Jane Neal Wharton." When asked why so many names she
replied with complete innocence that there were three men,
Lee, Neal and Wharton, and she didn't know which was the
father, so she had used all their names.

Mama had meant it when she said there would be
enough company to keep all the servants busy.

Everyone knew Papa liked to fish. So Mama suggested that
he make an effort to run down to the coast in July during the
encampment of the State National Guard. His old friend, Governor Longino, was coming to review the troops, or whatever
it was that governors did on such occasions, and it would be
nice if Papa would invite him to Ashton Hall for fishing at
Back Bay. Of course the Governor's staff would be expected,
too, and as these were young men, Mama would invite the
other maids-of-honor—I had already been appointed—to be
house guests at the same time.

Jerry was tied to his father's plantation during July. I knew
he would not be made happy by Mama's program, so I did not
write him about it. But this made me feel guilty; I wondered
if I should hide things from him. Would our married life be
happy if I had to do that? Yet I felt that he had no right to
object to my having other beaux—I was not yet his wife.

Also he knew I was not interested in these men! It was
Mama who wanted me to avoid being monopolized. I wondered if he thought Mama wanted to prevent our marriage.
Maybe she thought his jealous temperament would make our
marriage unhappy? I asked her.

"My child," she answered, "I haven't a trace of such an idea.
I know full well that no daughter of mine would ever do anything that would cause her husband to be jealous. And I'm
sure that Jerome Winston knows the same thing. As for my
wanting to prevent your marriage to him, that also is not true.
What I do want is to make sure that you do not rush into a
hasty marriage. Jerome is one of the most fascinating men I
ever knew. Every girl in the town is halfway in love with him,

and even some of the married women find him almost irresistible. But this is one of the dangers. Take time, and do not
let yourself be swept off your feet."

Papa managed to get away from court and came to entertain
the Governor and his staff of young officers, and I had some
extra beaux to dance with at the old Montross Hotel in Biloxi,
a landmark of earlier romantic days.

The National Guard was a matter of pride to all Mississippians, for these people of the Old South believed in military
valor and the duty of men to defend with the sword all noble
and right causes. The question of states' rights, or "the sover-
eignty of the state," had been such a cause to those who gave
their lives to the Confederacy. Today, the sons and grandsons
of these men, organized as "The Sons of Confederate Veterans,"
still carried the tradition. Thus the brave and the true and
certainly the aristocratic of young Mississippians were marching and parading and dancing in historic old Biloxi that July—
while the man I loved was "riding the plantation" in the hot
Delta sun, unaware that the girl he loved was engaged in some
heartlessly gay flirtations with valiant would-be warriors!

My teen-age oldest brother Orman sailed his race-winning
Juniper to Biloxi every day, to mingle with the military
crowd. One day he would wear the "fatigue" uniform of the
Kentucky Military Academy which he had just attended, and
the next day he would wear the dress uniform. Now he announced that he had invited "two of Sister's beaux" to visit him
at Ashton Hall after the encampment was over. Mama looked
surprised, but I suspected that there was play-acting in this
look.

Mr. Agar, a wealthy bachelor and a cultured Bostonian,
bought an old home two places from us. Mama sent Papa to
call and they began to talk about good food; Mr. Agar wished
he had a French cook who could make New Orleans-style crab-
gumbo. Papa told him he should come over to dine with us
and give Lou's crab-gumbo a trial.

Mr. Agar came and asked if Mama would let Lou teach his
cook the secret. Then they began to talk of the beauty of the

Gulf Coast. The New Englander said that he had traveled all over the world looking for the most attractive spot on which to establish a home for his old age, and lo, he had found it in his own back yard! "Right here in America," he said, "is this superbly beautiful body of water, with its snow-white beach sloping up to the grand old liveoaks draped in gray moss"— he stopped and looked at me, then added, "and, if I may be pardoned, the most beautiful women on earth." Then he added, to Mama, "May I tell you, dear Madam, that your young daughter is a beauty?"

Mama beamed and replied, "I think so, of course. It gives me great pleasure, sir, to have a man of such discriminating taste agree with me." Mama really believed I was all the things anyone ever said about me, and thus she risked making me into a vain goose. I would tell her that all young girls were beautiful, just as were young ducks and young chickens and young puppies. She would answer, "Young mockingbirds and many other young birds are horrid-looking."

Then came a letter from Jerry, saying that he had been to dinner with Papa twice since we left, and that they had a date to go fishing together at Back Bay in August. So Papa, the just and impartial judge of the law courts, had seen to it that there would be no injustice done in the court of love! I went around for days, laughing suddenly whenever I thought of this. Papa, who was so grave, and so big, so absorbed in important affairs, was taking a part, on his own initiative, against Mama's scheming! A fair field and no favors!

Jerry came in August and with him came one of those ill winds that blow no good. The dreadful scourge of stegomyia, the yellow fever mosquito, blew in on the west wind from the Louisiana swamps. There was no yellow fever in New Orleans this summer, but the fear of the disease, which was now known to result from a mosquito bite, troubled those August days when we had expected to be so happy.

"Every time I kiss my sweetheart, a mosquito bites me!" Jerry complained to Mama.

"I've never been sure you should be allowed to kiss her,"

replied Mama. "When I was a young lady, no such liberties were taken."

"Come, now, Mama," Jerry teased. "I don't believe the Judge would have asked for a permit."

Fishing at Back Bay was out of the question, so I had Jerry around the house all day. There was no way to keep the mosquitoes out—screen doors had to be opened by people coming and going, and even the small mosquito houses, little refuges of screen wire on square frames, did not give complete protection.

"Your visit is spoiled," I told Jerry. "Papa is leaving tonight. Go back to Greenwood with him and finish your work at the plantation. Then you can come again after the wind changes."

He begged that I come with him, but I knew Mama would not permit that. It took all the firmness I had to let him go, and I began to realize how near I was to loving him more than I loved my adored parents. I did not want even to think of this. When Papa was saying goodbye at the station that night, I held on to his hand and told him how much I loved him.

"Be a good little girl," he said, and stepped quickly on the train so that I could kiss Jerry last.

When Papa returned in September, Jerry came with him and they got their sheepshead at Back Bay. Jerry and I had a couple of happy weeks together, sailing with my brother in the regatta in Biloxi, gathering driftwood with the children, and sitting on the white beach in the evening while the bonfires burned. Driftwood made multicolored lights, and Jerry told the children it was Satan's fire, sulphuric, beautiful, but poisonous. We planned our home which was to be on the river on a lot Papa had given me. Jerry's father had put some shares of stock in my name as a wedding gift. He had also bought me a gold thimble by way of a hint, as Jerry had told him I did not know how to sew!

There were no longer any rivals to trouble Jerry, because poor Mama had developed a chronic case of "light nausea" and did not feel like entertaining. Before he left he begged her to change her mind and consent to November for our wedding. But she was as determined as ever on a long engagement.

United States Senator John Sharp Williams was Mama's cousin, so they could laughingly trace their mutual interest in politics to the same ancestral source. But the truth was that John Sharp loathed politics, and yearned for the day when he could retire to his plantation; while Mama, who wrote letters against woman's suffrage, liked politics as much as the Senator disliked it.

After Jerry went back to Greenwood, Senator Williams came to the coast. Captain Jones, a northern capitalist, had completed the harbor at Gulfport and invited the Senator to "christen" it. Mama sent me to meet him, and on the drive he said, "I haven't had a minute to prepare for this and I haven't an idea what to say about a harbor."

"Just tell them everything is shipshape," I laughed.

"That's fine," he said—and that is what he did tell them. When I told him afterward how flattered I felt, he said, "My dear little cousin, you belong in the diplomatic service."

Mama treasured all compliments to her paragon as proof that the gypsy fortune-teller had known what she was talking about. When I was only three years old, Mama had gone into the booth of this dark foreign woman and had given a hand for the woman to study. To the question, "Are you married?" she had replied, "No," and the gypsy had exclaimed angrily, "You are lying! You are married and you have two children." Then the seeress added, "The name of your oldest child will go around the world."

During the first two months after we returned to Greenwood Mama continued to feel too "uncomfortable" for social life, and by then she was too unsightly. She wore her pretty lace ruffled "tea gowns" to the dinner table when there was no guest but Jerry, thus proving that she had finally accepted him as a member of the family. More than this, she had given up calling him "Jerome," which was keeping him at arm's length.

Every day he became a more necessary part of my life, and

the popular love-songs he brought from Memphis and New Orleans, and we sang together at the piano, seemed to have been written for us. My Uncle Fisher went to Kentucky for some thoroughbreds, and he bought me a beautiful chestnut saddle horse, "the finest single-footer he ever saw." Jerry promptly bought one to match, and we went horseback riding along River Road and watched the dear old river growing wider as its tributaries became swollen from the winter rains.

There were still times when he thought he owned me, and I resented this, and told him I no longer loved him. Then he would walk out abruptly, with only a muttered word of farewell. We were too much alike for a placid relationship. But, oh, how happy we were when our pride allowed it!

Papa had said to me two or three times during those months that he was afraid Jerry was drinking too much. Jerry's father often sent him on business errands to Memphis or New Orleans, and Papa heard something to the effect that on these trips he had been on sprees with other young men from the Delta. But this was only hearsay, he said, and a man shouldn't be convicted on that.

Then one day the bottom dropped out of my world. Jerry had gone to the plantation for a couple of days. He was expected back the next day, so I decided to go to bed early and get up in time for a horseback ride tomorrow morning. But after dinner Papa told me he wanted to talk to me, and we went to the west gallery. There he began at once:

"Daughter, what I am going to say hurts me as much as it will hurt you. . . ." He paused, and drew a deep breath. I saw that he was struggling for composure, and so I laughed and asked him, "Where is your peachtree switch, Daddy?"

But he went on gravely, "I hope you realize that I would give my life for you; but some things I cannot do, and one of these has now come into our lives. It is something you must do for yourself." He paused again, and I saw how old and gray his face looked. I could not endure to see him suffer. I spoke quickly and, I hoped, cheerfully, "Don't worry, Daddy, I'll do whatever you ask. I always have, haven't I?"

Then his words came swiftly and almost harshly: "Jerome Winston is not worthy of the love of my little daughter. You must break your engagement at once."

I could not believe what I heard; I could not take in the meaning of the words. It was as if Papa had struck me. "But— but—" I stammered. "Why? What has he done?"

He looked at me sternly. "Do not ask me why. I cannot talk about it. I have to ask your promise that you will do what I say. Send for him and tell him that you will not see him again."

He waited, until I managed to whisper the words, "Yes, Papa." Then he turned and strode into the house.

I do not know how long I stood there—I felt paralyzed in mind and body. I knew that I would obey him, but I wondered how I could. All I wanted was to feel Jerry's arms about me. I began to cry now; then I choked back the sounds, and flew upstairs to my room so that no one would hear me. I got to bed somehow, blinded by grief and tears. I had only one thought, to see him, and to cry with my head on his shoulder. I kept on imagining that he would come in, and I would run into his arms, and he would comfort me. "Oh, Jerry, darling!—" I was sure that I could not give him up.

All night I lay, trying to think, trying to steel my mind to live in the world without him. But there seemed to be no world any more. He was gone, and with him everything was gone, everything! But I must have got to sleep finally, because when I woke up the tray with my morning coffee was on the table by my bed and the coffee was cold.

When I finally went downstairs, there to my surprise was Jerry in the hall, drinking coffee and reading. How like the picture in my mind of him in our own home, reading his paper while he waited for me to come to breakfast! And, oh, how handsome he looked, in a new spring suit and a blue necktie! He jumped up, a happy smile on his face, and started toward me. I stood still, fighting the impulse to rush to him, longing to feel his arms around me, to hear his voice calling me "angel," and saying, "I love you." But I was frozen where I stood, for I had given Papa my promise.

He too seemed frozen by the look on my face. Suddenly he burst out, "For God's sake, Craig! What is the matter?"

I don't know how I managed it, but I answered, "Go in the drawing room, please, Mr. Winston. I'll be with you in a moment."

I did not look at him, but turned and hurried upstairs. With shaking hands I gathered together the engagement ring and the other jewels he had given me at Christmas and on my birthday. I put them into a velvet box, and went down to the drawing room. The weather was chilly and there had been a fire in the fireplace; the embers were red and warm, and he stood by the mantel, looking down at them. His face was grim now, his lips pressed together tightly.

He raised his head and gave me a long look, his eyes dark with grief and love, and yet proud.

"Yes!" he said, hoarsely. "The sweetest, and the most beautiful!" Then, before I could move away, he had swept me into his arms, and his lips were on mine. A moment later he reached quickly for the box in my hand and tossed it into the fireplace. As I stooped to rescue it, he hurried from the room.

I got back upstairs somehow and ran to the window and fell on my knees, to watch him as he walked away and into River Road. I was struggling with the impulse to scream "Oh, Jerry, Jerry! Come back!" Then I lay down on the floor and sobbed until I was exhausted.

At last I got up and pinned a note on my door, reading, "Do not disturb. I am sleeping." Then I fell into bed again and cried for hours. It was over forever. I knew it, and I think he did, for he left town that day.

3. HOLD YOUR HEAD HIGH!

Now tears almost drowned me. I would open my eyes in the morning, while the beautiful freshness of the day poured in through the sunlit windows, and suddenly I would remember that my happiness had crashed into ruins.

But of course I must not go on grieving forever, though I felt sure that I would. Mama was thinking first of what people would say. It would be dreadful to have them say that I had no pride and was eating my heart out about a man. To Mama, pride was the foundation stone of almost all the human virtues. "Family pride" came first among the several kinds, and she explained why: a code of ethics, of behavior and a standard of living were built up by a family through generations. It kept wayward or rebellious members from wrongdoing, for once "the tradition" was invoked, it was a powerful deterrent. Another kind of pride was that of sex: woman was the nobler sex, and no woman should love *any* man enough to suffer a broken heart for him. There were other prides, but this was the one she now called on. "Put on your prettiest clothes, smile brightly, hold your head high, and above all, keep your beaux in attendance!"

So I ordered some new clothes. I accepted every invitation to dancing parties, dinner parties, card parties, afternoon teas, and to visit friends in Memphis, New Orleans and other Southern cities. But when it came to "smiling brightly," I simply could not do it. I held my head high when I entered a ballroom or a drawing room, but I'm afraid I looked as solemn as Julia Marlowe in a tragedy.

I did not lose my beaux; I probably had more than ever before, for now there was no jealous fiancé to object. "It would be a terrible thing for *you* to become an old maid," one of them told me. "Come on and marry me. I know you don't love me, but I love you enough for two. You will be happier with me than if you wither away and are put on the shelf."

Others gave similar reasons, all based on the idea that it was the next thing to disgrace to be an old maid. But there was a nightmare which often woke me, weeping, in the night: I had married a man I did not love, and it was for life. Of course I knew it was for life, for that was how all Southern women thought about marriage. Divorce was a disgrace.

Papa was less troubled than Mama by my increasing indif-

ference to parties, and the attentions of young men proposing
marriage to save me. He knew I was hurt, but he thought that
time was the great healer for such hurts. "Men have died and
worms have eaten them, but not for love," he would quote,
jokingly. But Mama would remark, "She is not a *man!* Women
are capable of a more deep and abiding affection than men."
However, she remembered that poor Winnie Davis had pined
away and died because she had been forbidden to marry the
Yankee; I must not do that.

It was Mama who thought of another year in New
York, where I could take a post-graduate course at the Gardner
School. I must become a "bluestocking"; only I must never let
the men know it, for men would flee from a bluestocking as
from a plague.

Back at the school there was a new lot of young ladies, all
younger than myself. I ate with them but was free now to
come and go as I pleased, and I got my instruction apart from
the rest in what was called the "second drawing room." I was
"majoring" in literature and the art of writing, for one day
Mama had come home from a meeting of the Winnie Davis
Chapter of the U.D.C. and said, "You must become a writer.
You are the only person who can tell the true story of the
love affair of Winnie Davis. You have suffered exactly as she
did."

I had one instructor, who came from Columbia University
two or three times a week. I paid him four dollars an hour, a
large sum in those days. His name was Clayton Hamilton—
Dr. Hamilton, I was taught to call him. He was very handsome and very dignified, with dark hair and eyes, and a slight
tendency to avoirdupois; he was only a few years older than I.
Being a mere man, he may have had some flutterings of the
heart in the presence of a "Southern belle" who had often
enough been told that she was irresistible to men. But I made
no conscious overtures, because my own heart was now dead.

He had read a great mass of literature of which I was ignorant, and it was his duty to form my taste. He began by asking
what I had read and I told him—it didn't take long. He

brought me books to read, and we discussed them chapter by chapter. But I'm afraid I did not apply my mind closely to my studies.

At a school reception I met an author who seemed most attractive. Mark Twain was benevolently tolerant of sweet young things dressed in their prettiest and gazing at a "parlor lion" in wonder. I was surprised to find him clad in a snow-white suit in midwinter. It matched his hair, and set off his rose-pink complexion charmingly. His bitterness was hidden deep within and only his kindness showed. The twinkle in his eyes seemed like that of a lighthouse, which came, and then disappeared in the dark.

One of my first duties, of course, was to call upon Mrs. Jefferson Davis. She had written me lovely letters about my happy engagement; in one she had said, "Beware the first quarrel; but stand on your inalienable rights." When she learned of the breaking of the engagement she sought to comfort me: "You have my loving sympathy. If your relations led to quarrels, perhaps the rupture was fortunate for when one of *our* women is married, she is, if unhappy, like Sterne's starling she cannot 'get out,' and she is truly miserable."

In that same letter she had commented upon my proposal to write the life of Winnie: "My Winnie's blessed birthday is the 27th of June. I am delighted to think anything is to be done to honor her name."

So now, when I called on her in the little apartment hotel, I first told her all the news about the older members of the family whom she knew and loved—my "sweet Aunt Susie and Colonel Yerger," my Aunt Sallie Morgan, who had been her lifelong friend, and "all the other dear ones." Then I sat with notebook and pencil and scribbled fast while she told me all she thought I should include in my story of her beloved daughter. It came to seem more and more like my own story— amazingly close in its details—except that I was not going to pine away and die!

When I left New York at the end of the school year, I went straight to Ashton Hall. Mama and the children were already there. Everything had been planned so that I could work on my book; no company had been invited, and Mama seemed as much interested in my career as a writer as she had been in my social success. This did not mean she had given up the idea that sooner or later I would marry one or another of the eligible men I knew; it meant only that she believed I had an unusual mind and it should be used. Apparently she thought it was not necessary to have a mind in order to succeed in the more desirable profession of "belle."

Her only reference to love and romance was in connection with the tragic affair of the "Daughter of the Confederacy." She again reminded me that I would have no trouble in portraying this affair, since I had suffered the same thing. But now I had to tell her I had decided there was a difference in the two cases; and I feared this difference would make my portrayal of Winnie's case unsympathetic to the Cause which was so dear to Mama's heart. It was a matter of ethics, and ethics was something not to be overlooked, even in a romance.

Because my father was a lawyer, as were several of my uncles and both my grandfathers and one of my brothers, I was used to discussions of moral and ethical questions. In my childhood there was a sensational case in which the only witness to a murder was the son of the suspect. Could a son be trusted to give an honest account when he knew he might send his father to the gallows? My father and some of my uncles debated this question among themselves, and with friends who came to our home, and I went around asking myself what I would do in that son's place.

Now I found myself confronting an ethical question almost as hard to answer. Had it been right for Mr. Davis to refuse his consent to his daughter's marriage, simply because the man was a Yankee and unacceptable, on this account, to the Confederate veterans? What right had these men to control her life—and what right had even the most austere of fathers to give them this extreme consideration?

If Papa had given me such a reason for his decision against my marriage to Jerry, I doubted if I would have obeyed him. But then, I lived in a later period than Winnie's; the wounds of a frightful war were fresh and terrible in her time. Still I decided against Mr. Davis and those veterans who had so bitterly voiced their opposition to the marriage.

Mama understood my question but she did not see why I had to bring this into the story. It had been Mr. Davis' and Winnie's problem, not mine. I could stress the Southern chieftain's devotion to the soldiers whose bitter fate he had shared, and of Winnie's devotion to her father's wishes. However, said Mama, it might be well for me to talk this over with some of Winnie's friends and learn how it had seemed to them at the time and how it seemed now. So I set out upon another tour of the South.

I went first to New Orleans, and visited the widow of the Confederate general William Preston Johnston, who had been the first president of Tulane University. She had known Winnie. Then I went to one of the most heavenly spots my eyes had ever fallen on—Avery Island, a dreamland floating in a vast sea of swaying green reeds, and peopled by one distinguished patriarch and his kin. Old General Avery was the master of this real "treasure island," with its rich salt mines and its tabasco-pepper plantation, from which came the fortune of his sister, Mrs. McIlhenny. There was also a sugar-cane plantation.

At the New Iberia depot I was met by a handsome young man who turned out to be the son of the old general. We drove to his home through the famous land of the Acadians— if salt marshes can be called a land. These descendants of Longfellow's *Evangeline* lived in shacks which, like our bathhouse at Ashton Hall, rested on pilings over the water. The "Cajuns" paddled around in their native *bateaux,* in search of a bare subsistence from fishing and trapping.

That evening at dinner in the big house, Mrs. Leeds, widowed sister of the general, told me about the miserable life of these people. They came to the Averys for help when they were sick, or had been bitten by snakes, and she was sure the famous tabasco sauce was a perfect cure for snakebite, if any victim could be persuaded to swallow a goodly dose of liquid fire.

And by the way, there was a snake loose in the house; I was
not to be alarmed if it suddenly ran across the room. "They
are deadly but they *never* attack," my hostess said.

This old home in the wilderness of the Louisiana marshes
was run in the stately fashion of antebellum days. All the family
dressed formally for dinner every evening, the Negro butler
and his aides wore their best uniforms, and the china and
silver of state occasions were in daily use.

Alice Roosevelt had just been a guest, and the family was
still talking about her visit. Like her father, colonel of the
Rough Riders and vote-getting organizer of the Bull Moose
Party, Alice had a flair for the bizarre. She was supposed to be
affianced to John McIlhenny, and I learned that she had slightly
shocked the primly elegant old lady of the house, John's aunt.
Mrs. Leeds would not tell just what Alice had done, but one
of the maids came to help me dress for dinner, and was less
reserved. "She jes' po'ed de dish uv mushrooms over Mr. John's
haid, dat's what she done!"

In a day or two, after I had been shown the wonders in
landscaping and other charms of this fairyland, I had a visit
with the lovely Mrs. Dan Avery, who had been a maid-of-honor
in the mystic court of Winnie Davis when she was Queen of
Comus at the Mardi Gras. Mrs. Dan told me that Winnie was
one of the most lovable girls she had ever known; but Mrs.
Dan was reticent on the controversial subject of the rightness
or wrongness of *anyone's* conduct in the matter of the broken
love affair.

During my stay I was entertained by a mild romance with
young Mr. Avery, whose role as resident heir no doubt required him to supply romantic interest to all young lady visitors. The setting for this pleasant affair was even more thrilling
than the affair itself. There was the "big house," with its formal
dinners; there in the remote wilds of the Louisiana swamps
were ladies and gentlemen in formal evening dress, with a
butler and aides pouring wines from antique decanters on a
priceless old sideboard. Outside were giant liveoaks and rose
gardens and flowering shrubs on all sides. The Spanish moss
on the trees was the longest I had ever seen, and there were

so many sweet-smelling flowers in the gardens that the evenings were intoxicating with their perfume.

There was a tower with a winding stair from which lovely ladies might lean on moonlit evenings to listen to the songs of a troubadour in the gardens below. My temporary troubadour preferred to climb the stairs with me to sit in the moonlight and let the mockingbirds do the singing. But how thrilled my prima donna mother would have been by this little opera! Or had she set the stage for it?

Anyhow, I could tell her about it and she would be consoled for my failure to find a solution of my ethical problem. She would remind me that I had just visited in the New Orleans home of one distinguished Confederate general, and in the island home of another—so to condemn either Mr. Davis or the Confederate veterans for what they had asked of Winnie would be a betrayal of hospitality!

After I got back home, I did a little writing, and began to find myself really against this book. Almost everywhere I had gone for opinions of Winnie I got only opinions of the inadvisability of publishing the facts. If I told about the letters in my possession from veterans, condemning Mr. Davis for ever having let his daughter be exposed to a Yankee suitor, I was told it would be a reflection on all veterans to quote, or even to tell, of these cruel letters. If I told that "the Yankee" had actually been a guest at Beauvoir, treated with courtesy, even consideration, by Mr. and Mrs. Davis, I was asked if I did not think even the loyal friends of the Davis family would be outraged. If I said that Winnie had died of a broken heart, I was asked what proof I had of this. And did I not know that both Winnie and her mother had left Beauvoir and gone to live like royalty in New York and Narragansett Pier? This was not the way broken hearts would behave. If I mentioned that Winnie had been called a "bluestocking" by some, I heard indignant denials—I must have misunderstood my informants.

The fury that had come down from the Reconstruction days was difficult for those of our happier time to imagine. A number of the letters that were written to the Davis family, and also

to her suitor, Mr. Wilkinson, were turned over to my father by
Mrs. Davis. I will quote one of them, addressed to "the Yankee":

Americus, Ga.

To Alfred Wilkinson   June 10th, 1890
   Atty at Law etc.
     Syracuse N.Y.
Sir:

As the Col of my regiment of the matchless R. E. Lee I
write you at the request of my comrades in arms '61 to '65, to
say to you that the choice of the "Daughter of the Confederacy" is by no means approved by us. No, Sir, and should
she bow our heads and crush our hearts in humiliation most
damnable by marrying the offspring of an Abominable Aboli-
tionist, she will have to go to some Northern city or burg to
do so. The very sleeping dead Southern soldiers would rise
from their graves, and hustle you back to Yankeedom ere they
would see the daughter of Jefferson Davis ruined, and shame-
covered forever, by marrying one whose only desire in marrying her is to get a Southern woman—preferring such an one
with warm feelings to the Salamander-like girl of Yankeedom.

No, Sir, a thousand balls would be shot into your Negro-
loving heart ere we would permit such an humiliating out-
rage consummated in our own Southland—and even should
Miss Winnie whom we so deeply love as infinitely purer than
any Yankee woman on earth, consent to go North, then we
will bind ourselves together to lay you in the dust.

I am, Sir, for myself and War Comrades,

————————   ————————

Col. Lee's Army, Macon, Ga.

How could I deal with passions like these? And when these
same veterans, wearing their old gray uniforms, were still gathering every year to march in their reunions!

4. DANGEROUS IDEAS IN MY MIND

AT LAST I had a book of a sort written. But it lacked reality, for I could not write any part of it in a straightforward way without offending someone. It was a stilted, uninteresting manuscript, but it was satisfactory to Mama, and that was the important thing. Also, the United Sons of Confederate Veterans approved me as the official biographer of Winnie Davis and sent me an impressive document to this effect.

Mama wanted me to take the manuscript to New York myself—she actually thought I might be able to charm a publisher! But suddenly, without any warning, she was stricken with a serious illness.

I begged her to let me go with her to the sanitarium in Battle Creek to see Dr. Kellogg. A girl cousin was already there, and getting some benefit. The buildings and grounds of this health resort were spacious and charming. Dr. Kellogg, founder of the institution, was a deeply religious person; he and all his staff were Seventh Day Adventists.

Both of us were happy because Dr. Kellogg gave Mama encouragement. She must relax, rest, shed responsibilities, and take the soothing treatments.

But Mama was a gregarious person, and couldn't bear to let her social talents lie unused. My young cousin, Susie Yerger, said to us one day, "There's an author here, very famous. Everyone wants to meet him. Would *you* like to?" Mama promptly answered "Yes!"

"There he comes, across the lawn," said Susie. "He's very sweet-looking when he smiles." He was attractive, in gray flannels and tennis shoes, striding hurriedly along. His blond hair was slightly curly, his eyes blue.

Susie had jumped up and gone toward him, and they stood talking for a few moments before she brought him to us, so we had time for a good look. "Not quite tall enough," said Mama,

whose husband was six-feet-two. She had said the same thing
about Jerry, but I saw no reason why a man of medium height
could not be as interesting as an oversize one.

"But he looks like a gentleman in spite of those clothes,"
Mama added.

"Don't mention my book, please," I urged. "I'd like to see
what kind of person he is. Then *maybe* he might read it and
give us some advice."

Susie arrived, followed by the man she was dragooning into
being bored by people who just wanted to meet an author.

"Aunt Mary Hunter, this is Mr. Upton Sinclair." And then
to me, "Craig, talk fast, if you want Mr. Sinclair to read your
book. He says if he read all the manuscripts that aspiring ladies
and schoolboys ask him to, he wouldn't have any time to write
his own."

"I have no idea of asking Mr. Sinclair to read my book," I
answered. "It would be presumptuous of me, since I've never
read any of his."

"Why, Daughter!" exclaimed Mama, smiling her sweetest at
the reluctant lion. "I'm *sure* you have read *some* of his books!"

"I'll give you one tonight, if you'll come to my lecture," was
the equally smiling response. "I'm in a hurry right now, but
drop in to the MacFadden health home this evening at eight."
And away he went.

"What could be more tiresome than a lecture?" said
Susie.

But Mama and I sat in the auditorium of the "health home"
and listened to a talk by the author of *The Jungle,* a novel
which had made such a stir in the country two or three years
previously by its exposure of shocking conditions in the meat-
packing industry. We listened now to his account of his experiments with diets recommended by MacFadden and other
"health cranks." He explained that he had been searching for a
diet that would permit him to overwork with impunity, but so
far he had not been able to find it. We had no tendency to fall
asleep as he kept us laughing over raw-food diets, nut-and-fruit

My sister Sallie. In this photograph she wears at her waist an ivory miniature of our great-great-grandfather. He was appointed Surveyor-General of the Mississippi Territory by his friend and neighbor Thomas Jefferson.

Jefferson Davis' widow was our neighbor. Her daughter Winnie Davis had once reigned as Queen of Comus in a New Orleans Mardi Gras. Here is Winnie, with her maids of honor.

Upton's father and aristocratic mother. She was Mama's
match when the conversation at the dinner table turned
to family trees.

Upton Sinclair, age eight, and at twenty-seven, when he
was writing *The Jungle* (1905).

diets, the Salisbury diet of nothing but ground-up beef, and MacFadden's idea of swallowing some sand every day.

At present, the speaker told us, he was on a diet of seven quarts of milk per day, with the juice of one orange or one lemon in the morning. Prior to this he had observed a twelve-day fast. He was staying in a cottage on a slight rise of ground, and near the end of the fast had gone for a short walk with a friend. Returning, he found that he hadn't strength enough to climb to the house, and had to sit down and wait while his friend went up and got him a lemon. I doubt if I had ever laughed so much in my life, and I surely never expected to see my dignified mother wiping tears of laughter from her eyes.

The woman patient sitting next to Mama asked, "Have you ever seen such a charming smile? I guess he thinks it cheers up the sick. But imagine making all of those experiments with one's health!" They agreed that he had done the experimenting for his own good, but that in telling about it, and without charge, he was trying to help others, and Mama said that she liked experimental people because the world would stand still without them.

When I ran into Mr. Sinclair again, he joined me on my walk, and I had decided to ask his advice about my book. However, he didn't give me a chance. He launched on his favorite theme, which was "industrial democracy," and sailed along with it, apparently determined to make a convert of me. I am sure he gave me an hour's lecture on this subject, and though he smiled his friendly smile whenever he paused, he had no sense of humor about this grave matter.

When at last he gave me a chance to talk, I remarked, "I agree with one thing you've said, though I never thought of it before. I see that every person on earth who isn't incapacitated and who doesn't work is a *parasite*."

"Exactly," he answered, quickly. "He is living on the labor of someone else. But understand, I don't mean only physical work; we say 'workers of hand *or brain*.'"

"But suppose my father *wants* to work so that I won't have to? He would be ashamed to *let* me work."

Mr. Sinclair stopped walking and stood looking gravely into

my face, as if I were trying to excuse myself from a duty. "He should insist that you work. If you are an idler, you are selfish! Besides, a person must learn to work, if only to develop his faculties."

"Well, I'm trying to learn to work now. But until recently I've spent my life just enjoying myself."

"You won't be a parasite if you write books," he smiled. "Good writing is hard work, and no fooling."

I asked him if he would read my book and advise me about it. He explained that he was writing a book of his own, but that later on he would read my manuscript. I should write and remind him. He was leaving the next day, and he urged me to take my mother over to the MacFadden place to learn more about fasting and the milk diet.

We did not see him again. I told Mama about our talk, and she said someone had told her that Mr. Sinclair was a "muckraker." That sounded so unpleasant that she had not asked what it meant. Had I found out anything about it? I said yes, it was a name President Theodore Roosevelt had given to social reformers during the uproar created by *The Jungle*.

Susie said, "You'll be thrilled by his background, Aunt Mary Hunter, and maybe Craig will want to put him in her book. His great-grandfather fought the British on the Great Lakes."

"Really!" exclaimed Mama. "Who told you that?"

"Everybody knows that!" said Susie. "There's an old lady here who belongs to the D.A.R. who told me all about him."

"Then he's the man, Daughter, to help you with your book. He knows the meaning of history."

Mama soon decided that she could follow Dr. Kellogg's instruction just as well at home. All the Kellogg foods were on the market, and she could teach old Aunt Millie how to give her the massage.

I had been impressed by Mr. Sinclair's account of MacFadden's cure, and urged Mama to try it. She agreed that our new friend was a very convincing person, but was he a competent judge? Did he have enough medical knowledge to know his own condition? However, she was really impressed by Mr. Sinclair's sincerity and was sorry about his departure, for she had wanted to tell him more about my book.

At Mr. MacFadden's health home a doctor prescribed a fast of considerable length. Mama managed to live on air and water for two days and then informed the doctor that she positively would not continue. In a day, she was ready to go home.

Soon there came to Mississippi from Mr. Sinclair a copy of a novel called *Looking Backward,* by a New England Utopian, Edward Bellamy. I read it and was greatly impressed, and gave it to Papa. I never knew whether he read it or not, as he became ill soon afterward and called in the doctor for a check-up.

Now I had a double anxiety—both of my beloved parents were ill. I sat down at once and wrote Mr. Sinclair, asking if he thought that a fast would help Papa. The author replied that if he were in my place he would waste no time but take them to MacFadden's.

Papa would not consider this, so I wrote to Mrs. Roney, the Swedish woman who had been Mama's nurse there, and asked if she would come to Greenwood and attend them. I believed that she and I together could persuade them to give the fasting cure a real trial. Soon she was on her way, and I felt that our meeting with Mr. Sinclair had been providential. I wrote this to him and he answered politely that he was pleased to be recognized as an agent of heaven. He asked me to send him a report from time to time on the progress of the "nature cure" in the Deep South.

The author no doubt knew enough about doctors to imagine what those in conservative Mississippi would think of so radical a remedy, and I soon found out. There was complete consternation among those in my little home town when they heard that Mama and Papa had been persuaded to undertake a fast—and under the supervision of a mere trained nurse!

Several days passed, during which Papa and Mama faithfully drank a lot of water and nothing else. Papa could not resist teasing his two guardians now and then by threatening to eat a square meal immediately, despite our protests that it would probably kill him. As for Mama, she actually did break her fast, consuming surreptitiously a whole breast of a broiled chicken! But she survived.

The town looked on as if it were a thriller at the little Greenwood opera house; everyone was sure that Mama and Papa would perish in the middle of some night. Relatives and friends came to try to talk them back to sanity; but Mrs. Roney was tall and sturdy, and made a good watchdog. I read to my patients, chatted with them, and kept their minds off their inner hollowness. All went well.

Papa was able to fast longer than Mama. On the other hand, Mama outlasted Papa on the milk diet. She didn't in the least mind drinking a glass of rich Jersey milk every half-hour and she liked to rest in bed and doze. But both of them became rebellious after a few weeks. The doctor, who had voluntarily dropped in to look them over every day, was relieved to see them become "normal" again. He pronounced them free from any diseases, but he was far too conservative to believe that a "crank" regime was responsible for their recovery. It might easily have been due to Mama's prayers! "You can kill a cow with enchantment if you use a little strychnine, too," said Papa, and none of us knew he was quoting Voltaire.

Of course the good news spread over the county; but only one other townsman applied for Mrs. Roney's services. He was Mr. Glover, an elegant, elderly citizen known to have some mysterious ailment. He came to Papa's law office and asked to speak to him privately. Might he engage Mrs. Roney during the day? He asked if she might remain with us, as he was a bachelor and it would be improper for her to stay in his home at night.

The arrangement was made, and Mrs. Roney delightedly took charge of her new patient. She reminded me to send a report to Mr. Sinclair and casually asked me to mention the progress of Mr. Glover's tapeworm. I, equally innocent, mentioned it jokingly in my letter.

I heard from Mr. Sinclair indirectly and in a most distressing manner. He was contributing a monthly article to MacFadden's widely-read magazine *Physical Culture,* and he included my letter in an article about the fasting cure. He thought he was disguising it by using fictitious names and describing me as "a young lady from Virginia"—not realizing that everybody in Greenwood had taken to reading the magazine and would recognize all the circumstances of the case.

So, an hour or two after the issue of *Physical Culture* appeared on the newsstands, Greenwood's most outrageous wag was running down the main streets of the town with a copy in his hand, crying, "Extry! Extry! Mr. Glover has a wild beast inside him! It's a T. W.! Read all about the wild beast inside Mr. Glover!"

Soon afterward came a letter from Mr. Sinclair, telling me what pleasure my letter had given him, and pointing out how carefully he had concealed all actual parties. He added, "It is fine propaganda for the fasting cure. It will amuse people, and at the same time teach them. So many have diseases for which no cure is known!"

I learned one lesson from that experience. From then on I would be careful what I wrote to any propagandist!

Out of trouble, Mama was again concerned about my career. The United Sons of Confederate Veterans joined Mama in zeal for early publication of my book. So I was soon on my way to New York.

I had mentioned the book again in one of my letters to the only professional writer we knew, and Mr. Sinclair told me to inform him when I arrived in the city and he would give me what help he could. I went to the Martha Washington Hotel, where unattended ladies could live safely. Men were allowed only on the main floor.

I learned that Upton Sinclair was out of town and Mama had told me not to take my manuscript to a publisher without his advice, so I left it in my trunk. All New York was before me, and there now began a new era in my life.

Never again would I feel as most Mississippians felt in those days—that life began and ended in dear old Dixieland! Below the Mason-Dixon line, life was lived in the dignified yet gay, the courteous yet exclusive, the only desirable and supremely

right way to live! But I had already questioned this on some
points, and was now prepared, without too much re-adjustment,
to let myself go in for free investigation of new ideas.

At the Finch School for Young Ladies, where a girl cousin
was being "finished," I met the principal, Jessica Finch, a
woman of broad and liberal views. She was an ardent suffragist, and no doubt was touched by my trepidation at the idea
of seeking a career of my own. She demanded "equal rights" for
women, and she granted these rights to her pupils. My cousin
was allowed to go out without a chaperone! Young men had
this right—why not young women?

My cousin offered me proof of the rightness of her school's
modern ideas. She was engaged to the "most adorable man who
ever lived," all because after meeting him at one of the Finch
receptions she had been allowed to go out unchaperoned to
dine with him in a restaurant. After the dinner they had driven
home in a hansom cab, and he had kissed her. Her first kiss—
and they were engaged by the time they reached the school.
The end of this affair a few months later was an elopement
which shocked her parents, but all ended well, for the young
man happened to be the eligible brother of another of the
Finch young ladies!

So it was that I began learning about "feminism" in action,
and found it interesting.

Upton Sinclair had founded what was then called the Intercollegiate Socialist Society and is now the League for Industrial
Democracy. It was holding a national convention during the
Christmas holidays, and Jessica Finch, who was on the directing
board of the I.S.S., invited me to attend the meetings.

I listened to talks by John Dewey, Harry Laidler, and Graham Phelps-Stokes, celebrated in the newspapers as a "millionaire Socialist." It was the opening up of a new world to me.
Never before had I met such learned persons, and such serious
young people. There was not even a trace of flirtatiousness, and
rarely even a smile. I remember one especially earnest young
man, just out of Harvard, where he had started an I.S.S. chapter. His name was Walter Lippmann. He asked me questions
about the state of things in the "Deep South," but I fear I was

not of much help to him. One question I recall: "What is the economic status of the Negro in the Delta?" My puzzled answer was, "I didn't know he had any."

I was soon invited to Greenwich Village, a locale quite different from Jessica's fashionable East Seventy-fourth Street school. There I met young people who were cultivating literature on a little oatmeal and a good deal of "dago red" wine. There were novelists and poets, painters and sculptors, and some were destined to become famous. But I had no way of knowing which. Their manners were free, and so was their talk—Freud was just coming in. I tried not to be thought prudish, for I knew I was a provincial and had much to learn.

One trifling episode impressed me; I sat at a table in one of those little cafes which the "villagers" loved, and next to me sat a tall, red-haired novelist-to-be, Sinclair Lewis. His talk was entertaining; and while it poured out he gently laid his hand on my knee and began to press it. If that had happened at home, I would have told one of my young brothers and they would have put him on the first train going North and told him never to come back. But here I said, "Is that the way you make love in New York?" His hand was withdrawn and the conversation was not interrupted.

I met Nellie, a lovely young woman who was a secretary to Fiske Warren, an immensely wealthy paper manufacturer of Boston. Nellie invited me to visit her; she had a cottage all to herself on the estate. I went because she was a highly literate person and offered to read my manuscript and advise me.

Fiske Warren seemed to me a kind but rather odd little man, with various notions strange to me. He was hoping to bring about the single tax by establishing "enclaves" in which the system would be put into practice. He had helped to start one in Delaware, another in Fairhope, on Mobile Bay, and one in Andorra, in the Pyrenees. These he visited at intervals. I had been taught as a social duty to seem interested in whatever ideas men put before me. Fiske Warren would often come to the cottage to chat with "two cultured young ladies" who might be converted to the single tax movement.

There was a curious ambivalence in Nellie's attitude toward her employer. He kept track of the postage stamps used in his office—and he a multimillionaire!—Nellie told me as we were walking in his apple orchard. To punish him, she tore branches off the trees we passed, saying she would rob him of at least some of his apples!

Then, a bit later, she confessed that she had fallen in love with her employer. It had happened when he stood by the fireplace in his splendid home, dressed for dinner; he had looked so aristocratic, so different from poor men. I asked her to consider whether she wasn't in love with his money and social position, and after thinking it over for a day or two, she decided that this was the case.

In the meantime Upton Sinclair had found time to read my manuscript. He wrote that when we met he would tell me why he could not recommend it to a publisher. But I did not return at once to New York, because Nellie also had suggested some changes. She could guess what Upton Sinclair would have to say about it. She knew him, and admired his moral courage, his determination to devote his talents to the ending of poverty and its offspring, ignorance, but she thought he was a reactionary in reverse; he was intolerant of what he called reactionaries. Nellie said that Upton would surely want me to include in my book a diatribe against slavery, and he would not like it because there was no propaganda of any sort in it. "He is a great man," she concluded, "but he has weaknesses. Don't take his judgment as final."

Mrs. Fiske Warren came one day and we sat under an apple tree and talked about Art. Art (with a capital letter) did not interest me at all, and I told her it might be because I had been crammed on it as a schoolgirl. Beauty was a vague term, and I could never be sure what it meant.

"It means different things to different people," said Gretchen Warren, who wrote poetry.

"Yes," I agreed. "That is why I don't know what *you* mean. To our Negroes, beauty means bright-colored glass beads."

"The Greeks knew the meaning of beauty," declared Gretchen. "And all true poets do." She looked dreamy, and her gaze was far off.

"What do you see?" I persisted, for that same faraway look had come into my art teacher's face.

"If you were a poet, you would know!" she declared.

She looked at me with suddenly flashing eyes, and exclaimed, "Away with these reformers, like your literary adviser, Upton Sinclair! I am not interested in the masses, the oppressed *mediocrities!* Mediocrities are not what the world needs for progress. I am a poet, and I ask, what matters it if they die by the thousands at my gate if I write one great poem?"

I asked, "What if there happened to be a great poet among those thousands?"

And she replied, "He would be here, inside, not out there."

She was a very beautiful woman, with the color coming and going in her cheeks, her dark eyes glowing and her golden-brown hair gleaming in the sunlight. According to my idea of beauty, she had it. But I wondered if she would be so considered in a cannibal community in Africa, where she would be attractive as a tender, juicy meal!

When I told Fiske of his wife's visit, he laughed and said, "She has reacted too strongly to my single-tax activities. She really has a very kind heart."

This was the era of the muckrakers, he explained, and Gretchen was repelled by the word itself, which was not really very descriptive of these earnest and quite effective reformers.

I asked Fiske to tell me what he thought of Upton Sinclair, and he said that he thought a lot of him, but that Sinclair had chosen the wrong remedy for our social ills. Why not accept single tax, which was so simple that any child could understand it? And so, off he went on *his* pet theme, just as had Sinclair on his. Surely I was in a different world from my dear Dixieland!

Oddly enough, Nellie agreed with Gretchen—reformers were a bore. She was a working girl, she admitted, but this did not blind her to the fact that "Beauty" was of first importance in this life. So here was a great debate, it seemed, in the world of the intellectuals: "Art versus Propaganda."

"God save you from ever falling in love with a propagandist," Nellie ended.

A day or two later Will Price arrived. He was an architect and a devotee of single tax. His heart was with the poor and oppressed, but his tastes and way of life were much the same as those of the fashionable Warrens. He also knew Upton Sinclair; everyone did, he said. Sinclair was a very famous man.

"He doesn't look it," I commented, and Mr. Price laughed, and replied, "His clothes don't, but his face does. He has a fine face, serious, determined, and aristocratic. He is an aristocrat, you know, with a whole line of colonial gentlefolk in his ancestry. His family has an honored place in both the United States Navy and that of the Southern Confederacy. He not only never refers to this, but I rather think he tries to conceal it."

"Why does he dress so poorly?" I asked.

"I suppose he is poor. He made a lot of money on *The Jungle,* but he spent it fast on his pet crusades. I think he'd be ashamed of having money and keeping it."

I lingered on with Nellie because she was one of the most interesting persons I had met. She was from the Middle West, and had brought along some of its locutions, strange to me. She talked about "watter," and she poured it into a "worshdish," to me a bowl. She had been a poor girl, but had managed to get herself an excellent education and a job as secretary to a wealthy man. She knew about all the "radical movements" of the day—socialism, single tax, philosophical anarchism, (quite different from just plain anarchy), and she explained them all to me. None, she pointed out, had the whole truth. Yet each was like a religion to its adherents, passionately convinced that their brand offered the only salvation from poverty and war.

By the time I returned to New York, I was sufficiently educated to be able to discuss "the economic status of the Negro" with Mr. Walter Lippmann if I should meet him again. And these new people discussed so many lively things which I had never thought of before, that I was able to write Mama I was happy.

She rejoiced as I knew she would. The book could wait, she

wrote me, so long as I was "learning something." I wrote that I had gone back to the great Metropolitan Museum of Art which had bored me so during my schoolgirl days, to take another look at paintings and sculptures. Also, I had gone to a concert at Carnegie Hall, where I had heard Paderewski, and been spellbound. But I did not try to explain Socialism, or any of the other "isms" of the times to the blessed darling who would have been horrified by my interest in them even though she had not the slightest idea what any of them were.

I did write her about Miss Helen Stokes, a "millionaire Socialist," who had a studio in Greenwich Village, and was an active supporter of the Intercollegiate Socialist Society, which Mr. Sinclair had founded. I said that her brother, J. G. Phelps-Stokes, was head of the New York chapter, but that these wealthy settlement workers were deeply religious persons, trying to help the poor. They were called "parlor pinks," not "reds"—as the newspapers called the Socialists who were not millionaires.

At a gathering of the I.S.S., for the first time in my life I sat down to dine with Negroes. One, a grave, soft-voiced man wearing glasses, sat beside me, and his wife opposite. So powerful is habit that I felt unnatural and ill at ease in this position of equality. I was used to black people "in their place," that is, behind my chair at the table or preparing food for me—Aunt Millie, who massaged my back and legs when I ached from too much dancing or horseback riding, or Ben, who came to my room in the morning with kindling and logs to make a fire for me.

Since I had come to know the "intellectual set" in New York I had heard every imaginable viewpoint expressed on the subject of color. I finally decided that it made little difference whether Negroes were mentally inferior or superior; they were here on this planet with me.

If the Negro was too primitive, the remedy was education and training. If his table manners were uncouth, he could be taught to eat properly; if he was a house-servant, he had already learned good American manners from his "white folks."

I had seen Jimmie teach himself to drive Mama's automobile —this without her knowledge or consent, and without wrecking it in the process! Likewise, Jimmie had learned to read and write merely by listening to a governess or tutor instruct my small brothers in the nursery.

Aunt Catherine was shrewd, philosophical and capable. Her grown-up sons were not, but this was no doubt due to the fact that they were lazy. They did not have to work, and nobody had ever suggested that they should go to school!

There were nine Negroes to one white person in my part of the Mississippi Delta. Yet two or three white families could live on remote plantations among hundreds of near-primitive Negroes, with violence a rare occurrence. In the small towns, where there were a handful of whites, the many "plantation hands" who came in to bring the cotton, milled around the streets on Saturday nights, with only a constable and a couple of deputies to keep order.

Thinking it over, it seemed to me only three things were necessary to civilize these good-natured, easygoing people: patience, education, and a better standard of living—in short, equality of opportunity! And this in turn depended on three things: the abolition of prejudices, friendly guidance and enough money to provide the better standard of living.

So I sat, a guest of the Intercollegiate Socialist Society, and cautiously watched my dinner companions at that gathering to see if they were playing their part in this program of equality of opportunity. The Negro on my right showed no concern when I told him I was from Mississippi. I had wondered if he would, for he probably came from some part of the South himself, and knew that equality of opportunity to dine together was not customary there. We discussed the problems of our time, and especially those of this society. They believed what I did, and that was all there was to it.

Nellie was the first working girl I had ever known. The lady clerks in the drygoods stores in Greenwood were all "gentlewomen," victims of the Civil War. The common workers, who were "red-necks" to some, and "plebeians" to Mama, made no effort to mingle with the planters' families. They must have been proud people, for they never asked for aid of any sort, even though they were in need of almost everything.

Nellie was not proud; she seemed merely unaware that some people might consider her inferior. She was independent, and knew no social laws forbidding her to come and go "unchaperoned."

Now and then she became tired of her quiet, bookish life in the cottage, and, as Fiske had several secretaries, she could take the opportunity to visit New York and mingle with the Greenwich Villagers. There was no such thing as formality here; all one had to do to get acquainted was to go into a "tea room" or some little cookery run by "Polly" or "Gwen"—penniless Villagers themselves—and over a pot of tea or coffee, start a conversation with anyone who looked interesting.

Nellie had a vacation coming soon, and I suggested that she ask Fiske to let her have it while I was in New York. She would make me feel as if I had a chaperone; I had been brought up to consider it almost a breach of decency to be without one, like going on the street without gloves! Nellie could stay with me at the Martha Washington, or we might rent a little apartment. Her presence would make it proper for me to invite Mr. Sinclair there to hear his criticism of my manuscript.

By now I had lost interest in the prim, sentimental story I had written about Winnie Davis; but I had become really interested in the idea of being a writer. So I dashed off a chatty, foolish little story about a girl named Mary Anna and sent it to the only publisher I had ever met, Bernarr MacFadden. He had probably forgotten even my name; but lo and behold, there came a letter from the editor of *Physical Culture,* accepting the story and sending me a check for twenty-five dollars! I walked on air for the next few days.

After I had wired Mama the thrilling news, I got on a streetcar and went to Huyler's on Forty-second Street, where I had sipped hot chocolates with the young millionairesses of the Gardner School. I ordered two hot chocolates and invited the waitress who served them to have one with me. "I'm celebrating," I told her. She looked at me as if she thought I was daft,

but she gulped the drink between attentions to her other customers. She was another working girl, and I had made up my
mind to know more of them. I realized by now that I did not
like parasitic women; I was one myself, but I did not want to
continue to be.

I was becoming a "radical." I was reading the works of
Henry George, given me by Fiske Warren, and thought that
his theory of the single tax was better than that of the Socialists,
but my budding radicalism was more emotional than intellectual. I did not yet fully understand Socialism, or even the single
tax idea, but I knew that poverty was a cruel and dreadful
thing, and that it was wrong, if there was any way to get rid
of it.

On a visit to Virginia I had seen poverty in one of its most
pitiful forms—the poverty of excessively proud people, clinging
desperately to the pretense that they were still the wealthy masters of slaves and lands. There in the antebellum houses I saw
children barefooted after the snow was on the ground. The
families had been offered great sums of money for "heirlooms"
—but these were regarded as a sacred trust, to be saved for the
undernourished heirs who had no shoes.

Now every day on the streets of the great, rich city of New
York I passed beggars, legless, armless or blind, dressed in dirty,
ragged clothing and sitting in the dust and spittle of the sidewalks. Couldn't these people be taken care of in warm shelters?

No one ever seemed able to answer the question I had been
asking for years: why does God allow His creation to suffer?
But the Socialists had a remedy for poverty, or so they insisted;
and they pointed out that if poverty were banished, most of the
suffering in the world could be abolished. I wanted to talk
about this with Mr. Sinclair again.

Nellie arrived the day after my hot-chocolate spree, and
a couple of days later we were installed in a pleasant little
apartment on the West Side. I wrote to Mr. Sinclair and invited
him to call on us and tell me about my book.

He telephoned, asking me to meet him for a walk on Riverside Drive the following morning. He was staying with his

mother in her apartment nearby. I was troubled by the idea
that it might be considered improper for me to go walking with
a married man. But nothing was further from Mr. Sinclair's
mind than either romance or impropriety. In fact, I got the impression that he was slightly bored, and in a hurry, as he had
been when I met him in Battle Creek. He had a promise to
keep and an unpleasant duty to perform, and set about doing
both without delay.

"Your book is terrible!" he said. "You can't write. I can't
honestly encourage you."

"You liked my letter well enough to give it a lot of *very* unpleasant publicity," I replied.

He laughed, and I joined him, for I, too, knew the book was
"terrible." I asked him to explain Socialism to me, and he
plunged right in.

I was not used to walking, and had trouble in keeping up
with his pace. More than once I suggested that we stop and rest
on a bench. He would sit for a few minutes, then inform me
that his circulation was not so good; he had been overworking.
He would get up, and I would have to get up also, and walk
some more, so that his feet wouldn't get cold.

"It is too late in the season to be wearing tennis shoes," I told
him. "No wonder your feet are cold."

"They are all I have," he explained. "I can't buy any clothes
until my new book is accepted. Then I'll get an advance from
the publisher."

I was appalled! I looked furtively at his shabby gray flannel
trousers, which were badly in need of pressing, at his worn
coat, which obviously belonged to a different suit, and at his
wavy blond hair, which was too long.

"I supposed you had made a lot of money out of *The Jungle*," I ventured.

"So I did," he replied; "but I spent it all on propaganda, one
sort or another. A man who believes as I do cannot honestly
keep money."

He resumed his Socialist lecture, explaining that poverty was
the cause of war, much disease and most ignorance. These different evils were all one to him, because all of them would go

almost automatically when poverty was abolished. If their energies were not spent in a blind competitive struggle for bread and butter, men could devote themselves to education and to scientific research; human brotherhod might become a reality.

I did not speak of my book again, which I am sure was a relief to him. But he was pleased to hear that MacFadden had accepted my story, and wanted to know what it was about. I told him it was nothing he would be interested in, just a silly story about a silly young girl. He said he might be very much interested, and asked if I intended to write more. I told him I meant to, and before we parted, he offered to read in manuscript whatever I might write. "You probably have some excellent material for a novelist," he said.

I corrected him. "You mean for a novel, don't you?"

He looked at me with his mischievous smile. "You might be good copy for a novelist," he repeated. "Ask Nellie to tell you what that means. And by the way, tell her she should ask George Sterling to call when he arrives in New York from California. I'd be glad if you and she would entertain him for me; I can't do much for him at present because I'm having some marital troubles."

He took out his watch, said he had an appointment with his lawyer, and bade me goodbye and good luck. He hurried away, suddenly looking small and pathetic.

Mama had been delighted by the news of my short-story sale, but she became worried because I was meeting so many people she had never heard of. Who were they, anyway? They might implant some dangerous ideas in my mind! I had thought I might gradually get her used to the idea of my actually becoming a convert to one or another of the "radical" social theories, but I realized that her mind could not open itself to such ideas. She was a believer in experimentation in many fields, but not in what she called "the very foundations of our society." Here her watchwords were *status quo* and *noblesse oblige*.

Nellie and I went to tea with Mrs. Gaylord Wilshire and she questioned me eagerly about life in the "Deep South." When

we were leaving Mary Wilshire cordially invited both of us to
visit her in London.

Like many of the Socialists I had met so far, "Gay" Wilshire
was a millionaire—or had been. An idealist, he could not bear
to live in unearned luxury while millions of human beings all
over the earth were cold, ill, and starving. So he had taken some
of his inheritance and put it into a magazine through which to
spread his Socialist beliefs.

He had squandered money on this venture, and was now
living a less spectacular life in London. But he was sufficiently
well known to attract to the salon which Mary held in their big,
rambling house above Hampstead Heath, the most celebrated
of the literary men and women of England.

Mary left New York the day following our visit, with my
promise to look them up if I ever came to England. I thought
it would be interesting to visit her, and told her that Mama
had wanted me to go abroad several years ago, and might still
want me to go. Nellie felt sure she would be going to Europe
soon, as Fiske would need a secretary on his proposed visit to his
colony in Andorra. Perhaps we would all meet again abroad.

5. LOVE FOR ART'S SAKE

WHEN NELLIE went to Greenwich Village to meet
Emma Goldman, the famed anarchist leader, she invited me
to come along but I declined. This would be going too far.
Nellie laughed a bit scornfully and said she had thought I was
too broadminded to be afraid to be seen with *anyone*. But I
stood by my prejudice. To "avoid even the appearance of evil"
was one of Mama's precepts.

I was alone in the apartment when the doorbell rang. The
chances were that some male Villager was outside, waiting to
come in and eat some of Nellie's vegetarian food. This might
be as improper as meeting Emma Goldman, but I decided to
take the risk, and opened the door.

There stood a tall, slender, dark-haired gentleman, who gazed at me fixedly. I returned his gaze for a moment; he was extremely handsome. I waited for him to speak. He continued to gaze at me as if he saw something he could not believe was there.

When at last he did speak, it was surely the most unusual greeting I had ever heard: "Goddess!"

His voice was low and intense. He was well-dressed, and elegant in bearing, and I couldn't be exactly afraid of him. I had been meeting writers and artists and assorted "radicals," and was prepared for strange things—but this was the strangest.

"Who *are* you?" he whispered.

My answer was, "I think it would be more to the point if you would tell me who *you* are."

"Star in alabaster!" he exclaimed.

That was too much. "Really," I said. "I think you are being rude." And I made a move as if to close the door.

"Let me come in," he pleaded. "I am not rude—I am a poet, seeing a vision from heaven. I am George Sterling."

So I stepped back, and he came in, closing the door behind him. He dropped down on one knee before me.

"Forgive me!" he pleaded. "I never dreamed that I would meet such a heavenly being on this earth."

I had had men on their knees in the romantic "Old South," but I had not expected it in Yankeeland. "Get up, please, Mr. Sterling, and sit in a chair. I'm not the least bit impressed. I'm used to men pretending raptures."

"You must be," he answered, "Only they were not pretending, I am sure."

He got up gracefully, and stood waiting for me to seat myself. He had a cultivated voice and manner, and I felt no concern about having him as a visitor; but he began to gaze at me in that rapt way again. I hastened to make conversation, as I had been trained to do in all emergencies. "You have just arrived from California?"

"I arrived two days ago; but I count those days wasted."

"You are Mr. Sinclair's guest?"

"Not entirely. I'm visiting an uncle out on Long Island. I'll stay in town if you will let me see you."

"Really, Mr. Sterling—"

"You have not told me who you are!" he burst out. "But I know—you are Beatrice." He pronounced it in the Italian style.

I replied prosaically, "I am Mary Craig Kimbrough, from Mississippi. Who is Bay-ah-tree-chay?"

A delighted smile crinkled his eyes and lips. "I am Dante, and you know the lady he worshipped." His face was rapt again. "God, what incredible beauty! What charm! How dare I gaze upon thy heavenly face!"

I heard Nellie's key in the latch, and she came in with a rush, her cheeks red and her excitement high. She was diverted only for a few moments by the presence of a caller. She greeted him warmly but quickly, and then exclaimed, "That outrageous woman! As if I would condescend to flirt with such a creature as Alexander Berkman! To be jealous of *me!* Incredible!" She removed her prim little felt hat and tossed it on the table.

"Sit down," I said, "and tell us about it"—for I knew that was what she wanted.

"I'm too nervous to sit." She began to pace the room.

"Emma got back late from her lecture, and found me sitting quietly in her apartment, to which she had invited me. That man—her lover, they say—had come in with a bunch of lovely roses for her. He had arranged them beautifully in a bowl of water on a table in the sitting room. 'She'll like those,' he said, proudly.

"Then he sat down beside me on the couch—too close, of course—and began to talk politely about the steel strike. In came the great Emma—super-radical, emancipator of womanhood, 'free lover' to all the bourgeois world. She glared at me and cried, 'Oh, so *you* are the reason he didn't show up at my lecture!' She seized the bowl of roses and hurled them at Berkman's head.

"I don't know what happened after that, for I left without saying goodbye. My fresh blouse was wringing wet. I got into the streetcar, and I suppose people thought I must have been in a fight, for they all kept on looking at me. And that's what I get for associating with those radicals!"

There came by messenger next morning two of George Sterling's books of poems, *The House of Orchids* and *The Wine of Wizardry*. Also there came what Nellie called "a magnificent sonnet":

TO CRAIG

I need not now a vision's light and pow'r
  To tell what loveliness was theirs of old,
  When Egypt's siren with her lures untold
Or Helen leaning from her eastern tow'r
Or Rosamund within her hidden bow'r
  The lords and kingdoms of the world controlled.
  Those were but dross before thy magic gold,
Earth to thy pearl, and nettles to thy flow'r.
All gracious things and delicate and sweet
Within the spaces of thy beauty meet:
  God hath set mystic jewels in thine eyes,
    And in thy face the rose of all romance,
    And in thy lyric voice, beyond mischance,
  Such chords as wake for Love in Paradise.

To me this seemed as amazing as his behavior of the day before. "I don't know, Nellie, what to think of such a man. I never before knew a poet. Do all of them write their poetry in a trance?"

"I think they probably do," she answered. "A real poet is inspired—I have felt a touch of it myself."

I laughed. "It sounds like Aunt Millie's rheumatism. She had a touch of it periodically."

"You can't be flippant, Craigie, about what has just happened. You are the inspiration of a great poet. Don't be too vain about it, though. You are not responsible for it, and neither is he. It just happens."

In the next mail a letter came from George Sterling: "I will be in town day after tomorrow and will telephone you. I must go on my uncle's yacht tomorrow. It will be a great bore to

me, but he brought me East, as his guest for his annual visit
to his summer home at Sag Harbor."

George Sterling telephoned to ask if I would walk
with him on Riverside Drive, and I said I would. He asked
if I had received his sonnet, and I told him, "Yes," and thanked
him. Before I went out to meet him I read it again, and thought
it was too beautiful to be real.

When I met the poet at the appointed place on the Drive,
he was smiling normally and looked more attractive than when
he had "discovered" me. He asked if his books had reached me,
and I told him they had, but I had had time for only a glance
into them. I was too ignorant to know what words of apprecia-
tion to use, and I told him so. This amused him, and he said
it would not matter. Just think what havoc had been wrought
by Eve's acquisition of knowledge. He told me about a poem,
"Lilith," which was taking shape in his mind, and I asked him
to tell me what it meant; I had never heard of Lilith.

We were walking briskly as we chatted, and as usual I began
to doubt my capacity as a pedestrian. When I began to feel
tired I took a seat on a bench, and he stood before me, threatening to begin his soul-gazing again. But the spell was broken
by the appearance of Upton Sinclair. He had evidently seen
us before we saw him. He looked so tired and careworn that
it was hard to realize he was the same man I had met at Battle
Creek.

"So you found her," he said to George. "I thought you would
want to meet her. But if she has any literary treasures up her
sleeve, they belong to me." He asked if I had finished another
story, and I told him I had finished several.

"In this short time?" he asked.

"Yes. By writing day and night."

"You had better lay them aside for a while and go on a milk
diet. You have really been overworking. You are pale and hag-
gard. You look like a skull!" At this George Sterling scowled,
and walked off, pretending to examine a statue near our bench.

"Save all of your stories for me, *please*," Mr. Sinclair begged.
"I might help you make them into something really good."

He told George Sterling that he was in the midst of a personal crisis, and that was why he had not called up sooner. The
other gave him a quick, warm look of sympathy. "I know," he
said. "Your wife wrote me about it. Let me hear if I can help
you in any way." The two men shook hands and Mr. Sinclair
called out goodbye to me and departed.

"Poor fellow!" said the poet. "They have been on the brink
of a complete smash-up for a long time. I'm very sorry for him
—otherwise I'd have been tempted to kill him for that idiotic
remark he made to you."

"But I do look like a skull," I declared. "I know it, and if
he were not a married man I'd want to marry him. He's the
first one who ever told me the real truth."

The next morning the name of Upton Sinclair was on the
front page of every paper on the news stands. "Upton Sinclair
Files Suit for Divorce." The famous author could not be located for comment, they said.

After that both Mama and my great-aunt Sallie, Mrs. Green
of California, wired me. Mama wanted me to leave at once for
home or for California. Aunt Sallie urged me to visit her without delay. It was as if I had been caught in a yellow-fever
epidemic in New Orleans. Divorce was such a terrible thing in
the South! There had never been one in our family, and my
mother and even my more broad-minded great-aunt were
alarmed by the mere thought of my being exposed to one, especially one which was making the headlines in newspapers
all over the country.

Aunt Sallie followed her telegram with a wise letter.
She said that as soon as the divorce story appeared, she realized
that my name might get into the affair through my literary
associations. Newspaper reporters were always on the lookout
for a romance, and were not always above a fabrication, if they
got even the faintest hint. Above all things, she said, I must
not see Mr. Sinclair while the reporters were on his trail! And
never, *never* speak a word to one of these sleuths!

The best thing for me to do, she was sure, was to leave New
York and come to her; for if I went home, it might attract the

attention of some society reporter in New Orleans or Memphis, who knew of my book, and of my intention to have it read and criticized by "Mr. S." (She was so alarmed that she did not dare to write his name!)

Mama's letter, following her telegram, was almost hysterical. "Oh, my child, do be careful! You are in real danger of becoming involved in that dreadful affair. Your tender heart may lead you to defy precautions. But you must not! Your sister Sallie is a young lady—think of *her,* not of that man we met in Battle Creek. He is kind and generous, I know, and doubtless is innocent of any wrong; but you cannot risk offering him your sympathy, even by one word, written or spoken. Aunt Sallie has wired you. Take your choice between California, or home, *at once.* May God spare us involvement in this sad, unfortunate affair. Maybe I am to blame for ever letting you leave the security of your home. Oh, I wish I had not let you go!"

It was fortunate that these warnings came without delay, for I was on the brink of writing Mr. Sinclair a note of sympathy. But even after the warnings from my family, I wondered if it was right to refuse one kind word to a man who had generously given his time to my manuscript.

Of course I had no idea of the sleuthing proclivities of news reporters, and of the dishonorable behavior of some of them. Even so, my impulse was not to desert a friend in trouble; and this is what I would feel I was doing if I failed to communicate with Upton Sinclair again.

George Sterling dropped in while Nellie and I were debating the question. He announced at once that he had come to warn me not to get anywhere near this dangerous situation. When I told him about the warning from my aunt and from Mama, he said that the ladies were right. When he grasped the fact that I had an aunt in California, he began urging me to visit her. There he could see me, and be inspired over and over again!

He said he was going to call on Upton's mother in order to learn the author's whereabouts; he wanted to offer to help his friend in any way he could. But when I said, "Then at least you can take him a message of sympathy from me," he answered,

"No, positively *No!* Upton is utterly indiscreet. He says whatever pops into his head. He might even be indiscreet enough to come here to see you and Nellie. I wish you would leave at once."

But I stayed on quietly in New York.

Nellie's comment on the divorce was that it was a good thing. No couple could be more mismatched. Her comments on my family's attitude were decidedly severe. The ideas of today, she said, made their attitude archaic. Only the Catholics believed that two people who were incompatible in their domestic life should remain together, even for the sake of the children. It was more harmful to bring up children in a discordant home than to have them divide their time between two parents relieved of the burden of each other's company. This seemed reasonable to me. I began to ponder Mrs. Jefferson Davis' remark, that "once *our* women are married, they are like Sterne's starling—they cannot get out." She meant Southern women. I was now questioning on one point after another whether I was any longer a Southern woman at heart. I differed with the opinions of my people on so many important matters. Why were they so self-satisfied, so certain they were superior to almost all other people—and so determined to remain as they had been for generations in our remote corner of the world?

But I always ended by realizing that I could never endure being separated from the parents I so deeply loved, or even from my dear young brothers and sisters. So of course I agreed not to see Mr. Sinclair again, and reminded Mama that I was more interested now in writing short stories than in meeting anyone.

Nellie's vacation was up; she went back to her job and I moved to the Martha Washington. I had never before known solitude, and I found it a wonderful experience. It gave me an opportunity to think, something difficult to do when surrounded by people. The old ladies in the hotel ceased to notice me as I came and went.

For some reason I have forgotten, I sent no more stories to *Physical Culture* or to any other magazine. Perhaps I hoped that I might accidentally run into Mr. Sinclair again and submit my writings to him as I had promised.

George Sterling telephoned me at the hotel and asked me to meet him for another walk. He wanted to visit the Cathedral of St. John the Divine, the building of which had been going on for a decade or two. I told him I had been in and out of Episcopal churches all my life, and had attended St. Thomas' in New York for two years. They seemed to me very much alike, the small ones miniatures of the large. But he answered, there was nothing in America like this one, and he wanted to see it with me. I asked him why these last two words, and he gave me a religious reason. I was named Mary, was I not?

I went with him, and we entered the enormous edifice which would require so long in building that he doubted if he would be alive when it was finished. I was more impressed by his feeling about it than by the architectural marvel. He stood still and gazed about him, and the tears rolled down his cheeks. He murmured, "Let's go," and so we went.

I am not impressed by bigness in anything. To me, size does not represent virtue, but only the supremacy of the body over the mind, which I resent.

Outside, George quickly regained his composure and became again just one of the pedestrian New Yorkers we were passing on the street. He wanted to know how soon I was leaving the city, and again he begged me to come to California. When I told him I had almost made up my mind to do so, he was enraptured. Now he could bear to start homeward.

We went over to Riverside Drive and sat on a bench. I thanked him for his sonnet and told him that I was going to the Public Library and find out all about Dante and Bay-ah-tree-chay. He asked me if I wanted to learn something about poetry, and I said yes, provided he would do all the talking. So he talked about poetry, and life among the California poets. George loathed cities—he was here at this moment only because I was. He longed for his bungalow among the pines on the craggy Pacific coast at Carmel.

George told me that he had been educated to become a

monk, and that, like my mother, he would always be grateful to the Catholics for the training given him. In contrast to his student days among these monks was his life at the Bohemian Club in San Francisco, where he found it hard to refuse to take a drink with a friend every time he was invited.

I informed him of my aversion to alcohol, and he immediately volunteered not to take another drink while he lived if I asked him not to. This I refused to do; I said that I thought a man should make his own choice.

George said he had not taken a drink since he had first laid eyes on me, and that he never would again if I would come to California where he could see me now and then. Now all that he dared ask of me was that I should not marry before he had time to show me what he could do as a poet if he had me to inspire him. "I'm afraid now of Upton," he said. "Oh, when he is free, he won't fail to beg you to marry him!"

Mama wrote me about Jerry for the first time since I had sent him out of my life. It was fortunate, she said, that I had not married him. He was drinking himself to death—she had heard that he spent most of his time in Memphis with some of his drinking cronies, and in Hot Springs, Arkansas, where drinking men from the Delta went every so often to have "the liquor boiled out of them."

I cried the rest of the day, and dreamed of Jerry that night. He stood before me as he always did, smiling that slightly mischievous smile. I loved him still, and my heart was breaking all over again! I wished that Mama had not written me about him. I had kept myself from thinking of him, but I had not succeeded in putting him out of my heart.

The next day the thought of him haunted me. He followed me everywhere I went. When I went out to do some shopping, I saw his face in the street crowds. Each time as I came near calling out to him and hurrying joyfully toward him, he would disappear. Once I cried suddenly in a department store where I was buying a gold-brown coat. He always liked that color, because it matched my hair and eyes. The girl who was fitting me asked if I were ill, and I said it would pass quickly—it always did.

But it did not. I bought the coat, gave my address, then went into a coffee shop and ordered some coffee. I drank it black, and hot. It braced me up, and I ventured into a shoestore. But when I asked for brown suede, I had to change my mind instantly—Jerry had admired the brown suede oxfords I wore with a brown tailored suit in Greenwood.

I bought some brown glacé kid ties, and got into a hansom and drove to the old apartment Nellie and I had recently given up. It was occupied again, but there was another, similar to it, only smaller. It was just what I wanted, and I took it. I would invite some people I had met in Greenwich Village to spend an evening. I could not bear to be alone with the memory of Jerry.

Back at the hotel, I found George Sterling waiting in the lobby. I went out to dinner with him. Did he know, I asked, of an eating place which was cheap and clean? I wanted to learn to live on what I could earn as a short-story writer. I was going to try to live according to my newly-acquired ideas, even though I might have to refuse to obey Papa and Mama.

George did not laugh at this, but offered to help me revise my manuscripts if I would send them to him. He often did such work, he said, for his friend Jack London. I thanked him and told him I was afraid he let himself often be imposed on.

His eyes twinkled and he shook his head—that would be wise advice, he said, from anyone but his goddess. I told him to please stop worshipping me and become a real friend—I needed one. He leaned across the small table and looked at me with a hurt expression. "You don't mean that!" he said. "You must know by now that I would die for you."

I thought I should remind him that I could never love him— my heart belonged to a man I would never see again.

"I told you to break my heart," he said. "That cannot matter —I mean, it does not matter if *I* suffer. All I ask is for my art to live. See me, write to me, pretend that you love me, do anything you wish; only let me worship you."

I told him I could not understand this attitude, but that I

must take his word for it, as he was an artist, and I was not. Then he said, "The next best thing to being the inspiration of art is to be the artist who is inspired." I was trying to find out, I said, what artists meant by that word "Art," which they tried to glorify; but I could not. This amused him, but he did not try to enlighten me.

We lingered a long time over our coffee-cups, and I told him about Jerry. When I got to my mother's account, I had to pause once or twice to get my voice steady; he reached over and caught my hand. "You poor darling!" he murmured. "It only makes me love you more."

I told him about a poem which Jerry had once brought to me. It was a poem of a man's regret for his wasted years. Jerry had come upon it in some magazine and had cut it out. I might have gathered from it that he had a troubled conscience, but I was too young and too ignorant of the world to get that meaning.

"What was the name of the poem?" George asked, and I told him, "The Man I Might Have Been."

He said, quietly, "I know *just* how he felt—for I wrote that poem." And he recited it. The last stanza ran:

> Clear-visioned with betraying night,
>   I count his merits o'er
> And get no comfort from the sight
>   Nor any cure therefor.
> I'd mourn my desecrated years
>   (His maimed and sorry twin,)
> But well he knows my makeshift tears—
>   The man I might have been.

I was able now to realize what the verses had meant to both men, and I was so moved by it that I kissed George Sterling goodbye when he left for California. That night in my dreams Jerome Winston stood holding out to me a copy of "The Man I Might Have Been."

I decided that I wanted to fight it out with my memory ghost. It interested me to realize how vividly an image lived on in the subconscious mind. I knew that I would never see Jerry again. And I was no longer a child; I must learn not to weep. I must learn to master what I now knew to be my very emotional nature.

No one from Greenwich Village could help me in this struggle. I must do it myself—and now was a good time to sit down alone and say, "You can and you *must* take control of your own mind!" The brave spirit of "do or die" pervaded the Village, but its aim was merely to win some kind of worldly success—fame, or social justice, or both. But what I wanted was to understand life; self-understanding came first, in my opinion.

Someone had once told me that introspection was dangerous, that one should go out and mingle with people, look for entertainment, do anything but sit and look into one's own heart and mind. I had tried to lose myself in writing. The acceptance by a magazine of one poor story had thrilled me for a brief time, and I had worked tirelessly for a time far into the night, drinking too much coffee. But look what had happened when Mama wrote me that Jerry was drinking himself to death!

What could I read that would help me to understand my mind? Surely someone had written something more helpful than the psychoanalysis the Villagers were talking about; that did not draw me. Religion, as I then knew it, threw no light on my problem. I was "seeking the kingdom of heaven," as far as I knew it. But I wasn't finding it.

Then I met the Norwegian-born critic, Edwin Björkman, who greatly admired the French philosopher, Henri Bergson, and in answer to my questions about the mystery of the human mind, advised me to read this Frenchman's *Creative Evolution*. Bergson felt that a memory was never erased, but lasted as long the body did—possibly longer! That it might outlive the body was such an interesting idea to me that I began a reappraisal of Mama's religion. The Old Testament taught that death was a sleep forever, but Mama was sure that death released the spirit, which went at once to either Heaven or Hell.

One other of Bergson's ideas remained with me. He didn't believe in the supreme importance of Art. I was glad to have an ally! Philosophy now became my chief study. I read William

James' *Psychology,* two large volumes packed with information new to me; also his *Will to Believe,* which I surely had.

One of George Sterling's sonnets came every day, as he had promised. But they only added to my bewilderment. Here was more human suffering—and of the most mysterious sort! A man who actually *wanted* to suffer, who believed that suffering was necessary to great art!

I wrote him that I had read the volumes of his poetry he had sent me, and that *The Testimony of the Suns* made me unhappy about him. Why was he so pessimistic? I knew that he gave the reason in that long poem, but I could not see why he should worry about the destiny of the universe a billion years from now. Was there not enough tragedy in it today to occupy all of a man's concern?

I ended this impertinent criticism by saying that he must forgive me for my lack of understanding—it was due to the fact that I was not educated. I had found out how very ignorant I was.

I wrote Mama and Aunt Sallie that I was back in the same apartment house in which Nellie and I had lived. I assured them I was in no danger of becoming involved in Upton Sinclair's divorce. I tried to make it clear why I wanted to stay where I was; I had access in New York to a great library, and I was still in need of those "cultural advantages" which Mama had always wanted for me. I told them that at the rate at which I was proceeding a new book would soon be finished. It was all about the people back home, and would make it clear that I was learning something besides radicalism.

One of my old beaux, a distant cousin, showed up without notice at the apartment. He said he had been waiting patiently for me to come back where I belonged, and had decided to see if he couldn't persuade me. Papa had given him my address, and his blessing.

"What do you mean by his blessing?" I asked.

"I'm your cousin by marriage only, you know, so if you are superstitious about kinship, you are mistaken. The Judge has no objections to having me for a son-in-law. That's what I mean."

"This wasn't Papa's idea, was it—I mean for you to come here?" I asked, anxiously.

"It wasn't his idea. But Mary Craig, you surely can't believe that your long absence is not a source of anxiety to *every*one."

"Papa and Mama haven't expressed anything of the sort to me," I answered, coolly. "I'm not a child any longer."

"But you know I've loved you since you were a little girl. You'll always seem like that to me—the sweetest, gentlest, the most lovable child I ever knew. Why can't you love me? I'm not bad-looking, I've made a success of my financial affairs; as young as I am, I've become one of the substantial men of our county. What's wrong with me?"

"You ask me, and I'll tell you the truth," I said. "You don't know there's a world outside one little piece of land below the Mason and Dixon line. You are provincial."

"And that means I'm a bore to a sophisticated young lady like you? Is that it?"

"You don't have to be a bore," I answered. "You just *want* to be. You don't have to stay in one spot all your life, satisfied to live according to a long-since-dead code. You are young and have money. Yet I doubt if you see any reason to do anything but stay where you are."

"And why not?"

I laughed at him because I felt like crying. It was the Old South that I was taking to task; I hated to scold it because I loved it. "Why not? Well, for one thing, it has led you to believe that it is actually dangerous for a young woman of my age to live alone in New York. You think I'm crazy or something. You think that 'Woman's place is in the home.' And I believe in women's suffrage. Stop being so intolerant of all ideas except those you learned when you were a tot. Stop judging people until you have a yardstick!"

My would-be knight-errant gave a long, low whistle. He got up from his chair and came and stood before me.

"I love you," he said, quietly. "The same golden-brown eyes, and that golden hair. But the roses in your cheeks are fading and the dimples are almost gone."

"In other words, I'm no longer a child. I look like a woman."

"Dear child, won't you please come home before the woman decides to marry one of these long-haired anarchists?"

"I don't know any long-haired men," I said, "except one— and he lived next door to us in Greenwood. Now forgive me, dear cousin, I don't want to be unkind. But you traveled all the way here to save me, and I thought I ought to tell you the truth. I don't want ever again to be anything but frank with men."

George Sterling had joined Aunt Sallie in a tireless plea for me to come to California. He was keeping his promise to write me a sonnet every day for a hundred days. He wrote a letter with almost every one. I considered it a duty to keep them in order, and got a tin breadbox for the purpose. Soon it was overflowing.

A letter came from Mary Wilshire, saying that she had told her friend, the Countess Russell, about the interesting "Southern belle" she had met in New York who was trying to write a book. Lady Russell, who wrote many books, told her she hoped I would come to England. She would like to study me, presumably as a character for one of her novels. Very soon there came a letter from her, inviting me to be her guest.

I wrote Mama about Lady Russell's invitation, and this relieved all of her worries about divorces and newspaper reporters. I should accept at once. Nothing could go wrong with me under the wing of an Englishwoman of the nobility! Mama even knew of this particular noble family; Lord John Russell, grandfather of Frank, the present earl, had negotiated with Jefferson Davis. Mama was not quite certain what these transactions were, but I must look it up in Davis' *Rise and Fall of the Confederate Government*.

Fiske Warren was in town and offered to attend to my steamship ticket, which I hadn't an idea how to do. I drew a large check and tucked the extra money into my corset, that ancient place of hiding for the valuables of traveling ladies. A week later I was on the high seas, alone.

When I arrived in London, there was the historic fog, dense and dank. But my hostess welcomed me so warmly that I was soon completely at home, with everyone questioning me about my native South, and my intention to pursue a career as a writer.

Lady Russell was Irish, petite—that is up and down, if not sidewise. She said she was too stout, but since she was a writer, it was no longer necessary for her to worry about her looks. Writers usually spurned appearances, living in their minds instead of in their clothes.

She did not like titles, and told all young people to call her "Aunt Mollie." She told me she hoped to read my Winnie Davis book; I replied that I wasn't proud of it, but was writing another book, which I thought she might like. She suggested that when I was in the mood to write I take her little hideaway cottage in the country. I could use it, rent-free, as long as I wanted to. She would send a woman to keep house for me. But I told her I had been writing too steadily for a long time now, and wanted to see Europe.

In London it was the same as in New York—everyone I met knew Upton Sinclair, or felt that he did. Everyone asked questions about him, some foolish, some intelligent. Did he live on shredded wheat, and if so, did he eat it dry, or with cream? Was it true that he fasted about half the time? If so, did he try to write on an empty stomach? What was he writing now and why had he never been to Europe? But no one mentioned his pending divorce; that was his private affair. I was certainly grateful for this example of British good manners.

I went out for a walk, and the fog came up, so thick that I could not see my way across the street. But I stood on the corner, and heard the calm, quiet English voices as the passersby helped one another to grope their way. I loved it, fog and all. I did not want to return to the cozy house of my friends until I had wandered around and gotten lost several times in the "pea soup."

I felt I belonged here. Passing these silent, dim figures, I felt safe, with no sense of haste or bustle such as I felt on the streets of New York or even in lazy old New Orleans.

I went into one of the little teashops which seemed to be in every block, and asked for a pot of tea and some buttered muffins. The English voices and pronunciation were quite different from those in Mississippi and New York; but they spoke the same language, and I was able to compare the gossip of the teashop girls with what I had heard when I ordered hot chocolate or coffee at home. One of them referred to "our betters," and at first I thought this had something to do with horse racing. Then I discovered that they meant the people who were socially "above" them. But I did not know enough about white working people to judge the English working-class.

My friends the Wilshires had a visitor from Holland, Dr. Frederik van Eeden. He wanted to study their little boy, Logan, who had the mind of a prodigy. He had met the child on a former visit, and been so impressed that he asked to be allowed to return a year later to see what developments had taken place.

Dr. van Eeden was recognized all over Europe as a psychiatrist, a poet and a novelist. Besides his native Dutch he spoke three languages fluently. He believed ardently in a revolution from the top. Modern machines had made drudgery unnecessary, and as a humanitarian he was eager to prove it, even at his own expense. He had established and financed a cooperative colony in North Carolina.

He regarded Upton Sinclair as a man after his own heart, a man who set the welfare of his fellow men above his own, the "truest kind of Christian," said this author of a successful novel about a return of Jesus to the modern world. Van Eeden had met Mr. Sinclair in New York. Was he in good health? Was he writing at present? Had I read his books?

Very soon the scholar discovered that I didn't know much about economic theories; he began asking me about the South, which I did know. The novelist in him had awakened, and he sat before me, his broad Dutch face keen with interest in a new country and a new type. I told him that we Mississippians felt that Virginia, Kentucky, the Carolinas, Alabama, Tennessee, Mississippi and Louisiana were the only *real* South—all the other Southern states were "redneck," or hillbilly states. The Georgia "rednecks" we called "crackers." Texas was the wild West in which criminals and desperadoes, escaping from the law, went on being criminals and desperadoes. Oklahoma we regarded as similar to Texas, but so wild that no one knew much about it; it was dangerous to go there at all. It was in these states that despised demagogue politicians rose to power on the theme song, "Keep the nigger in his place."

The earnest seeker-after-truth sat back in his chair and looked me over. Finally he said, "Do you feel contemptuous of those poor whites, as they call them in the South? You see, I have traveled in your country, and heard this same thing about the classes there." I answered that I did not know any of these people—they kept to themselves. Now and then at home I had seen a poor, weatherbeaten wagon drawn by a skinny horse on the road. There would be a man driving it—a "tow-head" with a pinched, unkempt face, pale, weak eyes—carrying some jugs of sorghum molasses in his wagon to sell to householders. Papa used to buy some now and then for the Negro servants, who liked its acrid flavor. What the "tow-head" could not sell would be taken into town and traded for cloth and tobacco, or snuff.

Dr. van Eeden was distressed by my account. "Can't you see," he asked, "that all of this bitter class feeling from which so much of your so-called Negro problem springs is a purely economic one? These poor whites cannot buy the good land and they take what they can get—the poor land—and lead substandard lives on it. They are proud of their race and angry because of their poverty. They take out their feelings of inferiority on the poor black man. Thus the rise of your demagogues; a loud, shouting politician can keep a lot of dangerous feeling boiling in the breasts of the people. But at bottom, it's all economic."

Mrs. Wilshire came in with the maid and the tea things, and soon other guests began to arrive, all of them men. "Gay" appeared, and with him the labor leader, Tom Mann, and Hyndman, founder of the Social-Democratic Federation. Dr.

van Eeden was excellent company—he entered into the political
discussions which soon were waxing excitedly. The British coal
strike came first, and militant women's suffrage next. The suffragettes, it seemed, were smashing art treasures in the British
Museum and emptying vials of acid into mail boxes. I listened,
and learned something new every minute.

Later on I found myself again chatting with Dr. van Eeden.
This time he was the novelist instead of the economist.

"What is a 'Southern Belle' made of?" he wanted to know.
"I am sure you are one who can tell me."

"Sugar and spice and all things nice," I answered, with a
smile.

"I'm sure of the spice," he said. "But what brand of sugar
is used?"

"Flattery," I replied, and he looked shocked.

"Oh, surely not!"

"But that's true," I told him. "That is why I grew tired of
the game. I want people to be frank and straightforward."

"I wonder," he said, thoughtfully. "If the truth were always
spoken, would we not hate one another? Hate is the thing we
must drive from the world."

I told him I had never thought of that. But surely no one
should mind hearing the truth, even about himself. "That is
what I am seeking," I said, "to understand myself."

He replied that I was a wise person, and as a psychiatrist,
he could assure me no search was more important. But at the
moment he was a novelist, and on the trail of Southern belles.
They were famous for their charm. What was this charm
made of?

I answered, "I have already told you—sugar and spice and
all things nice! It is just as simple as that. My grandmother
gave me the recipe when I was still in school. Flattery was the
basic ingredient, the sugar; and a little mockery is the spice.
Men like to feel that they are powerful—brave, capable, important. This isn't a wholly bad idea—they do have to take
care of a family later on, so why not let the poor dears feel
as superior as they want to?—it makes them more willing slaves.
This is my wise 'Gram-ma' speaking:

" 'Here, child, is the whole recipe. First, get for yourself the most alluring background you can. As an artist, I stress the importance of background: a carefully chosen lampshade, which will not dim the freshness and glow of your lovely complexion, yet will add a touch of shadowy mystery to your face. Put a bowl of roses—preferably red or white, near you so that they become a part of your face in *his* line of vision, so!'—and my slender, agile 'Gram-ma' would arise and remove a bowl of flowers from a stand and set them on a table beside my chair. 'Of course you must choose for your costume the colors which suit your skin, hair and eyes—though in the evening by lamplight almost any girl can wear red becomingly, and men like red. This is about all—now you have only to ask some question that will lead your "intended" to talk about himself; then sit gracefully, listen intently—and you have him snared! Remember, the most important of all of these is, *get him to talk about himself!'* "

I stopped and looked solemnly at the great man before me, trying not to seem embarrassed at the shoddy devices of the game of coquetry which I had exposed. "You asked me," I said, apologetically.

I discovered, to my further embarrassment, that conversation had died out all over the room, and everyone was listening to my too-frank confession. I had to save myself—so I remarked to my hostess, whose sense of fun could always be counted on, "You see, Mary, it works! Look at all these men—they want to hear about feminine 'charm'—they want to be 'charmed,' because it means *they* are worth the effort of the charmer!"

Dr. van Eeden leaned back in his chair and laughed. "I'll stand behind you," he said, "if Mary doesn't." But Mary did! She had brought me over to show her English friends what a "Southern belle" was like.

When Nellie arrived, she and I went to Paris. The air was gleaming with golden tints, like the famed French champagne, and the cleanliness everywhere was, by contrast with grimy, fog-bound London, as refreshing as the sunshine. The treasures in two more great museums failed to impress me, just

as had those at the St. Louis World's Fair and in the museums
of London and New York. Nellie stood rapt before the can-
vases and was shocked by my indifference. Yes, I admitted, the
clear, deep atmosphere in a Corot came close to that of the
country outside Paris. But one was static, the other was quivering with wondrous life, changing every instant, lifting my imagination out of the realm of dead, flat art. Nellie scolded me
for my incredible materialism, and I was mystified by the idea
that art was spiritual. I did not know how to argue with her,
for she had a far better art education than I had.

We rented bicycles, which were common on the city streets
as well as on country roads. We donned our new "divided
skirts" and off we went daily to see how the other half of the
world lived. (Our world was composed in those days, of the
United States, and Europe which included the British Isles.)
We went the rounds of fashionable Paris shops by day and ate
at sidewalk restaurants in the evening, where we chatted with
any strangers who knew how to speak English. I tried out my
Gardner-school French once or twice, but only to the bewilderment of the population, some of whom shook their heads politely and then addressed me in excellent English.

There were painted women everywhere—not merely rouged,
but with painted green shadows around their eyes, or lavender
all over their faces. I was "short-changed" so often that I decided there were no honest people in Paris. The policemen
seemed to have no idea of law enforcement, certainly not of
the kind the tall, dignified "bobbies" of London represented.

But we were having a fine time, and I was learning that
chaperones were an expensive superfluity, though I knew it
would disturb Mama if I were to write her this.

Back in London, I settled down to read the books George
Sterling and Upton Sinclair had sent me. Each was generous
with his own books; and I, remembering my grandmother's
teaching, felt sure they wanted to be praised. But I would not
deliberately praise them! I wanted to be free of all artificial
things, including most of my family traditions, but especially
the necessity of praising men.

Mama wrote that she hoped I would be able to explain to the Russells that the South had not fought to preserve slavery; the South had fought for a principle, the sovereign rights of states. The issue had been secession. Mama had been consulting the Jefferson Davis book with reference to Lord John Russell's part in Britain's adopting a course of neutrality, during our Civil War. But for this, the North would never have won the war, and the lives of so many innocent men would not have been lost on the bloody battlefields. I must say this with tact, of course, for no doubt Lord John had felt that he knew what was best for England. "To be sure, we knew," Mama wrote, "that the Confederacy had the sympathy of the British, and we were grateful for at least this much."

But Papa was not so certain that tact was appropriate. He thought that Lord John should have come out openly for the right against the wrong—no man should be neutral when the right was at stake. Papa did not think so well as Mama did of this long visit.

Aunt Mollie did not think that I should do any more writing for a while—I really did show signs of possible injury to my health. The trip to France had not achieved the good results it should have. What was it, she wanted to know, that was draining me? Was it a love affair, or simply too much coffee and writing?

I told her it was both, with a third thing added—I was trying to wean myself from complete dependence on the love of my parents. After I had given up the sweetheart I loved, I had felt that I wanted to live only for them. But since I had lived among the New York intellectuals, I had acquired many ideas which gave meaning to life. I needed this, for I felt that its pain was greater than its joy; this made it hard for me not to question the goodness of a heavenly Father—and I did not wish to do this. Now I had found that there were able and competent people, not just dreamers absorbed in their dreams, who believed that much of this pain was unnecessary. They knew why they believed it, and some were actually putting their theories into practice.

I admired such courageous experimentalism. I told Aunt

Mollie of Fiske Warren's absorption in his single-tax colonies, to which he gave not only money but his own time and thought. And there was Jessica Finch, with her school—fashionable in spite of her bold experiment in "freedom" for women. Dr. van Eeden had spent most of his own money on the two colonies he had founded, one in the United States and one in Holland. He wanted to prove the soundness of his program to abolish poverty. And the same was true of Upton Sinclair, whose Helicon Home Colony near Princeton had failed only because it had burnt down and the insurance had not protected him— he had paid off all the debts of the enterprise himself.

All these, and other bold spirits I had come to know, had given me new hope and interest. It was a cruel paradox that my dear parents, who had been struggling tirelessly to restore my interest in life, would be shocked by most of these ideas. And I did not want to go home to Greenwood until I had found out which of the current "isms" seemed most practical to me. Then I would be able to argue with my scholarly father, who had written me that Socialism sought to tear down everything he had spent his life building up.

Papa thought I should come back to my own people. But my happy-hearted mother still felt that all must be well with me, here where my birthright lay—in England. With dear indolent Aunt Mollie, so utterly indifferent to "society," in the sense of smartness and fashion! And the grandson of Lord John Russell, who cared even less for the social conventions and habits of the peerage! He never went near the House of Lords.

Aunt Mollie's cottage in the country sounded just a bit too lonely. So I persuaded Mary Wilshire to let me stay with her as a "paying guest" while I finished my novel.

Mary's rented house was old, but bright and cheerful. The furniture was covered with flowery chintz, and there were vases of flowers on stands and tables. The hard-worked, frowzy little English maid was always gasping under the burden of carrying scuttles of coal to replenish the many fireplaces. Somehow this sole servant managed to keep the house clean and to prepare and serve three good meals a day to the family, as well as tea in the afternoons. How different from the ways of the many Negro servants it took to care for Mama's household!

Gaylord Wilshire agreed with Upton's economic theories, and he said that he had done so for a long time; in fact, he had converted the author to Socialism. But he had decided that no capitalist government would ever permit Socialism to be brought about by political means, and so he had recently become a Syndicalist, looking to labor union "direct action." He added that Upton would make it hard for him if they ever got on a platform to debate the matter. Upton, in a debate, was as light on his feet as a cat! There was something about his platform manner that got him the applause, whether or not he had the better argument—so said his old friend.

I went for a walk on Hampstead Heath in bright sunshine, and came back with a letter for Mama in my mind. But I did not write that letter; for there in the Wilshire drawing-room sat Upton Sinclair, debating Socialism versus Syndicalism with the editor who had changed his mind. What would poor Mama say *now!*

I soon discovered that I would not have much of Upton's time on this brief visit. He was going at once to Holland to establish a residence, so that he could get his divorce there. The New York courts had ruled against him. The reason was "collusion." This seemed to me one of the strangest things I had ever heard —if both parties in an unhappy marriage wanted a divorce from each other this made it wrong for them to have it, while if only one wanted it, the divorce might be granted!

Gay urged Upton to meet a few of his friends before he left, and persuaded him to stay another day. Upton refused to stay longer—he had stopped longer than he intended in Italy where he visited a good friend, George D. Herron. Herron had been a churchman who wanted freedom from a galling marriage contracted before he was mature enough to know his own mind. Upton was in a mood to crusade against that New York law and against any other law which could make it so hard for a person to win his freedom from a marriage which he had tried again and again to make into a success—and when the cause

had been infidelity acknowledged by the wife! But Gay advised
him not to. He reminded him of Lord Russell's crusade against
the British divorce law, which had met with no success. It was
a matter of religion.

Upton Sinclair looked so forlorn that no woman could see
him without wanting to treat him as an unhappy little boy.
Both Mary and Gay treated him that way, and Aunt Mollie was
so sorry for him that tears came into her kind Irish eyes whenever she spoke of him; she called him her "poor baby" when
she talked to me of his plight. She herself had fallen in love
with a man who had been through the divorce mill, so she
knew how it could hurt. She had married her man—and now
she must find a tenderhearted wife for a wandering, unhappy
American. In short, like most of the women I knew, she was a
born match-maker, and she picked me out as the future Mrs.
Upton Sinclair.

Upton asked if I had read the books he had sent me. I
told him I had not. He looked disappointed for a moment,
then said for me to try to read them soon; he seemed sure I
would be converted by his propaganda. He was certain of the
validity of his doctrines and of his ability to present them
convincingly.

I told him I was going to work on my own novel now, and
would be very busy—just as he used to tell *me!* But he did not
smile; instead he invited me to let him help with it. He was
sure that my girlhood environment was wonderful material for
a book, but he was not certain about my ability to handle it. I
was impressed again by his simple, direct way of saying exactly
what he thought.

After he had gone, Mary and I talked about him and I began
to feel a sympathy for him again, because she did. I proceeded
to read *The Jungle* and *Manassas* at once. *Manassas* was the
first volume of a Civil War trilogy which he had never finished.
It touched me deeply. As I read the manhunt scene in this
Civil War novel I thought of Aunt Catherine's kind and humble black Henry sitting on our back steps waiting for his corn-
bread and turnip greens, and I felt as if I were being stabbed

in the breast. A helpless fugitive fleeing before yelping blood-hounds was to me far more terrible than anything that happened in the Chicago stockyards. This was because I knew nothing about white working people, nor were the griefs and joys of foreigners real—they were so different from "us." I tried to express all this in a letter to Upton.

But now I myself must flee from the bloodhounds! Here I was again in contact with their victim, the "celebrity" whose name always made headlines, and a would-be divorcé. I was sure the newspaper hounds would discover him in Europe. During the next few days I thought of little else. The whole thing seemed so unjust and so unnecessary. No wonder Upton Sinclair, Fiske Warren, Gay, and others were crusading for social reform. What a foolish and unkind world it was—and here was I, brought up in such ease and pleasure that my old home and my dear ones in their peace and security seemed to exist in a dream world.

But I must go home, for if they heard that Upton Sinclair was in Europe, they would be panic-stricken. Mama's vision of me as a lady returned to the ancestral English home of the Southworths would be shattered like a glass vase dropped on a stone.

I told Mary that I must go before the news of Upton's presence in Europe could reach my parents. I took passage at once on the *Lusitania*.

6. CHILD, WANDERING DOWN THE WORLD

MAMA AND THE CHILDREN were at Ashton Hall, and I was glad to be on the coast again. My dear mother was as young and beautiful as ever, smiling brightly in a summer dress of yellow dimity. She did not like the way my hair was done, and she was shocked at the clothes I had worn in Europe. What had

my hostesses thought? I had owed it to them to have better
things! She hoped I was not going to dress the way Mr. Sinclair
did. She had heard somewhere that the novelist George Eliot
was indifferent to her appearance. Was it necessary for a writer
to be shabby?

She settled down in her hammock on the front gallery to read
my manuscript. As she progressed, she became more and more
thrilled—it was a beautiful story, she declared. But other people
might not like what I had written about them—I had not sufficiently concealed the identity of some of my characters. This
meant a lot of rewriting.

Papa came to the coast earlier than usual. He was so happy
to have me home again that I put off day after day my intended
efforts to try to make them see that Socialism was not dangerous but humane. Two or three of my old beaux from the Delta
"dropped in" on their own initiative, and of course were invited to stay long enough for some fishing and sailing. They
took me driving, in order to have an opportunity to warn me
again how fast I was becoming an old maid; I should marry
before I had "faded." Each offered himself as my last chance to
escape this fate.

But they treated me as if I were a child or a doll, when I
wanted to be an equal. They said I was on a pedestal—what
more could I want? Why would I want to come down, and
stand as an equal with a man? Were men so bad, I asked—and
was fervently assured that they were!

After I had tried out on them some of my new ideas, we had
nothing to talk about. They were too polite to express their extreme disapproval, so we could only return to personalities. I
concealed my boredom, and grew restless for the day when I
could return to the North and look up my new friends and discuss the ideas I was still trying to assimilate.

The story on which I had been working had taken its name
from the lines of Shakespeare—

> Who is Sylvia, what is she,
> That all our swains attend her?

I had been working hard on this manuscript because of the insistence of both Dr. van Eeden and Upton Sinclair that my stories of a Southern belle were "priceless"; they had begged me to put them on paper. Having done so, I sent a copy of the manuscript to each of these men of letters, and waited eagerly for their replies. Both complimented me on the material, but agreed that I had no plot and that without it there could not be a novel. They were both in Holland, meeting frequently, and combined to deliver this verdict.

After reading van Eeden's letter about *Sylvia,* Mama consented to my return to New York. I would come home as a famous author, and how proud she and Papa would be! Half in fun and half seriously Mama said, "There were seeresses in Greece in ancient days who could really look into the future. Do not ever forget that your name is to go around the world!" She was referring again to her gypsy fortuneteller.

Back in New York, there came a letter from Upton Sinclair. He had, without informing me, set to work to write a novel based on my material, and had got well along on it! As soon as he had his divorce, he wanted to come home to work out with me the terms on which he could publish it. In my girl of the Old South, he said, I had given him a heroine around whom could be woven a wonderful story. He had not waited to hear from me before setting to work, because when an idea for a story took possession of him he found it next to impossible to wait. "The characters come alive suddenly in my mind, and give me no rest. They speak and act as they please, and compel me to write down what they are doing." Thus he explained his astonishing behavior.

But there was nothing improper in it. If he wanted to expend his time and mind on the gamble that I would give my consent, that was in no way injurious to me. As George Sterling had once remarked, "No one can ever tell what Upton has up his sleeve. And whatever it is, when it appears, it is sure to be something different. It's uncanny, for it doesn't seem as if he were acting on his own volition. It is this that makes him such good copy for newspaper writers."

"Maybe he is possessed of a devil," I had said, and George's mischievous smile indicated that this was probably the truth.

Now George was writing to warn me against this "ethical monster." He had told me in New York before he went West that though Upon was his friend and he would do almost anything for him, there were moments when he didn't like him. Now he clearly didn't like him as a possible suitor of mine. Of course Upton would try to persuade me to marry him, wrote George; and of course I thought that George was jealous.

Upton Sinclair brought back from Europe, besides his divorce, a whole trunkful of surprises. First, he asked Nellie if she thought I was too ignorant for him to try to collaborate with on a book, and forgot to swear Nellie to secrecy. She was so indignant that she asked me never to speak to him again.

"But I *am* ignorant, Nellie dear, as you well know. I like him for his truthfulness. I want to be treated honestly by men. I'm tired of coquetry and flirtations and insincerity."

But there was an even greater surprise. "I have been thinking it over and trying to decide if you are the woman for me to marry," Upton said, the worried look on his face expressing real uncertainty.

My first impulse was to say something haughty. Instead I answered, quietly and with no resentment, "Think it over a bit more, while I do the same. Remember, I haven't thought of it before, and I shall need more time than you."

Here it was again—this complete frankness—and suddenness —which people like Nellie resented, and which Dr. van Eeden and I liked.

"There is my young son, David," Upton was saying. "I have put him in a German boarding school, and he is to stay there. I agree with Charlotte Perkins Gilman that 'the home is no place for children.'"

I thought this was the most revolutionary thing I had yet heard in this world of novel ideas in which I was thinking of spending my life. I asked who Charlotte Gilman was. He told me she was a feminist and Socialist writer—a Fabian, not a Marxist. He said he would send me one of her books. I laughed and reminded him that I could not read all the time, and that during the last few months he had sent me several rather heavy volumes.

He invited me to have dinner with him, and attend a concert at Carnegie Hall. I accepted the first, but declined the second. "I'm fastidious about music," I told him. "Most of it bores me."

We went out, he in his everyday clothes, and I in my street dress. With no apology he hailed a streetcar and, as the car was crowded, we stood holding onto overhead straps for several blocks. It was the first time a man had ever taken me to dinner by way of a streetcar.

A few minutes later, I was following him into a cheap restaurant. It was hard to talk, for the place was crowded. But Upton seemed to be hungry, and apparently had no idea that this was a time for conversation. He ate his simple one-course meal, pausing only now and then to comment on the benefits to his health from a diet of beefsteak, raw vegetable salad and shredded wheat.

He told me of the luncheon he had had at Bernard Shaw's country place. Shaw was a vegetarian, as Upton had been before his stomach protested. Shaw's vegetarianism was due to his belief in the right of all living things to remain alive—certainly not to be eaten by a civilized human being. Upton had put to him "Mr. Dooley's" question—whether it was not just as cruel "to cut off a young tomato in its prime or to murder a whole cradleful of baby peas in the pod."

I had ordered more than my host, and coffee. After Upton had finished I asked for an extra cup. My host leaned across the table and said, with great earnestness, "I'll have to teach you better than to drink stimulants. They are really bad for you."

I told him I liked coffee too well to give it up. Everyone I knew drank it, and it had never hurt any one of them. But he had a fine explanation for his objection to my favorite beverage, and I heard it all in the earnest, yet smiling manner in which he would plead whatever cause he espoused. Finally I told him I didn't think I should marry him—I liked coffee better than I liked him.

He decided that he would not go to the concert; he preferred to spend the evening with me if I had no other engagement. When we returned to the apartment we found a note from Nellie, who had a key. She had gone out to eat and would return in half an hour.

Upton sat in front of me, looking at me intently as he talked. Did I think that two people who were unhappily married, and had agreed to a divorce, should go on indefinitely without a divorce when there was nothing left of the marriage? He was hurt because he had been forced to demand a divorce although he had given his former wife the use of his name and his home, and had supported her long after there was nothing between them but a memory, because she asked for these things while she sought the right man to marry.

I was deeply touched by his conscientious feeling. I thought of him as Aunt Mollie did—in some departments of life he was "a babe in the woods—a very lovable one." She had told him not to brood, and now I told him the same thing, explaining that I knew how he felt about the death of a love that had once filled his heart. I too had been compelled to give up such a passion.

His face brightened, and he asked eagerly, "Tell me about it! It may be just what your manuscript needs." So here I discovered the true passion of the born storyteller—"copy" for a book!

Nellie came in and I told her what we had been talking about. "The brute!" she exclaimed, looking at Upton in disgust. "Do you think," she demanded, "that a sensitive creature like Craigie would be happy with a writing machine? Above all, one that tells her he is grieving about another woman!"

But Craigie disagreed. "If I am to marry him," I said, "the more I know in advance of what is in his heart, the safer I'll be. And maybe I won't marry him because I know too much!"

"Even I get sorry for him," said Nellie. "But I'm warning you seriously, Craigie—pity won't help you to be safe with this man."

For the next two days I thought of him almost constantly,

and always he was a dual personality—a helpless child in his
personal affairs and a brave and skillful fighter in the cause he
loved. I saw him as the true heir of his forefathers, on the
quarter-deck of a warship. One of his admirers, Harry Kemp,
had written a sonnet about him:

> Child, wandering down the great world for a day
>   And with a child's soul seeing through and through
>   The passing prejudice to Truth's own view.
> Immortal spirit robed in mortal clay,
> Striving to find and follow the one way
>   That is your way, none other's—to be true
>   To that which makes a sincere man of you.
> Still be yourself, and let tongues say their say!

The next morning Upton came early to work on my manuscript. I had named the book *Sylvia,* and he approved of that,
but when I read his idea of the kind of girl that "all our swains
attend," I had to tell him that his heroine was neither my
Sylvia nor Shakespeare's. In my opinion, no swains would "attend" his Sylvia. She was a bluestocking, and made of cotton,
at that!

"She's my ideal woman," he informed me.

"Then I'm out of the running, Mr. Sinclair. If I married
you, I'd be jealous of every dowdy, strong-minded character
who showed up."

"You might learn to be like her in time," he said, sweetly.

"As if I wanted to!" I exclaimed, with such obvious amusement that he set out to explain what he meant.

"You are really like that," he said. "You are fundamentally
an ethical person. This veneer with which your mother has
decorated you will wear off—you are already wearing your old
clothes on the street."

He told me that his mother had invited me to dine with her
tonight, and he hoped I would accept. Her invitations helped
to reconcile Mama to my longer sojourn in New York. Mrs.
Priscilla Sinclair served as a proper chaperone, being, like
Mama, "to the manor born."

Upton and I struggled through several chapters of *Sylvia* together, disagreeing about something on every page. But now and then each of us admitted that the other had improved something. I was learning fast now that this novelist was not much of a psychologist. He thought of characters in a book merely as vehicles for carrying his ideas. But the ideas of Upton Sinclair were important, I reminded myself. The better I understood them the more important they became, and the more convincing.

I wore old clothes that evening to dine with his mother; I was keeping my unspoken promise to darling Papa not to draw so many checks. But Mrs. Priscilla looked me over with the same disapproving frankness I liked in her son. Before the evening was over she said, "You are foolish, girl! You know the value of attractive clothes, and your father has plenty of money. Don't neglect your appearance."

She was not pretty—she was too stern-looking; but she had lovely, soft, pink skin, and bright blue eyes like her son's. Her hair was white, and perfectly dressed. She surely did not neglect *her* appearance. But she disapproved of her son's ideas as thoroughly as my mother did, and made no effort to apologize for him. "But he will not listen to his mother," she ended, each time she spoke of his intellectual waywardness.

Upton's mother was an embittered Baltimore lady. Life had not been kind to her; she had lived it as the wife of an alcoholic, and had hoped that her only child would be her comfort; but now he was grown, and had turned into a Socialist! What was there to sweeten her lot?

I helped Mrs. Priscilla wash the dishes, and admired her rosewood heirlooms. I invited her to go to a matinée with me the next day. Afterward we had hot chocolate together at Huyler's, and I bought her a large box of candy. She toddled off on her high heels, considerably sweetened.

After several weeks of polite argument over the *Sylvia* story, the manuscript was almost ready to be offered to a publisher. But my peace of mind was considerably upset by Nellie's sudden marriage to a Socialist organizer! He was a fairly pleas-

ant young man, not bad-looking, but in no way measuring up
to Nellie's esthetic tastes. He was penniless, and during a brief
courtship she had taken him out to meals for which she paid.

When I asked her why she had kept the affair secret until it
was too late for anyone to dissuade her from an apparently un-
suitable match, she replied that was the reason. She did not
want to be dissuaded! He was the only man who had ever asked
her to marry him, she said.

Her Socialist organizer received a small salary from the local
he represented, but it was not much. Nellie was quite willing
to pay the rent, the grocer, and even to darn Jim's socks. But
she simply would not press his pants!—she bought an ironing
board and an iron so that he could learn this art—which he
never did. Upton was his god, and Upton took him to his heart
as a young idealist. So it was not long before poor Nellie's husband was absorbed in the throes of authorship, while Nellie
grudgingly pressed his pants.

Jim depended on Nellie for everything. She was practical
and efficient, and managed their little establishment well, in
spite of his dreamy attitude toward preparing a meal or cleaning up the apartment. And she was happy. He loved her, she
said, and beneath all her swagger and defiant talk which I had
so much admired, there had always been a longing to be
necessary to some attractive man's welfare and happiness. Un-
doubtedly she now was.

She found a new job easily—she had been highly recommended by her former employers, and she had the appearance
of an efficient and dependable secretary. Jim would invite Sinclair to lunch, and then as a matter of course would let the
successful author pay the bill.

Nellie told me, "I'm not sure that I admire Upton's naïve
faith in his fellow-man. He must have this faith, of course, or
he couldn't be a Socialist. But what concerns me is *you*, Craigie.
I'm afraid George Sterling is right when he says that your tender heart may lead you to marry Upton. I just don't believe in
martyrdom."

I did not point out to her that she was making a martyr of
herself.

It was after this talk, and while Nellie was present, that Upton renewed his strange marriage proposal; so I was well armed for the assault. He was still in mourning for his other marriage and had never tried to conceal it. "If I had given less time to causes, and more to our own affairs, maybe she would not have gone off in search of the kind of love she wanted,"— so he had told me, on more than one occasion. But it was not within the possibility of his character to seek personal happiness ahead of everything else. Humanity was one brotherhood, and, in the words of Eugene Debs, "So long as one is hungry, so am I."

Now he turned to me and asked, in a matter-of-fact tone, "Have you given any more thought to the idea I suggested a while ago?"

"You are a man of many ideas," I answered, just to gain time. "To which one do you refer?"

Nellie jumped up and stood between us, facing him. "You infuriate me!" she exclaimed. Then she turned to me. "Don't give in to him, Craigie, I beg you! He is an incorrigible martyr. He *wants* to die for others. Let him have what he wants."

"Do you think I could save him?" I laughed.

"Of course you could. You have an iron will, and a capacity for self-sacrifice equal to his. The only difference is you don't *want* to be a martyr. And so why be one? The herd will run right over you!"

Upton went over to the window and stood looking down into the crowded street. "Down there on those sidewalks is the herd. They hurry to their jobs—overworked, undernourished, densely ignorant. But they are men and women, and in them lies the future of our species. They are the workers of the world—they produce its wealth, on which all culture feeds. They should be given a fair share of what they produce, whether they are intelligent enough to demand it or not. They need only to be taught their own powers."

"I came from among them," declared Nellie. "And no one helped *me*. What helped me most was that very fact; I *had* to do it for myself. Can't you see that, Upton? Can't you see that you are what you are because you *had* to help yourself? If there had never been a Civil War, if your father had owned slaves, would you have got out of the comfortable nest to find your own worms and seeds? You *had* to find them or starve. You were compelled to use your own mental and physical muscles, and so they grew strong."

"You don't understand economics, Nellie," said Upton quietly, without turning from the window. "You waste your time trying to talk about it."

She picked up her little brown hat and set it on her head without looking in the mirror. "I've done my duty, Craigie. I've been a good chaperone." And she was gone.

I felt that Nellie's reasoning was sound, and that Upton's arguments were up in the clouds. He wanted to lift that enormous swirling mass of humanity out of its ignorance and teach it to exercise the prerogatives of self-governing people. But was there enough native intelligence in the average man? Were all men born equal in mind and body? Certainly not in body. The weakness of Upton's case lay in the naïve idea that one frail little man like himself could do much about this basic situation.

But at least he wanted to *try!* Rational or irrational, he would do what he could to improve the lot of all humanity. And I had seen enough of suffering by now to want the same thing.

I went over to the weary-looking man, gazing so sadly down on that noisome crowd below. I stood five-feet-seven and he was not much taller. But he seemed small because he had no tailor and his ready-made clothes were too tight.

"I think you are right," I said. "Maybe it can't be done. But we'll go crusading together."

Upton swung around and caught me in his arms. "Angel!" he cried, his face shining, as if a lamp had been lighted suddenly in front of it.

I said, "You have forgotten that you once told me my father should make me go to work. Well, now I shall have to. That will make a real person of me, won't it?"

"You're the only real person on earth!" he exclaimed. "I'm in love again!" and he gave a war-whoop which sounded like a

rebel yell. It was the way Jerry might have behaved, and I felt
the blood fly into my cheeks. I laughed, and we both decided
that at last we were happy again.

That night we had dinner with his mother, and her comment on our engagement was, "Now I hope you can make him
get some decent clothes!"

I wondered if it was my duty to write George Sterling.
I thought this over from every angle and decided that I should
not. In the first place, I had warned George from the start that
my affair with him was not to be taken seriously, except in the
strange artist's way he asked for. So there was no excuse for him
to be hurt—only his art would suffer, and the longer he remained ignorant of my interest in Upton the longer his "inspiration" would last.

Having come to this decision about the poet, I put my mind
on my own problem—did I really love Upton? There was no
doubt about my great admiration for him; I was a Sinclair fan!
But being an author's "fan" was a different thing from becoming his wife.

I had never doubted for a moment that I wanted to marry
Jerry; but I was too young then to have even the faintest idea
why, unless it was just wanting to be near him all the time and
being miserable when I was not. But my love for Upton had
reason behind it. As I thought it over, it seemed to me that the
strongest of these was what Nellie called "maternal." Was there
in every man a little boy who never grew up? And was all the
so-called brave, strong, self-confident behavior just whistling
in the dark?

I asked myself, did Upton really understand what he was
doing when he championed the cause of the poor? What had
started this in his mind? In his earliest years he had known
poverty and wealth. What could a child make of the changes
back and forth from the sordid home of his hard-drinking
father to the homes of his wealthy uncle and grandfather?

He was always a lively and happy-hearted child, as his pictures indicated. He did not require constant entertainment by

an adult, as an only child usually does; he would invent ways to entertain himself. He was taken to an Episcopal "high" church service every Sunday, and was impressed by the drama. One day as a tiny tot he came to his mother, asking if it would be wicked to "play church." She gave it a moment's thought, then said, not if he did it reverently. So he got a broom and imagined it was a cross, and marched up and down, singing "Onward, Christian Soldiers." He remembered much of the elaborate ritual and went through it with due solemnity.

In the country he picked blackberries and hunted birds' nests with his young cousins, and when he was in New York he rollerskated on the sidewalks, and played ball on vacant lots, along with the other urchins of a poor neighborhood. His mother sent him out to play because a doctor had told her his mind was too active for his young body. He was not sent to school until he was ten, but at five he taught himself to read with a set of alphabet blocks. Thereafter, he asked his many aunts and uncles and cousins to send him only books for Christmas.

Once in New York when he was eight or ten years old, he came upon a second-hand bookstore which had a whole set of *The Leatherstocking Tales* for one dollar. With them he was happy for weeks. When he went to Baltimore, there was the wonderful library of his Uncle Bland. On one Christmas vacation he read the entire works of Shakespeare, and finished off with the poetry of Milton. That was when he decided he was going to be a writer!

Through all of this he had not minded poverty very much for himself. What worried the boy was his mother's worries, her humiliation when she could not pay the rent and landladies were insulting. Beginning college at 14, he had lived on four and a half dollars a week, and in a year or so he was earning it by writing jokes and verses for newspapers. When he was 15 he was writing a novel and trying to sell it to an editor. He had done the job in a week. This won for him the friendship of the editor, who soon gave him a paying assign-

ment. At 18 he was turning out "half-dime" novels at the rate
of 8,000 words per day in order to support both his mother and
himself. When he wanted to begin serious writing he refused a
business offer from his wealthy uncle and went off into the
wilds, put up a tent and lived in good part on fish and berries.

But what turned his drive against personal poverty into a
drive against poverty for all mankind? What really lay behind
the impassioned attack he made in *The Jungle?*

He had been deeply stirred by the story of the sufferings of
the strikers in the meat-packing industry of Chicago, and decided to investigate that situation. He had gone to Chicago and
settled in the stockyards district. The story of what he had seen
—diseased and filthy meat being doctored, canned, and sold to
the public as food—had made a world-shaking book. The New
York *Evening World* had declared: "Not since Byron awoke
one morning to find himself famous has there been such an
example of world-wide celebrity won in a day by a book as has
come to Upton Sinclair. Yesterday unknown, the author of *The
Jungle* is today a familiar name on two continents. Paris, London and Berlin know him only less well than New York and
Boston. They know about him even in far-off Australia."

This was the same man who now presented himself to me as
a suitor. Surely he was not a little boy whistling in the dark.
He knew what he was doing and he did it with unbreakable
courage. He had heard without a shiver that the meatpackers
might have him killed; he had been assured by people of the
stockyards that if old P. D. Armour had still been alive, the author of *The Jungle* would not have been. And he knew by now
from much experience that he would always be misrepresented
in the newspapers, unless he changed his tune and played love
songs to industry. An author could become a parlor pet instead
of a "parlor pink" any time he was willing to give up his convictions.

Then why was he crying like a child about his broken marriage, and rejoicing so ecstatically in the hope of a new one? He
was still the little boy in need of a mother! He had outgrown
his real mother, who did not understand him and disapproved
of him so bitterly.

The doorbell rang, and I called out "Who is it?"

"Who else could it be?" came the answer, in Upton's jubilant tone.

He looked younger and better-dressed than usual. The day was damp, and his blond hair was almost curled by it, and his eyes were so lively they seemed a deeper shade of blue. "You look like your mother today," I told him. "Quite handsome."

"That's odd," he said. "I just came from her—the good soul had bought this blue shirt and tie, and made me put them on. She told me to ask you if they were becoming. You are going to be her ally, she says."

"Tell her they are quite becoming," I replied. "But tell her also that I love you because you have the courage to ignore fashion."

"Are these clothes good enough for a wedding?" he asked. "If so, why can't we go out and get a marriage license?" He got out his watch. "We've just got time before they all go to lunch."

"Sit down. I want to talk to you," I said. He had been dancing around the room like the little boy I had been thinking of. So I told him what had been in my mind. "I'm not sure that I love you enough to marry you."

He took me by the hand, and tried to pull me up from the chair. "Hurry," he said. "Registry clerks don't wait for reluctant brides."

"Very well, young man. If you are not warned, it's because you don't listen."

He laughed. "Of course I don't listen. I don't want to listen; I want you before you begin to ask ethical questions. I'm a divorced man, but I did not want to be. Now I want to be married again, and that's all there is to it. I love you, and I think you love me. So get your hat on."

"I'm too ignorant to be an author's wife," I replied.

"Leave that to me," he said. "I'll teach you."

"But that's something to think seriously about," I insisted.

"I've already thought about it. I've thought about it a lot. Nellie will tell you so—it infuriated her when I asked what she thought."

"No wonder!" I exclaimed. "It infuriates me, too."

"You told me a long time ago that you liked me because I told you the truth."

By now he had tugged at my arm until I got up in self-defense. I kissed him, and then hurried into my little bedroom and put on a hat and coat. When I came out he gave a shout of victory which made me burst out laughing.

"Egotist! I'm just going to lunch. I want two cups of good, hot coffee. I'd give a dollar for just one made by Aunt Catherine." I had moved over to the door and opened it.

"What was that kiss for?" he asked, dejectedly.

"So I could escape with my arm intact." I started down the hall.

After we had finished our soup, I told him why I was hesitating. I had loved Jerry so long I wouldn't dare marry anyone until I was sure I had got over that. Maybe the way to find out how much I loved him was to go home and see if it would break my heart to talk about Jerry. I had discovered that lately I could think of him calmly; I could even imagine meeting him on the street and passing with just a friendly smile. This was real progress. But could I actually do it? I was tempted to try! To this Upton said an emphatic No. He was afraid Mama and Papa would not let me marry him, and he had good reason.

"I have gone over that hurdle," I said, positively. "I cannot let them tell me to give up another love."

Soon I had a visit from one of my relatives; his aunt had married a cousin of my father, and so, Southern fashion, he was a cousin. I politely invited him in, and after I had seated myself, he stood in front of me. He was tall and broad and bold-looking. "I'm here to take you home," he declared, positively. "How long will it take for you to pack?" Both his face and his voice were stern.

"How did you learn to be so masterful?" I asked, a bit irritated.

"I'm president of several enterprises," he announced. "After my father's death, I had to take over and learn how. I have learned. When a situation arises, I take charge."

This was going too far, even for a cousin. "There *is* a situation," I said, firmly. "But it isn't the one to which you refer. It's right here, in this room. Please take charge, and get this absurd young man out of my apartment right away." I rose and walked over to the window to look at the crowded street below.

"You have a view of turbulence there," my cousin remarked, as he joined me. "What is it you like about this noisy town, Mary Craig? Who is the man?"

I was glad he asked that question. It would be a pleasure to tell someone from Mississippi the kind of man I liked. "It doesn't matter who he is," I assured him. "It's a matter of *what* he is."

He was thoughtful for a moment. Then his whole manner changed; he took my hand and asked, humbly, "Come, let's sit down and talk it over, won't you?"

I moved away from him to the far side of the window, and turned to face him. I hadn't seen him since he became so many kinds of president. He was really impressive-looking. He had matured; his fine hazel eyes were like Papa's when he held a switch over a naughty child.

I had to control a sudden, unaccountable impulse to rush to him and cry on his broad shoulders. Here was a man of the big, brave, all-powerful kind. He needed no mother to comfort him or buy him becoming clothes!

He was a protector, and I needed one. I was so terribly afraid of what I was going to do to my beloved Papa and Mama! I was tired of struggling with the problem of how to make them see what I saw. I couldn't make anyone from the South see it. "Yes, let's talk it over," I said, wearily, and went back to my chair.

He took a seat in the big armchair which was too heavy for me to move when I ran the carpetsweeper.

"I like your salt-and-pepper tweeds," I said, trying to be casual—just to put off the hopeless battle of words.

He leaned back and looked me over. "I can tell you why you aren't wearing an equally good suit," he said. "You are interested in a poor man."

"That's a good guess. He *is* poor, and I'm glad of it."

"Tut, tut, Mary Craig! Money is a great thing!" He stood up and squared his fine shoulders and strode up and down the room. "I've *got* it—*money!*—and I like it. And I intend to get more!" His eyes narrowed and his lips came together in a tight line. "It's power! Power! *Power!*" One arm went out in front of him, his fist clenched. "I've got it—and I'm going to *keep* it!"

"Are you talking to me, or to the man you think I love?"

He turned on his heel and faced me. "Yes, I'm talking to him! He's a Socialist, isn't he? The son-of-a-gun!"

I felt that I was being run over, pressed down, trampled. I had to get out of the way of this power machine.

"The South must be changing," I said, just to get my self-control. "I've always thought that Southern gentlemen considered money a vulgar topic."

He gave a short laugh. "I'm no Southern gentleman, Mary Craig. I'm a half-breed—part aristocrat and part redneck. Didn't you know that the other side of my family are hillbillies from Texas? I'm proud of the fact. They were he-men once—that's why they had to flee from the law and hide in those hills. They never became effete."

"Are Southern gentlemen effete?" I asked.

"Aristocracy always becomes effete," he answered. "Idle minds are the devil's workshop."

"History's stairway," I quoted back—"wooden shoes going up and silken slippers coming down!"

"Quite pretty!" he agreed. "My version is less poetic: 'Three generations from shirtsleeves to shirtsleeves.' "

"Then what will happen to your grandchildren?"

He gave a quick laugh. "They can never be real aristocrats—you know that much about Mississippi!"

The doorbell rang, and I opened it without the usual protecting question—I had a he-man in my apartment! Outside was the different kind of man. "Upton," I said, "I have a visitor from Mississippi. He is my cousin, Stephen Johnson. Come in and tell him why he should be a Socialist."

The slender, blond man in his cheap gray suit smiled cordially at my cousin-by-marriage. "I'm glad to meet you," he said, in his quiet, friendly way. He was always glad to meet anybody, except when he was writing.

"At least you can see Upton has a Southern voice," I remarked. "But maybe that is effete. Is it?"

Stephen had given the little man with the scholarly head a swift look of appraisal. "My fears are relieved," he said genially. "You had led me to believe he might throw a bomb at me."

I decided they were going to get along, so I went back to the kitchenette for the cup of coffee I had set down when Stephen had come. It was cold, but I was learning to drink cold coffee. I forgot it often when I was writing, and I never threw it away because it was such trouble to make. How I missed Alberta—every day of my life. I heard Upton's voice, keeping up a cheerful discourse on his favorite theme, so I took my time. I would invite Stephen to go to our cheap restaurant with us.

But Stephen had not come to New York to discuss any sort of theories. He made this clear by the businesslike way in which he ignored the cheapness of the crowded restaurant.

"This cousinship is remote," he informed Upton, as soon as we were seated. "The real relationship is that of a suitor toward his lady. I've loved this girl for a long time. No man is going to win her without some real competition! I'm ruthless when I go out to get something I want." His face and his tone were ominous, and he meant them to be.

Upton listened politely. Then he said with his innocent smile. "I am honored by the challenge. If you play tennis, I'll take you up to Croton where my friend Margaret Mayo will let us fight it out with rackets on her court. I won a cup in England a few months ago." It sounded like two gentlemen from Kentucky, where dueling with pistols at so many yards was sometimes practiced, without consent of the law.

But Stephen had no time for trips to Croton. He had to get back to his business without delay. A few days passed, and I discovered what weapons he had chosen. There came a telegram from my Aunt Sallie. She was coming East. Would I

make a hotel reservation? Or maybe I had room in my apartment for my old auntie?

After I had made it clear to Stephen that I wouldn't
see him again, I went to my apartment alone. I wanted to face
the fact that Stephen had somehow got me into a practical ad-
mission of my intention to marry Upton. Now Mama and
Papa would soon know everything, and before I could present
my case in the way that would hurt them least.

When Upton came back he brought me a bunch of violets,
and I told him I would not thank him, for I knew he had no
money to spend on flowers. His mother had told me that he
always spent every dollar as soon as he got it, and often be-
forehand.

"They cost only twenty-five cents," he pleaded, as if he had
committed a crime. "And I got a check today for an old article
I sent to an English paper before I left there."

I asked Upton if we could take his mother out to dinner. I
did not want to be alone with him—I knew he was worried
about Stephen, and I was afraid I would accuse him of jealousy.
I would take the violets to his mother, to teach him not to
spend even twenty-five cents when he had only twenty-five dollars in his pocket.

He went out and telephoned his mother and she told him
she had friends coming for dinner. So I would have to spend
the evening with Upton; he would be hurt if I told him I
wanted to be alone to think. He would want to help me think.

I put my problem before him. What could I do to convince my parents that he was not a person who wanted "merely
to tear down," as Papa had expressed it?

He answered that he would write it out for them if I wished.
He wanted to tear down evil, but also he wanted to build up
good. He wanted to end poverty and war. That would require
some tearing down, of course. He wanted to tear down the
evil of hired gunmen shooting workingmen who wanted to
build up labor unions. He wanted the workers to have strong

unions; but maybe this would not please anyone who lived where there was only black labor.

I could hear Papa saying that the Negro was not yet capable of exercising such rights. No, I could not persuade my Mississippi father to approve that plank in the Socialist platform. My state knew little about white labor, and the Socialists knew nothing about Negroes.

If I said the Negro must be educated, I would be asked who had the money to pay for it? The white South had not yet recovered from the poverty inflicted on it by the war. The white South wanted no ideas on the subject from any Yankee, whether Socialist or Republican. It had not forgotten the "carpetbag" era!

"It looks hopeless," I said.

Upton was fidgeting around the room. "It *is* hopeless," he declared. "Look at my mother. I have been trying to get her to understand me for a dozen years. She doesn't want to, and the reason is, I'm her own, her precious private possession. You are the same thing to your parents. But you have to live your own life, sooner or later. You are no longer a child."

"You are ruthless!" I cried. "If that's the way Socialists feel, I just can't ever be one!" I was suddenly angry with him. It wasn't reasonable, but I must have someone to blame for my fear that I was not strong or wise enough to solve my own problem.

"Your friend Stephen told me he was ruthless. You didn't get angry with him."

"I was angry with him, too. I wouldn't marry a man like that for anything! I don't want to marry any man. They are all brutes!"

"Now you *are* making yourself sick." He came and knelt down by my chair, and took my hands.

"Listen, beloved," he said, gently. "We can end all of this misery so easily. We can get a marriage license tomorrow, and in three days we can be married. Your parents would face what they must face sooner or later."

"Heavens, Upton! Think of letting them get the news from the papers!"

"You are right—that wouldn't do. Then let's go over into New Jersey and be married there. No license is required in that state."

"Do you imagine the reporters wouldn't learn about *that?* Marriages must be recorded somewhere—I suppose in the town hall; and your name is easy to recognize."

"We could use fictitious names."

"You mean that would be legal?"

"Yes. But I will look it up before we go, if that will reassure you."

I said, "Go home now, and I will think it over. I must be sure I love you enough."

"Kiss me good night," he said. Then he whispered, "*I'm* sure enough for two."

There followed several days of indecision, during which I made sure in my mind that I would never be able to find happiness without Upton. He had become to me everything desirable, and the idea that I still loved Jerry had really become lifeless. I could at last think quietly about the image of him in my mind. There was no longer any emotion, there was even astonishment that I could have felt so deeply for so long.

I hadn't known what Jerry's ideas about anything were. The truth seemed to have been that neither of us had any ideas! Again I asked myself the old question: What is first love? I could not answer. It had been something powerful, blinding; but it no longer existed.

I was a thinking, reasoning person at last. And I not only could see reason for loving Upton, I felt this love as something permanent, tender, sweet. I had wanted to see Jerry every day without knowing why, but I knew why I waited happily for the doorbell to tell me that Upton had come. His presence constantly haunted the plain little apartment, and filled it with warmth and fun. We laughed at the same jokes, the most amusing of which, to him, was that I had chosen him from among so many other candidates. I realized that all my hesitation and unhappiness had been due to only one thing—my deep love for Papa and Mama, and my profound distress at what my marriage to a divorced man would mean in their old-fashioned world.

I still had an impulse to delay about everything. I was baffled by the realization that I could never change their minds, and I simply could not confront them with an accomplished fact. They had expected so much of me.

The one who would be the most disappointed was Mama. Dear emotional, ambitious Mama! Always girlish, almost a child in her everlasting zest for life, its glamor and romance! Now this lovely mother was to see all her romantic dreams for her eldest daughter transformed into something almost disgraceful! This was how she would see it, I knew, and all her world would see it so.

But Upton finally said, "Don't you know, Craig, what you would do to *me* if you sent me away? I have come to think of you as an angel; you were sent from heaven to save me from my blunders, and to guide me—and love me!"

He had been marshaling his forces for some time now. Aunt Mollie had written me, and Mary Wilshire, and only yesterday, Nellie had capitulated. "He is really worth saving, Craigie," she said, earnestly. "I'm no Socialist, as you know, but maybe you can save him from even that!"

Upton's mother could not help me with my problem. All she would commit herself to was that my father and mother had reason to worry about Socialism. She couldn't see why her son, who was born a gentleman, had to waste his talents on these "low, ignorant foreigners."

Stephen Johnson, however, had helped to clarify my thinking, for he would be the choice of my parents. He had everything they believed in, except for that Texas blood—of which there must have been only a drop, or Mama would not have approved him.

I loved my parents, but I must also love the man I married. I loved Upton because he looked at the world outside himself and the narrow orbit of one man's family. To be sure, he wanted a home and family, but he wanted everyone else

to have them, too. He saw the world with no boundaries anywhere on the globe. Mankind was one family to him—white,
yellow, brown, red and black. Modern machines were making
plenty for all not only possible, but necessary. Upton wanted
to speed up the process, and save untold suffering to mankind.

I thought I knew Upton Sinclair well by now. He was a
truly sincere man, truly dedicated to one "cause." This cause
was abolishing from the world the demon poverty. "The demon
rum" he hated equally. He had suffered since childhood at the
hands of this second evil. Not only his father but three of his
uncles had been destroyed by the monster; one had died a
suicide. Upton had seen their sufferings, and that of their
families at close range, and had sworn to himself to seek the
cause of this terrible craving which burned up the will power
of some of the best men in Virginia, as well as in Mississippi.

Nellie came to tell us she was going to Nevada to divorce Jim. He had given up his job as a Socialist organizer
and had settled down in the apartment, expecting her to support
him while he kept on with his scribbling! "If there is one
thing I do know," she declared, "it is what good writing is.
He hasn't even an aptitude, to say nothing of talent. And I
think he knows this. He uses it as an excuse for not getting a
job under the capitalist system. And he won't even do the
housework while I hustle off to my job."

Remembering Upton's distress when he had parted from his
first wife, I asked Nellie why she was weeping.

"Because I love him," she said. "Don't ask me what that
means—I haven't been able to find the answer to my love for
an unworthy husband."

"Maternal, perhaps?" I ventured.

"Yes. But oddly enough, I don't like children. I'm anti-
maternal! I think all children are brats!"

I laughed. "Not little angels, 'trailing clouds of glory'?"

"Little images of the worst, most primitive elements in their
parents. What is good in their elders has not yet been pounded
into them."

"Maybe no one ever pounded any civilization into Jim.

Wouldn't it be a solution of your problem if some man he respected—"

She stopped me with a positive "*No!* Not Upton! He is too tolerant. He would spoil anyone—man, woman, or child. He trusts everyone. But Craigie, you are happy—that is a surprise. I'm *so* glad!"

"Yes, I am happy," I told her. "I believe in Socialism—the Fabian kind, 'the inevitability of gradualness.' I haven't read Karl Marx and don't want to. He teaches class hatred, and I could never believe in hatred of any sort. Besides, I know too many good and generous men who would be called 'capitalists' by a Marxist. My father, for instance."

"Upton draws the same distinction," she said. "So does Bernard Shaw. The Socialists of England are practically all Fabians. But not these New York Socialists! However, I'm not for either kind, as you know. Jim has made me less and less interested in the whole idea. It won't work, Craigie. Human nature isn't fit for it, and may never be."

"What you are saying is that men are not good and will never be. This is despair."

She began to cry again, suddenly. Then she got up and said she must go. "I *am* in despair, Craigie! But don't worry about me—I'm a tough little nut, not easy to crack. I'll come out on top. I always have."

Upton came in a half-hour later. I told him Nellie had just gone. "Yes," he said. "I met her downstairs and walked home with her. Poor girl—I know how she feels. She said she knew now how I had felt. So I told her, 'Look how I feel *now!* There's always another chance.' "

I paid a call on Upton's mother, and found her slightly more hopeful about her son. At least she was smiling when she said, "I hope, Craig, that this new book of his isn't just another Socialist tract."

"You can be happy about that," I told her. "It is not a Socialist book at all."

"What is it?" she wanted to know.

"Social diseases," I answered, cautiously using the polite term.

"What's that?"—and when I told her, she almost fainted. "Mercy me! *Why* does my son have to go around picking out the lowest thing he can find to write about? Why doesn't he write about something nice and make some money, as other authors do?"

I tried to divert her by joking. "He's a muckraker, you know. He *has* to rake muck!"

"Indeed he does not!" she declared, indignantly—as if I had implied that he had inherited this evil tendency from her. "I never discussed such things with him, or with anyone else in my life!"

Then she gave up again and sighed resignedly. "I see you are going to take sides with him."

Sylvia was at last ready for a publisher. At my insistence it was going out to the world as Upton's work. He was sure it would be a best seller. "But even if it isn't," he said, "it is a book which is needed. That is always enough."

"But what good can a book do if it doesn't sell?" I asked.

"It will reach a few key people, and that is one way to spread knowledge. Then, too, I can always find translators and publishers abroad. I'm far more popular over there than at home."

"Why is that?"

"I have never committed the sin of attacking the vested interests of those countries, so their press does not falsify about me. Though of course I didn't intend it, my attack on the meat packing industry in this country was an advantage to the meat packers of other countries. So, in Germany, *The Jungle* was a best-seller. No one over there wanted to eat canned meat from the United States."

John S. Phillips, editor of the *American Magazine,* read the manuscript of *Sylvia* and said that she was "the loveliest heroine in all fiction," and that it was a crime for Upton to use her for his propaganda. But his propaganda was the heart of the story to him, so I had not asked him to cut it out.

Now that our collaboration on the book was done, he was urging me to marry him without further delay. I asked him again if he was not afraid of marriage after his dreadful experience, and he quoted Dr. Samuel Johnson: "A second marriage is a triumph of hope over experience."

Now I had become a rebel. I did not use that word in my letter to Papa, though of course it was a common word in the South, and every Southerner knew how to give the famous "rebel yell." At the same time Southerners would deny that they were rebels. They were Mississippians, or Virginians, or South Carolinians, exercising their inalienable right to secede from the Union.

Writing to Papa, I carefully avoided anything which sounded rebellious. I wrote firmly, but with tenderness, pleading my case as one who loved him more than my own life, but to whom it was a matter of principle. He had great respect for "principle," also in common usage on Southern tongues in connection with the Civil War. "Secession was a matter of principle," it was said.

Now it was such a matter with me. I was not needed at home; other children had grown up and could take my place. But this man, this truly great crusader, who believed in the poor and lowly just as Jesus had, and who only wanted to drive the money-changers from the temple—he did need me; he needed me terribly, I was sure.

I had not felt that in the case of George Sterling. Great poet though he was, I was not necessary to his cause—and besides, the cause of "Beauty" did not appeal to me. However, I did not compare the two men in my letters home. I wrote only of Upton and his crusade.

When a second telegram came from Aunt Sallie, telling me that Mama was coming with her, I knew what to expect. They were coming to take me home!

I made reservations for them at the Martha Washington, and then went to see Upton's mother. Would she dine with them the night they arrived? Mama believed, just as Priscilla did, that Socialists were dusky foreigners, unkempt and untrust-worthy. Priscilla was fair, and had a lovely black chiffon dinner gown, with a little toque to match. "Wear your baby-lamb coat—and bring your lorgnette," I told her. "I want to show you off."

She beamed at the prospect of a good dinner, good company and the box of chocolates I had just brought along. Upton came in before I left and ate more than his share of the choco-lates. "It's his only vice," said his mother.

He went home with me, and we sat talking of the impending threat to his happiness. I tried to assure him that I had made up my mind and given him my promise. I told him he should realize that I kept promises—I had never even considered see-ing Jerry after I had given my promise to Papa.

"It will be an ordeal for all of us," was his reply. Then he asked, "What can I do to make it easier for you?"

"Get a new suit of clothes!" I told him.

"What's wrong with this one?" he wanted to know.

"Everything. Ask your mother to go with you to get a new suit—I know you won't let a tailor make one for you."

He said he would do anything he could, but a new suit was out of the question financially. His son was in a boarding school, the trip to Europe and the divorce had been costly, he had been working on *Sylvia*. During the past year he had earned very little.

"I want to lend you some money," I said casually. "You don't mind borrowing from Gay Wilshire. Why not from me? You believe in equality for women, don't you?"

He hesitated. Before he could object I went over to my little desk and wrote a check. Down in the corner, for Papa, I wrote, "For literary help on my books." He looked at it and smiled. "You do things I would never think of."

Then I told him how he could earn it. He could take the trouble to be nice to my great-aunt. She was not so old-fashioned as Mama, and I had a feeling that she was going to take him to her heart, as Aunt Mollie had done. This would go far to convince Papa of Upton's worth—Papa had never re-gretted her judgment of *him!*

Upton and I rode downtown on the Ninth Avenue elevated railway, and walked across Desbrosses Street to the ferry; that was the way you met arriving friends in the days before there were tunnels under the Hudson River. The April day was showery and we sat in the cabin of the big ferryboat. We waited at the gates until the train arrived and the passengers came streaming down the long platform; our two were among the last, for both were plump, and the elder one in her eighties. I hugged and kissed them, and Upton grabbed Aunt Sallie and kissed her, which obviously pleased her. She knew what he meant—that he was a member of the family, or determined to be.

On the ferryboat he sat next to her and wooed her. He could be charming when he took the trouble; he was using his lovely smile. We didn't talk about serious matters in a ferryboat, of course, but a taxicab was different. Upton helped the two ladies in; Aunt Sallie, who must have weighed two hundred pounds, needed a lot of helping, and Upton remarked, "You carry great weight, Aunt Sallie. I hope you'll throw it on my side." My shrewd great-auntie got this, too, but made no answer. He hadn't won her yet!

Aunt Sallie had gone out to California as a schoolteacher and had married General William Green, who was known as "the father of irrigation." When he died the flags were at half-mast all over the state. She had inherited his newspaper, the Colusa *Sun,* and had both published and edited it, and written a book called *Tahoe.* She was what at home was called a "strong-minded woman." With it all, she had as tender a heart as Mama.

Upton talked to her about what was going on in the world, and what he thought about it, and what he was trying to do about it. "My husband was a man of action, too," said Aunt Sallie. "But he did not get into trouble as you do."

I thought this was my call to defend my fiancé. "That's why I love him," I said. "Because he acts without considering what will happen to him." I went on to explain that when he saw something evil he didn't turn his back on it; he figured out what should be done about it and went to work to get it done.

He had convinced me that he knew what to do, and I wanted to help.

My proud mother was keeping back her tears; but she was as brave as she was proud, and I was sure she was going to meet the inevitable with grace. When the taxi arrived at the Martha Washington hotel, we three ladies went upstairs, while Upton sat in the lobby and read a newspaper.

"Remember, Mama," I said, while she and Aunt Sallie were dressing for dinner, "I'm happy at last! And though I haven't chosen the man of your choice, you will realize in the end that the man of my choice has the spiritual qualities which make him much nearer to you and Papa than any of the others."

"My dear child, I pray God that you are not mistaken. Aunt Sallie wanted to come alone to try to persuade you not to break your father's heart. I came with her, even though I am not well, because I could not bear to hurt you by not being with you when—" She was silent, struggling with her emotion, then continued—"when you made your decision. I knew you would suffer."

Aunt Sallie had been busying herself with her toilette, seeming to be paying no attention to us. Now she announced in a matter-of-fact tone, "If Craig is going to wear that suit she has on, I can wear my traveling dress. It's getting late, Mary Hunter."

Then she said to me, "I'm glad you invited Mrs. Sinclair. Men don't go far wrong if there's a good mother near."

Upton's lawyer was the husband of his feminist friend, Charlotte Perkins Gilman. Upton had arranged for him to bring Mrs. Priscilla to meet us for dinner. When we were at the table I hastened to lead the conversation into channels where I knew the ladies would be happy. Upton's eight Virginia uncles and cousins, plus a grandfather, who had been officers in the Confederate States Navy, would thrill Mama. I mentioned the uncle who had commanded the ironclad *Mississippi*, being built at New Orleans; the Yankee navy had seized the port in order to get her. This was close to home, and moved Mama to tell of the *Star of the West*, a gunboat sunk just around the bend in the Yazoo we could see from our Green-wood home.

Mrs. Priscilla told about the Sinclair family tree. Her son was a direct descendant of King Robert of Scotland and King Edward II of England. Mama told of her family tree, starting from Charlemagne; and Upton could not refrain from inform-ing her that he, too, was descended from that father of trees. "Then," said Mama, "both of us are descended from at least a dozen French kings. But I've never been happy about those French ancestors, even though they were kings. I do not feel that I'm anything but Anglo-Saxon." Priscilla told about Uncle Bland's Virginia tree, which had hung in the billiard room of the home where Upton had spent part of his childhood and youth, reading volumes never before taken from the shelves of the library. His Uncle Bland had been given the name John Randolph, after the Virginia statesman, a member of the family; that name put us on the trail, and behold, there were other cousins of my family who were cousins of Upton's! And so it turned out that everyone present belonged to the F.F.V.s—First Families of Virginia—except dear little Mr. Gil-man. I think we must have made the genealogical trip from Virginia to Mississippi and back again a dozen times in the course of that evening.

What the mothers were trying to do was to establish a bond of stability between the two parties of the coming alliance. The life of Upton's mother had been embittered by the pov-erty which she felt was not natural to her family. Her son had perversely chosen to take his place among the lowly ones of the earth, but now it appeared to her satisfaction that he was about to marry into affluence as well as aristocracy. As for the ladies from Mississippi, they were hearing reaffirmations of what their child had told them, the gallantry of Upton's her-itage. To be sure, this heritage had been financially impaired by the loss of the Civil War; but all Southerners understood that, and it appeared there were branches of the family tree still flourishing.

It was Priscilla who gave us our final lift. She produced from

her jet handbag a letter from a lieutenant-colonel in the War
Department and gave it to Mama. It read:

"In the interesting conversation we had on subjects genealogical you mentioned that your ancestors, the Sinclairs, Earls
of Orkney and of Caithness, were descended from Robert
Bruce, King of Scotland.

"The following pedigree which I have located and which
I vouch for as absolutely correct, shows such descent, and I am
sending it to you because I am sure you will be interested.

"ROBERT BRUCE, King of Scotland, had by his second
wife, Lady Elizabeth de Burgh, daughter of Richard, Earl
of Ulster:

"Princess Margaret Bruce, sister of King David II, who m.,
1344 (his first wife) William, Earl of Sutherland, d. 1370,
and had:

"John, sixth Earl of Sutherland, only son, d. 1389, who m.
Lady Mabilla Dunbar, daughter of Patrick, tenth Earl of
March, and had:

"Nicholas, eighth Earl of Sutherland, second son, d. 1399,
who m. Elizabeth, daughter of John MacDonald, Lord of
the Isles, and had:

"Robert, ninth Earl of Sutherland, d. 1442, who m. Lady
Mabilla, daughter of John, second Earl of Murray, and had:

"Alexander Sutherland, of Dunheath, third son, who had:

"Lady Margaret Sutherland, m. William Sinclair, third Earl
of Orkney, and Earl of Caithness,

and left issue from one of whom your distinguished ancestor,
Captain Arthur Sinclair, USN., is descended."

Whether or not Mr. Sinclair's legal adviser was able to figure
out the purpose of all this talk of "family," he enjoyed a good
dinner, and he finished earning his fee in a few minutes after
the meal. He sat with us in a quiet corner of one of the hotel's
reception rooms; and Aunt Sallie relieved Mama of the embarrassment of questioning him. "Is this Dutch divorce decree
valid in the United States?" she asked.

And the answer was, "I have studied it carefully and have

looked up the law. It is unquestionably valid, and I offer congratulations to all parties concerned."

Mama invited him to be the family's guest if he ever came to Mississippi. "We have the best crab gumbo anywhere on that coast," she said.

Everything was now clear for a wedding, except the question of how we could reconcile Papa. I had given up Jerry because Papa asked me to, and without demanding to know why. Now I wanted to know why I could not marry Upton Sinclair. I had been told only that I could not marry a divorced man. I decided that it was a remnant of Papa's early training in the Episcopal Church.

Aunt Sallie made up her mind at once after she heard Mr. Gilman's affirmation of the validity of the divorce: there was no reason to forbid this marriage. The one thing left to settle was where the wedding was to be. Surely not in New York, or near it; for the newspapers would revive the divorce story, photographs and all—the desertion of the author by his wife and her flight with "the other man." Such publicity would spoil the dignity and beauty of a marriage ceremony, especially for Papa.

Aunt Sallie was ready with an answer: we would go to one of those lovely old family homes in Virginia. The home chosen was that of an elderly cousin in Fredericksburg.

As soon as we arrived, Upton went to call on the rector, who began an interrogation. It was his duty, he said, to make absolutely certain that the divorce had been granted for the cause of infidelity and that Upton was the innocent party. The entirely innocent party produced an impressive document issued by the court in Holland; unfortunately it was written in Dutch. Upton translated some of the words, pointing with his finger. The saving word "infidelity," having a Latin root, could be recognized in any language, and soon after it came the word "vrouw," which the clergyman knew meant wife. So he expressed himself as satisfied, and consented to perform the ceremony.

It was after we got back to New York that Upton happened to be looking in his trunk, and with an exclamation produced

a second and still more imposing document in Dutch. It was
the divorce decree; the one he had translated to the minister
was the decree granting him custody of his son!

The Fredericksburg house was big, rambling and
painted white a long time ago; it stood on the banks of the
Rappahannock River and was almost hidden by ancient trees.
The month was April, and the sun was bright on our little wedding party, which stood bareheaded on the lawn, with golden
jonquils dancing in the gentle breeze. On one side was the historic hill that had been the scene of a dreadful battle just half
a century earlier. There twelve thousand blueclad Union soldiers had laid down their lives to keep us under the stars and
stripes instead of the stars and bars.

Upton and I stood solemnly before the clergyman. The ladies
stood near us, trying to hide their tears. Mama tugged nervously at her wedding ring, which she found hard to remove;
she had just discovered that we were being married without
this time-honored symbol! She got it off, slipped it to Upton,
and so we were correctly married.

Poor Mama dried her tears, then put her head on Upton's
shoulder and shed some more. Our hostess tactfully walked
down to the water's edge with the clergyman.

Aunt Sallie said to Upton, "I have a respect for history. I believe in *noblesse oblige,* for a great example inspires later generations to great deeds. This is a part of our common Southern
tradition. As you look around this garden and at this old home,
has it occurred to you that it was in this countryside your distinguished ancestors lived and planned the future of your
native land?"

Upton saw what the dear old lady was doing—leading him
gently to express his feeling about his country, and those ancestors about whom his mother had told us last night. Upton
stepped in front of her and took her hands, and with his best
smile, as bright as a child's, he answered, "Aunt Sallie, what do
you think my work as a Socialist means?"

"That's what I asked *you,*" countered my lively old auntie.

"It means," said he, "that I love my country because of its

ideals. They are the same as mine—the same as those which moved my great-grandfather Commodore Sinclair to fight the British on the Great Lakes. He believed there should be no 'taxation without representation.' I am sure this means there shall be no work without just compensation. Isn't that the same thing?"

Aunt Sallie thought it over for a moment. "Yes," she answered. "But let's get it entirely clear. Your mother told us last night that this great-grandfather was one of the founders of the Democratic Party. How do you reconcile that with Socialism?"

"I don't think my great-grandfather intended to found a party to represent only the privileged classes. That would surely not be democracy."

Aunt Sallie gave him a pat on his cheek. "You have a good case," she said. "Now, kiss me."

It was necessary to receive the reporter of the local newspaper. Three-fourths of the party were in a state of great concern about this, and there was agitated discussion—about reporters here, and reporters in Mississippi, and reporters in New York, and what would we say to them and who should say it, until my newly-acquired husband burst out, "Oh, damn the reporters!" This shocked the elders but perhaps pleased them a little, too, as normal masculine behavior.

"My darling mother," I said. "Have a good laugh—my name is going around the world! Go find that gypsy fortune-teller and let her know that her prophecy has come true!"

Aunt Sallie was ready to start for Greenwood at once, to relieve Papa of his groundless fears. She said, "I'll restore that lovely oil painting of Craig to the wall of the drawing-room where it belongs." Papa used to call it "the sweet young face of my first-born," but when he realized that his child was really considering marriage to a Socialist and a divorced man, he had taken the picture down and carried it up to the attic, and turned the "sweet young face" to the wall.

Mama would first visit my youngest sister, Dollie, at her finishing school up the Hudson. She confided to me that she

wanted Upton to travel to Tarrytown with her. Someone had
told her that all Socialists despised religion, and she must have
one real talk with her new son-in-law on this subject. I decided
not to go with them; I would let my devout mother have all of
my husband's attention. So they set out, Mama determined to
make a Christian of Upton—and Upton, as I well knew, determined to make a Socialist of Mama.

I could guess pretty well what was going to happen, for I
knew that Upton had written of himself as a practicing Christian and Mama was already a Socialist in spirit, without having
the least idea of the fact.

Mama started explaining her idea of Christianity as soon as
their train pulled out of Grand Central Station. Upton listened
politely, and apparently with considerable interest, for a couple
of hours passed before he suddenly became aware that they had
traveled some forty miles beyond Tarrytown! They had to get
off, and wait for a train back; and by the time they had arrived
at Tarrytown and got off the train, Mama had told Upton, "If
the purpose of Socialism is to bring about the brotherhood of
man, then of course I am for it!"

Two people so sincere and so truly good had come to a working agreement that was never to be broken. Mama went back
to Mississippi prepared to do her share of converting Papa to
both Upton and his faith. Soon after they reached Greenwood,
Aunt Sallie wrote us with some amusement what had happened before they got there. The news of the wedding had
been telegraphed over the country, and a reporter had called
Papa on the telephone. "Does your daughter share her husband's ideas about Socialism?" Papa had replied sharply, "My
daughter does not share *any* of her husband's ideas!" And then
he had hung up.

We never knew what caused the newspapers of the country to
give our marriage respectful attention. One of them stated
twice in the same report that the bride was "very beautiful."
The *New York Times* reported that the bride's father was "one
of the wealthiest men in the section and controls large banking
interests." My bridegroom informed me that this had done the

trick, but I thought the *Times* had been interested when it heard that Upton's wife did not agree with him about anything!

7. I NEVER DREAMED OF THIS

MAMA'S ACCEPTANCE of her new son-in-law was so complete that I hoped for a letter from Papa inviting us to come home. But no such letter came. I was so hurt by this that I wished at times that Upton went to an office to work instead of being in the apartment all day; I wanted a chance to cry.

Upton called me *"himmlische Engel,"* which he translated for me as "heavenly angel." I objected on the ground that I had no intention of living up to anything of the sort; no man had a right to expect it. But he proposed, with shining eyes, "Let's keep it like this! Let's never have a cross word!" Here, indeed, was the eternal optimist.

There was a silk workers' strike in Paterson, New Jersey, accompanied by the violence customary in those days; the strikers blamed it on the police. Greenwich Village took an interest, and John Reed and a group of friends designed a wonderful pageant representing the events of the strike, and a thousand workers were brought over to Madison Square Garden to rehearse. When the great evening came, twenty thousand of New York's "reds," "pinks," and all shades between paid a dollar each to come and cheer themselves hoarse.

We decided to go, and my sister Dollie from Tarrytown begged to go with us. I discovered how easy it is to enlist the enthusiasm of youth in a cause, provided there is noise, excitement and a rebellious spirit. My sister had no understanding whatever of the complex economic causes of the strike; all she knew was that someone wanted something, and the way to get it was to make a big fuss. She wore around her neck a large red silk handkerchief, which she said she had bought from a girl on the street who was peddling tickets to the pageant. Also, she had a leaflet on which was printed the *Marseillaise.*

John Reed came to the speakers' platform, and the cheering crowd welcomed the handsome young revolutionist who had just been in Mexico as a war correspondent. Up jumped Dollie and climbed into her seat, wildly waving her red handkerchief.

"Congratulations, Joan of Arc!" laughed Upton when she resumed her seat. "You should have been on the stage!"

"Take me up there!" was the reply. "What did you say his name was?"

Sylvia was accepted for publication by the John C. Winston Company and we received a good advance. So we decided to spend the summer in Europe with Upton's boy, David.

During the winter Dollie had grown up rapidly into an attractive young lady. She preferred tailored clothes to ruffles and frills, and looked well in them. She did her blonde hair in a saucy coiffure of her own design, and flashed her black eyes roguishly.

I wrote Mama of our plans, and told her we would be glad to take Dollie with us. I knew that Mama considered a European tour a necessary part of a young lady's education, and Dollie could not find a more scholarly guide than my husband. Also it was my wish to have a sort of playmate for David; Dollie was a few years older than he, but she was something of a tomboy and always ready for a lark. Dollie could take singing lessons and a dance course at the wonderful new Dalcroze school near Dresden where David might also take lessons.

Mama's answer was "Yes!" Perhaps Papa was persuaded that this show of family confidence would add to the general acceptance of our marriage. So I was able to leave for Europe with a lighter heart.

Dollie brought one large trunk filled mostly with evening gowns and picture hats trimmed with ostrich plumes—things she usually disliked. I wondered if she envisioned herself as being introduced at court. Upton and I carried another large trunk in which Upton had packed a few well-worn clothes and an enormously heavy overcoat he had bought after the Helicon Hall fire when he escaped in the snow with his nightshirt half burned off. Also there was an iron frying pan, a hatchet, a hammer, a pair of high-topped hunting boots and a poncho— all of which had served him well during the poverty-stricken years he had lived in a tent in the woods. The rest of the space in our trunk was filled with books and writing pads and a few street clothes I had stuffed in. We used only the few street clothes. When David joined us, his luggage was a rücksack which he had acquired in his German boarding-school, and a cigar box containing an active, voracious gray mouse.

Bernarr MacFadden had come to live in England, and invited us to visit his fine new sanatorium at Brighton. We enjoyed seeing him again, but we found the coast chilly and stayed only twenty-four hours. MacFadden told Upton that he looked ten years younger than at their last meeting, and Upton made the same answer he had made to Aunt Mollie and the Wilshires: "It's because I've married a *himmlische Engel.*"

Nearby lived Peter Kropotkin, who had been born a prince but refused to use the title. Upton had read all his books, and they had corresponded for years. Now we went to call on the old man. He held his arms wide open and took Upton to his heart in a warm embrace, then he kissed the hands of the ladies and the forehead of young David, who said "ouch" when a curtain of gray whiskers fell over his face.

We were eager to meet the head of the Dalcroze dance school. Eurythmics, which Jacques Dalcroze had created, was so beautiful that we named it "music made visible." After one of the Dalcroze performances we ran into Bernard Shaw. It was on the edge of a meadow, on a sunny, windswept day, and I have never forgotten the charm, the sweetness and kindness, which seemed to surround that tall, golden-haired, golden-bearded man as he stood chatting with us. Shaw introduced us to Granville-Barker, a young playwright who endorsed our opinion of the Dalcroze miracle. Since our two young people were clamoring to enroll immediately Shaw suggested, "Why not come to London, and enroll there? Dalcroze will be there soon to open a school."

We decided to take Shaw's advice and return to England for the rest of the summer. But first there must be a few days in Paris for Dollie to see the latest fashions, and for David to go up the Eiffel Tower. Also we wanted to pay a brief visit to our friend Dr. van Eeden in Holland. He repeated what everyone had told Upton, "You have shed several years."

Then he took me for a stroll to give some psychological advice to a bride. "Keep him below boiling point," he said. "But let him have his way now and then." I promised not to boil over myself, if I could help it.

We were happy to be in England again, with our friends the Wilshires and Aunt Mollie nearby. We rented a cottage with a gorgeous flower garden all around it, except for one clear stretch of lawn where we drank tea and played croquet. Upton enjoyed visiting his confrères: lunch with Shaw at Shaw's country home at Ayot-St. Lawrence, and again at his town flat overlooking the Thames; with H. G. Wells at the New Reform Club and at Aunt Mollie's; a meeting with George Lansbury, where both of them spoke from the back of a truck; a day at the country home of Havelock Ellis, whose six enormous books I refused to read; lunch with two of the less dangerous suffragists, Mr. and Mrs. Pethick-Lawrence—he destined to become a lord. Frank Harris, a former Texas cowboy, now editor of one of the great London magazines, bought him a twenty-four-dollar lunch at the Savoy Hotel. But Upton was not impressed.

When autumn came, we put David in an English boarding school, and Dollie went to live with the Wilshires during the Dalcroze School term. During the summer Upton had worked at turning Brieux's French play, "Damaged Goods," into a novel. Now he was ready to return home to see his publisher. Again we said au revoir to England and sailed to New York. Upton liked to write outdoors, but could not do so in winter, so after he had delivered the manuscript we left for Bermuda.

But before we left New York I had an experience which would greatly have shocked my parents had I told them about it. We went to dine at the home of a wealthy physician, Dr. James P. Warbasse, who busied himself with cooperatives and other humanitarian projects. There we met and sat down to dinner with Mary Goode, a notorious "madam" of the great metropolis. She had recently testified as to the rapacity of the police in collecting from the world of vice.

Dr. Warbasse had read the Brieux story of veneral disease, and he invited Mrs. Goode to discuss that subject with us and give to a novelist of social themes a first-hand account of her world. I had learned much about these social evils while helping Upton with his novel, and had a feeling of pity mixed with horror. There sat this richly-dressed woman of the underworld between my husband and the elegant Mrs. Warbasse, quite as much at ease as her hostess.

I asked few questions, for I was in a strange world. Both my husband and the surgeon asked many, and Mary Goode replied with quiet dignity; they understood the tragedy of the world's outcasts. There was one main cause, she said—poverty! Take the poor girl who fell in love during her teens; the man betrayed her, and she was pregnant with nowhere to go—nowhere but Mary's. I asked her about the psychological attitude of the average woman prostitute. "What happens is this:" replied the "madam," with sudden bitterness, "the girl trusts a man when she is young; and when he betrays her she says, 'Never again! The next time, they pay!'"

So many of Upton's friends had voluntarily advised me how to manage him that I had come to believe it would require constant effort on my part. But as time passed, I began to feel more at ease. Besides instructing me, he gave me many books to read, until I was firmly based in his world. This made it easier for me to go along with his various crusades to put his social reforms into action.

His weaknesses were obvious, for he was neither subtle nor secretive; in fact, his very lack of reserve might be a form of weakness. Some of his friends thought he wore his heart on his sleeve. But was it a weakness or was it a virtue? Some thought Upton simply did not want to bother with being discreet. But I was inclined to believe it was due to his hatred of sham and insincerity; he was determined to tell the truth and the whole truth at all costs. And he thought other people would do the same.

Taking stock of my marriage, I could write home with a clear conscience that I loved my husband and was happy. This would make up, in part at least, for the divorce and Socialism. I did love him. He was so game, and so charitable! The world was full of pain and sorrow, but with him at my side, there was hope.

In Bermuda we had a book to finish—a sequel to *Sylvia* —which required some collaboration. We worked steadily and conscientiously, for in Upton's mind the theme of *Sylvia's Marriage* was the same as Brieux's—venereal disease.

We rented one of those lovely small houses made of white coral, and from it we looked out on the clear blue waters of the Atlantic. Back of us, and on each side, were patches of plantains, fields of Easter lilies, and gardens of poinsettia, scarlet hibiscus and bougainvillaea interspersed with clean white roads and cottages. Not too far away for Upton to ride on his bicycle was the Princess Hotel, where he would go in the afternoon for a game of tennis.

One of his former secretaries, a pratical young woman like Nellie, lived a mile from us. Ruth had married a Bermudian who raised acres of Easter lilies for the New York market, also Bermuda onions and "new" potatoes. They were eager to show us the wonders of their island home and we accompanied them on various excursions. Automobiles were not allowed at that time, and we traveled by bicycle and occasionally by horse-drawn vehicles. At night we drifted in a boat on placid Harrington Sound.

It was a joy to me merely to be alive in this dreamy, brightly-colored place. I had never outgrown my love for the peace and quiet of the Delta countryside. Always with me was the memory of the deep, dark "River of Death" which flowed in tawny grandeur past our big house and on into the setting sun; the rich green of drooping willows on each side, the wide dusty roads along its banks, the sheen of dew on the rose garden under our windows, and the vast fields pink when the cotton was in bloom, white when the bolls had matured and burst

Aunt Sally Morgan Green. She was a strong-minded woman, but she had as tender a heart as Mama.

Upton and his young son David in 1905. Upton's first marriage ended in divorce, and Upton won custody of David.

My sister, Dollie. She was studying dancing under Dalcroze in Germany.

Upton's great-grandfather, Arthur Sinclair, known as "The Commodore," commanded the American forces on Lake Huron in 1814 and captured three British vessels. Many years later a naval destroyer, the U.S.S. *Sinclair*, was named in his honor.

"Commodore" Arthur Sinclair's son, shown here in the uniform of the United States Navy, later joined the Confederate Navy. He died in a shipwreck and was buried in Fleetwood, England.

Upton liked to write outdoors but could not do so in winter, so we spent a few months in Bermuda after a trip abroad.

Bernard Shaw and his wife Charlotte came to California
on a world cruise and we renewed our acquaintance, begun many years ago in a German meadow. He sent us
this photograph, inscribed as shown, and once wrote
Upton, "When people ask me what has happened in my
long lifetime, I do not refer them to the newspaper files
and to the authorities, but to your novels."

This is me in 1948
G. B. S.

To Upton Sinclair

Ayot Saint Lawrence
6ᵗʰ January
1949

open. Bermuda was even more beautiful. I had not been "thrilled" by the art treasures in the galleries and museums of Europe, but sometimes my breath was taken by the sudden splendor of crashing white and green waves on a coral ledge at the end of a turn in a Bermuda road.

All of the tension clouding our wedding now suddenly and mysteriously fell away. I thought it was because Bermuda was so remote from the rush of cities, so quiet, and so lovely in every direction. But maybe Upton was right when he suggested that it was due to a letter from Mama in which she said, "I read your letters about beautiful Bermuda to your father and he enjoys them as much as I do. He would like to go in a boat to spear lobsters." That truly sounded as if Papa, too, was relaxing his anxiety about me; but I wanted *everything*—I wanted him to write me himself!

Of course I had heard from other people about the sensation produced by *The Jungle,* but I wanted to hear how my husband felt about it after seven years. Sitting one afternoon on a rocky point looking out over that boundless blue ocean, I questioned him about it. He had been living on a small farm near Princeton when he read about a strike in the Chicago stockyards. As usual, he became indignant over their mistreatment. He had finished his novel *Manassas,* which dealt with chattels. Now he wanted to write such a novel about wage slaves. The *Appeal to Reason* offered him five hundred dollars for the serial rights to such a book and this advance enabled him to write it.

He settled down in the stockyards district. Dressed in his usual cheap clothes and carrying a dinner pail he could walk through any room in any plant without attracting attention; it would be assumed that he was a worker in some other department. He spent seven weeks studying every aspect of the industry, and the district known as "Back of the Yards," where the workers lived. Every night he would return to his hotel room and make notes of what he had observed. One Sunday afternoon he followed a wedding party into the back room of a saloon; he sat against the wall and watched these Lithuanians who knew only a few words of English. The opening scene of his story began to take shape, with these Lithuanians as his characters. He wrote this wedding scene in his mind, and when he was back on his farm at Princeton, he put it on paper—as he told me, sometimes blinded by his own tears. After the book was finished, Jack London wrote: "It is written with sweat and blood and groans and tears."

Five publishers declined the book because it was too full of horrors, but Upton wouldn't cut them out. He got the book into type, intending to publish it himself, with the backing of the *Appeal*. Then Doubleday, Page agreed to take it over, allowing him to have his own edition. The book created a terrific sensation everywhere. Winston Churchill wrote a two-part account of it for one of the leading English weeklies.

I asked Upton the usual question, "How did this sudden change make you feel?" He said, "I wanted to run away and hide from all the excitement. But of course I was glad to know that now I could use fame and my writing ability in the cause of industrial democracy. To me this meant democracy for everyone."

President Theodore Roosevelt invited Upton to Washington to discuss the charges made in the book. He told the author that during its serialization he had received two hundred letters a day asking him to make an investigation. At lunch in the White House he said, "Believe me, Mr. Sinclair, I have no love for those packers. I tried their canned beef during the war in Cuba, and I'd as soon have eaten my old Army hat."

There followed a battle in Congress lasting for weeks, with Upton in New York issuing a blast in the newspapers every day. After his fashion, he wore himself to exhaustion. Mark Sullivan in his book *Our Times* records: "Roosevelt appointed two commissioners to investigate conditions and they found them even worse than Sinclair had reported them. They found proof of all his charges except the one about the men falling into vats. The uproar forced Congress to pass the Meat Inspection Act and the Pure Food and Drug Act, both in 1906."

Before we left Bermuda we stopped at a tiny wayside grocery to buy some cookies. While the grocer was weighing and wrapping them, Upton happened to glance up at a shelf in front of him, and observed some cans of a shape very familiar to him. They were covered with the dust of many years, and Upton was moved to ask, "What are those cans of Chicago roast beef doing up there?"

The grocer answered, in a tone of resentment and disgust, "Oh, some fellow wrote a book about that stuff, and I haven't been able to sell a can of it!"

We paid for our purchase and departed, and Upton quoted to me the remark he had made when *The Jungle* uproar was at its height: "I aimed at the public's heart and by accident I hit it in the stomach."

In Bermuda, Upton had taken time off from *Sylvia's Marriage* to write a fantastic drama called "The Millennium," set a hundred years in the future. One of the imagined wonders was an airplane which would allow the members of the ruling class to follow the sunset around the world. Another was a man standing before a device describing what was going on at a ball to the people of all the world. Supersonic planes and international radio are commonplace today, but in 1913 they represented a leap of the imagination.

There was a further leap; a character rushed in, exclaiming: "Professor Holcombe has discovered a new element, which he calls radiumite, and this develops a power of an intensity never known before, penetrating all substances, and destructive of all animal life . . . Think what this means! Here is power enough to turn all the wheels of industry in the country! And think of what wealth it will create! Why, sir, from a single thimbleful of sea water, Professor Holcombe can extract sufficient power to drive a freight airship around the world. Think of it! And it is all yours!"

This is a synopsis of the rest of the play:

What came of this discovery? One evening over the world-radio device came the news that the scientist, forbidden to continue his work, intended to explode a bomb that would kill every living thing on earth. A party of wealthy people attending a ball on the top floor of an immense "pleasure palace," crowded into a flying machine on the roof; this carried them to safety high above the earth. On their return they found everything but themselves dead.

The last act of this fantasy was a picture of a Utopia, or perhaps I should say an Uptonia. These people organized a cooperative colony, and went to work to restore the world. In the autumn they harvested their only crops: pumpkins and a baby.

"A return to vegetarianism," I remarked, when I read this scene.

"Yes," said Upton. "What else could they do? There was no livestock in the machine."

To which I answered, "I suppose the chef at the ball had some pumpkin seeds in his pocket."

Upton's friends the Selwyns took this manuscript to David Belasco, and he expressed delight with it and agreed to produce it. Utopian dreams were swarming in my Utopian's mind when he came home from an interview with this all-powerful stage-master. He had no idea how freely promises were made and broken in the theater world.

Belasco had been fighting a concern which controlled theater bookings all over the country. His method had been to produce expensive spectacles in New York and force the country to come to the Belasco Theater. That was what he had in mind for "The Millennium," but suddenly the syndicate came to terms with him, and after that he wanted small shows which could travel cheaply on the road. He dropped Upton without apology, and put on a play by Eugene Walter called "The Easiest Way."

But for my husband the world was still young, for he was young! We could be happy and hopeful without Mr. Belasco's help.

Winston accepted the new book and made an advance. After our debts were paid, we had fifteen hundred dollars to live on for the next year—unless the novel was a success—in the United States, or in England, where Upton's publisher was waiting for the manuscript. Altogether, this wonderful English

publisher issued sixty-five of Upton's books and never declined
a single manuscript.

Each time we received an advance we planned how we would
live during the year in which he would write his next book.
Upton's mind was now busy with the idea of compiling an
anthology of the literature of social protest, to be called *The
Cry for Justice*. He would need access to a good library and the
full time of a secretary. Upton saw nothing to worry about in
this, for he was used to living "from hand to mouth," but it was
otherwise with me. I had come to feel more and more insecure
in a world where I could not draw checks.

During the peaceful days in Bermuda, there had been little
need for money—only the rental of an inexpensive cottage, too
small for most visitors, and simple meals which we prepared for
ourselves. Upton had learned, from much camping in his early
life, how to cook steaks, and I had learned how to make coffee.
Also I had learned to get along on Upton's diet of beefsteak,
whole-wheat bread, green salad and fruit, with now and then
a can of tomato or vegetable soup. Together, we were able to
prepare a meal quickly. But now we were back in New York
City and needed a living room in which to entertain friends, so
we rented a respectable apartment on Morningside Heights.

For the first time I was beginning to feel the pinch of poverty. Suppose I should have to ask the landlady to wait for the
rent? I still had a diamond necklace which I might sell and
other pieces of jewelry. I passed the windows of pawnshops,
wondering if it would be safe to leave anything of real value at
such a place.

I did not tell Upton of my worry—he was sure that *Sylvia's
Marriage* would be a success. I did not want to spoil his peace
of mind. I had never forgotten his depressed condition after
those tormented days when he was suing for divorce. I wanted
to keep him fit in every way to do his work. I loved him for his
zeal, his optimism, his eternal naïve faith in the benevolence of
the universe.

When I questioned this benevolence, observing the misery of
every sort imaginable, he would answer that it was the duty of
men to exert themselves to remove this misery. Evidently the

Creator expected us to use our faculties, mental and moral as
well as physical, for misery did not remove itself. But with the
faculties of mind God had bestowed on us, we could move
mountains—and Upton was out to prove it!

My questioning could not continue for long in the presence
of such faith. Life had hurt me, but it had hurt him, too, and I
could be as brave as he—especially when he looked at me across
the table with that shining smile.

There was a mass meeting at Carnegie Hall. I was asleep
when Upton came home about midnight, but he woke me to
tell me what he had heard. During the past half-year there had
been a strike of Colorado coal miners, demanding the right to
organize. The operators of the Colorado Fuel and Iron Company bitterly and determinedly opposed their right to organize.
They had driven the strikers out of the isolated company camps
in the mountains; the strikers had thereupon set up tent colonies. Some 11,000 men, with their women and children, had
been living there all through the winter. Machine-guns had
been trained on the strikers and at Ludlow company gunmen
had poured gasoline on the tents and set fire to them. Three
women and 14 children had been burned or suffocated to
death.

This was the story to which Upton had listened. Laura Cannon, wife of one of the United Mine Workers organizers, had
been an eyewitness of this "Ludlow massacre," and when she
told about it 3,000 New Yorkers cried out their indignation
and subscribed money for the support of the homeless and hungry strikers.

The great newspapers of the city had published almost nothing about the strike or about the Ludlow atrocity. My husband
said that something *must* be done to break the conspiracy of
silence by which the newspapers kept the public from hearing
what was going on in those bleak and lonely mining camps.

For a couple of hours we lay discussing the problem. Here it
was again, the denial of basic rights to workingmen in a democracy; here was the refusal of all-powerful employers to recognize that working-men were human beings. Upton knew the

wiles of the press and was determined to find a way to outwit them. They were the owners of that commodity called publicity, which is essential to the operation of democracy. The case of the helpless strikers must be brought before the bar of public opinion.

The Colorado Fuel and Iron Company was controlled by the Rockefeller interests. John D., Jr., at this time about 40, was our target. He denied that he had anything to do with the handling of the matter, but later on, when the Walsh Commission forced him to produce his correspondence files it was shown that he had been giving the orders.

We must do something spectacular, Upton declared, in order to enlist the public's sympathy. As the night wore on, an idea came to him at last: we would ask a group of sympathizers to put on bands of mourning crepe in memory of the murdered women and children of Ludlow and walk up and down in front of the Rockefeller offices all day. We would not block traffic, we would not provoke violence and we would keep absolute silence; no matter what was said or done to us, we would look straight ahead and keep on walking.

"They will surely arrest you," I argued.

"Of course they will; and that is what is needed. The newspaper reporters will certainly be there and their editors will not suppress the story—they will be afraid their rivals won't. Once the public knows the truth, public opinion will force action."

My heart sank, for I thought of my people at home. And I thought also of myself; I was still a Southerner, and had a horror of crowds, noise, uproar—and above all, of seeing my name in the newspapers. The worst thing was that the story would not stop in New York, it would go to the Memphis *Commercial Appeal,* which Mississippians read. Why should Upton try to tell Mr. Rockefeller how to run his business? My husband was stirring up the working class—why couldn't he attend to his own business? That was what Mississippi would say.

Upton said, "We will make the announcement this morning." I think he didn't intend to sleep at all. But I checked him;

it was to be my lifelong fate to try to make him think twice. He always wanted to act instantly.

I said, "We must give Mr. Rockefeller a chance. Let us go to his office with Mrs. Cannon, and ask him to see her; if he does, that is a story, that will be publicity—without anybody going to jail. If he refuses, we have improved our position. People will see that we have been fair."

We argued it back and forth, and Upton gave way, so we got a little sleep.

In the morning we phoned Mrs. Cannon at her hotel and made a date to call for her at ten o'clock. Upton typed a letter to Mr. Rockefeller, telling him that the wife of a United Mine Workers organizer who had lived through the events at Ludlow requested an opportunity to tell him what she had seen and experienced. Both of us signed the letter, and we took Mrs. Cannon down to the office of the Standard Oil Company at 26 Broadway.

In the anteroom we presented the letter to a secretary, and after taking it in he returned and asked us to come back in one hour. We did so, and were told that Mr. Rockefeller would not see us. We then presented a second letter, prepared in advance, saying that if he persisted in his refusal to see us, we would hold it our duty to indict him for murder before the bar of public opinion. The secretary took this in, and came back and stated— not so politely this time—that there would be no answer.

We went home, and to work at the telephone. An international lawyer, Edmond Kelley, author of *Twentieth Century Socialism,* had organized the Liberal Club in Greenwich Village. That was the place for meetings of this sort and we made an arrangement for that evening. With a secretary's help Upton got off special-delivery letters to the editors of all the newspapers, and we telephoned a score of sympathizers and put all of them to work at spreading the news. So when we went down to West 10th Street we found fifty or more sympathizers, and, even more important, a dozen newspaper reporters. At that time picketing was common in strikes, but so far as we knew this was the first time it had been done off the premises, so to speak, and for an altruistic protest. It set a pattern widely followed since.

I was learning about the newspapers of my country. To Mrs. Cannon's detailed story at the Carnegie Hall meeting the New York *World* had given two inches, and no other newspaper except the Socialist *Call* had given it a line. But now, when the author of *The Jungle* told the story, every reporter was scribbling diligently. When he told of the visit to 26 Broadway and read our two letters to the gathering, every reporter wanted a copy of those letters—and Upton had been foresighted enough to provide them. The poor coal miners were news now, by proxy!

The program of silence and the strictest nonresistance was outlined to our group. Upton called them "mourning pickets," but the newspapers chose to speak of them as the "free silence movement." They might have called it free advertising for the coal miners.

There was much discussion as to action among the free-lance reformers. One man stated his idea: we should organize a group to raise money to buy arms for the Colorado strikers. Upton instantly pointed out that there was another room in the club to which all those who wanted to buy or use arms should withdraw and hold their own meeting; they did not belong with us. A few did withdraw, and we were interested to observe, when the Russian revolution came, three or four years later, that these went over to the Bolshevik cause, while those who stayed in the front room with us remained Socialists, pacifists, Christians or whatever they were.

A dozen or so men and women promised to join Upton on Broadway in the morning. One was George Sterling, just arrived from California. There were also the poet Clement Wood and Leonard D. Abbott, one of the editors of the *Literary Digest*. Also there was Elizabeth Freeman, an ardent suffragist who had visited us in Bermuda. The rest I did not know. They pledged their word to conform to the agreed program; the reporters hurried off to write their stories, and Upton and I went home.

First thing in the morning he bought the newspapers. Sure enough, the story had a column or more in every one, most of them on the front page. Between readings, Upton took a few bites of breakfast, and then hurried off to his post. I did not go with him, for I did not think I would be needed and I dreaded the ordeal of publicity.

When Upton arrived at the scene he found a crowd of persons who had read the morning papers and wanted to see the free show, as well as a number of reporters and cameramen. Three of the pledged ladies were also on hand, and a strange person who had provided herself with a flag with a bleeding heart on it and stood on the steps of the Standard Oil Building shrieking Upton's name at the top of her lungs.

The reporters besieged my husband for statements, but he was pledged not to speak. He started to walk up and down quietly on the sidewalk, and the crowd gave him room. The ladies fell in behind him, including the one with the bleeding heart. There were a number of uniformed policemen on hand, and presently one of them ordered Upton to stop walking. The reply was that he had made sure he had a legal right to walk quietly on the public sidewalk and intended to continue. He was placed under arrest, as were each of the ladies in turn. The officer started to hustle Upton along, and my mild-mannered crusader said, "I have no idea of anything but to go along with you. Please behave like a gentleman." So they walked side-by-side in "free silence."

Clement Wood telephoned to tell me what had happened. He said George Sterling was with him; what should they do? I asked him to wait for me.

My only respectable coat, a white camel's-hair, was too sooty to wear. I left it at a cleaner's, and stopped at a department store enroute, where I bought a spectacular white military cape of exquisite broadcloth which covered me to my knees—it was the only thing that would need no alterations. I couldn't put crepe on the sleeve, as it had no sleeves. So I had bought a small crepe-trimmed mourning hat.

Later Upton told me what had happened at the police station. He didn't know whether the sergeant at the desk was a secret sympathizer, or just curious—anyhow, he held up the process of booking the prisoners and allowed Upton to talk freely for the benefit of a dozen newspapermen who had crowded into the room. The story of the Ludlow massacre was told all over again as well as the all-important fact that the company had denied the right of the miners to form a union. Our visit to the Rockefeller office was described, and our aim. What charge could be made against five people who had walked up and down on a sidewalk in perfect silence? The pencils of the reporters flew and the barricade of silence that had been built around the Colorado coal fields was blown sky-high.

Charged with "disorderly conduct," Upton was taken to the prison known as "The Tombs." The four ladies were taken to the ladies' department of the same. They sang the "Marseillaise" and Upton promptly wrote a poem, "The Marseillaise in the Tombs," and for the second time discovered how he could get his poetry published in the New York papers.

Upton had told me that he might very well be arrested, and that I was not to worry. I had no time to, for someone must let Mr. Rockefeller know that this war was not over!

George Sterling and Clement Wood were waiting for me. I put these two on their honor that they would not resist anything that was done to me, and then I took each one by the arm and we began our siege.

I cannot say that the Rockefellers employed ruffians to harass us; I can only say that ruffians were there. They did their best to provoke resistance, jostling us and snarling; finally one of them stepped in front of me, and shook his finger in my face and called me a name. George doubled his fist, but I held his arm, and said, "Smile!" I knew that we would ruin everything if we broke our rule, and so did he.

A couple of reporters crowded up and one said in low tones, "Those fellows are paid thugs!" I was so ignorant of the criminal world that I did not know the word. So when another reporter asked me if I was afraid, I said "No, but I don't like those slugs."

We were not arrested. More policemen appeared, but it was evident they had received orders to let us walk; they busied themselves to keep a passage clear so that we could do so. The

crowds grew so dense that presently there were mounted policemen in the street, to keep a passageway for the street cars and
other traffic.

It was fortunate that I had good dancing muscles in my legs,
for I walked until five in the afternoon without stopping except
briefly to answer a reporter's questions. My escorts stayed with
me, and new ones joined us. It was a challenge to believers in
the cause of labor unions.

During the afternoon, Upton and the four lady "criminals" in The Tombs were brought into court. The magistrate
was courteous, and allowed them to make speeches. The charge
was using threatening, abusive and insulting behavior, but the
policeman who arrested Upton testified that his conduct had
been that of a perfect gentleman. One of the ladies was accused
by a policeman of trying to make a speech on the sidewalk, and
the lady promptly arose and exclaimed, "Oh, you ungram-
matical prevaricator!"

All five were judged guilty and sentenced to pay a fine of
three dollars each. They had agreed in advance to pay no fines,
so back to The Tombs they went. The law in New York was one
day for each dollar. Upton was used to fasting, and prison food
did not appeal to him. Although he didn't call it a "hunger
strike," he remained in his cell.

I did not discover until the next morning that the report
which the Associated Press had sent out all over the country had
included a statement that Mrs. Upton Sinclair had been among
those arrested. Mama threw a few things into a suitcase and
took the first train North. I sent a hasty telegram to Papa, but it
was too late—and anyhow I doubt if Mama would have stopped
even if I had caught her.

Mama bought newspapers on the way and learned that I was
still free to go on picketing, so she was not so alarmed when she
arrived. She stayed in our apartment and was allowed to meet
several of my not too "radical" friends. She was horrified when
I told her of the children in the tent colony who had been
burned alive. She had always known, she said, that the Yankees

Clement Wood, who worked as my husband's secretary for a time, George Sterling and I were photographed in 1914 just after Upton was arrested for picketing in front of the Standard Oil Building in New York.

Papa, "The Judge," with two of his beloved grandchildren.

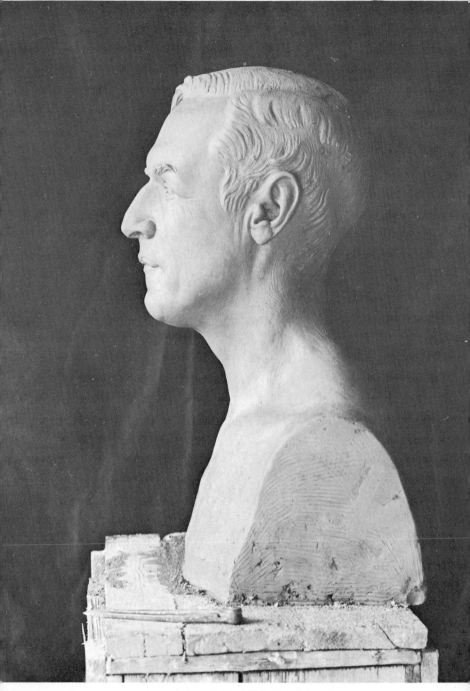

Bust of Upton by Carl Eldh, Swedish sculptor.

were "a cold-blooded and calculating people." She would stay near until I was out of danger.

The second day I was on the picket line at nine o'clock and we marched until five. Many sympathizers showed up, most of them strangers; lumberjacks from the Oregon forests, sailors from all over the world and half-starved boys from East Side slums. The papers had faithfully printed our rules of conduct, so these men knew what to do and did it loyally. When the "slugs" tried to make a disturbance, they were driven away by the police.

I even dared stop for an hour or so to read the papers and learn from them that my husband was enjoying himself in jail. In the meantime the demonstration was led by Alexander Irvine, an Irish novelist and ex-clergyman. George Sterling took time off to wander down to the Battery and give his overcoat away to a shivering beggar. He had told me when we first met that "Upton might soil his wings" if he wished but that he would not; now the ivory tower was abandoned and the poet had come right down into the mud. He sat on a park bench and composed a poem to the symbolical bronze lady out in the harbor, the Statue of Liberty:

> Oh! Is it bale-fire in thy brazen hand—
> The traitor light set on betraying coasts
> To lure to doom the mariner?

Upton learned from his lawyer that if he wished to appeal the magistrate's decision he would have to pay a fine, since otherwise there would be nothing to appeal for; he could not ask to get back the time he had spent in a jail cell. So on the last day I set to work to get him out.

I left Ryan Walker, the cartoonist, and his wife in charge of the "mourning pickets," and took a taxi to the Criminal Court Building. It seemed to be especially constructed for the confusion of visitors; it was built around a central court, and its numerous balconies all looked exactly alike. I managed to find the District Attorney, and that gentleman kindly told me what to do and made out a paper for me. Then he told me that I should go to a certain justice in a certain room and tell him what I wanted.

I went out, wandered about, and found myself completely lost. I saw a gentleman coming out of a courtroom and I stopped and asked him the way. Maybe I looked exhausted, or maybe he was impressed by my white military cape and thought I was the Army. Anyhow, he asked, "Why do you want to see Justice So-and-So?" I answered, "Some imbecile of a judge has sent my husband to jail." "Thank you, Madam," said the gentleman, "*I* am that judge."

He showed me how to find the right courtroom, where I was told that the court was in session and His Honor could not be interrupted. But, my father being a judge, I felt that His Honor might be interrupted. I walked down the aisle, and when His Honor saw me coming he waited in silence; I told him what my trouble was and he immediately signed my paper and instructed the clerk to take my one-dollar bill.

From the Criminal Court Building I crossed the Bridge of Sighs into The Tombs and led my happy and amused husband out of jail. I thanked heaven for that happiness, in sunshine or shadow, in danger or in play—and above all when sitting at a typewriter in a cheap apartment, with only a few dollars in the bank!

The reporters had learned that Upton was coming out, and there they were. We went to a building on a nearby side street for a policy discussion. I had realized that we must have a place for such sessions, where tired men and women could rest their feet and hungry stomachs could be filled with sandwiches and milk. So I had sent one of our young men to rent an office room west of Broadway; it had a couple of tables and chairs, and we bought some old camp stools. Nobody had any money, apparently, except me, so I paid for everything.

I had never imagined I would meet lumberjacks, sailors or garment workers; I had thought of the intellectuals as the "radicals," at least as the only kind an author would know. The demonstration was a memorable experience for me. I had once read an essay by John Dewey on "education by doing," and that was the way I was getting mine: a whole term's course in a few days.

Upton and I went home and talked things over that evening. He considered that our work was done, so far as it could be done in New York. The "concrete wall," as he called the Associated Press, had been shattered, and the country had been told about Ludlow. But the strike in Colorado was still going on, and he wanted to go to Denver to see what could be done there. He wanted to call off the street demonstration, for he knew that I was wearing myself out. I told him I would think it over, and meantime he could go to Denver.

I could not give up. I believed that our continuing publicity would help his work in Denver, so I went on for three weeks, spending every dollar left in our bank account.

I cannot prove who it was who paid the thugs, but I do know that the Rockefeller people paid some spies, for soon Clement Wood came to report that one of their people had come to him and offered him a weekly salary to make daily reports. He said, with a grin, "I took their money because I need it, and I knew you have nothing to hide."

I said, "Of course not. Mr. Rockefeller himself can come with us, if he wants to. Invite him."

During all this struggle, the Socialist Party had remained aloof. Mr. Gerber, secretary of the New York local, announced early that the party had nothing to do with the affair. Victor Berger, newly elected Socialist Congressman whom Upton thought of as a friend, took the occasion to state, "Sinclair is an ass." Upton had belonged to the party for a dozen years and, at the urging of party leaders, had been its candidate for Congress. But now the party disowned him! I was shocked, and decided I would never join such people. But Upton stayed with the party for three more years, until the question arose whether or not the United States should enter the war.

One evening Mama came to the apartment with Upton's mother; they looked like two guilty schoolgirls who had sneaked out to a delicatessen. They confessed that they had gone down to 26 Broadway in a cab to see the "show." Both of them had wept, Upton's mother in an upsurge of embarrassment because her only child—so gifted that he might have gone to the top of the political or business world—had attracted to himself and to his new wife the motley crew which was picketing Mr. Rockefeller's own private property! But she added that those shivering boys, so poorly dressed on a chilly day, deserved sympathy; she felt they did not know what they were doing. They were blindly following her son and his wife—and poor Priscilla was almost ready to shed tears again.

Mama tried to comfort Upton's mother by suggesting that we were heroic, like the brave people of the South; the women had stood proudly by their husbands through all the hardships of war and the shame of defeat—they had stood for a principle, and that was what we were standing for. My adoring mother was still at the side of her wayward daughter!

I tried to assure them that Upton was enjoying our war, for he felt certain of ultimate victory. Also, I said, I wasn't being one bit heroic—hadn't they seen those mounted policemen? Mama's face brightened and she exclaimed, "Yes! They looked very kind and handsome. I would have liked to thank them. I'm sure they knew they were protecting someone who would never commit a crime because she is a lady."

Priscilla said she knew there would be no violence because her son did not believe in it and would not tolerate it.

So Mama decided it would be safe for her to leave me for a couple of days. She had been invited to Washington to dedicate a memorial window in the Red Cross Building. President Wilson would officiate and Mama had been chosen to make the formal presentation.

Our friend Daisy McLaurin Stevens, President-General of the United Daughters of the Confederacy, would meet her in Washington and they would sit together on the platform. Mama became her old-time merry self as she told us of her plot to make a match between Senator McLaurin's daughter and President Woodrow Wilson, at this time a widower. Daisy, a charming young widow, was the daughter of a governor of Mississippi as well as a United States Senator—what more suitable qualifications! Of course, Daisy did not know of this plot, but that would not matter.

I told Mama I had a project of my own. I had sent a long telegram to Upton; and three days later there arrived from Denver a document signed by the officials of the United Mine Workers petitioning President Wilson to compel a settlement of the strike by setting a time for withdrawing federal troops from the mines of the Colorado Fuel and Iron Company.

When I showed this to Mama, she consented to put it into the President's hands when she gave him her dedication document. It would be her "widow's mite" in behalf of the needy! She kept that promise, but then was aghast to find that a reporter had got hold of the story from someone. It might go all over the country! What would Papa think now?

Her matchmaking intentions vanished; her only thought was to get home as fast as she could and explain to Papa. And so one little newspaperman changed the course of American history: President Wilson married the handsome widow of a Washington jeweler instead of the widow from Mississippi.

Though Upton's efforts in Denver were baffled there by the Associated Press, he gathered a mass of evidence which five years later he put into a book called *The Brass Check*.

When he returned from Denver, the demonstration on Broadway perforce came to an end. We had no money and badly needed a rest. But the protest did not stop when we did; a group of the "mourners" would not give up, and transferred their activities to Mr. Rockefeller's country estate near Tarrytown-on-Hudson. Their palatial estate there was surrounded by his armed guards.

The first contingent of "mourners" was composed of the poor fellows for whom I had bought shoes and sandwiches on Broadway. They were rough-looking, cheaply dressed and no doubt looked dangerous to the police of Mr. Rockefeller's town. They undertook to hold a street meeting and were arrested.

Upton and I were exhausted, physically and financially, and I felt now that we had done our duty. We had let the public know what was wrong, and now surely it was up to the public to protect its own free institutions. But this, apparently, was too much to expect. Upton said he couldn't leave these young men stranded.

John Reed wrote: "If I were in New York now I would certainly go to Tarrytown with you because I believe thoroughly in what you are doing there."

It was a matter now of free speech, which Upton considered one of the foundation stones of all freedom. He went to call on Georg Brandes, famed Danish literary critic who was on a visit to New York. Brandes expressed surprise to learn that there was a town in America in which speakers were arrested for attempting to tell the public about public affairs, and he gave Upton a letter to this effect.

Armed with his eminent support, and that of Leonard Abbott and Theodore Schroeder, tireless friends of civil liberty, Upton appeared at a meeting of the board of trustees of Tarrytown. The trustees voted down the request for a street meeting, but the discussion was a friendly one. Upton told me he had had a talk with the president of the board and had never met a more kindly person. To our surprise we read in the New York *Herald* the next day that Upton had threatened this gentleman with violence. In the words of the *Herald:*

> "Suddenly Frank R. Pierson, president of the village, leaped to his feet and said: 'We shall not be intimidated by threats. We will hear no more of this kind of argument. For one, I was willing to listen to what these people had to say, and to hear them fairly and honestly, but when they come here with threats of death, of assassination and of mob rule, I will not hear them further.' "

Upton traveled back to Tarrytown to see the president of the board, who declared that he had made no such statement to the reporter and that he had at no time criticized the conduct of anyone before the board; he had voted every time in Upton's favor, and had been overruled by the others. So Upton sent a letter to the *Herald,* stating these facts, and threatening a libel suit. They sent a reporter to him in a hurry and he explained the basis of his complaint. They published Upton's letter, together with a statement in which they reiterated the details of their former false report and quoted three of the trustees as supporting them! Furthermore, they quoted Mr. Pierson as saying, "The *'Herald'* did not misquote either Mr. Sinclair or me."

Upton went up the Hudson again. The long-suffering Mr. Pierson again avowed that he had given no such interview, and that he would appear in any court and testify accordingly. A second member of the board wrote that the interview with him also was a "fake." So Upton put the matter in the hands of a college friend, Bernie Ernst.

A suit for libel was filed, and it became a case of endless delay. A long time passed and we had actually forgotten about the matter when there came a letter from Ernst, telling us that the *Herald* was prepared to settle the case out of court by a payment of $2,500. It was too late to repair the damage done by the libel, so we accepted the settlement.

The trustees of Tarrytown had agreed that the free-speech crusaders had the right to hire a hall or a theater; they tried to find one, but with no success. East of Tarrytown lay the Pocantico Hills on which were palatial estates, including that of the Rockefellers. My husband was told that the owner of one of these estates, a Mrs. Charles J. Gould, was a sympathizer. She had a sense of humor and was pleased to make her open-air theater available for a Sunday-afternoon "free-speech meeting"—almost next door to the Rockefellers'! Some three hundred people, rich and poor, swarmed in, including some of the workmen on the Rockefeller estate. (We wondered what the spies made of that.) A resolution was offered to the effect that Mr. Rockefeller's treatment of his strikers had been such that we called upon the President of the United States to take over his mines, and that resolution was carried unanimously.

One of Mr. Rockefeller's advisers, L. M. Bowers, chairman of the company's board of directors, considered the strikers, and especially their leaders, to be "disreputable agitators, socialists and anarchists." He wrote to John D. Rockefeller, Jr. as follows:

> "When such men as these, together with the cheap college professors and still cheaper writers in muckraking magazines, supplemented by a lot of milk-and-water preachers with little or no religion and less common sense, are permitted to assault the businessmen who have built up the great industries and have done more to make this country what it is than all other agencies combined, it is time that vigorous measures are taken to put a stop to these vicious teachings which are being sown broadcast throughout the country."

But the public had the story, and time was all we needed for public opinion to move Mr. Rockefeller and his advisers from their determination not to yield a step to the miners. The "vicious teachings" that encouraged workingmen to organize into unions were indeed being sown broadcast throughout the land.

In *John D. Rockefeller, Jr.,* from which the Bowers letter is quoted, Raymond B. Fosdick gives a full account of this stage in the education of a philanthropist. He lists the grievances of the Colorado miners in more detail than I have space to recount here, summing up the situation thus: "This oppressive vigilance on the part of the operators was understandably one of the chief sources of tension and insecurity among the workers, and the absence of any adequate grievance procedure only intensified their dissatisfaction."

Mr. Fosdick also provides an amusing picture of the attitude of the older generation of the plutocracy toward the progress of this education. Old John D.'s closest associate and friend was a man named Gates, and at the time when John D., Jr. was being crossquestioned by the Walsh Commission, Gates relieved his feelings by noting in his private papers his resentment at the "conciliatory" character of young John's behavior.

"I would have engaged," said Gates, "an array of the most brilliant and able counsel to be gotten in New York—men not afraid, if necessary, to make a scene in court. . . . I would have demanded, in a tone to be heard 'way across the continent, my legal rights of appearing by counsel and cross-examining witnesses. I would have used every legal method, if necessary that of injunction. I would have called upon the President of the United States in open speech and public letter. I would have exposed the record of this man Walsh. If necessary, I would have carried the matter so far as to invite arrest, and been carried struggling and shrieking from the courtroom for the purpose of getting my case vividly, powerfully before the people of the United States."

Mr. Fosdick, in his book, adds: "Fortunately, the younger Rockefeller was not built on this pattern." What the younger did, not long afterward, was to go out to the Colorado coal camps and visit every one of them, meet the miners, hear their stories and dance with some of their ladies. He engaged Mackenzie King, later prime minister of Canada, to work out a program of employee representation. The camps were opened to union organization and the chairman of the company's board of directors was fired—"this doughty gentleman of the old school," as Fosdick describes him.

This biographer of the new school does not say anything about the part which Upton Sinclair played in the education of his subject, but I think that history will be less discreet.

According to Fosdick, John D., Jr. said many years later, "The Colorado strike was one of the most important things that ever happened to the Rockefeller family." Fosdick's comment on this was: "What he meant, of course, was that it bred an awareness of the inequities and injustices of ignorant and outdated industrial practices. It dramatized for him and his associates the responsibilities of management for the economic conditions of the community of employees. To John D., Jr. himself it brought a conception of what he called 'the kinship of humanity'—the common hazards, anxieties and suffering that face all men alike. During the decade that followed the Colorado strike John D., Jr. proceeded to use every means to advance his plan of industrial representation. Urged by King to get his message before the public, he began to accept some of the speaking invitations which flooded his office after his trip to Colorado."

As a result of all of the excitement, Upton became ill, and I set my foot down; we had surely done our share. We were free to retire to the country and work on a new book.

8. HOW DO YOU STAND SUCH A FELLOW?

IN THE COUNTRY we could live for half of what it cost to live in the city. Upton went to Philadelphia and persuaded the Winston Company to give him an advance on a proposed anthology, and to furnish him with five hundred dollars' worth of books from which to gather material for it. (Books didn't cost so much in those days.) Clement Wood volunteered his services as Upton's secretary; as a poet, his advice on the anthology would be helpful.

Soon we were settled in the picturesque bungalow of Frederick C. Howe at Croton-on-Hudson. It was built on a hillside, and Clement lived on the "ground floor," which opened into a forest sloping down to the heavily shaded Croton River. The second story of the bungalow opened to a road on the ridge. We were soon joined by another young intellectual, Frank Shay, who had been attracted to the mourning parade. He offered to do our cooking and dishwashing in return for room and board. He and Clement were congenial, and both adapted themselves cheerfully to our customary diet.

Clement loved life ardently because he was very young and healthy. He had gone wild over Vachel Lindsay's poem, "The Congo," and improvised a form of sing-song declamation to suit it; he went swinging off into the woods, chanting "Boom-lay, boom-lay, boom-lay, boom!" every day before lunch and again before dinner, and sometimes when he should have been typing Upton's correspondence. The hills and glades rang with his voice, and the echoes turned it into a chorus of cavemen.

Frank Shay was a shy bookworm. As soon as he had done the last dishes, he settled down in the den to pore over our books. Later on he became a bookseller in Greenwich Village.

We were happy again in the improvident way of social re-formers—we had a roof over our heads, and enough money to buy food for a summer—even with two extra young giants to feed! The forest around us was ours, for Croton was a small village, with a few shops down by the railroad station and scattered homes of artistic and literary people on the higher land.

Inez Milholland, the suffragist beauty married to a handsome Dutch gentleman, lived on another hill, and Isadora Duncan's sister had established a dance school just down the road. Our neighbors were not close enough to intrude into the stillness of our wooded domain, and, besides, they had their own forests.

Edgar and Margaret Selwyn had their country home on another hillside less than a mile away. Edgar was a distinguished actor and Broadway play producer, and his wife, Margaret Mayo, had made a dramatization of *The Jungle* in collaboration with Upton. They had a tennis court where Upton played while I sat with Margaret, Grace George and other stage folk, and chatted about their activities. Among those who gathered at another tennis court were young Max Eastman, Floyd Dell, Boardman Robinson and other intellectual "rebels" from "the Village." Floyd Dell became Upton's good friend, and one of his most charitable critics. Perhaps that was why Upton and I considered him the best literary critic in America.

Upton worked tirelessly on *The Cry For Justice,* consulting hundreds of books, and asking advice of half a hundred special-ists in the literature of the world. I listened to impassioned arguments among the three literary men of my household over the relative amount of space that should be awarded to Walt Whitman and Edward Carpenter, and often I was appealed to for support of this or that newly discovered poet.

Papa had at last written to me. He said he had studied the evidence, and there was no doubt that we could have won a libel suit against the Associated Press and its papers. But he was glad we had dropped the suits as they would have dragged on for a long time, and from one city to another, causing end-less publicity. What a series of shocks I had caused him, one after another—first my marriage, then my supposed arrest and then Mama's public participation in our crusade!

Now came a letter from one of my girlhood friends in Greenwood, telling a story about which the town was gossiping. It seemed that Upton, in his role of dutiful son-in-law, had set out to educate his newly acquired father-in-law. He had purchased, autographed and mailed to Papa a recent English publication, *Socialism and the Great State,* a collection of essays by eminent writers such as H. G. Wells, Ray Lankester, Chiozza Money, Herbert Trench, Conrad Noel and the Countess of Warwick, on the problems of world organization and peace. Upton had been sure that this dignified work would impress a scholarly lawyer, and apparently it had, for Papa took it with him on a trip to one of the county seats where he held court and was reading it on the train coming home. When one of his lawyer friends approached, Papa hastily tried to hide the book under the tails of his coat; but the friend pounced on him, laughingly demanding to see it. So Papa had to produce it, and now the story was all over town that Judge Kimbrough was reading the books of his Socialist son-in-law and trying to hide the fact!

The winter snows fell on the Croton hills and woodlands, and the deer came out of hiding and posed on the roadside for our delight. The hardest part of the work on the anthology was finished, and Greenwich Village beckoned to Clement Wood. Frank Shay went back with him to New York, and we were left alone in the isolation of frozen roads and icy winds.

When Lincoln Steffens, a friend of Upton's for a dozen years, came for a visit I was awakened by my husband's cheerful early morning voice, urging "Steff" to come for a stroll.

"Stroll?" growled Steff. Then, sorry for his surly tone, he said resignedly, "Give me time to get dressed."

Upton had astonished me during the first months of our marriage by being wide-awake the instant he opened his eyes in the morning. I had lived in a world of coffee-drinkers, and no one in my mother's home ever got out of bed until after coffee had been brought to him or her. When the two walkers returned I was getting the fire started in the living room. Upton hurried into the kitchen to prepare breakfast for his guest, and Steffens sat down close to the blaze and asked grimly, "Does he wake up like that every day?"

"Yes," I said, sweetly. "Isn't it wonderful?"

"Maybe so," said Steff. "But he won't get another chance to take *me* strolling before I get my coffee. He talked a steady stream of politics for half an hour! How do you stand such a fellow?"

I hurried away and brought our guest some drip coffee, Southern style, which he found so good that he promised to stay out his intended visit, with the understanding that he would join me in the kitchen while Upton took his morning stroll alone.

Edgar Selwyn had very little time to spend in Croton during the winter. Upton would drop in to see him in the city when he went there. On one occasion, when Edgar invited him to dine in a fashionable restaurant, Upton wore his Croton outdoor costume, including a wool cap with ear-flaps to prevent frostbite. When he showed up in the lobby, Edgar growled, "Maybe you can't afford a tuxedo, but did that cap cost any less than a hat?"

Moving pictures had spread all over the world, and fortunes were being made with them. The Selwyns formed a company, the All Star Feature Corporation, which was going to make four- and five-reel pictures out of full-length novels—the first time this had been done. *The Jungle* was one of those chosen, and once more Upton saw himself a millionaire overnight; it was my job to keep him from spending the money before he got it.

"The Jungle" was our first experience with the movies. The picture was banned from Chicago, home of the meat-packing industry as well as of the packers themselves. But it ran for several weeks in New York. We got no money from it, for the producers went into bankruptcy. The same thing had happened to the stage version which Margaret Mayo and Upton had made. I decided that never again would I expect to get rich but that somehow I was going to get a little money and hide it.

Dollie had finished her London course in Dalcroze dancing and was ready to return home. I wrote her that we would meet her in the city, and bring her up to Croton. Vachel Lindsay, young poet who had traveled over the country "trading rhymes for bread" in the homes of farmers and villagers, wrote Upton that he was in New York, and we made an engagement to take him to lunch at the time Dollie was arriving from England. He was an unsophisticated country boy, simple and direct in manners. We picked him up and then went to meet my little sister.

She came toward us, with banners flying; she almost danced as she walked, her gay black eyes sparkling with fun and mischief. The poet ceased to notice Upton or me, and gazed at this saucy girl as if he were hypnotized. Of course Dollie saw what had happened, and under this stimulus became more coquettish, while poor Vachel became more incoherent in his replies to our remarks. Finally he burst out in an agonized tone to Upton, "I don't believe you *like* me!"

Upton wondered if the young man could be drunk, but I explained later, "That remark was really meant for Dollie!"

Dollie said she had become "emancipated" in London while crusading with the suffragettes. She told us about the thrilling things she and the other young women of the Pankhurst army had done. One thing she had found most exciting was slashing priceless paintings in the National Gallery. Naturally I was shocked, and used the word "rowdyism." She answered that according to Mrs. Pankhurst, it was symbolic of the militant determination of women to get their rights at any cost.

"Those Englishwomen mean business," said my sister. "The real suffragettes hate Englishmen for the indignities English women have suffered for centuries. Do you know that in England a man can legally beat his wife provided he uses a stick no thicker than his thumb?"

"Did you actually slash a painting?" I asked, and she said no. What she had done was to carry the hatchet, concealed under her coat, into the art gallery. She was not known to the police, while the suffragettes of course were, so she could go into the gallery without being searched. She had delivered the hatchet surreptitiously to a real suffragette who did the slashing —and who was, of course, arrested and sent to prison, where she went on a "hunger strike."

"That's why I was so useful," declared my sister, a glow of pride suddenly suffusing her young face. "The painting can be fixed—and the purpose was right."

"The end does *not* justify the means," I told this youthful crusader; but all I got in reply was, "It was fun and I'm glad I did it. If they get the vote over there and we don't get it here, I'll go over and marry an Englishman."

I thought it might be wise to keep Dollie near me for a while, so I suggested that she might like to talk to Mrs. Harriet Stanton Blatch, of the suffrage movement in New York. Mrs. Blatch was not a "militant" but she was a determined propagandist and the daughter of Elizabeth Cady Stanton, one of the pioneer champions of women's rights. Upton, who knew her well, took us to the office of the Women's Political Union and introduced us.

We met a woman close to sixty, sturdily built, frank and decisive in manner. She looked Dollie over, listened to her story and exclaimed: "She is just what we need! She is young, pretty and full of life. We think the old-fashioned way to win men is best; we have to charm them into giving us what we want—and when we have got it, then they'll see a difference! Come, Dollie, there's a job for you in this office!"

Mrs. Blatch was the shrewd woman who had picked out Inez Milholland, set her on a white charger and sent her into battle at the head of a huge parade of marchers on Fifth Avenue. We knew she was correct in her judgment, for even Upton had bowed in worship before that Joan of Arc as she gathered her army of men-for-women's-rights that day.

Dolly stayed on with Mrs. Blatch in her Fifth Avenue headquarters. Mrs. Blatch pushed her out in front whenever a masculine prospect came in, and Dollie assured many a hesitant male that woman's suffrage would not turn women into either icebergs or Xanthippes.

But she was so shocked by the "free love" ideas of some of the well-known feminists of that time that she came up to Croton to tell me she didn't want to associate with such women any longer.

"I thought you called yourself emancipated," I reminded her.

"Why, sister, you don't think I meant that I would ever be immoral, do you? All I believe in is the right to flirt, just as men do. That is equality."

"Is that all you have learned about men?" I asked, and found out that it was.

The snow on the trees and shrubs was beautiful to one who had never seen much of it during a lifetime in the far South. But after a while the shut-in life at Croton began to tell on my health. Upton decided that I should adopt a milk diet, and according to his temperament, to think was to act.

I was called to the front door one freezing day by loud yoo-hoos from down the road, and when I looked out, there came my city-bred spouse leading a lean, rickety-looking cow! Our hillside was steep, and the only level place was the road itself and our front porch. When Upton arrived on the porch, the cow arrived there, too. I shut the door hastily to keep out the cold, and the possibility that the cow might be led right in.

Upton tied the animal to a post of the porch, and hurried in to tell me of the bargain he had just made. He had bought a whole cow for only seven dollars! We could have our own fresh, sanitary milk, instead of the stuff we had been buying from a farmer.

"But where can we keep her?" I asked, in amazement.

"Right where she is. What better place could there be? There's a roof over her, and the house wall on one side—and the wonderful thing is, we only have to step out the door to milk her."

"*We?*" I managed to ask. "You don't imagine I know how to milk a cow, do you?"

"Oh, I'll do the milking," he declared, cheerfully. He was always ready to do everything, from washing the dishes to re- forming the national economy.

He worked earnestly at the job, and received kindly advice from various villagers, but no milk. One of them said that a worried or scared cow would not "let down her milk." Give Bossy time to get used to her new home. But Bossy continued her strike, so her new owner went again to the village for advice, and ran into a country boy who offered to see what he could do. Upton brought him home and came in to get the pail and other equipment. But when he returned to the porch, the new milker was standing indifferently on the roadside, ignoring the cow. He turned and announced in a disgusted tone, "That there's a *dry* cow."

Upton asked him if he had a shovel at home and he said he did. So he was employed to take the cow to the butcher, and then bring his shovel and wheelbarrow and tidy up our front porch.

George Sterling came to visit us, and I found myself more interested in him than before, because I was no longer in the strange category of the Beatrices and Dulcineas. He delighted Upton with his prowess as a woodsman. He chopped down some dying chestnut trees behind our house and converted them into logs for the fireplace. Now and then he would gaze at me soulfully, but for only a moment; then he would make some mundane remark of the kind he had once resented coming from Upton. "You are too sad-looking—too thin—too pale," he would say. Or, "You look frightened. Tell me what you are afraid of—if it's human, I'll chop him into firewood!"

I told him I liked humans better than poets, and he was up in arms because of this insult to Art. We argued about the subject and I insisted that anyone could be an artist. "Every child likes to play with paint, and with clay—even the cavemen did very good murals. It is a form of communication invented by primitives before they had a written language, and its use now is pure affectation."

I might have got away with that, but never with his own

most sacred art form. When I pointed out how children delight
in jingles and rhymes, he said, "I suppose you think a child
could write a sonnet."

"*I* could," I announced.

"Oh, that's different," he said. "Angels can do anything."

"I'm a *himmlische Engel,*" I reminded him.

"That's Upton's idea," he declared, scornfully. "You are not
heavenly. You are from hell. You are the infernal kind who
burn men's hearts to cinders!"

"Explain the sonnet to me," I told him, "and I'll write one
for you!"

So he sat by me and pointed out patiently the measure called
iambic pentameter, the groups of lines called octet and sestet,
and the various rhyme schemes from which I was free to choose.
It seemed to me needlessly complicated, and there were troubles enough in the world without it, but it was a challenge.
"I'll have to wait till I have something important to say," I
remarked. "Upton hasn't educated me yet."

But I read Upton's manuscripts, and often hurt his feelings
by telling him they were bad—inhuman even, for his people
were not people. I read everything he selected for *The Cry for
Justice,* and often the books from which the extracts were
taken. Bernard Shaw became my favorite, and I read a lot of
Wells, Bellamy, Blatchford and Veblen.

The great *New York Times,* in its solemn, stodgy way, was
opposing the suffragist arguments. I read one of its editorials
on the subject, and there came to me one of those moods of
teasing with which I had brought so many youthful gallants
to confusion. Why not try that same banter on a ponderous
editor? So I looked up the notes I had made of George's teaching—iambic pentameter, octet and sestet, and a rhyme scheme—
All right, let's go! It went fast, and presently I had a sonnet:

SUFFRAGE

Oh, come! Forget this foolish talk of Rights!
  Are you not on a pedestal, my sweet?
  But you are lonely there on that high seat?
What woman's jest is this! Man loves you, plights
  His heart and soul to you: to all your sex

> He holds himself as slave. Why should you vex
> Yourself and him with questioning? Why talk
> Of "Rights," "Equality," the while you walk
>   The earth as goddess in men's eyes? You say . . .
>   You are a goddess for a summer's day,
> And then you are forgot? Well, does the rose
> Ask more than that? . . . In sweet content it blows,
>   And bares its perfumed heart unto the bee.
>   Oh, come, my sweet, and be a rose to me!

I sent that to the *Times,* and lo, they accepted it for publication and mailed a check in payment. I showed the check and the sonnet to Upton and he was hilarious. It has often happened that irony and mockery are mistaken for solemnity, and Upton wondered, could it be the *Times* believed that the lady who had led the "mourning pickets" on Broadway considered herself unworthy to cast a ballot? And that she would be content to bloom for one summer's day, and then be forgot?

Later, the Germans took seriously a sonnet I wrote on their *Kultur;* it was reprinted in the Berlin and Frankfurter *Zeitung* and Frederik van Eeden wrote that it was sent to him by triumphant but humorless German friends as "a crushing blow, the conversion of Uppie to the Kaiser."

Now in my far-off home in the land of cotton and tradition, the two people I loved more than all others, except my husband, were nursing the wounds I had inflicted. This seemed part of the cruelty that was inherent in the universe—for I would have died rather than hurt them. But if I had refused to marry Upton, I would have hurt him more. He was a man of such intensity of feeling that grief could literally eat him up. I had this same capacity for feeling, so I knew what it meant.

I put my feeling for Upton into a poem, and when he found it in the trash basket, he was aghast. He had it typed, and the columnist, John D. Barry, published it in a San Francisco paper. George Sterling wept when he read it. Luther Burbank wrote to Upton that it was "the finest thing of the sort ever born of the human mind."

LOVE

You are so good, so bountiful, and kind;
  You are the throb and sweep of music's wings;
The heart of charity you are, and blind
  To all my weaknesses; your presence brings
The ointment and the myrrh to salve the thorn
  Of daily fret of concourse. That you live
Is like to bugles trumping judgment-morn,
  And stranger than the cry the new-born give.
And yet, some day you will go hence. And I
  Shall wander lonely here awhile, and then—
Then I, like you, shall lay me down and die.
  Oh, sweetheart, kiss me, kiss me once again!
Oh, kiss me many times, and hold me near:
  For what of us, when we no more are here?

Worried about the war which he had seen coming before we left Europe, Upton had decided to bring David back to America. He happened to mention his fears to his friend Phelps-Stokes and learned that the latter's butler was about to return from England. This man brought David across with him to a school in North Carolina conducted by C. Hanford Henderson, an educator whom Upton had once visited in California. Henderson believed in locating his schools as far as possible from wealthy parents, so they would not be visiting his students and demoralizing them. The quality of self-reliance Upton felt strongly was his own best gift from adversity. He wanted his own boy to develop it, and had chosen schools in Europe which emphasized this quality.

Now the summer was again approaching, and David was to spend it with us. But what was there for a thirteen-year-old boy to do in Croton? None of our friends had children. We were poor, because *Sylvia's Marriage* had had almost no sale in America. Maybe Upton's mother had been right; it was because, just before the book's publication, Upton had challenged the right of the great Mr. Rockefeller to run his own business! Whatever the reason, only two thousand copies were sold in the United States, while a hundred thousand copies were sold later in England alone.

Now we talked over our problem, and I wrote Mama about it. There came a prompt and happy letter from Papa: "Come home!"

The L. & N. train stopped to let us off at the little De Buys station in the pine woods near Ashton Hall. There on the platform in a gray cadet uniform was my teen-age brother, Hunter.

Around the little station towered the ancient pine trees— their fragrance mingling with that of the yellow jasmine which grew profusely throughout this dear, familiar woodland. I had stood on this same platform and kissed Papa and Jerry good-bye, that summer, long ago, when a mosquito had bitten Jerry "every time he kissed his girl."

Now my young brother had just said "Hello, sister!" and Upton had caught him playfully by the arm and tried to pull him away from the porter who was holding our bags.

"You can't carry but one," my husband was insisting. But Hunter was big and tall and he firmly grasped both and held on. To Hunter, Mr. Sinclair was a guest. "That yellow boy I hired yesterday promised to be heah, but he musta fuhgot," said Hunter. "The pony for the cart hasn't come yet, either. We'll have to walk."

"I've walked it many times," I told him. "I may be a stranger to you, Hunter, but not to this road. Let me see—how old were you when I last saw you?"

Upton laughed. "I believe you told me he spoiled your début party by being born."

Hunter ignored this. "I've never met Mr. Sinclair before," he reminded me. "I'm glad to meet you, sir," he added gravely, to be sure he omitted no courtesy due a guest at Ashton Hall— even if I had forgotten to introduce him.

"Glad to meet *you*, sir," said Upton, with equal gravity. "I hope we'll see a lot of each other. My son David will be here soon. I hope you'll like each other."

"Thank you, sir," replied Hunter. "That's why I'm here. Sister wrote that she wanted a friend for David. I've transferred schools—I like the Gulf Coast Military Academy here just as well."

The glittering blue waters of the Sound stretched before us now. In a few minutes we would turn to the right on the white shell road and Ashton Hall with its memory-ghosts would welcome my husband. I caught his arm suddenly and murmured, "*You* are the one I love!"

He laughed. "Of course I am! Welcome to our heavenly city, *himmlische Engel.*"

Mama had written that she had engagements, made before she knew we were coming, which she could not break. She and Papa would come to Ashton Hall together as soon as these and Papa's court duties permitted. So it was Aunt Catherine who was waiting to throw her arms around me and exclaim, "Ah sho is glad teh see you, honey! Miss Ma'y couldn' come, so she sont me. You ain't so pretty as you was, honey—what you been doin' up No'th to git so pale?"

"Aunt Catherine, this is my husband, Mr. Sinclair," I told her, and Upton surprised her by offering a handshake. The faithful old friend was shocked, I was sure, but she beamed and accepted the courtesy. She believed in "quality" not "equality."

Upton lost no time in exploring this place about which he had heard so much; he set out, eager as a boy. Hunter was a solemn youngster, full of concern over his duties as host, and he accompanied his guest, gravely pointing out what he thought would be of interest to a visitor. "That boat under the house belonged to Miss Winnie Davis. Mrs. Davis gave it to us after Miss Winnie died. That old phaeton on the back gallery belonged to Mrs. Davis. These things are dear to Mama and she keeps them close by so no one can steal them. Do you want to see the grape-arbor first, or would you rather go to the beach?"

"I'd like to meet Mr. Bebb," Upton replied, and Hunter told him that the poor old Welshman was dead. He was very old when he died—maybe a hundred, Papa had said.

Aunt Catherine and the other two Negroes had gone back to the kitchen, and now I went out to ask what she had for lunch, and to have a look in the pantry, for I was sure there would be no shredded wheat, or salad of any kind. Upton would starve!

Worse yet, when Upton and Hunter returned, Upton asked if there was any place where he would be able to write without being eaten up by mosquitoes. His mind was full of the novel he wanted to write about the Colorado coal mines. I suggested that with so much local color at hand he should write a sequel to his Civil War novel, *Manassas*. But no, his mind was in Colorado, and only his body in Mississippi.

In order to write he wanted to get away from all disturbances; a tent in the woods had been his solution of that problem for several other books. He was going to order some lumber and have a small tent sent out from Gulfport. He would build the platform himself, put up the tent, make it mosquito-proof and after that he would be in a Colorado mining camp most of every day.

Next day came the lumber and the nails. Upton had chosen a spot as near the beach and as far from the house as he could get, and now he went to work with hammer and saw. The Negroes looked on from a safe distance—they had never before seen a gentleman working with such tools, but it never occurred to my husband to be concerned as to what anybody would think about him. Aunt Catherine shook her head with disapproval. "These niggers here ain't gwinteh have no 'spect feh Mista Upton," she said to me. "You knows dat, Miss Ma'y Craig. Dat's not a white gemman's work."

The platform was eight feet by ten, which gave him room for four steps while pacing back and forth, thinking out the next episode in his book. When the tent arrived, there arrived also a high wind off the Mississippi Sound, with reinforcements for the mosquito army. The task of handling that billowing spread of canvas was too much and Upton called for aid. "Dude," a young Negro boy, tied the guy ropes to the base of oleanders—no tent pegs would hold in the sandy soil. Presently came the job of tacking the bottom of the canvas to the sides of the platform to make it mosquito-proof; and then Dude had the job of picking tacks out of the sand where Upton had upset them.

The author wasted no time. When he had a theme in mind, it was the hound of heaven that pursued him and would not let him rest. Every morning while the west wind lasted he would dash out of the house, carrying his heavy typewriter, and run for the shelter of his tent. Once inside, he would shut tight the little frame door covered with mosquito netting, and set to work with a flyswatter to get rid of all the pests that had gone in when he had. This completed, he would soon be living with the miners in the Rocky Mountains.

In the middle of the afternoon he would quit work, and perhaps take the trolley which now ran alongside the white shell road. At the Great Southern Hotel in Gulfport were young men to play tennis with him; or he would have the saddle put on the pony, named Winnie Davis, and ride over the pine woods country.

It was summer, the sun shone brightly, and the new book was growing into a masterpiece, as usual. My husband was happy, and so was I, for I was at home again. And Papa and Mama would be with us the next week.

The roads had been improved and it now took only a day to drive the three hundred miles from Greenwood. All day I waited, on tiptoe; then, late in the afternoon, came the big dusty car up the drive, and stopped, and out jumped black Jimmie, the self-chosen "shofa," followed by Duke and Allan, my two youngest brothers. Upton was in his tent, so I welcomed them alone—Papa the most. Would he like my husband? I hoped so, for his sake as well as my own.

We sat on the gallery, and cold fruit juice was brought—not mint juleps, Upton being a teetotaler. First Upton kissed Mama with filial affection, and then he shook hands with Papa, in his warm way of welcoming all the world whenever he met a new member of it.

I knew how curious each of these men would be about the other. Neither would say one word about the past—I had taken the precaution to warn Upton against that. Let *me* handle it! They talked about the drive, and the wonderful advance in transportation; then Upton asked if Papa had read *Socialism and the Great State.* Yes, he had; they talked about those thirteen scholarly essays, and Papa voiced his objections. Upton, whose pen had been pouring out books, pamphlets, and magazine articles in a flood for fourteen years, knew all the objections before they were spoken, and his answers had been repeated, over and over, through all those years.

Presently he went into the house; and then, with my heart in my mouth, I said, "Well, Papa, what do you think of him?" He smiled and replied, in his quiet voice, "I guess I overspoke myself."

Oh, heavenly words! I knew my stern father so well; I could guess that this might be the first time in his life that he had ever apologized, at any rate for a considered action. Over and over again he had said, and put it in writing, "Daughter, you cannot marry a divorced man." And now Papa had accepted him without reservation! My heart was whole again, my life was whole, and I was literally dancing everywhere I went.

Papa wanted to get acquainted with his new son-in-law, and Upton enjoyed the process. They went fishing together and took walks on the beach. These were for Papa's pleasure, while Upton's explanations of Socialism and the right of workers to strike were for Upton's.

Papa chose a time when we were alone on the gallery to tell me how the value of the waterfront properties had been increased in recent years by the trolley line and the rapid growth of the harbor of Gulfport. Rich Northerners had come in, and one of them had offered Papa three hundred thousand dollars for our place. He had turned the offer down.

His five oldest children were now married and four of them had families and homes of their own. Only Upton and I were homeless. "What I want to do," he said, "is to give you a deed to this property, of course in the hope that you will live here. I must tell you frankly, however, that Upton should consider us—and by us I mean your brothers and sisters and their families—as far as his conscience will permit. He should not start any crusades in Mississippi!"

I told my father that I wanted no more crusades, except those which could be carried on by books. I was as sick of the newspapers as he was, and hoped never to see my husband's name in print again, except in a book review.

One evening just before dark Papa left the house alone, while Upton was finishing a scene for his novel which he could no longer contain without an emotional explosion. Mama was taking a nap, and so this was my chance for a talk with Papa about our future. I wandered around the place looking for him, then down to the beach, and there he was, some distance away at the water's edge, walking alone.

It was the same beloved figure, looming against the white sands and placid water, the twilight gathering around him as the years were. Yes, he was growing old now—though I could not define just how it was changing his appearance. He was still erect, and had not gained weight, and he still moved easily. He loved every inch of "the coast," as he called our summer place. He always longed for the day when he could get away from his Negroes, his office in the bank, and his law office, for a month of rest at this quiet and beautiful place.

He was a good man. He had faithfully done his duty in the way tradition pointed: he had a large family, as he thought the Bible taught, a sheltered and honored wife, a home in which there would be health of mind and body for those with whom God had entrusted him. For them he was willing to serve his country in war or in peace—for the country was their home, even more certainly than the houses built of wood and stone. His ancestors had risked their lives to make the country the home of freedom-loving men, and had given their services as lawmakers to provide a constitution in which these freedoms were clearly defined. He believed in divine law, as in civil law He was a judge, like his father before him, trying to dispense justice and uphold all law. This was the traditional model of a Southern gentleman.

I caught up with him and put my arm through his. "Listen,

Papa," I said. "We can't accept Ashton Hall. Don't make any deed yet. I must not tie you or my husband with any promises. Don't misunderstand me. I intend to try to spare you and the family any more shocks. But if I should fail—"

We walked in silence for a few minutes, then he answered, "I understand."

It was President Theodore Roosevelt who first applied the term "muckraker" to reformers. Upton had raked up no end of muck and sent it all over the world in *The Jungle,* and his chief aide in this performance had been President Roosevelt himself. Now ex-President Roosevelt came to the Mississippi Coast and Upton had the hope of using his enormous power on behalf of the Colorado miners.

He was a guest at the summer home of Governor Parker of Louisiana at the old resort town of Pass Christian, Mississippi. This was a short ride from Ashton Hall, and Upton telephoned for an appointment. He was told that he might have ten minutes. David and Hunter clamored to go along to meet the famous head of the "Rough Riders," and Upton agreed to take them if they would be quiet. When they reached the Parker home they found a large number of guests assembled to meet the great man. No doubt these were distinguished persons, but Teddy chose to leave them and go out to the gallery to hear Upton's account of the miners' plight.

Twice the Governor of Louisiana came out to try to lure his eminent guest inside; but Teddy was used to having his own way, and his way was to dig in the new muck which this young "raker" had assembled. Teddy had been abroad and had heard little about the strike. He expressed his indignation at the lawless conduct of the great coal company, and he said, "I will see what I can do." He did not make any public statement, but soon thereafter young John D. went out to the coal camps and personally reversed all his labor relations.

Instead of ten minutes Teddy had detained Upton for an hour and three-quarters. The baffled guests never knew that outside on the gallery history was being made. But Upton came home elated, and his hopes were justified. Teddy's influence turned out to be powerful indeed, when added to all the other pressures of public indignation which had been steadily mounting ever since our Broadway demonstration.

The scuppernong grapes were swelling and turning brown, and would soon be sweet and ripe. So would the figs on the Judge's enormous tree. Wagons filled with watermelons were stopping at the gate; I would send Walter, "that yellow boy," out to thump and find ripe ones, to be brought in for chilling in the ice-box. Upton said that the color was coming back into my cheeks. It was Utopia again in my world.

Upton had just written a scene in his novel about an explosion in a coal mine—when something exploded in my world. There suddenly flamed across the front pages of the newspapers of the country the story that "Mrs. Upton Sinclair," on a visit in North Carolina, was being named by her hostess as corespondent in a divorce suit! Two days later this same *former* Mrs. Sinclair was at the Great Southern Hotel in Gulfport, advising us that she had come to demand the custody of David. No wonder Papa thought that a marriage was a permanent thing! There was indeed no way to end it!

Upton's writing had to be laid aside. All "inspiration" was gone, of course. He was never daunted by a political enemy, but this was something he did not know how to face. I saw that it was almost unendurably humiliating to him and I assured him my family would think no less of him. Together we pledged ourselves to keep what Upton already had, the custody of his son.

Papa telephoned an old friend, Judge White, who lived not far from us, and asked him to see us, and do whatever was necessary. Papa himself would come without delay. There were two other lawyers in my father's office now, my brother Orman and another young man. Both of them came to Ashton Hall with Papa, and after a talk with us, all of them went at once to Gulfport. One of the lawyers advised us to send David away to some secret place, with a "trusted caretaker"; the child's mother had threatened to send the sheriff to take him into legal custody.

We had no "trusted caretaker," but we dared not run the risk of losing possession for even one hour. We explained the situation to Hunter and sent him off with David to camp in the pine woods a mile or two beyond our house. They carried enough food for a couple of days.

Papa returned to Greenwood after having gone into the situation thoroughly and instructed the younger lawyers, who stayed in Gulfport. Upton and I were now alone at Ashton Hall, the two younger boys and Aunt Catherine having gone back to Greenwood with Papa. For the first time in my life Ashton Hall was not a refuge of peace and safety. The big old house, the beach, the giant liveoaks, where children had always played happily—all this was now a place into which the law might reach a cruel hand to carry off a little boy. "The long arm of the law" which I had respected was now revealed as an iron arm, harsh and destructive, for certainly it might destroy one good man's power to work again for a long time, if not forever. Also it might undo everything a father had done for the boy for years past. At this moment this child had to be hidden in the woods like a culprit, as a civilized community could not protect him—not even his own father could go near him for fear of being seen by some passerby and reported to "the law."

For our lawyers thought that someone had "gained the judge's ear." They were worried because he was a Catholic, with no love for Socialist "agitators," and no belief in the validity of a divorcé's second marriage. This was indeed a weapon against us. Papa had warned me not to let Upton go into the courtroom until he was called—"he might try to make a Socialist of that Catholic fanatic," my father had said! I wondered if he was so convinced of Upton's righteousness that only the Catholic was a fanatic.

But our fears proved groundless. When that ordeal was over, Upton still had custody of his son. We were truly thankful, but Upton was still too upset to get back to his writing—it was that old demon, memory, this time haunting *him*. He would deny this, and force himself back to his work, pound on his typewriter for an hour or two. Mama thought he was ill, and wanted me to persuade him to see her doctor. But I knew that Upton's sickness was in his heart, or wherever memory resides.

Captain and Mrs. Jones were at the Great Southern Hotel, which they owned, along with most of the harbor, the trolley and the railroad. One day, soon after the custody trial was over, Mrs. Jones came to call and invited us to lunch with her the next day—her husband wanted to meet mine. I took this to mean that the great lady was letting us know that we had not damaged the family friendship. Perhaps she also wished to let some other people know how she felt.

I happily accepted the invitation. Upton had recently been treated with some disrespect on a streetcar by the son of a "hillbilly" United States Senator, and I wanted this man to hear about our being guests of Captain and Mrs. Jones.

Captain Jones met us in the lobby and invited us to await his wife there, so the local gossips, whose tongues had been busy since the former Mrs. Sinclair's arrival, would be certain to see us. As the Senator's son came stalking through the lobby on his way to the dining room I understood for the first time Aunt Catherine's contempt for "hillbillies." They were just "po' white trash," after all.

Captain Jones was an old man, white-haired, ruddy, stout and enfeebled. His lifework was done and he wanted to retire, but this had turned out to be not so simple as he had expected. When we were safely in his private apartment, out of earshot of the populace, he began immediately to tell his troubles to my husband. I suppose it was because he knew that Upton was for "the underdog," and Captain Jones thought that he was the underdog in this case.

"Mr. Sinclair, you can't imagine how it makes me feel to have come here and done all I have for this state, and then to have these 'pineywoods' people fight me at every turn. They are the ones I have most benefited, yet they seem to hate me, and try to make my life miserable. Maybe you won't believe it, but they were so poor and hungry they actually ate clay!"

He paused and looked at my husband as if expecting him to dispute this assertion. I laughed and said, "Mrs. Jefferson

Davis called them 'clayeaters,' years ago. She wrote about them, and her articles were published in New York."

The old millionaire's face brightened. "Ah! So you know about them!"

He went on without waiting for an answer. "Call them what you will, 'rednecks,' 'clayeaters,' 'po' white trash,' they are *mean!* They hate the Negroes, but they've done things to me that no Negro would! I've had no trouble with the Negro—he is a useful citizen, kindly, polite, decent as far as I can see. But these white pineywoodsmen hate him, call him 'nigger', shove him around."

He poured out his story. When he had come to this region the lower half of Mississippi was a wilderness except for the fringe of summer estates and resort towns along the beach. There was nothing the eye could see in the interior but vast forests of pine trees. Captain Jones had a vision of a harbor at Gulfport, and a railroad from it, straight up through the state, to join the Illinois Central at Jackson and on to Chicago from there. He saw those pine lands converted into farms, the trees into lumber for homes and factories. It was a wonderful vision —and the millions he had made out of oil in Pennsylvania would thus be of service to the people.

"Think, Mr. Sinclair," he said. "When I came into this state, these people had no cattle at all. But some of them worked at building the railroad, and so they got money and bought cows. And then what? The cows were turned loose and wandered onto the railroad track and some were killed; so then, of course, I paid damages. So many cows were killed that I had to put a fence along both sides of the line. And then what? When the cows got old and worthless, the men would take down the fence and let the cows in, and when they got killed, of course they were prime cows, worth prices never before heard of in Mississippi."

Some "shyster" lawyers from up North had come into Gulfport with the boom—it had been one of these who had advised the former Mrs. Sinclair, thinking to extract money from my family. These lawyers knew how to work on the hillbilly juries and make them shed tears for the sufferings of the poor oppressed farmers, brought to ruin by a heartless railroad corporation. "Can't you see how that is, Mr. Sinclair?" asked the capitalist.

Upton had no trouble in seeing, but he was somewhat staggered when Captain Jones went on to tell of heavier damage suits, brought by men who had deliberately put a foot under a railroad train and had the toes cut off. That would bring enough damages so that the men could retire for the rest of their lives.

"What is there that people won't do for money? It's the dishonesty," he exclaimed, and tears actually came into his eyes. "I am an honest man myself—and so is your father, Miss Mary Craig. But are the poor dishonest? And is that why they are poor? Or is it the other way around? Did poverty make them mean?" "Yes," said Upton.

I had the feeling that Captain Jones was not thinking so much of the money as of the hatred of the railroad. This railroad through the center of the state was essential to everyone who lived near it, and it ought not to be hated, it ought to be loved! Its builder loved it, and not merely for the money—it was his dream, his pet, and why couldn't people appreciate all the good it did?

He put this question up to my husband; and of course the answer was automatic: railroads were public utilities and should be state-owned, then everyone would have an interest in them. Captain Jones of course didn't think the state could run a railroad economically. Upton quietly pointed out that the Post Office delivered his mail fairly well, and if it came to a war, the Army and Navy would defend us efficiently without being privately owned. I had heard all these arguments before we were married, and many times afterward; I wasn't too much bored by the repetition, because it was always a new person to be convinced, and I was interested to watch the reactions of anyone in the process of having a new idea put into his mind. Upton always seemed to feel that if it were good the new idea would be accepted, but I had heard that human nature must first be good, or it wouldn't accept a good idea. And I wanted to know if human nature was good. I never forgot Papa's maxim, "Trust every man, but watch him."

Upton tried to comfort this good old capitalist—I knew he was good, for Papa thought so—by explaining the psychology of a poor, undernourished man, striving to exist on nothing, illiterate and utterly ignorant, trying to understand why Captain Jones had so much money while he had none—how could he distinguish between a great corporation and the United States Mint? "Build some schools for these people, Captain Jones," said the Socialist, "and when the children grow up they will have better minds."

Captain Jones had discovered nothing that I had not heard all my life about the rednecks; and I had told Upton about them.

But Upton was always fascinated by the contrasts between rich and poor. He had struck this vein in *The Jungle,* and was now tapping it in his novel of the coal mines. He knew about the coal miners—he had been to Colorado and talked with them. He had heard what they thought about the Rockefellers. That was the bottom looking up at the top; and here was the top looking down at the bottom, a dramatic reversal. How did this "hillbilly" underdog appear to the top dog, master of oil millions, who had built a harbor, a railroad, a trolley and a luxury hotel?

Not long after our discussion with Captain Jones, the handful of Socialists from the North who had come into Gulfport with the boom sent an emissary to invite Upton to speak at a Socialist meeting. By using his name, they could attract a crowd. The effort to organize the Italian shrimp-pickers and the dockers into unions, would be useful to the cause of labor. Upton said, "Of course."

Several friends came to talk to me about this. Some were shocked, others uncertain as to where Upton's duty lay. It was not a "crusade," such as Papa had mentioned when he offered us Ashton Hall. But neither was it exactly what he had hoped for. And now, if the dockworkers should go on strike, what would that mean to Captain Jones? We did not know, and Upton did not ask. He said he knew his duty, and I felt that

no one had the right to expect him not to do it. I doubted if
even Papa would.

Aging United States Senator Hernando Money, a family
friend, had a beach home a short distance from ours, and his
daughter Mabel, a lifelong friend of mine, came to see us. She
had just arrived from Washington, and had not met Upton
before. I never found out whether she had come to remonstrate
or to sympathize, for she seemed to feel immediately *en rapport*
with my husband and began to talk to him about books like a
regular bluestocking—something I had never suspected her of
being. I felt encouraged by her visit, for it was clear that she
liked Upton, and she had always been an ardent champion of
whatever she believed in. She was not provincial, like so many
of my friends; she had lived in Washington for years, and
would know how to argue our case, just as Aunt Sallie had.

And then, most unexpectedly, came another supporter. Mrs.
Jones, who had sat quietly listening while my husband debated
with hers, drove out to Ashton Hall and asked if she might
accompany us to the meeting! And would we dine with her in
advance? We ate in the luxury of her fine private dining room,
and then set out for the dingy hall the Socialists had hired.

When we arrived, a couple of members of the party were
waiting for us on the sidewalk, and they grabbed Upton and
hurried him off to the side entrance so that he would not get
his ovation until he was in full view on the platform.

I suggested to Mrs. Jones that we take a seat in the rear of
the hall so as not to attract attention; but she caught me by
the arm and said "Nonsense!" and firmly guided me down the
center aisle to the front row. There was no doubt that she
meant to be seen there with me. And she certainly was, for
Upton came out and after bowing to the first applause, he
stood for a moment and threw kisses at us.

There was not one word about this meeting in the papers
next day, so at least Papa wouldn't have to read it and decide
whether it counted as a "crusade." But I learned that there
was a lot of underground excitement in the town, and I realized how impossible it would be for me to keep Upton quiet
in Mississippi!

The time came for Hunter to return to his military academy. Upton did not want David in a military school. He longed to abolish war from the world, and felt that even a military uniform encouraged martial pride. So we accepted Mama's invitation to let David spend the winter with her younger boys in Greenwood, and go with them to the public school. Dollie took him home with her, and Upton and I were left alone at Ashton Hall.

We had time to think over the difference that events had made in our future. The memory of the lawsuit and the sensational newspaper publicity, which included photographs of all concerned, would linger in the minds of our neighbors and no one would ever see us now without thinking of it.

Publicity is a powerful force and the essence of this power is suggestion. A picture of a celebrated man and two young women, his first wife and his second, side-by-side on the front pages and displayed on every newsstand in town—with the accompanying story as exciting as a reporter could make it—all this together stamps an impression on a reader's mind which recurs whenever the name of one of the principals is mentioned. It finally becomes that person in the mind of the whole community. I surely did not want everyone I met to think of the former Mrs. Sinclair beside me, or with my husband between us. And it would be the same for my family in Greenwood, if ever we went there on a visit. Yes, a divorce was a dreadful thing!

It made me desperately sad to think of leaving, for I knew how Papa and Mama wanted to have us near them. I wandered around the dear old home, looking at all the familiar things that I loved. On the front gallery near the lovely pink crepe-myrtle trees was Papa's big armchair in which he loved to sit and watch the changing beauty of the sky and the waters of the Sound. He had looked so tired and worried the last time he sat there during the lawsuit, trying to explain to me the legal complications which made things so uncertain.

In another chair his mother, my grandmother used to sit, making little water-color pictures for her grandchildren. Mama was asleep in that hammock at the far end of the gallery. The little boys ran by on silent bare feet, on their way to the beach or the grape-arbor. Soon my older brothers would come up the walk, sunburned and tired, after a sail to Biloxi. So many happy memories!

Now I must think first of that good, hard-working man out there in that silly tent. Memory had been the reason he had put up a tent instead of a screened "mosquito house," such as we used to have scattered on the wide galleries. Tents had been his salvation when he was a penniless youth, in search of the cheapest possible shelter while he wrote a book. So he had put one up here.

What is memory? I kept on asking. Most people take it for granted, but not students of the human mind. I was interested in the human mind above all things. "As a man thinketh in his heart, so is he."

A storm was coming up, and I wondered if Upton would be too absorbed in his writing to know it. He might be, for he lost all contact with the world of reality when he was constructing a world of his own on typewriter paper. I recalled the time when he had sat writing for hours, then suddenly gave a loud groan and called me. I ran to him and he exclaimed, "I'm paralyzed!" I called a doctor, and the doctor stripped off his shirt. There on the "paralyzed" back were deep imprints of the chair's back. "Apparently you haven't moved for a long time," said the physician, and began to massage away the scars of literary travail.

But this time Upton moved, for a sudden powerful gust of wind roared into his tent and nearly lifted it from its moorings, platform and all. The shaken author lost no time in rushing for refuge to the strong, solid old house which had withstood many such assaults during a century. With him into the front hall came the wind of a familiar Gulf-Coast storm. It did no harm except to bric-a-brac and other small objects, but Upton found that he could not shut the double front doors. He called for help, but there was a wild five minutes before a frightened Negro awoke and hurried into the house. The three of us finally got the piano against the doors, then piece by piece, all the other movable furniture in the room. We were safe now;

these violent storms had never damaged Ashton Hall, which had been built before the Civil War.

But Upton's tent was a total loss. We could see it being shredded and carried off piecemeal to the treetops of the brake, to terrify the poor little mockingbirds blown from the big live-oaks around the house.

"Well," I said, when the storm abated, "that is the voice of our guardian angel, telling us that all is over for us in Mississippi. Papa will understand that you couldn't write without a tent."

And for me it was goodbye forever—dear old Ashton Hall!

9. SO MANY UNHAPPY RICH PEOPLE

UPTON AND I had decided that we should go to California. Above all things he wanted to be warm. He had gone ahead to find a house while I had stayed on a bit longer with Mama and Papa.

Soon there had come a letter from Upton in Coronado. It was typical of his handling of financial affairs.

Jan. 27th

Dearest:

I am in a pickle owing to having made an error in adding up my bank account. Same old story—no need to go into details, suffice it to say that I have sworn off on that once more—I mean, on not keeping my bankbook carefully. Well, I had overdrawn my account. I had to hustle up and deposit a New York check, the last cent I had in New York. That makes the check I sent you N.G. I relied upon sending you a wire not to cash it, but—horror of horrors—I find that the wires are down from the new and worse storm that is raging, and I can't wire you, and either your check or the one I gave the bank will be N.G. I am sending you this letter in a rush, also I am writing Pris to deposit 30 for me the instant she gets my letter. She will do this, no doubt; so you, if you have not cashed the check I sent you, make it over to Pris and mail it to her to reimburse her. I am telling her not to cash it if she has not deposited the money for me. Damn! It may be these hellish rains will stop, and I'll be able to get a wire through to you. I am stuck here with $2.—will have to borrow a little from the Fentons or someone. Brennan's check should be on the way, so that will clear it all up. I am surely going to economize and put an end to all this mess. I am really and truly through with it.

My little house is leaking under all the doors, and I am being driven to the center. If it keeps up I shall have to climb up and live on the table. Such rains never seen in the history of the country. Don't I beat the Dutch?

But I'm still doing the book. Have only 20,000 words more to do. Lots of love to you, and try not to let your dear blessed self be too much worried by this money misery.

Uppie

We were far from happy in Coronado. At the outset Upton, and then I, developed whooping cough. He had rented a wretched little summer beach house full of cracks through which all the winter winds of the Pacific poured. We were poor now, but we had decided that I should never draw another check on Papa.

I had not yet got used to discomfort, but Upton had, and I kept up my courage by remembering what he had been through. And I had his optimism to sustain me—he was sure that *King Coal* would abolish the oppression of labor all over America, and help to establish industrial democracy. He had finished this novel and sent it to his latest publisher; but alas, it came back! All Europe was at war, and all Americans were taking sides, either trying to get in or to keep out; nobody would care to read a book about coal miners away off in the Rocky Mountains. Or so the publisher said. We must try another publisher; it had been that way before, and would be so again. Upton never changed publishers voluntarily, but his books were so different from one another that no one publisher could approve them all.

Throughout that winter we tried, and four or five publishers said no. I read the manuscript, some parts for the first time, and pointed out defects. This was still a risky procedure, but if I had not been willing to take risks I would surely never have spoken the words of the marriage service, "until death us do part."

The heroine in Upton's story, Mary Burke, was a daughter of the mining camps; the author had failed, however, to tell how such a girl would look. I called on him to tell me, and he said he didn't know—he never thought of how people looked— it was not important. So I begged to describe the poor girl, and her clothes. The phrase "putting clothes on Mary Burke" be- came my formula for what the story needed, meaning of course the psychology as well as the looks of the characters.

There came a letter from George P. Brett, president of the Macmillan Company. He had published *Manassas* and later had declined *The Jungle,* because Upton was unwilling to cut out some of the "blood and guts." Mr. Brett now declined *King Coal,"* and took the trouble to tell Upton his reasons—which were the same that I had been telling him for months.

I wrote to him saying what I thought the book needed, and asking would he read it again if Upton and I revised it to- gether? He kindly said that he would; and so began the tough- est ordeal that any woman can undergo for the love of a man. Jacob wrestling with the angel and Laocoön with the serpents out of the sea had no harder time than anyone who tried to tamper with Upton's adored manuscripts. If anyone had heard us, he would surely have thought it was highly personal. But we had a magic word that eliminated hard feelings between us in an instant. We just said *"Manuscript!"*

The whooping cough had not been easy to get rid of in our little house, and both of us were depleted. Upton became gaunt and colorless, while I became nervous and irritable, sitting up half the night to rewrite scenes in *King Coal* only to have him spurn them. Finally we decided to move to Pasadena where, so we were told, there were no wintry winds, but only sunshine and the Tournament of Roses! Upton had a friend there who wrote him there was lots of tennis, and it was really warm. It was then a small city, occupied mostly by retired millionaires and those who served them. It had a good library, a theater, a reasonably liberal newspaper—all those things which Upton had missed on the Mississippi Coast.

We received some money from a foreign publisher, so we rented a more comfortable cottage, with a tiny garden behind it and one cherry tree. We looked forward eagerly to those cherries, but one morning we woke up and discovered a flock of birds just finishing the last ones. Then I found a larger house for half the price, and with an entrancing view of the stark, unpopulated foothills.

> Like honey pouring from a golden jar
> > The days of autumn pour upon the hills
> > Whose peaks are purple while the sunlight fills
> The vistas where the valley winds afar.

Thus I celebrated this view in verse, and made up my mind to own it. I had never dreamed that such natural beauty could be bought for twenty-five dollars a month, with a comfortable if dingy cottage thrown in! A rosebush aflame with crimson blooms covered half the lot outside the row of living-room windows. On the other side of the cottage, a jacaranda tree waved fernlike branches laden with violet blossoms. Over the front porch was a vine with cream-colored roses. *"Himmlische Engel!"* cried my happy-hearted "Uppie." "Let's never have a quarrel!"

"I've written four lines of a sonnet already," I said.

But soon the sunlight pouring from a golden jar got too hot, and our little cottage on a hillside heated up unbearably. The vistas of the valley quivered at a temperature of 110 degrees. We couldn't plant trees to shade our living room, for that would cut off the western view. So would awnings, and anyway, we had no money with which to buy awnings.

Since we had no furniture, I went to town by streetcar and shopped around in second-hand places. I knew nothing about modern furniture; we had only antiques in Mississippi. I did know the good woods, however, and one of these, black

walnut, turned up in the places I visited. I found two old rocking chairs for five dollars the pair, and bought them, though
the original upholstery had been poorly replaced with cheap
calico. They looked shabby but, like all old-time furniture, they
were sturdily made.

The deliveryman said, "If that's the kind of stuff you like, I
have a friend who is selling out the furniture from her lodging
house. She has some old beds like these chairs, and you can get
them cheap. Two dollars apiece, with springs and mattresses."

I went to the lodging house early the next day and bought
two enormous walnut beds—not antiques, but old. I had worried a long time the night before whether I could bear to sleep
on second-hand mattresses. But the thought finally came to me
that I slept on them in hotels and furnished apartments. And
an old house could have as many germs and other disease-
carrying things in it as old furniture.

But Upton had written two books about social diseases, and
this was in my mind.

I asked a druggist if he had a fumigant that my husband and
I could use without danger. He offered me some sulphur can-
dles which we could put in pans and light, then run out of the
house holding our breath. We did this; but later Upton decided
that sulphur wouldn't kill anything except flies and moths. He
wanted to do a real job with cyanogen gas, such as he had done
on a flea-infested cabin he had once rented for a study. This was
a deadly gas if you inhaled it—but he could move fast, he said.
However, I preferred to risk the germs. Upton said I was silly;
he was as capable as the poor workingmen who did such jobs
regularly for the fumigation companies. "Can't you trust my
judgment?" he asked.

I was tired and cross, and told him, "You haven't any!"

This irritated him more than was justifiable, and so I told
him he was vain—I had offended his ego! We were on the way
to something as deadly as cyanogen gas when my husband suddenly smiled his nicest smile and said, "Let's not have the first
quarrel, *himmlische Engel.*"

I recalled the words Mrs. Jefferson Davis had written to me

when she heard I was engaged to Jerry: "Stand fast on your in-alienable rights—but avoid the first quarrel!"

Other pecuniary problems arose to mar the charm of our pic-turesque little bungalow. The roof leaked, which in turn dam-aged the plaster in the living room, and before we could get a roofman on the job, a severe storm came up and soaked the plaster so thoroughly that water dripped through and damaged the varnished floor and the built-in bookshelves. The roof was old, and needed to be replaced, but we couldn't afford that. So we had a patching job done, and the man who did it used some kind of black oil which leaked through at the next rain and made unsightly stains on the plaster.

I had become so newspaper-conscious by now that I never used my husband's name when giving our address, even to a deliveryman. But it was unpleasant to live in hiding; I wondered if we were developing a fugitive psychology. So one night we yielded to the temptation to attend a meeting of some people who were proposing to start a cooperative grocery. Upton had always been interested in "co-ops" as one of the ways to end poverty in the world.

We had employed an elderly stenographer, recommended by the city's Welfare League, to type *King Coal,* and this lady told someone that we were in the hall. So it was the end of our seclusion in Pasadena! A man came immediately, urging Upton to say a few words in behalf of the proposed co-op; and then our stenographer came and asked me to come and meet a "Mrs. Gartz." She explained in almost reverent tones that this lady was one of the richest in America, and a supporter of the Wel-fare League and other philanthropic groups.

In Gulfport a very rich woman had helped us with her pres-tige, but in our new home all we wanted was to be left alone to write. So I politely said that I did not care to meet Kate Crane-Gartz, daughter of the founder of the great Chicago Crane Com-pany, makers of elevators and plumbing supplies.

Our stenographer was astonished—how could I refuse, and how could she explain my refusal to her employer?—for she also did part-time secretarial work for Mrs. Gartz.

"She surely won't blame you," I said. "Just tell her that I will be glad to meet her sometime, and leave it vague as to when."

But Kate Crane-Gartz had a will of her own; she was not used to having anyone decline to meet *her,* and she had no idea of letting me have my way against hers. So over she came to meet *me.*

She was a beautiful woman, with tender blue eyes. But there was great sadness mingled with hauteur in her face. "She looks and acts like an empress" a mutual friend once said, and she did.

"I hear that you have come here to live," she said, in a low, soft voice. "That is nice." And then the meeting was called to order, and she went back to join her friends.

The next day she stopped by our house, driving a little electric coupé. She turned into our short, unpaved entrance drive and almost immediately said, "There's too much dust here. You should have it oiled. That's not so expensive as concrete."

In Mississippi we had only pebble drives and crushed oyster shell. "I'll attend to it for you," she volunteered, and when I said, "Oh, no," she replied, firmly, "Nonsense! That's all I have to offer—just money, while you and your husband have everything else!"

She was stout, and she now seated herself with caution in one of my decrepit rockers. "This is very comfortable," she went on, "but the upholstery is not good enough."

I told her I did not like the way the chairs looked, but they were all we could afford, and I never wanted better ones until *everyone on earth* had enough to eat and a roof over their heads.

"I'm glad you feel that way," was her answer; "for sometimes I feel the same. Everything is just handed to me—I never have to do a thing for myself. It isn't right!" And so we could be friends; we understood each other.

The next day a furniture van arrived in our dusty drive, and a couple of men jumped out, rang our doorbell and began to unload a sofa and chairs. When I opened the door one of them asked, "Mrs. Sinclair?" I told him yes, but I had not ordered any furniture, and there must be a mistake.

"Mrs. Gartz bought it yesterday," he replied, "and asked us to deliver it at once."

"But she doesn't live here," I told him.

"I know that," he answered. "She said it was for you."

"I don't want it. Take it away."

He was astonished. "It's one of our best—very fine, and expensive. Look at it. You couldn't find anything prettier!"

It was certainly pretty—modern mahogany, done in soft blue brocade. "You'll have to take it," the man informed me. "It's paid for."

But I told him to take it back to the store, and return Mrs. Gartz's money—it was all a mistake. The bewildered deliveryman reluctantly returned the furniture to his van and departed, and I went back into our little living room and sat in one of my own rocking chairs which had seemed so wonderful only yesterday. Had I been silly? What right had I to be so proud?

Our money was giving out rapidly, and I was beginning to wonder if we would be able to make our monthly payments on the bungalow. But Upton showed no signs of worry. He said he never crossed bridges until he came to them, and by that time something had always washed them away. I was not cheered by this philosophy. There was not only the rent, but the leaky roof, we needed some clothes and we owed the stenographer more than I liked to remember when she came to invite Upton to speak at a meeting to raise funds for the new co-op.

Then the prophet of Utopia was justified; we had no bridges to cross in order to enter, for Macmillan accepted *King Coal!* Better still, Mr. Brett wrote us a complimentary letter and sent us an advance of five hundred dollars. *I* had been the "something" that had abolished the bridge by the simple device of "putting some clothes on Mary Burke."

"You certainly did," Upton admitted, then called me his best pet name again and hopped on his bicycle and rode away. When he came back, he said he had been down to buy that blue brocade suite for our living room. It had been sold, but he had ordered another, to be charged.

"And with a leaky roof over our heads to protect it? I won't have it! Go to the nearest telephone and cancel it!"

He went out to telephone and came back with six carnations. "They cost only twenty-five cents," he pleaded, when he saw my look of disapproval.

"But we haven't got that much to spare," I protested. "This is the second time you've wasted twenty-five cents on flowers for me, when you couldn't spare it. Haven't you ever heard that a penny saved is a penny earned?"

"But why save pennies when you have a book like *King Coal* at the printers?"

"I want a roof on this house!" I insisted. "Besides, look at all those free roses out there!"

We had that supposedly magic thing, a home of our own, and there came some royalties from abroad—enough money to make Upton miserable. He never wanted to save money, and I decided to put some into needed improvements before it burned holes in his pockets. The first thing, after ordering a telephone installed, was more furniture, of the inexpensive but durable kind I had found in the second-hand stores.

Now, I told Upton, he could spend some money on a full-time secretary. Next on the list was a filing cabinet, so that grocery cartons full of letters, book reviews and duplicate manuscripts could be taken out from under our beds. But we discovered that a filing cabinet was a more expensive article than we could afford, so I went in search of a carpenter who could construct some shelves.

While the carpenter was working on this job, he suggested enclosing our small back porch, making it into an office. This was done, and now we were comfortable; a tireless author was happily working away on a sequel to *King Coal*, as certain as ever that he had another *Jungle*.

But the war which was raging in Europe looked more ominous every day; German militarism might really force us into it. Upton became restless and dissatisfied with his daily writing job, and wandered around the place, absorbed in the problem of what our country ought to do—and what he ought to advise the country to do.

Then came the beautiful blue-eyed "empress" to call, this time in a huge Packard limousine with a chauffeur. Her sons Crane and Richard were both of draft age, and she was a pacifist! At a meeting of the fashionable Friday Morning Club in Los Angeles she had heard a lecturer tell of the atrocities the Germans were committing. She could not believe that these things were possible—they were too horrible for civilized men even to imagine. What did *we* think?

Upton agreed that they were horrible, but were the German Junkers civilized? The German people were orderly, law-abiding and completely obedient to the Kaiser's military machine. Even the Socialists in the *Armée* were marching with patriotic fervor. The Socialists in other countries were talking about resisting by peaceful means the use of the working-class as "cannon fodder"; but those of Germany would never join in a strike against the war machine. This would be against the "Fatherland"! Upton had been told this by no less an authority than Karl Kautsky, intellectual leader of the German Social Democracy, in Kautsky's own home in Berlin.

Mrs. Gartz thought I should go with her to the next meeting of the Friday Morning Club, for there was to be another lecture on the war. I agreed to go, though from what I had heard of the lecturer, I felt that my husband was a better-informed person. But I had no clothes fit for such an occasion and I had no idea of buying any. Wouldn't she be ashamed of me?

Again I had given her the chance she wanted to supply some of the things we needed! The next afternoon her secretary-companion, a sweet and friendly spinster, arrived with several boxes of moderately-priced ensembles. Mrs. Gartz had been careful this time to see that nothing would be sent me that I might consider too expensive. But I said no again.

There arrived at our front door one day a very old man, seedy and tired-looking. He asked if he could see Mr. Upton Sinclair. By now I was used to tired and seedy-looking people calling on my husband, and I still felt sorry for most of them.

Kate Crane Gartz, who looked and acted like an empress.

Aline Barnsdall, of Los Angeles, whose money gave her no peace. (1932).

But don't write me dear Bolshevik. I'm a Wilsonite. For the first time in my life there is a man in the world that I am content to follow. Lenin I can assure you is a little beast like this

He just wants Power & when he gets it he has no use for. He doesn't eat well or live prettily or get children or care for beautiful things. He doesn't want order; he hates machines almost as much as he hates life. He's just a Russian dodging Webb, a rather little incessant sophistical intriguer. He & the Kaiser

Upton published a 16-page monthly magazine "dedicated to a clean peace and the Inter-nation." One contributor was H. G. Wells, who included in his letter a caricature of Lenin. A portion of the letter is shown here.

This was an especially pathetic figure, slender and bowed, sweet-faced, gentle, well-mannered. No one could reach our hillside home on foot without a considerable walk, and I invited him to take a seat on the porch.

"Have you an appointment?" I asked. When he said no, I explained that I never interrupted my husband during his writing hours; if he would tell me what he wanted I would deliver his message, and he would get a reply.

He introduced himself as N. O. Nelson. I had never heard the name and when I told him this, he said, "Of the N. O. Nelson Company, plumbers." I thought this was some little local concern, perhaps soliciting business. I suggested that he should leave his card, and I would let him hear from us if we ever had any trouble. He smiled gently and answered that he was retired; he would just wait, if I did not mind.

I left him sitting there and went inside. A few minutes later Mrs. Gartz arrived, and I heard her ask if I was at home. Then she wanted to know if he was one of the carpenters. I opened the door and heard him tell her that he was a plumber. I was not willing to invite a conspicuously rich-looking woman inside while leaving an old working-man outside, for he had taken a long walk in order to see my husband, while she had arrived in a limousine. So I invited her to sit on the porch, and I got a camp chair and joined them.

"This gentleman represents the N. O. Nelson Company, " I told her, and then, to have something informal to say, I added, "But Mr. Nelson is retired, so don't call him if your plumbing gets out of order."

Mrs. Gartz was cultivating the grace of being democratic so she immediately followed my lead. "Isn't that funny?" she replied. "I'm a plumber, too. I belong to the Crane Company."

"Indeed?" said Mr. Nelson. "Once my rival. But you outgrew me, I believe."

She looked at him questioningly. "Are you N. O. Nelson himself?" she asked.

"I am," he told her. "And I take it that you are a daughter of Richard T. Crane."

At this point Upton arrived, and Mrs. Gartz introduced Mr. Nelson, then explained to my husband who our caller was.

But Upton had been corresponding with the elderly "plumber" for a dozen years. He was, it appeared, a disciple of Bellamy, Gronlund and Robert Owen. He had bought from Upton a large number of copies of the "Sustainers' Edition" of *The Jungle,* and thereby, of course, earned Upton's undying loyalty. He was an ardent "co-opper," and after building up an immense plant which manufactured plumbing supplies in the Midwest, had tried to turn it over to the control of the workers. He had discovered that they were glad to take the profits, but preferred to leave all the responsibility to the boss. So now the old man, greatly saddened, had retired and gone out on a search for idealism—outside the plumbing industry.

While he was telling this story I excused myself and hurried off to our temporary kitchen in the basement, where I was afraid the soup might be burning. When I returned, Mrs. Gartz had gone, and Upton told me that Mr. Nelson would be our guest for luncheon.

"But we're eating in the basement!" I protested.

"I like that," said our guest. "I'm for the simple life. That is why I am here—I thought I would find it in the home of Upton Sinclair."

"You don't know his wife," I laughed. "I *hate* it!"

When we went down to lunch, I asked him if our dirt floor was simple enough, and he said the human race had used dirt floors for millions of years and had been well satisfied with them. His life experience had led him back to nature. "I'm a mechanic, and as founder and owner of a great plumbing corporation, I've learned whereof I speak. It is my belief that civilized man is under a vast and dangerous delusion: the idea that technology is progress."

That was his theme, and Upton listened, and then told him about his old friend Prestonia Mann Martin, who had the same philosophy. She, like Mrs. Gartz, was the child of a manufacturing entrepreneur and had rebelled against it; she had become a kind of Socialist, looking backward to Plato instead of forward with Bellamy. She had written a whole book to prove that modern culture was a highway to destruction, and that the Greeks had had everything better. And so she continued to occupy alternately her splendid country estate, and another fine home on Staten Island.

Upton told of their intellectual duels—and oddly enough the weapon with which he had beaten her down was a plumbing pipe! Prestonia had been forced to admit that there was one feature of our civilization which the Greeks had lacked and which she would not be willing to give up; that was plumbing. But of course that was giving up her whole argument, because you couldn't have plumbing on any large scale unless you had lead mines and steel mills, and the tools and technical processes, and transportation.

"I've spent my life building 'a house on the sands,'" said Mr. Nelson, sadly. "I have wasted my years, and now at the end, I can't see why I was ever put here. But there must be a reason."

I was deeply interested in his arguments, but I remained unconverted. I was sure I wanted plumbing, and floors. I preferred automobiles to horses, and screen doors to flies and bees and bugs. But neither Upton nor I made any impression on a man who had spent his life making gadgets for human cleanliness and comfort—and incidentally a great fortune for himself—but who at the end was desolate because he had accomplished nothing!

He wanted to convert us, he said, for we were good people, and the world needed goodness, and we were wasting ourselves, as he had, trying to get gadgets for the poor. He asked if we had a spare room—he wanted to live as we were living, in the simplest possible way! He was lonely, as any man is who is out of step with his generation. He was old, too, and I had always been sorry for old people. I invited him to stay with us for a while, if he could climb stairs. We had only a small upstairs room with a single bed.

The elderly "plumber" trudged off toward the streetcar tracks on his way to Los Angeles to get his suitcase. He would return the following day.

Mr. Nelson stayed with us long enough to find that he could not change Upton's ideas. We were made sad by the fact that we could not heal his pessimism. As time passed and I remembered how the disillusionment of an idealist could desolate his heart I was thankful for my husband's invincible optimism, and confirmed in my resolve not to weaken it.

Rob Wagner was a well-known California painter and writer. He had made a life-size portrait of Stewart Edward White, the novelist, which we had admired, and he was a highly-paid writer for the *Saturday Evening Post.* Upton met him, and the two became warm friends. Rob was also a friend of Charlie Chaplin and introduced us to him. Rob was a sociable fellow, and everyone who knew him loved him. He told us that all travelers from Europe wanted to meet two persons, Charlie Chaplin and Upton Sinclair, and it kept him busy making excuses for two hard-working hermits.

When we first met them, Rob and his wife, Florence, lived between Pasadena and Los Angeles. Rob had two boys by a previous marriage, and in order to have quiet for his writing he rented a cabin, somewhat isolated, on a small hill nearby. When the war came, there were spy scares, and one day two sturdy citizens came to Rob's shack, showed him credentials as police detectives, and proceeded to subject him to a questioning. They told him that neighbors had reported this mysterious man who stayed alone and spoke to no one, sometimes flashed lights at night, and by day gave mysterious signals in a tree near his cabin. Rob didn't know about the lights, but supposed he made them by walking up and down while thinking over his next paragraph, thus passing between his lamp and his window. As for the tree signals, there was an old Chinese peddler of vegetables and fruit who passed every day with his wagon, and to avoid being bothered by his visits Rob had arranged to hang a large colored card in the tree whenever he wanted to make a purchase.

Charlie Chaplin invited Upton to drop in at his studio when he was in Hollywood. On one occasion I was with him when the director-comedian was running an unfinished film. We were escorted into a darkened projection room, and there was the little "funny man," both on the screen and "in person." The latter,

well-tailored and without a mustache, was as animated as the
small make-believe figure scuttling around in baggy trousers
and shoes too large for him. He kept up a running fire of comment on each silent scene as it unrolled before our eyes, and got
so excited that he would jump up and down as if he were going
to climb bodily onto the screen to show the tramp how to do a
better job.

Afterward he invited us to dinner, and we told him we had
to catch a streetcar before the evening rush began. But he
wanted to hear everything Upton thought about the film and
said he would drive us home in his car if we would stay. He was
then at the height of his fame, but as simple and unspoiled as
he must have been when he left the slums of London to seek
his fortune in the land across the ocean.

When Charlie looked at our poor little cottage in the nearest
thing to a slum to be found in Pasadena, he said, "Now, Upton,
you can't deny that my car beats a streetcar. Don't you see it is
more sensible to have money than be poor?"

Upton was wishing for a sight of his boy, so Mama
wrote that she would bring David out; she was wishing for a
sight of her girl. She was many times a grandmother now, but
younger-looking than I, and more debonair. She had never
been on a mountaintop, and when from our windows she saw
a track leading up Mt. Lowe, she wanted to go up. There was a
car that took you; but I told her that after she got as far as the
hotel, she would have to ride on a burro to the top. I said she
would ride on a trail so steep that if the burro lost his footing
she might be dashed to death in a canyon far below. Her answer
was, "Don't you know how I love to ride wild horses?"

Upton and I were too busy to go up the mountain, but David
was happy to escort her. They went, and came back safely, well
pleased with the adventure. Soon after that Mama was having a
nap upstairs, when there came an earthquake, threatening to
shake our old house off its foundations. I screamed to her, "It's
an earthquake, Mama! Come down at once!"

She, too, was shaken, for her voice trembled. But her answer
was, "Not until I get my stockings on!"

"You'll be killed!" I cried.

"I can't help that—I'm going to have my stockings on when I am." My same proper mother—though she did not think the earthquake was a lark. There had never been an earthquake in the Mississippi Delta.

David had become aristocratic in that so-different world, the far South. He didn't want to ride a bicycle to high school because the rich boys came in cars. His father told how he had walked to school when he was younger than David, and the distance far greater. But what the youngster wanted was a car.

After Mama left we put our minds to work on the problem of what a young boy could do to earn the cost of a car. He was not old enough to be trusted to drive—he told us how he had driven one "anyway" in Greenwood and had got it wrecked, trying to beat an oncoming train to the crossing. He could not earn enough money for a car very fast; the important thing was for Upton's boy to learn to work, as all boys should!

I suggested to David that he take the school course in arts and crafts and be a carpenter's helper while we enlarged our house, with money from the sale in England of *Sylvia's Marriage*. To the north of us, looking toward the mountains, lay a row of vacant lots. I made a down payment on the one next to ours. My idea was to fix up a separate study, so that Upton would be free from household affairs. In my shopping walks I had spotted an unoccupied one-room cottage and a garage. Now I bought the two of them for seventy-five dollars and had them moved for twenty-five more. We recalled our carpenter and work began.

The one-room cottage was small, and too dilapidated for restoration, but it furnished material for turning the garage into two rooms. The principal duty of our carpenter's helper was to extract old nails and straighten them for re-use. Morning and afternoon David straightened nails for twenty-five cents per hour, and was happy because he was earning the price of a second-hand flivver.

Mrs. Gartz came and went during all this building, and would ask, plaintively, "Why won't you let me give you *any-*

thing? I have so much!" I told her she should give her money to causes. The Socialist Party and other groups working to abolish everyone's poverty, always needed money, while charity to individuals was like dropping things into a bottomless pit— there was no end to it in a world teeming with poor people.

Several times then she reached into her large handbag and got out considerable sums of money and asked me to use it for causes. But I always refused. "You must give it yourself," I said. "It will be good for you to take an active part in such work. Make sure what is going on, so that you won't be putting funds into unworthy hands."

"Oh, I can't do that!" she protested. "I trust everyone!"

Georg Brandes, the Danish critic, had written in praise of Upton's books, and Upton had sent him a set of the proofs of *King Coal,* asking if he would care to write a preface to it. We were delighted by his reply, with a little essay in which he said:

> "Upton Sinclair is one of the not too many writers who have consecrated their lives to the agitation for social justice, and have also enrolled their art in the service of a set purpose. A great and non-temporizing enthusiast, he never flinched from making sacrifices. . . . This time he has absorbed himself in a study of the miner's life in the lonely pits of the Rocky Mountains, and his sensitive and enthusiastic mind has brought to the world an American parallel to *Germinal,* Emile Zola's industrial masterpiece."

Now the book came out, and the *New York Times* called it "Better than *The Jungle.*" Eugene Debs wrote to say the same thing, and added that having served as a special organizer for both the United Mine Workers and the Western Federation of Miners, he marveled at the author's "mastery of the subject in its minutest details."

By the time summer was over, David had got homesick for the boys in Greenwood with their many games. Mama did not believe in having an only child growing up with adults, and begged us to let him come back for school there. So we paid

David what he had just invested in a second-hand flivver, and assumed the debt for the rest. It was a welcome addition to our household. Upton learned to drive it, but he never quite mastered the art of cranking it. As a result, not long afterward he was in a hospital to be operated on for hernia.

At this time we had a new house guest in David's upstairs alcove, a young clergyman from Boston named Albert Rhys Williams. Albert hated automobiles, but Upton insisted that Albert must learn to drive. He took his guest out and gave him full instructions and a quick demonstration. The two of them took a spin around a couple of quiet blocks near our house, with Albert at the wheel. Now, since I had no one else to take me to visit Upton in the hospital, Albert consented to "risk both our lives" in that deadly machine.

Then came a letter from novelist Zona Gale, telling us that she had arrived in town and wanted to call on us. I cordially informed her that I would send my car and chauffeur to fetch her!

She arrived breathless with excitement, and declared "Oh, what a wonderful driver your friend Mr. Williams is! He miraculously avoided being run down by a foolish old woman who kept jumping in front of him. But every time she did, our car jumped the same way, just missing her. It was one of the most incredible things I ever saw!"

Edna Ferber came to town, and we took Kitty Gartz and a school-teacher friend to call on her. She was stopping at one of the de luxe hotels, and Upton remarked that he had known few writers who could afford such splendor. Was she an honorary guest? he asked.

"Oh, yes," she replied. He told her that we had also been invited to be honorary guests at one of the local hotels, but had declined.

"It is well that you did," she answered, "unless you know how to protect yourself."

She said that instead of paying your bill in cash, you were expected to pay in time and boredom. You were a "lion," and must roar for the entertainment of other guests. Every day

you would be called downstairs by the management and introduced to new arrivals. That was an interruption of your writing, and in every way too high a price.

"How do you protect yourself?" asked the schoolteacher.

"With chewing gum," answered Edna. "I come downstairs
and step out of the elevator, a-chewing with vigor and vim.
You can't imagine how lustily I can chew! This is not wrong—
it wasn't forbidden in the contract."

King Coal earned very little money. No one we knew
doubted why; it was the war in Europe, just as several publishers had foretold. But Upton had no idea of abandoning his
second volume. It was called *The Coal War,* and dealt with that
great struggle in which he had tried to help, both in Colorado
and on Broadway in New York. It was a struggle that was going
on all over America at that time, for the elemental right of
labor to organize and bargain collectively. The emotions of that
struggle had been deeply graven into Upton's soul, and he was
working on the story grimly; but the bigger war in Europe was
crowding in on his thinking. His mind was torn between two
tremendously important themes.

He was used to being poor, doing his writing under the
strain of physical discomfort and interruptions, also to working
without considering the question of a possible audience. If a
book did not sell now, it would be read later on, provided that
he could get it into print. He had always managed to do that
somehow, and it was all he asked.

But I was not reconciled to seeing him work under such
strain. I wanted every material comfort the world had to offer,
and I wanted him to have them. "Then why are you a Socialist?" a friend asked me. "You and your husband call yourselves
friends of the underdog—yet you want comfort."

I was irritated by that foolish question. "Do you think we
want to perpetuate 'underdogs'? Never! We want to abolish
them!"

I refused to live like one a day longer than necessary. But I
was not willing to compromise with my sense of rectitude in
order to escape. I would not be supported either by my family

or by a rich friend. Nor did I want my husband to give up his dedication to causes, in order to provide me with comfort. Even more than I disliked poverty I disliked a parasite!

Mrs. Gartz would hear me say this at her tea parties, and would ask, "But I'm a parasite—why do you like *me?*"

"Because you are trying to get over it. You are trying to work. You are working as custodian of the wealth your father bequeathed you, not just spending it on your personal pleasures. Giving money to a cause is work, if you take the trouble to investigate before you invest."

"I'm finding that out," she said.

She was finding out, also, that her rich friends disapproved strongly of her new ideas and activities. And this also put her to work, answering their objections.

I was determined to earn some money and I thought I had found a way. I noticed an old house on Fair Oaks Avenue for sale at a low price. I thought I saw what could be done with it and persuaded the owner to sell it with no down payment. It would keep my carpenters busy, and they needed the work. If I sold it at a profit I would have earned some money, all by myself!

One afternoon during my girlhood I was driving a friend in a new Stanhope, behind a pair of beautiful Kentucky thoroughbreds. Suddenly I said, "Let's go back. Mr. Barry is at the house." My friend protested, "What makes you think that? He would not come without being invited." I answered, "I had a feeling; it's just as if I saw him—sitting on the front gallery." We started home reluctantly and when we arrived, there was Mr. Barry, sitting on the front gallery.

I had such experiences often, but paid no attention to them. But now I was married to a man who had read books about every important subject in the world, or so it seemed to me, and one of the many was psychic research. In his youth he had met Minot J. Savage, minister of the Unitarian Church of the Messiah in New York, and Dr. Savage had assured him quite seriously that he believed in what were called "psychic phenomena." Upton had read Dr. Savage's books, those of Profes-

sor Quackenbos of Columbia University, and the classic
F. W. H. Myers' *Human Personality and the Survival of Bodily
Death*.

Now I said to Upton, "I have the strangest feeling about Jack
London, that he is in trouble."

Upton and Jack had been corresponding with each other for
a matter of a decade and a half. They had met only twice, when
Jack came to New York in 1905, but they had sent each other a
new book every year and had discussed them by mail, agreeing
on every subject except drinking. Jack had been a hard drinker
from boyhood, and Upton had learned the details from Jack's
terrible book, *John Barleycorn*. Of late, under the influence of
drink, Jack's character had deteriorated—he had become so
rude and domineering that George Sterling, his dearest friend,
had decided to go no more to his ranch.

Now I said to Upton, several times, "Jack is in trouble. You
ought to try to help him. You ought to telephone him." Upton
had spent so much energy trying to help alcoholics, and all in
vain, that he felt he could do nothing. Next day came the news
that Jack London had died by poison. There followed a letter
from George Sterling, saying that it was suicide. Jack had acquired what he called in his book "the White Logic"—John
Barleycorn gives to his victims the ability to see clearly that life
is a swindle and a thing of no account.

Within two or three weeks came Charmian, his widow, to
call on us. She was arrayed in bright-colored silks, and sparkling
with rubies and sapphires, and her manner was as striking as
her costume. She exclaimed, "Oh, my friends, I have had sound
sleep for the first time in ten years!"

She had come all the way from Glen Ellen, the London
ranch, five hundred miles distant, to see us and we did not
know why. It was a strange thing, for I had never met her, and
by what she said, and by her gay costume, she made it clear that
she was not in need of comforting. Upton and I speculated
about it, and he wondered if Jack had not told her to see us;
but she did not mention it if he had.

And now one day our telephone rang, and a woman's voice
asked, "Is this Mrs. Sinclair?" When I told her it was, she said,

"I am a medium. I have a message for you from Jack London. I would like to see you and tell you about it."

I was a bit startled, for I did not believe in ghosts, nor in "fortune tellers," not even in Mama's gypsy. I did not want one coming to call on us, so I politely told the voice that we had just had a visit from Mrs. London, and she had not brought any message, so I thought there must be a mistake. The woman did not persist. Afterwards I regretted that I did not see her—as other strange things happened on which she might have thrown light.

George Sterling came down from San Francisco, and told us how Jack's suicide had depressed him. He said he wanted to stay with us for a few days, hoping a new environment would soften the blow. He prowled around our place haunted and bereft, and I was worried. He seemed to feel that because he had so often drunk with Jack, he was partly to blame. Upton, always prone to draw moral conclusions, said he hoped George would take the lesson seriously; "social drinking" was an anti-social custom.

George's distress continued, and he went on talking about alcoholism, and what it had done to literary men and women. Upton was right, it had blurred some of the finest minds and ended them in suicide. I asked if he would care to talk on the subject at one of Mrs. Gartz's weekly tea parties, but George said he was tired of rich people—they never listened, they wanted people to listen to them.

Then I recalled that our neighbors, who were far from rich, had expressed their pride in having an author so near; the woman next door had hoped to meet some of our literary friends. So I invited some of these people to a "literary evening," and informed George that he was to give a talk to the working class.

About a dozen of our working-class neighbors came to hear a famous San Francisco poet tell about his fellow poets and story writers. George was the poet-laureate of the wealthy Bohemian Club, and had written a masque for their "High Jinks" on Mt. Tamalpais. That, of course, was a bacchanalian affair. I am not sure if George realized how his descriptions would strike our church-going neighbors. Really it was a prohibition lecture, a heart-breaking recital of the dreadful thing that alcohol had done to some of the finest literary talents of our time. Our poet spoke with sorrow because he had known them personally; several beside Jack London had become suicides. He did not name any of them—he did not think he should "drink and tell," but it was certainly no advertisment for California literature. Upton was deeply moved, and so was the simple, poorly-dressed audience.

My next-door neighbor said, when she was leaving, "If that's the way literary people behave, how do they have the nerve to tell us what to think?" And there were several audible "Amens."

Without notice from home, there arrived by freight a used Dodge sedan. Next day a letter from Papa told us that this one had a "self-starter." It was Mama's, and had been driven very little. We simply must get rid of that other "contraption" before Upton got a second hernia! There was nothing we could do but accept this gift, for the cost of returning it would have been more than we could afford.

Aunt Sallie was feeble now, but wrote that she wanted to come to see us; she would even be willing to try our diet! Upton and I moved upstairs to give her our ground-floor bedroom. She was distressed because I was climbing up and down stairs all day. Why didn't I lock up that basement, and send our clothes to the laundry?

She was not able to get up from her chair without help, and she weighed "a ton," according to her own estimate, so she had to sit and wait for Upton to pull her out by holding on to both her hands. She had a Chinese houseboy who did this service for her at home. They were wonderful servants—why didn't I get one? He could do the laundry and everything, as hers did. She had had him for years and he was completely reliable. I told her we were not able to pay for "help," as servants were called in Pasadena, and we were determined not to accept support from anyone.

She thought this was the first foolish thing she had ever

heard from my lips. Then she asked if we would not sell this ridiculous house, with its rooms all on the perpendicular instead of on the ground, and come live with her. I explained that Upton always did his writing outdoors, and had found a climate suitable for this.

She was worried about us, and urged me not to become a "crank." She had decided that our diet was a "crank diet," served in a "crank house." When she went back to her own comfortable home, she sent me a box of lovely new clothes. At least I must not let myself become dowdy!

I knew that this good, kind aunt was not long for this world, and that if we accepted her invitation it would mean inheriting her money. But what would have become of Upton's books? And what would have become of her peace and security, with two irresponsibles in her house? It was like Papa's offer to give me Ashton Hall.

There came one day, in a shining blue Lincoln roadster, a tall, sweet-faced country girl in pale blue chiffon who said simply that she was Esther Yarnell and wanted to know us. The name meant nothing to me, but I invited her in, and she proceeded to inspect my old walnut furniture.

"I love old walnut," she said. "I'm building a house in the country; it is something of a monstrosity, I'm afraid—I wouldn't dare tell you the cost. It frightens me! When it is ready, I'll bargain with you for this furniture. I'm not joking."

Her twangy Western voice reminded me of those accents of some of the Gardner School girls, and her background turned out to be the same. Her father was an old-timer on whose ranch oil had been struck. "Haven't you ever heard of Yarnell Oil?" she asked.

No, I hadn't. "Sometimes I wish *I* hadn't," she said.

She was as direct and straightforward as Kate Crane-Gartz, and like her also in the look of bewildered sadness in her face. While she was spending some of her unearned wealth, she was troubled and unhappy about it.

"Sometimes I want to go back to those times before I had an income of five hundred dollars a day, and that increasing with every well they bore! I was happy in those old days, I had friends. Now I sometimes think I haven't a friend in the world! Nobody thinks of me, only of my money."

Esther said that she had studied Socialism, for she wanted a philosophy to give clarity and meaning to life. She had been to New York to investigate Greenwich Village, where writers and artists were said to live free and comradely lives; and what had happened? At a nearby beach resort, she had come near drowning. A young "comrade" had rescued her and then informed her that he was a writer, and broke. She wrote him a check for a thousand dollars. Since then he had been "broke" a half-dozen times, and each time she had sent him a thousand dollars.

"How much money do you owe a man for saving your life?" she asked me.

I had come to know so many unhappy rich people by now that I had begun to wonder if wealth was worth having. But why was the plantation-owning class in the South happy, while these Northerners and Westerners were not? The Southerners were not rich by comparison with "oil princesses" and Crane Company "empresses," but they had enough money to live in considerable luxury, and they did so in carefree enjoyment.

Of course the rich who sought us here in the West had somehow developed what Upton called a "social conscience," or else they would have felt about us as did some of Mrs. Gartz's tea-party guests. Did this mean that my people, like Kitty's "girls," had no social conscience? This was a painful idea, and I decided to postpone consideration of it by calling them merely ignorant.

We were invited to visit Luther Burbank the next week at his experiment station. Esther asked to be taken along to see the "plant wizard," and she wanted to bring her sister Jessie. Luther Burbank was a great public figure at that time, known and honored as a genius. But the simplicity of his living room and of the dress of our host and hostess equaled that of the Sinclairs.

Burbank spoke with quiet admiration of both George Sterling's and Upton's books. He was slender, frail-looking and white-haired, but showed no sign of strain, or even of intensity. He loved his work and believed that evolution could be controlled by intelligence for the benefit of all mankind.

Upton told him we had come to see and hear him, so he must do the talking. He smiled and said, "Then ask me questions."

There was silence for a moment, and so I asked, "What caused your genius?"

"I must decline the term; I do not think I am a genius, and I do not think genius had anything to do with my success. It was caused by unrequited love! In my youth I loved a girl who was the whole world to me then. When I lost her, I had to create a new world for myself. My work became that world." He smiled quietly at his young wife and she returned his smile.

He showed us many of the fruits of his work out there in the warm California sunshine, and after that Mrs. Burbank gave us some fruit juice and little cakes. We left them standing contentedly in the doorway with his arm around her.

During the drive home Esther Yarnell asked me when and how I became "a rebel." I answered I did not think I ever was one; I was a questioner. I was molded to a great extent by the life of the South in that part-white, part-black atmosphere, which had in it still so many factors of the Reconstruction chaos. (This sounds like a paradox, but what was called Reconstruction was never that. It isn't that yet.)

I went on questioning everything—and wanted *cures*. So, when I met Upton, I was fully ripe to accept something different. He, too, had been a seeker after cures—he, too, had been a victim of that Civil War and its aftermath. He thought he had found the cure for everything. He was sure he had! He was so convincing that I became a part-time or part-way convert to his "cure."

He could see all the ramifications and effects of poverty in every aspect of life. It was "economics" (of which I had never heard until I met him) that had to be changed, so that poverty could not exist anywhere on earth. It was economics that had caused the Arabs in Africa to sell Negroes to the slave-traders, the latter being merely products of a false economic system. It was ignorance, too, but that also was due to poverty. The ignorant cannibals in Africa had to be given houses, sanitation, schools, doctors, laboratories; then they would not be ignorant, and the Arabs could not steal them, nor would they want to, and the slave-traders would become college professors and physicists, and leaders in a co-operative commonwealth!

When I had finished this sermon, Esther laughed and said, "That's the rebel yell!"

Young Bobby Scripps was another of the very rich, restlessly seeking for a purpose in life. His father had amassed a fortune, building the Scripps-Howard newspaper chain, but was off on a yacht to spend his last days alone. Young Bobby, destined to be head of the newspaper chain, wanted to be a poet, and brought us a book of poems he had written and had printed in expensive format. They were good, and Upton and I encouraged him to follow his bent. But that wasn't all that Upton suggested as a panacea for Bobby's discontent. There was a penniless Canadian farm-worker named Gerald Lively who also had written good poetry, but no publisher would take it because it was full of social protest. Bobby should pay for the publication of Gerald's *Songs of a Soil Slave.*

But this was not the panacea Bobby wanted. He preferred to bow to his destiny, to be a newspaperman, so left it to us to take care of the "soil slave." Like his father, he became an alcoholic, and went to sea on the same yacht which had been his father's last home, and there, like his father, he died.

I sold the house I had remodeled, for enough to cover what I had invested in it, plus two vacant lots near the beach. So the return for my time was just more real estate in which I would have to invest more time. Then I read in the morning paper that one of the big companies had "struck oil" in that area. I made up my mind to hold those lots and see if the oil boom would swing my way.

Upton, who did not want us to own any property, advised

me to forget about oil. Surely I could do more important things
with my mind!

"But how will we be fed?" I demanded.

"The ravens will feed us," was his response.

"Better to say, 'God takes care of children and idiots'."

But a few days later came a raven!

It was Upton's habit to do his writing in the morning,
while his mind was fresh; he would sit and hammer at his typewriter for three hours or so, and his secretary's orders were "No
interruptions," no matter who called. But one morning she
tapped on the door and whispered that there was a gentleman
outside who looked "most important," and who had handed
her *"this."* Upton took it and it was a crisp new hundred-dollar
bill, with a card reading "Mr. King C. Gillette." We forgot to
ask either the secretary or Mr. Gillette whether the bill was
for Upton, or was a bribe for the secretary to let him in!

The name in those days was known to all the world, also
the face, which was on every package of Gillette razor blades.
He was middle-aged when the photograph was taken and his
mustache was black; now he was elderly and portly and his
mustache was gray. He was "the razor king," inventor of the
safety razor, and he had managed to hold on to a share of the
profits. So now he owned several mansions in Southern California and rode about in the most expensive car of that day,
with a chauffeur in livery.

He was known to Upton for a different and most unusual
reason; he was a Socialist of a sort, though he did not know it.
He had sponsored two immense tomes called *Gillette's Social
Solution* and *Gillette's World Redemption,* and had sent them
to libraries, where Upton had come upon them. It occurred to
Mr. Gillette that he wanted his ideas put into more readable
form and that Upton Sinclair was just the person to do this.
They had a chat, and Mr. Gillette was pleased to learn that
his ideas were already known to the author. So he explained
them all over again—that being his one delight in life. Upton
replied that he had a book half done and it was therefore impossible for him to think of anything else; but later, perhaps—

So the millionaire idealist went away, and Upton came in and told me about the visit. By that time I was thoroughly tired of being without money; I saw no sense in it, and I had become a bit skeptical of the mood in which Upton did his work—the certainty that the next book (the one still in his mind) was going to make the world into paradise. I just didn't believe in turning down a multimillionaire when he wanted just what Upton wanted. I wrote a letter to Mr. Gillette pointing out that I had some influence with my husband, and that it might be worth while to explain his ideas to *me*.

So he came again, and this time the meeting was in our living room, humble but with, by now, a touch of old-fashioned comfort. I had never met anyone more lovable than this man who, when he was young, had worn out his shoes trying to find someone to manufacture and market his invention. He had never forgotten that once he was an underdog.

I had been trained from childhood to listen to gentlemen, old and young, telling me their ideas about everything from running a cotton compress to killing Moros, from handling a torpedo boat to planning a regatta or a Mardi Gras, so it wasn't at all difficult to listen while the razor king explained his idea of making over the American industrial system. I wasn't much good at economics, or even at addition and subtraction, but I could see at once how much waste there was in having a dozen firms making razor blades, and spending millions for competitive advertising which might or might not tell the truth—and how could the buyer know? Upton had admired a book called *The Cost of Competition,* in which an engineer, Sidney A. Reeve, proved that seventy per cent of the social effort was wasted because of it; and now the razor king laid it all before me.

What he wanted was a mammoth enterprise called "The People's Corporation," to be a holding concern for all the basic enterprises. It was to be run democratically by all the citizens of industry, and it was to systematize production and distribution and eliminate waste. It sounded to me exactly like Gaylord Wilshire's old formula, "Let the nation own the trusts." But I quickly learned that Mr. Gillette dreaded the word "Socialism."

He had heard about a man named Karl Marx who was a Socialist, but who had talked about confiscation and violence. Mr.
Gillette had a horror of these. He was a lover of peace and
order, just as Upton was, and he wanted Upton to drop the
Socialist label and come over to the new dispensation, with a
new label. He said to me, with the utmost earnestness, "Mrs.
Sinclair, if you will persuade him to do that, you will never
have to think about money again as long as you live."

He told me about his own early struggles. He had been a
traveling salesman, and sitting on trains all day, he had evolved
the idea of a shaving device with a blade that could be inserted, used and then thrown away. He had a model made and
set out to interest someone with money. It had to be mass produced; otherwise the device would cost too much. It had been
years before he could find anyone to back him. Then had come
tremendous success, and he had a great deal of money, and an
idea that was too big to finance alone. Many men of wealth
would have to get together on "The People's Corporation."

He seldom mentioned his family to me, and I could guess
that they lacked interest in his idea. Alone with his dream of
national order and international peace, his solace for all the
world's sorrows, he wanted to talk about it.

We worked it out that Mr. Gillette was to visit us two morn-
ings in the week and explain his ideas, and as Upton and I
found time we would put them on paper. For this service he
would pay us five hundred dollars a month.

Our friends the Wilshires had come to live in Pasadena.
Mary had become interested in psychoanalysis, had gone to
Zürich and studied with Carl Jung, and now wished to set up
in practice. She had been so tirelessly kind to me that I wanted
to make a return. By now I knew some of the influential people
in our community and I invited as many of these as my small
living room would hold to hear a lecture.

I was aided in this by the arrival of the gay British earl,
Frank Russell, on a tour. After his divorce from Aunt Mollie,
he had acquired a new wife—the author of a popular novel,
Elizabeth and Her German Garden, and she was with him.

Mary Wilshire was lovely and very striking in her cream satin dress, heavily embroidered in red and gold. She gave a clear explanation of the general meaning of psychoanalysis according to Dr. Jung, a dissenter from Freud's over-emphasis on sexual repression as a cause of neuroses.

At this time I had in our home a young woman as a part-time secretary and household-helper. She had been brought up on a small chicken ranch near San Diego, and was a veritable young Juno. After his lordship was settled in a comfortable chair just across the room from her he had no eyes for anyone else and no ears for his old friend Mary Wilshire. The course of the evening's events was summed up in a brief stanza which Upton composed the next day:

> She was smiled at by a lord,
> Then he fell asleep and snored—
> By a lecture he was bored!

Upton had told Mr. Gillette that, regardless of what he called his program, it *was* Socialism, and would be called Socialism, especially by the big businessmen. Gillette said this could not be because it was *not* Socialism! So it occurred to Upton to make a test. We would invite some of the important businessmen of Southern California to meet him at our home.

I asked Mr. Gillette, and he said he would be glad to try out his ideas on such a group. So one evening there met in our living-room half a dozen of the most powerful persons in the community: an oil man, a banker, a newspaper publisher, a lawyer and our own Kate Crane-Gartz. They listened silently while Mr. Gillette, in his clear and quiet manner, set forth the program to which he had devoted years of thought. Then he stopped and waited for their reaction.

What happened appalled me. They were not rude to him personally—he was too important for that—but as for his ideas they were ruthless. Merely to talk of such a plan was a threat to the *status quo;* and the more Gillette tried to explain, the more indignant they became. By the time that session was over, the razor king had wilted like a flower on a cut stem; the per-spiration stood out on his forehead and melted his collar. Kitty and I came near shedding tears of pity for this good but naïve humanitarian.

Our next troubled visitor, dissatisfied with the destructive aspects of great wealth, was Prince Hopkins of Santa Barbara. Prince was not a title, but a family name, and it embarrassed him, especially when traveling abroad, where it got him too much attention in hotels and interfered with his privacy. He had no taste for this, and finally changed the spelling to Pryns.

But he couldn't change being a poor little rich boy; his millionaire parents had done him that harm from infancy. With loving care they had sheltered him from every trouble, and, as Kitty expressed it, "everything had been handed to him." Money had created in their minds the belief that he was indeed the American version of royalty. He was never allowed to play the rough games in which other boys learn to use their bodies and match their wits. So, when he went off to a select boarding school in Europe, attended by some real princes, he discovered that even they had learned to play games while he had not.

When he became ill and was confined to a sanatorium, he began to do some thinking and resolved to find out about the real world. He ordered books by authors such as Upton Sinclair, known to have something to say about the evils of unearned wealth.

He became convinced that he must do something useful in the world, and decided that education was the key to all progress. He set out to use some of his money to combine education with manual labor—and his devoted mother proceeded to build for him a palace in which to establish that kind of boy's school!

Now he wanted to know personally the author whose books had helped to clarify his thinking, and he came to call. Later Upton went up to visit his school, and was much impressed with the spirit of devotion and kindness he found there. Prince had the idea of "learning by doing." Besides teaching in the school he did manual work there himself, and the boys worked with him gladly. I had discovered the same thing myself, for I now had two schoolboys who came after school and on Saturdays to work on my place, and I made it a rule to work with them in the garden at least part of the time. It not merely made them happy, it turned the humblest job into something important. (One of those boys now holds a high position in the Pasadena schools.)

When the war came Prince, a devoted pacifist, joined with three others in issuing some kind of manifesto opposing our entry. There was terrific excitement in Santa Barbara, and the four Tolstoyans were arrested by the federal authorities and charged with sedition. They stood to receive prison sentences of ten to twenty years—and for the leader, with his predisposition to tuberculosis, that would have been serious.

His lawyers came to Upton, who obtained permission to talk to the judge. This is allowed if both sides consent. Judge Bledsoe put my husband through a cross-examination for two or three hours, first about his own attitude and then about what he knew concerning the four accused. Fortunately Upton knew all the answers on the subject of conscientious objectors. He described the evening he had spent in the school, talking with Prince while all the boys gathered around, an obviously happy family. He was able to convince His Honor that this was the case of a young idealist and not a secret agent of Kaiser Wilhelm.

If the four would plead guilty and agree to drop their anti-war propaganda, the judge said he would let them off with fines. Prince would have to pay twenty thousand dollars, and the fine of the other three would come to ten thousand more, which Prince would pay. There was nothing for him to do but accept this settlement, and because of the uproar the school was closed. It was sold and converted into a fashionable inn.

But Prince's determination to have such a school was by no means ended. He bought for the purpose a magnificent château in France. "A million of my 'unearned wealth' I spent on boys' schools in America and in France," he wrote. He gave not merely his money, but his time and teaching ability to these schools. But the troubles of great wealth enslaved him, and still do!

Esther Yarnell's mansion was finished, and she came to look at my old walnut furniture. I had bought a number of pieces since her first visit—a bed, old chairs, a table and "what-nots." She was delighted with some of it, and finally said, "Craig, it is exactly what I want, but I feel it would be wicked to take it. I know how much time you spent finding it."

I wanted to give her the furniture; I was used to giving people things, and felt better that way. But she insisted it would be robbing me. So finally I said, "Pay me fifty dollars, and that will allow me a profit."

She hurried off happily, saying she would invite me over soon to dine—then I would see how beautifully my big table fitted into her dining-room. A week later she sent me a check for twenty-five hundred dollars, and a letter saying, "That's what the appraiser says. Please spend some of it on some clothes for both you and Upton."

But of course I did not do this. Upton considered "fashion" a matter of crude commercialism, while I was more concerned with its power of demoralization. In the matter of women's clothes it was especially degrading, as it automatically made every woman who ignored it a freak. But no one could per-suade me to waste my time and money discarding perfectly good clothing because advertisers decreed that it was no longer the style. I was becoming a crank, said my elegant sister Dollie, now married to a successful businessman. But I replied that I knew many women who spent days looking for the most stylish and becoming coat, at a "bargain" price, when they should be at home reading a book. And how much of a woman's time, thought and money went into cosmetics and beauty par-lors! More than enough to found orphan asylums and research laboratories where scientists could work on finding cures for diseases. I thought of a crusade of my own on this theme. When I told Florence Wagner, she agreed with Dollie. She looked at me thoughtfully, then said, "You'll be awfully unpopular."

Of course I knew I couldn't afford any kind of crusade;

Upton had a monopoly on this in our family. He knew how
to promote his, but I had no idea how to promote mine. The
best I had been able to do so far was to stick to my determination to appear anywhere and everywhere in inexpensive clothes.
Kitty had adopted a way of announcing my arrival at her parties: "Here comes Mrs. Sinclair in her *cal*-i-co!"

One of her fashionable friends called one day and said, "I
hope you won't mind if I ask you to let me see your house.
It's your austerity which so appeals to Mrs. Gartz."

I laughed. "I'm sorry, but I don't like austerity. I wish I had
the best mattress made, and every labor-saving device on the
market!" I explained to her, as I was always explaining, that
I did not believe in poverty, I wanted to see it abolished from
the world. It was a hindrance and a crime, unless necessary. It
was necessary in my case, because Upton wished to put everything into "causes," and I had married him with full knowledge
of that fact. Was I to break the bargain? No.

Not long afterwards Esther Yarnell died, quietly and un-
complainingly. I think the indirect cause was a broken heart,
which is a real and killing thing. She left some money to me,
which I did not expect, for I had done nothing for her. But
she had meant a lot to me, and she was another tragic example
of how hard it is for a kind and sensitive soul to live happily
when she has more money than everybody else she knows.

Upton tried to accommodate his mind to that of Mr.
Gillette. He believed in Gillette's plan, as an orderly way to
bring about democracy in industry, without violence or economic waste; it was a completely American way, in accord with
our psychology and our vocabulary. But that wasn't enough
for the plan's creator; he dreaded the word "Socialism," and
kept on insisting that his plan had nothing to do with it. He
wanted Upton to agree to that, and promote the plan as the
entirely new and original creation of King C. Gillette—which
he sincerely believed was true. Of course Upton, who knew history as well as economics, couldn't say that. It was one of the
many American forms of Socialism!

He tried to write the book as Gillette wanted it; but there

again a clash developed. Upton had a sense of form, of structure; he wanted to begin at the beginning and proceed step by step, proving each point and then going on to the next. But that was not the razor king's way. He would take the first chapter, which Upton had carefully constructed, and bring it back three days later, with writing in between every line, and with the top and bottom margins covered solid with fine writing, done with a sharp lead pencil. Mr. Gillette tried to put the whole book into the first chapter; it was all so important, nothing of it could wait for the second!

And that went on until the manuscript became illegible. That was all right, because at home Gillette had a secretary who had nothing to do but sharpen his lead pencils and make a new clean copy. But my impatient husband said to me, "I can't go on with this forever, and apparently Gillette can. My time had better be spent on my own work."

I said I was sorry for this truly good rich man whose heart was wedded to his world-saving plan. "I'm wedded to my plan, too," said Upton.

"Yes, but yours is the same as his."

"Yes, but I can help the world with one of my books," declared Upton, "while I'm never to be allowed to help it with Gillette's. That makes a world of difference."

I realized that Gillette valued the chance to come twice a week and tell his plan to people who understood it. For five hundred dollars a month, I was willing to listen and Gillette would be glad to double the price. But Upton's answer was that he wouldn't stand it for a million a month! He was going to write his own books, and in his own way.

So he told Gillette that he had done all he could, and Gillette sadly took his bulky manuscript and got someone else to help him. We had a visit from him now and then, and when the book was done, Upton wrote his publisher friend, Horace Liveright, about it. Horace accepted it, and Gillette put up twenty-five thousand dollars for advertising of the book, although he felt that it should sell without a line of advertising because the world had been waiting for it. Alas, even with the advertising it had very little sale.

10. THE RAVENS FED HIM

THE GREAT MUCKRAKING ERA in American history had drawn to a close. It had begun about the time I left boarding school, but I had known nothing about it until I met Upton Sinclair several years afterward. Such writers as the American Winston Churchill, David Graham Phillips, Ida Tarbell, Jack London, Lincoln Steffens, Ray Stannard Baker, Samuel Hopkins Adams, Ernest Poole and Upton Sinclair had spoken out against the corruption of politics by big business, which was poisoning our national life and threatening the constitutional rights which made our country a great democracy.

The American Socialists had always backed these reformers, circulating their writings and organizing meetings at which some of them spoke. The rank-and-file Socialists, the "Jimmie Higginses" as they were called, were dearly loved by my husband. They were "the people," whom all politicians claim to love, and who are truly loved by only a few. They supported all strikes as best they could and were punished for it. They were often dismayed by the strikers themselves, who only wanted higher pay for their own little group.

Here in California were the "I.W.W." (Industrial Workers of the World), who advocated "one big union," and for so doing were reviled and jailed. Yet many years later America's two great labor federations finally did become one.

All these forces, the muckraking writers, the Socialists, the then hard-pressed, unpopular labor unions, were merged—that is in the mind of the public—by the forces of reaction which lumped them together under the name of "the radical movement." In this movement were also included such alien and contradictory theories as anarchism, which advocated no law but each man's conscience, and Socialism, which advocated government ownership under democratic control. These theories were wholly unlike, dissimilar, except that all advocated a

change in the methods of big business by which the public was
bled, politics corrupted, and big business became bigger.

Despite these differences in theory, this "radical movement"
gave a great impetus to the rise of the "welfare state" which
was to follow later on, and to the labor unions as they gradually and painfully won power. The muckrakers had been the
voice of this movement; it was they who first made its purpose
articulate to those who did not want to hear—for the writers
had the prestige of letters, and sometimes of aristocratic background.

I understood this radical movement and my heart belonged
to it. I loved my husband because his heart had always belonged to it and had refused every temptation to desert it. But
at times it was hard for both of us—harder for me than for him,
for his was a lion's heart while mine was that of a rabbit.

To deny myself physical comforts was not so very painful,
because I was young and strong. But I was full of resentment
when Upton was ridiculed and grossly misrepresented by the
"kept press," ostracized and discriminated against by petty local
politicians, and spurned by rich women whose standards of
morality were based on the conspicuous display of wealth.

I had been indignant when some of Mrs. Gartz's friends had
told her that she was "dishonoring the name of her father, the
founder of the great Crane Company, by associating with a
Socialist like Mrs. Upton Sinclair." So when I went to her
weekly luncheons I deliberately challenged the friends by ele-
mentary lectures on Socialism and the rights of labor. And my
hostess, now my good friend, gave me her powerful endorsement—which strengthened my rabbit's heart and won my deep
affection.

She had told me how, as a young matron, she had gone to a
great office building with her father one night and had seen
for the first time, women, mothers of children, clad in dirty,
dingy clothes, crawling with their scrub-pails across the floors
on which men had walked and spat all day! She had never forgotten it, and her blue eyes filled with tears even now as she
told of it. So she was able to understand what Upton and I

were speaking out for. She, too, took fire, and now began to speak out, as she had never done before.

Frederick C. Howe, who was President Wilson's Commissioner of Immigration, came on a visit to Los Angeles and wrote to Upton. It was he whose bungalow in the snowclad woods of Croton had been our home one winter. Upton invited him to Pasadena, and I asked Mrs. Gartz if she would like to meet him. She said she would—her brother, Charles R. Crane, knew him well. I invited her to dine with us, and then sent Upton to buy a beef roast, some potatoes and celery. I had no icebox, so I could not have ice cream, but when Upton returned he brought with him several boxes of graham crackers and other cookies. Company was an excuse for more cookies than he usually allowed himself.

It was the first "formal" dinner I had ever attempted. Upton always cooked our steaks in a frying pan, and I do not know why I was inspired to try roast beef. He left for Los Angeles to fetch our old friend, Fred Howe, and I beautified our living-room table with a bowl of cream-colored roses. I had no china and no silver, no tablecloth, no cloth napkins, but I polished our few pieces of plated ware, and laid out our heavy earthenware plates, with paper napkins beside them.

Then I went to put on the roast. We had a "biscuit pan" in which we toasted our shredded wheat when the weather was damp, so I laid the roast in it and put it into the oven with no water to keep it from sticking to the pan. I put the sweet potatoes into the same pan, without peeling them. I had meant for Upton to bring white potatoes, but he had seen some yellow yams at the small grocery near us, and bought them instead.

I had the idea that it took a long time for a roast to cook, so I felt free to leave it until our guests arrived. I had no idea how long that would be, nor how hot our small gas oven was. I went upstairs and read some manuscripts and then dressed and waited on the porch for the company.

When Mrs. Gartz came she said it was too bad my kitchen was so close to the living room—she could smell the meat cooking. She opened a couple of casement windows and sat near them. Then Upton and Fred Howe came, and Upton hurried off to the kitchen, exclaiming, "The roast is burning!" It was—but just a little. He brought it to us on a platter with the butcher knife and fork he had used to dislodge it from the biscuit pan. The potatoes had also been pried loose; they were black on the outside, but not inedible when you cut them open.

Our guests continued to chat calmly, while Upton struggled to carve the roast. He finally gave each of us a thick slice of half-dried beef, and completely dried potatoes. I left for the kitchen, remembering that I had not made the coffee, and I was glad to stay there while Upton made jokes about my cooking. No one could cut even a potato without a struggle, and soon no one tried to keep from laughing.

I came with the coffee, and after a taste or two Mrs. Gartz made no further pretense of drinking it. She said, sweetly, "Everything is very nice, but next time, bring your company to *my* house. I have a cook, and you shouldn't have to be one!"

Fred Howe and Upton ate celery and sweet cakes cheerfully, and talked about world affairs as if they had feasted; but I was miserable the rest of the evening. The first time was the last time I ever tried to cook a meal, though finally I did learn to make the thick vegetable soup which became our chief article of diet.

Mama and David came to California on another visit. David was going to spend the summer with us, and said he would miss swimming at Ashton Hall. He asked why we couldn't have a swimming pool, and Upton told him he could have it if he would dig it. The two of them went to work with zeal, because Upton also wanted a "swimmin' hole." David insisted it must be deep enough to dive in, and Upton wanted it long enough to turn around in. So they labored happily until the pit was dug, and a cement man came to complete the job. After this, life was one noisy party after another until schooltime.

Mama stayed only long enough to satisfy herself that I was happy, and to be entertained by Mrs. Gartz at a luncheon, where she and her hostess mourned together over the austerity of life in the Sinclair household. David also found it austere by comparison with that of the harum-scarum Greenwood family, and went back happily to attend school with my young brothers.

When Upton finished *The Coal War*, it began the rounds with publishers. Mr. Brett turned it down, and so did half a dozen others; it was too factual to be a good novel, and, as in the case of *King Coal*, nobody was interested in a labor war when they had a constantly more ominous World War to read about twice a day.

Upton had been pondering the causes of war all his life, and the various groups in society which profited by them. The groups which seemed to him to represent the greatest betrayal were those who went to war in the name of the Prince of Peace. And so he set to work on a new book, *The Profits of Religion*. I did not like either the title or the book, for I knew that both would be misunderstood.

I knew that Upton was a deeply religious man, and considered himself that. He believed in the spiritual nature of life, and had written more than once that "an atheist is as dogmatic as the Pope." In his student days he had taught himself Latin, Greek, German, French, and Italian by reading the New Testament in those languages and all through his books are Biblical quotations. What he objected to was the use of this proletarian carpenter, this friend of the poor and lowly who had nowhere to lay his head, as a shield for privilege, a buttress for exploiting classes.

His book is a history of nineteen hundred melancholy years, in which the example and teachings of Jesus have been distorted in order to keep the poor humble and submissive and the rich glorious and safe. Such a book is, of course, easy to misunderstand and to misrepresent, especially if you do not get as far as the closing chapters in which the author sets forth a vital religion for the young rebels of the time. The book was acclaimed by ministers of the gospel such as John Haynes Holmes, but also by scoffers such as H. L. Mencken.

Many visitors came now, and they were of many kinds. Some, like Sinclair Lewis, who had been the furnace man at Upton's

Helicon Hall Colony, were too interesting to be considered "interruptions." "Hal," as Upton called him, brought his first wife with him, and she and I sat still and listened to the two friends who had shared the pleasures and displeasures of "co-operative" life—which, as they agreed, had ended in one individual, Upton, paying all the bills after the place burned down. This was the way "co-operation" often ended, so I was naturally a bit doubtful as to its feasibility. "Hal" was one of those who wrote enthusiastic letters about *The Profits of Religion* when it appeared.

Upton had never been a "peace-at-any-price" man; he favored wars of self-defense, and wars in defense of other countries having democratic institutions. As early as 1907, in *The Industrial Republic,* he had predicted that the German Kaiser would start a war of aggression and that the United States would be drawn into it. To prevent that catastrophe, he and Dr. van Eeden had advocated an international movement of labor to pledge a general strike in all countries to prevent the start of a war. The crux of this problem was Germany, of course; and Upton had an exchange of correspondence on it with Karl Kautsky, intellectual leader of the German Social-Democracy, who said that such a movement could not be attempted in that country; it would be high treason. "Perhaps after a defeat in war," he said, "but not before."

"What that amounts to," said Upton, "is that you, a Socialist, must want Germany defeated in a war." A few months later Upton visited Kautsky's home in Berlin and threshed out the question with him and his wife and son, and this point of view was frankly confirmed. But when the Kaiser ordered his troops to march, the German Social-Democracy proved to be what van Eeden had sadly predicted, German, not Socialist.

However, the Socialists of America went on clinging blindly to their faith in "peace at any price." Many of them, like Victor Berger, were more German than Socialist; no matter how many *Lusitanias* the Kaiser's submarines might sink, Deutschland must remain *ueber alles.* So, when Upton had fully made up his mind, he drafted a manifesto of resignation from the Socialist

Party of America and it was signed by a number of the intellectual leaders, including J. G. Phelps-Stokes, William English Walling, and W. J. Ghent.

I was with Upton through this period of decision, and I saw the careful study he gave to the issues. I read what he wrote and sometimes revised it, and I knew many of the people with whom he exchanged views. When the hour of decision for our country came, I was on the platform with him at a mass meeting in the Pasadena High School, when he was jeered by the Socialists and cheered by a group of patriots. Mrs. Gartz was also on the platform, although I knew that she was against every word that Upton said. This situation was to endure for a quarter of a century—she would disagree with us constantly, but we continued to be close friends.

At this meeting Upton outlined a program to keep the peace of the world after this war was won: an "Internation" with real power, and the internationalization of all those border territories which had been bones of contention throughout modern history. The Los Angeles *Times* published a full account of this meeting and the Associated Press carried it. He sent a telegram to President Wilson urging that the Allies be required to agree to this program as a condition of our support in the war. Alas, Wilson did not take this precaution.

The Russian Tsardom was overthrown and the Socialist, Kerensky, became Premier. This event was hailed with delight by every sort of liberal in the world. It was the coming of a new age, and there was no limit to our expectations—

> Bliss was it in that dawn to be alive,
> But to be young was very Heaven.

However, it soon appeared there was a Satan in that Heaven, and a great number of his imps, known as Bolsheviks. The Satan's name was Lenin; we had never heard of him but read that he had been hiding in Switzerland and the Germans had shipped him home in a sealed train, so that he could make trouble in Russia but not on the way there.

What to think of all this was difficult indeed. Obviously, if our ally, Kerensky's Russia, could be overthrown by the Communists under Lenin, the Germans could then move all their forces to the West, and our task there would be doubled. The Russian people were starving and their armies were falling to pieces, with the troops deserting and going home, plundering on the way. We did our best to send help, but the only route was by way of Archangel, through cold seas haunted by the Kaiser's submarines. Under these conditions "agitators" could thrive in Petrograd and Moscow; apparently they wanted to make a separate peace with the Germans. What were we to make of them?

In New York was a widely-read weekly, the *Outlook,* edited by a clergyman, Lyman Abbott. He asked our ex-clergyman friend Albert Rhys Williams to go to Russia to report on it, and soon we had both Albert's articles and his personal letters. He was a big fellow, warm-hearted and naïve as to politics, as perhaps young ministers should be. He fell in love with all the Russians; it was his job as a reporter to meet them, high and low, and he did. In his articles he had to be more objective, but in his letters he poured out his enthusiasms to us.

When the Socialist government was overthrown and the dread Bolsheviks seized power, Albert was still there and saw the fighting. The cadets of the Military Academy were supporting the Kerensky government, and when the Bolshevik mob stormed their building, Albert, who knew the leaders on both sides, was able to intervene and arrange for a peaceful surrender—quite a feat for a visiting correspondent. He saw it all, and then came home by way of Siberia, and told us about it.

An Austrian in Los Angeles wrote Upton a furious letter, calling him all kinds of names, and threatening dire consequences if he continued to support the war. We made no reply, though the letter alarmed me. I told several friends, including Mrs. Gartz, so that if anything should happen to us, the police would know where to look for the perpetrator.

One or two more such letters came, and then one evening as we were dining with Mrs. Gartz and two of her friends, Dr. and Mrs. Melton, at the Hotel Maryland, a rough-looking man came into the lobby and peered at us from the dining-room door. After dinner Dr. Melton went out to call Mrs. Gartz's chauffeur, and the man stepped up to him and began to denounce Upton. He shouted in German, "Shame on you, who are a German, for being one of his friends!" Dr. Melton knocked him down, and then came back and told Mrs. Gartz that he had ordered the chauffeur to meet us at the side door. He did not tell us why until we were on the way home.

So I was really frightened when our telephone rang the next day and a snarling voice said to me, "I'm on my way to your house to kill Sinclair! I'll crush him like a louse!" I hurried to Upton's room and asked him to go out the back door at once and then to our next-door neighbor's house. "Wait for me there, and ask me no questions," I said.

Then I called Mrs. Gartz and told her what had happened.

Fifteen minutes later we were on our way to Los Angeles in her limousine, with Upton out of sight in a corner of the back seat. He wanted to ask the advice of Harry Carr, a newspaperman who had become a friend; for Upton wanted to avoid publicity as well as danger. A curious thing for the editor of the *Times* to take a liking to the man who was to write *The Brass Check*. But it was this Harry Carr who wrote in a letter to Upton, "I like you so much, but you make me so damn sore!"

And Upton knew that the one way to keep a secret from a newspaper was to entrust it to such a member of the staff.

Harry Carr went with him to the Los Angeles chief of police, for the Austrian lived in Los Angeles. The chief said Upton should buy a gun, and then report at once to the Pasadena police and get a permit. Upton did not like this advice. But he went to the Pasadena police station, and there was given the same advice. "You might be killed, and we don't want anything like that to happen in Pasadena!"

So Upton got a gun but I thought he might decide to talk peace to a mad dog. As a girl in the Delta I had never thought of danger, because my big, strong father had a shotgun and a rifle in the hall closet. But here in Southern California there were periods when I found it hard to think of anything but danger.

Once Upton had made up his mind that our country could not stand apart while others poured out their blood in defense of democracy, he put his whole heart into doing what he could to insure victory. But of course victory was not enough —for after it there must be what enlightened thinkers in Britain were calling "a clean peace," or there would again be world war. He decided that a monthly magazine of his own would enable him to reach the readers of his books with his ideas of how to obtain that "clean peace."

When he presented this project to me my first thought was that it was so utterly out of the question that I would not have to worry about it; he would wake up from this nightmare without my help! So I smiled, made no answer and went about my household chores. But soon I was the one who had to wake up— for Upton had employed a full-time secretary, interviewed the parents of two nearby schoolgirls as to whether they could help address envelopes and agreed on the cost of printing with the manager of the local newspaper. Now he was composing a circular to be sent out to prospective subscribers!

"But," I cried, in consternation, "where is all this work to be done? In our living room?"

"You won't have to do a thing!" he answered. "I'll find a big second-hand table, and a couple of extra chairs—"

I stopped him in mid-flight as he soared off to heights of unbelievable extravagance. "You don't think that *'finding'* is all there is to getting those things, do you? How will you pay for them?"

"We haven't starved yet," he pleaded.

"No," I answered, bitterly, "but when we do, *you'll* starve alone! I refuse to go with you!"

Upton was an eloquent pleader—he should have been a defense lawyer. Now my life of moderate order and comfort, won by so many efforts, was turned into a daily debating society on the question of how to make the world *permanently* safe for democracy. Upton had no doubts as to how—it was through the conversion of humanity by means of a sixteen-page monthly magazine entitled *Upton Sinclair's: for a Clean Peace and the Internation.*

"We have everything necessary," he was pleading: "Credit with the local printer, a tip-top secretary, office help, even a perfect delivery service free of charge—a rainproof Dodge in which I can deliver the magazines to the post office—"

"Stop!" I cried. "You can't *have* it!"

But of course I hadn't married him in order to be just a housewife; he was a muckraker, a crusader, and that was why I loved him. And after all, I hated war and loved democracy, just as much as he did. What else was I in the world for, if not to help make it a more decent place for humanity? What is anyone here for, but this?

So I wrote Mama that I had dedicated her old Dodge to the cause of world peace! And then, late one night when all the rest of Pasadena was asleep, I poured out my heart in an editorial for the first issue of that small magazine:

Spring Song

My husband is going crusading again! Shall I go with him?

If you have never been poor and ill, and unable to buy the chance to rest, this will have no meaning to you—this talk of a Crusade. It will seem "crude," exaggerated. The poor are often that—especially those among them who have the intelligence to realize the devilish absurdity of poverty, in a world of abounding wealth.

My husband is going Crusading again! Shall I go with him? That is what I have been asking myself for the last four days. I have sat with fear and hesitation. It means to work sixteen hours a day, and then not be able to sleep because your mind is driving on. It means to risk your last dime, and maybe your last modicum of health.

I sit frowning over endless manuscript; and then I look out of the window, and oh, it is springtime out there! I see jonquils, and a breath of them floats to me with the warm sunshine; beyond are the mountains where I know there are trails calling for footsteps. Is not my duty there—when all my being yearns for sweet, calm hours under the skies? I am so weary of Crusades! May not this Crusade be deferred—just a little while?

Or is this, as my husband says, the supreme hour for the world, when to act on the call of conscience may be to answer the need of the whole world? Is it, as he says, no time to think

of beauty, peace, and health, when young men are going to face
the cannon, answering the call of their conscience?

My husband and I are going Crusading together!

There was no limit to the speed with which Upton
worked when his heart was in a job—and he never undertook a
job that his heart was not in. Here was the civilized world being
deluged in blood; the world's youth was giving it on the battlefields, and Upton thought he could contribute at least his own
vital energy. His circular announcing the magazine would be
ready for the printer before I could buy a table and chairs on
which the schoolgirls could work at addressing envelopes and
stuffing them.

With Upton as chauffeur, I hurriedly made the rounds of
the dingy used-furniture stores, and finally found a marvelous
bargain—the most enormous dining-room table I had ever seen,
made of cherry and larger even than the walnut one I had sold.

My next errand was to find an office large enough to hold the
table and the girls. Of course it would be another old house to
move. I was in the real-estate business once more! I hired a
schoolboy to drive me, and went in search of another second-
hand house. A considerable distance from our home, I found a
two-room affair that had once been part of a larger house; someone must have bought the other half and moved it away. The
remaining half was in good enough condition to keep out wind
and rain. The owner lived next door, and had apparently not
known what to do with it.

"You may have it for seventy-five dollars, provided you'll pay
for the moving," he said.

I paid him, then hurried off and got our old carpenter. He
said he could get a man to help him roll some big rocks in place
for the foundation, to save the cost of the customary concrete wall.

"Then move it as quickly as you can. In the meantime I'll
buy that lot next door to put it on."

"That lot ain't worth nothin'," he told me. "It's all sand and
rocks. You couldn't grow a potato on it!"

But I didn't want to grow potatoes, so I bought the lot. In a few days we had two plastered rooms with a homemade sign reading "Office."

The subscription list continued to grow, and Upton's world-saving hopes likewise. The piles of mail increased, and many readers inquired as to where copies of *The Jungle* could be obtained. It had been out of print for several years, so Upton had bought the plates and now decided to reprint it. Soon we would be in the book-publishing business!

Another house was bought, this time for fifty dollars. Still the magazine and book business grew, and letter-files and card catalogues and tables and desks and bookcases piled up, and again and again the neighbors were astonished to see another house come rolling up our street. The structures were joined end to end: the study, at the left, dark green; the first house, yellow; the second house, gray; the third house, white. The last house, terracotta, was torn to pieces to patch up the cracks and joints, and so the whole structure looked like a camouflaged battleship on the way to France. It was assuredly the most wonderful architectural spectacle since the days of Noah's Ark. The fame of it spread, not merely over the millionaire city of Pasadena, but to all the surrounding country, and on Sunday afternoons a procession of people in automobiles came by to stare.

In the early numbers of the magazine were three sonnets signed with my initials, "M. C. S." Then there were no more; when readers asked for more Upton explained that M. C. S., wan and anxious, was busy racing back and forth all day as yard-boss, making life miserable for two carpenters and a plumber who were performing the hitherto undreamed-of feat of telescoping five houses into one—and without disturbing the wrapping, pasting and addressing of magazines and books that was going on in all the houses.

The price of the monthly magazine was ten cents, or one dollar a year. The circulars went out and right away our mail was full of dollar bills; some people sent us lists of names, with checks for five or ten dollars. Upton, in his usual fashion, was "rich" at once; we would have money to pay the girls, the printer and the post office—I had nothing to worry about any more. Go and get a larger house, for very soon we'd have half a dozen girls! He left it to me because he had to write the magazine, everything in it.

He brought me his editorial which was to occupy the front page, in twelve-point type. The time was April, 1918, and American boys were lining up, getting ready to drive the Germans out of France. The opening paragraph read:

> "This is the hour of a world decision; the greatest crisis which ever has confronted mankind. Upon the course of history during the next few months depends your whole happiness, your whole future. No matter who or what you are, no matter what you wish to do or be, what you wish your children or your children's children to do or be—all depends upon this world decision."

He meant, of course, what we were to do with our victory, which he knew we would win; what we would do, and force our allies to do, if we had the clearness of vision.

In the first issue he reprinted the circular he had written in 1909, which van Eeden and a number of other eminent Europeans had signed, urging the labor movements of the various countries to *prevent* the next war by holding out the threat of a general strike. He told how the idea had been welcomed in Britain, France and half a dozen other countries, but absolutely rejected in Germany. So he insisted that the democratic world must defeat German autocracy. "But at the same time," he wrote, "we propose to hold out to the German people the hand of friendship, the promise of a Clean Peace and the International." By the "Internation" he meant, of course, the League of Nations which our country refused to join at the end of the war, thereby rendering it impotent, and make World War II inevitable.

Before publication there were friendly warnings. George Sterling reminded us that California was called the graveyard of periodicals—"But then all the other states are." And Mencken wrote:

"What we need in this country, beyond everything else, is absolutely free discussion. At the moment, of course, it doesn't exist. You will be barred from the mails if you are not very careful."

Our little magazine was printed on good 9 x 12 book paper. When it was mailed to all the subscribers and to thousands of other persons likely to be interested, letters poured in, and we sat up half the night opening and reading them. Some praised and some blamed, but none were neutral. William Bross Lloyd, millionaire Socialist and pacifist of Chicago, wrote: "You are a renegade from the Socialist movement, a deserter in the face of the enemy. . . . You go, in my mind, with Judas Iscariot and Benedict Arnold." A local lawyer wrote: "Anarchism! I.W.W.! Beautiful for Pasadena!" An anonymous critic wrote: "I could punch the pith out of a horsehair, and put your brains inside, and hear them rattle!"

On the other hand there came laudatory letters from Mencken, Colonel Edward M. House, Louis F. Post (then Assistant Secretary of Labor), William Allen White, John Haynes Holmes and Senator John Sharp Williams. John Sharp wrote to Upton:

"Dear Husband of My Cousin: You may call me 'yours' all you please, because I think you are honest, and I do not care for much else in the world. I have read your article on 'A Clean Peace' and I send you back in this enclosure the article with lead pencil marks on the side to indicate the part that I agree with."

This letter was important to us because of what happened to the magazine in Washington. In order to obtain second-class postal rates on our magazine we had to file an application at the Pasadena post office, with samples of the magazine. These had to be sent to Washington; in the meantime, we had to pay first-class rates—many times higher—on our first issue. We would get the difference back when our application was granted. But we waited and waited, with no decision. We worried a lot, because we just didn't have the money to pay the higher postal rate on the next issue—we wouldn't even be able to have it printed unless we could be sure of getting the large refund from the post office. We besieged Washington with telegrams, and at last word came; the second-class entry was refused, on the ground that our magazine was held to be seditious!

I telegraphed to my cousin John Sharp Williams, who, for a Southerner, had been surprisingly liberal. He argued all his life for government ownership of railroads, and was the Senate whip for President Wilson's reform program. He claimed the honor of having sponsored the precedent-shattering provision for an income tax. He called himself a "Jeffersonian" Democrat, meaning not that he had followed Jefferson literally, but had tried to meet the problems of our time in the spirit of Jefferson. In time he would refuse to stand as a candidate for re-election to the Senate because of his dismay at the failure of our country to join the League of Nations.

Now there came a long letter from Senator Williams, saying that he had gone straight to Burleson of the Post Office Department—who came from Texas, and so understood Southern talk. Burleson had shown him a copy of the magazine with the passages marked to which objection had been taken. John Sharp went off and prepared "a thirteen-page brief," answering the objections. One of his replies was, "I will take those words to the President and I will eat my hat if he doesn't say the same thing."

I had also telegraphed the other Mississippi Senator, James K. Vardaman, who was an interesting character. A Texan, he had come to Mississippi to start a newspaper which he spoke of as "iconoclastic." The planter class despised him, charging him with ushering in the era of "nigger-hatin'" which has disgraced our state for a half-century. Vardaman knew all the prejudices of the poor whites, because he had been one. He saw a way to fame and fortune by playing upon these prejudices, and he set himself up as champion of the poor, who were in the majority and who despised the Negroes, their economic rivals. This was the opinion of the planter class, which controlled the Negro and resented what they called Vardaman's demagoguery. He went to the United States Senate on a campaign promise to bring about the repeal of the 15th Amendment.

Vardaman had married a rich widow and bought a home

next door to us in Greenwod. There was a high board fence on our side of the property line that had stayed through my childhood. Then one night a violent wind blew the fence down. In the morning I went out to see the wreckage, and standing on the other side was our neighbor. I was a young lady then, and on an impulse of sociability to this handsome and magnetic person, I said, "Let's take it away." He answered, "Let's," and we called our servants and had it done. Now I was repaid for this; Senator Vardaman wrote that he, too, had intervened for us.

Upton had telegraphed also to Colonel House, who replied: "Your recent telegram was forwarded to me while I was in Washington and I happened to be with the President when it arrived. I read it to him and I hope some result may follow." With all this powerful help, we got the second-class entry!

The next issue of the magazine, dated "May-June," started off with a column headed, "Our Smiles to the Censor." It contained a lovely letter from H. G. Wells in his own hand, and we published it in facsimile, along with his caricature of Lenin. In the course of months we published letters from Gertrude Atherton, Frank Harris, Israel Zangwill, Sinclair Lewis, Eden Phillpotts, Newton D. Baker, Luther Burbank, E. A. Ross, Will Levington Comfort, Eugene V. Debs, Charmian London, Norman Angell, Ellen Key, John Haynes Holmes, Minnie Maddern Fiske, Ryan Walker, Louis Untermeyer, Frederik van Eeden. W. L. George, Helen Keller. I submit that is a list any magazine might boast of. We had extensive debates with John Reed, Mencken and Sir Arthur Conan Doyle. We published poems by Maxwell Anderson, George Sterling, and the editor's no-longer-beautiful wife.

I enjoyed working with the carpenters, who were old men, full of wry humor and the milk of human kindness. The only trouble I had was when I wanted to do something they did not approve, as when I insisted on more windows for the lighting of desks and tables than was customary in a certain size room. I would say, "Can it be done? Just tell me that."

"Oh, yes, it *can* be, but no one ever did before." This, of course, was against the philosophy which guided our lives;

Upton and I worked every day to do something that had never yet been done—the ending of poverty and war.

While the ultimate decisions which made history should be those of the people, Upton knew that one man could and usually did show the way. And I had faith in Upton's ability, for I had seen him change the lives of the working people in the Chicago stockyards, as well as the quality of the meat the public ate. Of course he had help before it was over—he even won the support of the President and Congress. But it was he who had driven them to action. All the muckrakers had worked alone at first and I knew what great things they had done for our country.

So, no matter about new clothes, or a better house to live in, until that office was in order.

When the carpenters wanted to install floor furnaces, because everybody else did, I found that we could buy small second-hand wood-burning stoves for a fraction of the cost, and burn the scrap lumber with which the place was littered. But I had to make the fires every day, and take out the ashes, and Upton had to gather and bring in the wood. Such chores were not in themselves tiring, but when they had to be done in haste while a dozen similar ones were waiting, it added up to drudgery. When night came, we were tired! But there was still work to do, such as signing letters or revising manuscript. This was Upton's job, while I wrote memos for the next day.

Mrs. Gartz, an increasingly vocal pacifist, naturally thought our magazine was a tragedy. Both her sons were in the service, and we could not help feeling great pity for her. She was desperately unhappy and spent most of her time, and a considerable amount of money, in support of groups opposing the war. She bailed out conscientious objectors when they were jailed, and gave money to their families. It was a difficult time indeed for friends to hold opposite opinions.

One day I was at work in our basement when a pleasant-faced young man appeared in the open door.

"Hello," he said, breezily. I was used to informal and unexpected callers; I waited a moment to see what he had to say for himself, and when he said nothing, I asked, "What do you want?"

"Oh, nothing much," he said, casually. "I'm your new neighbor."

I was not appeased, for he had startled me by coming noise-lessly to the obscure back door of the house. "Do you know my husband?" I inquired.

"No," he answered, still casual.

"Well, he is not at home; and he doesn't see visitors without an appointment."

"I'd just as soon talk to you," he informed me, hastily. "I'm not after Mr. Sinclair. I'm after Mrs. Gartz. I want to talk to you about her. It is very important."

"Go upstairs the way you came down—by the outside stairs. I'll meet you on the front porch. I'll be glad to talk to you about my dear friend."

He thanked me, and I met him on the porch and invited him to a seat.

"I won't take much more of your time," he said. "I've sized you up, and I think you will tell me the truth—in the name of our country. I'm a federal agent."

I laughed with relief. At least he was not a lunatic. "Ask me anything you want to," I said.

"Then tell me, is she a German sympathizer, or just a plain fool?"

"To use your language, she's just a plain fool," I replied—for this was his idea of a woman who cared only for an ideal!

He rose, thanked me and walked away. That evening an old acquaintance, the official host from the Hotel Maryland, came and cautiously began talking about my friend, Mrs. Gartz. I soon realized what he was doing and I laughed. He blushed and asked why.

"Because I'm amused," I answered. "I know what you are fishing for. She is neither a German agent nor a German spy. Is that satisfactory?"

He was embarrassed, and answered, apologetically, "I don't like this job. But I must see it through. Please take me to call on her, won't you?"

"That won't be necessary—she isn't hard to see. I'll make a date for you right now"—and I called Mrs. Gartz. "There's a federal agent here who wants to talk to you. May I send him up?"

"No," she answered, mildly, "I'm ready to leave to attend the opera."

"But you mustn't refuse to see a federal agent," I told her.

"Oh, well," she answered, in a bored tone, "send him on up— I'll take him with me, and convert him on the way."

The next day she reported to me, "I took him to the opera, and I tried to convert him, both going and coming. But isn't it funny, I can't convert anybody!"

For the first time in her life, she was taking some of the snubs which true crusaders have to endure. She was amazed when her banker—who saw the checks she was signing for those who were working against a continuation of the war—asked her firmly to remove her account to some other bank.

Her two sons in the service, the idols of her heart, opposed her, insisting that German militarism must be overthrown or it would engulf the world. Her brother Richard wrote, "If we do not stop the Germans this world will not be a fit place for human habitation." Her younger son, the dearest human being on earth to her, had first gone in as a volunteer, driving an ambulance for the French. He wrote eloquently from the front, trying to comfort her, and explaining that "the longer we stay in, the better will be our chances of a humanitarian settlement." But she could see only the horror of war and the risk she ran of losing both her sons.

On the whole, our effort in behalf of "a clean peace" was progressing well. We were taking subscriptions at the rate of a thousand a month, which meant a thousand dollars; and it took several months before we could believe that we were actually paying out more than we were taking in! And then Upton went to the hospital.

He had been working day and night, at a breakneck speed, and now Nature exacted her price. After the surgeon operated, Upton was told he must stay in the hospital for a while to rebuild his strength. This would have been a severe punishment for a man of his impulsive temperament, if he had not acquired the reading habit in his childhood. He read steadily, and then supplied several thousand words of book reviews for the next issue of the magazine. Also, with the help of his secretary, he read and answered his mail every day. Everything else was handled by me and the office force, as best we could.

In the midst of many worries, Upton had a new inspiration—or whatever name you choose to give to an idea which comes as a sort of illumination in the mind. He was in contact, both personally and by mail, with numbers of Socialists, old and young, who had made peace their religion and war their hell, but who now were either changing their minds or refusing to change them, and in either case undergoing mental strains and moral agonies. What a theme for a novel, portraying these people and their reactions in the greatest crisis that had come to modern man!

American Socialists had a name for the humble party worker who was never seen or heard on a platform, but who did all the drudgery that built the Party—attending meetings, distributing leaflets, putting up posters, selling books. His name was "Jimmie Higgins." Now some of these Jimmie Higginses were in jail as pacifists and others were in the Army; in either case they were arguing and worrying, doing their best to solve new problems. So now Upton wanted to celebrate in a novel these humble people, their hopes and dreams, sacrifices and activities. He told his readers that the next issue of the magazine would contain the first chapter of *Jimmie Higgins Goes to War*.

This opening chapter brought a letter of unbounded delight from Eugene Debs, then a prisoner in the Atlanta penitentiary for his opposition to the war: "It is the beginning of a great story, a story that will be translated into many languages and be read by eager and interested millions all over the world." That was the sort of letter that Upton liked to get! It was followed by one from Gertrude Atherton, who stood close to the opposite pole of thinking. Upton printed both. And now, when she saw us struggling so hard to hold on to our magazine, Mrs. Gartz came again, urging us to let her make a contribution—to *it,* not to us, she carefully explained. She reminded me that I had been helping her by editing letters of protest. So I told Upton he should let her pay our present debt to the printer.

On November 11, 1918, the last shot of World War I was fired, the Germans surrendered unconditionally, and the Armistice was signed. The American people went wild with joy—including ourselves and our dear friend, Mrs. Gartz. We rejoiced as much as she did; and we had a double reason—peace on "unconditional" terms could mean "a clean peace and the International," and no more war forever. That is what our magazine was for; and when President Wilson went to the Paris Peace Conference, we felt that it was the greatest crisis in human history, and we redoubled our efforts to make it clear to our readers: that and the struggle for justice for the working people, which we saw going on both at home and abroad.

In the December issue of the magazine Upton addressed the Merchants' and Manufacturers' Association of Los Angeles, which had issued a manifesto warning labor that it must not get the idea that war wages could be paid in peacetime. Upton warned these gentlemen to "wake up quickly from this perilous dream." He told them: "The wave of labor revolt, which began in Russia, and is now rolling over Austria and Germany, is a movement that will not be stopped by any barriers of mountain or sea; it will spread wherever the human heart protests against servitude."

But the strain of editing and running a magazine and at the same time writing a highly emotional novel threatened to send my frail husband back to the hospital. It was breaking both of us. All the fine letters couldn't make up for the fact that we were running "in the red," physically and financially. It was just impossible for any magazine to exist without advertising! But we had bound ourselves to our ten thousand subscribers; the first ones had received ten copies—but what about the later ones, who had received only one or two copies? We would have to refund their money; and where would we get it? We would owe six thousand dollars.

Upton, to look at and talk to, is the most "utopian" man I

ever knew; but he is something of a strategist and his "inspirations" are not only literary—he can come down to earth and be practical. There came a letter of praise for *Jimmie Higgins* from Haldeman-Julius, publisher of the weekly *Appeal to Reason*. Upton said to me, "Maybe that is our out." He wrote Julius explaining that he wanted time to work on the novel, and would Julius care to take over our ten thousand subscribers and send *his* paper to them, and publish in it the rest of *Jimmie Higgins*—about three-quarters of it still to be written? When that novel was done, Upton could easily furnish enough copy to fill up a weekly newspaper page.

It would be impossible to portray our relief when there came an acceptance of that offer. "Manuel," as we called him, agreed to call the back page of his four-page paper "Upton Sinclair's," and to pay us fifty dollars a week for it. Instead of having a weekly deficit of a hundred and fifty dollars, we would have enough to pay the secretary who would take the dictation of the new page. The cardfiles were boxed and shipped to Girard, Kansas.

Upton's inspiration had got us out of the magazine business but not out of debt, and I had two unfinished houses on my hands! I must forget everything else now and sell something, and get some money. I decided to move out of the "perpendicular house," into the one which had "all the rooms on the ground." This would enable me to sell the perpendicular house.

Our fine, trustworthy secretary had proven himself a true friend. I offered him, in part payment for his services, one end of the still unfinished "office" as a home for himself, his wife and baby. Upton and I would live in the other end. This would save us some money, for rents were high now, due to the shortage of men and building materials.

Six newspaper columns, in small type, every week for five years; and six big books written during the same time—*Jimmie Higgins, 100%, The Book of Life, The Brass Check, The Goosestep, The Goslings*—this was the program before Upton. These books went all over the world, some in a score of translations. The bound volumes of the *Appeal* are today too big for me to handle, but Upton leafs them through and reminds me of things which both of us had entirely forgotten, and would have denied as having happened. For example, in the second issue of the paper, an article headed "Good-Bye, Teddy," told of the arrival of a letter from Ex-President Roosevelt on the day that the morning papers reported his burial at Oyster Bay. Like a voice from the grave, the letter read:

Dear Sinclair:

Perhaps I shall be less shocked by your book "The Profits of Religion," than you imagine—although I will not guarantee this! I have an idea that I often use dogma or theology or ecclesiasticism where you would use religion, which to my mind is an entirely different thing.

Faithfully yours,
T. Roosevelt.

And so Teddy Roosevelt agreed with me that Upton was careless in his choice of words.

It was winter, and Henry Ford spent it on a hillside estate a couple of miles from our home. Upton wrote asking to see him, and an appointment was made. There were guards at the gates and at the house. We were told that Mr. Ford was in the garage "tinkering," and as that did not appeal to me I stayed in the car. Upton went in, and met Mr. Ford and his son, Edsel; the latter he described as a shy or perhaps subdued person, who seldom spoke and never disagreed with the old man. They had come upon a mystery in the garage; amid a lot of junk was a disused carburetor, of a type they had never seen before, and they were trying to figure out how it had worked. Upton knew that carburetors were found under the hoods of cars, but that was the extent of his knowledge, so he couldn't be of any assistance.

They had a chat and Henry said he liked to walk in the foothills and invited Upton to accompany him some afternoon. Upton went more than once, and they talked over many problems. Upton reported to me that this manufacturer of motorcars by the million was a strange combination of business autocrat and idealistic dreamer; he had ideas on almost any subject that was brought up, but unfortunately so many of his ideas were wrong. He believed that the remedy for poverty was the production of more and more quantities of material things, and so it was, said Upton, provided you could distribute them. To Henry, that word meant trucks and freight-cars to carry them; as to over-production and lack of purchasing power, all he could say was that the problem could be solved by education. Upton would ask, "But education for *what*, Mr. Ford? What are you going to *teach* about this problem?" But Henry wanted to leave that to education.

Also he had developed a strange mystical streak. He had been reading Jack London's *The Star Rover*, and had adopted the idea of reincarnation. He said, "We are living in the Eternal all the time." Upton was ready to admit that, but he didn't want that idea used to tangle up men's minds on the subject of social justice. He grieved at the thought of the "Flivver King" living in the Eternal, while oppressed workingmen, women and children so desperately needed him to live in Michigan politics, and in Wall Street finance and in Washington diplomacy.

However, Upton thought he had made an impression on this man of millions. Henry revealed that he had bought a broken-down weekly paper in Dearborn, Michigan; he was going to turn it into a national organ, in which social problems would be discussed freely and fairly. This was a fine idea, and Upton pointed out to me that when Henry really got an idea in his head, he showed no fear of ridicule or rebuke—his "Peace Ship," for example.

My hopeful altruist could not rest until he had done his utmost to teach Henry what to put in that paper. He told him about the ideas of King C. Gillette—a mere industrial baronet compared with a flivver king, but even so a member of the nobility. Henry said he would like to meet him and discuss the idea of "a people's corporation." Upton promised to bring them together some afternoon, and I was to play the hostess at my lumber-burning fireside.

I got an idea of the enormous importance which great wealth meant to Americans from the schoolboys who came to work on my place in the afternoon. When I told them that the great

Flivver King and the smaller Razor King were coming to call
that afternoon, they were in such a state of excitement that I
couldn't get them to work at all. They just wanted to stand by
the front drive so as not to miss that sight. And when the visitors arrived, one of the youngsters ran to my bedroom door and
whispered, "You are mixed up, Mrs. Sinclair! The little one is
the big king, and the big one is the little king!" They were
right, for Gillette was tall and massive, while Henry was slim.

Mr. Gillette was as ardent in behalf of his remedy for the
world's ills as Henry Ford was in behalf of more and better
gadgets. "Look at that poker," said the Flivver King. "If it stays
where it is it will soon be too hot to pick up. A hot poker causes
inconvenience enough to waste a lot of human energy. Save that
energy by inventing a heat-proof poker handle. It's the same
wherever you look—some labor-wasting device where a labor-
saving device is needed. The sum of all this wasted labor is
great. We must invent more and better things, and sell them at
lower prices."

"But who will sell at a lower price?" asked Upton.

"I will," said Henry.

"But look at the waste of competition," exclaimed Gillette,
"the small-scale manufacturing, and the advertising, in efforts
to persuade the public that one poker is better than the next!
What we need is a People's Corporation—the people will be the
owners, and they will not charge themselves high prices, nor
will they waste time and money and brains in competitive selling." Thus they argued for two hours, and no one converted
anyone. No one but the Razor King was depressed by the
wasted afternoon, for Mr. Ford was sure he had won the debate,
and Upton was sure that Socialism would win Mr. Ford, sooner
or later.

The two kings of industry departed, and I, who had sat still
and listened, was still wavering in my mind on the subject of
the best way to end poverty. With three such experts disagreeing, surely I could be excused.

"If you pay any attention to what the newspapers say
you'll have a very unhappy time in your life"—so President

Theodore Roosevelt had told Upton a dozen years ago. But Upton did pay attention on more than one harrowing occasion, and now the time had come when he was determined to make the newspapers pay attention to *him*. He would write a book about them, and whereas they had lied about him, he would tell the truth about them. He did not shrink from the tremendous amount of documentation and verification required by *The Brass Check,* his muckraking story of American newspapers. All I had to do was to try to prevent too many people from interrupting him.

When the bulky manuscript was completed, Upton took it to an old friend, Samuel Untermyer, who was wintering at the Hotel Huntington in Pasadena. He had long been the most highly-paid of Wall Street lawyers, and in spite of that was a staunch Democrat. He had served as counsel to the Pujo Committee of the United States Senate, investigating the monopoly control of credit, and he had subjected a string of the country's money lords, including J. Pierpont Morgan, to a relentless grilling.

This highly-paid lawyer read the manuscript of *The Brass Check* and gave his legal opinion, free of charge. "Upton, you can't possibly publish this book. It contains at least twenty criminal libels and a thousand civil suits."

"You mean my statements are not true, Mr. Untermyer?"

"No. I mean that you couldn't prove them."

Upton explained his attitude: he found out what was true, and then he told it, and was prepared to risk the consequences. It was the only possible way his work could be done. He had risked it with *The Jungle,* and later on had learned how J. Ogden Armour had spent three days and nights with his lawyers, avowing his determination to have the author of that book indicted for criminal libel. The lawyers had forced him to realize that he couldn't face the evidence that a muckraker might rake up.

Now the great Sam made a gesture of despair, and said, "All right, my boy, if that's the way you feel."

The printers in Hammond, Indiana, got the book into type, and soon there was a first edition of twenty-three thousand copies. When the first shipment reached Upton he took a copy to his friend Gaylord Wilshire. A few hours later he received an alarming telephone call. "Upton, it is absolutely inconceivable that the big powers will permit that book to be circulated!"

"How can they stop it?" asked Upton.

"They will find a way to stop it! They will call it criminal libel, sedition, anything! They will seize those books at your home, at the printers, anywhere they can find them. Take my advice and get those books scattered over the country! Ship them to bookstores, to Socialist groups, to old customers—anybody who will hide them!"

Upton took this advice; but it proved to be needless. There was no attempt to stop the book. There were a few denials but no suits of any sort. The scattering of the books was a calamity, for orders poured in upon Upton, and he had no books to fill them with! He ordered another printing, only to get the painful news that the printers were unable to get any more book paper. It was one of the postwar shortages. Upton began telephoning to Los Angeles, and learned that there was no paper to be had there, or anywhere. He wrote to several of the wholesale paper houses, trying to buy a little here, there, or anywhere—but all in vain. This was an agony to him—to have hundreds of orders pouring in by every mail, and be powerless to fill them. It was not merely a year's work being ruined, it was a war being lost!

Upton had often reminded me that the ravens came to feed Elijah, and now, providentially, one came fluttering down into our refabricated dwelling. Our old friend, Fiske Warren, arrived—and he was one of the largest paper manufacturers in the country. He protested that he had no book paper in stock—no paper of any kind, for that matter. "Then *make* some for us," Upton insisted. Fiske declared that his mills were booked six months ahead, and that pulp was as hard to get as finished paper; it would not be fair to his regular customers and stockholders if he gave precedence to a buyer so financially unimportant in the publishing world.

Before my muckraker gave up, Fiske had promised to let us have a carload of book paper in four months. However, before he could even book the order, we would have to put up the full price, five thousand dollars!

Upton paid another visit to Samuel Untermyer. He listened to the story, asked questions about Fiske, and about the printer, and then he said, all right, he would lend the five thousand. He wrote the check, and Upton came home convinced that not all rich men should be barred from heaven.

But there would be four months' wait before the carload of book paper would be ready; and Upton's mail was full of clamor from would-be customers. "I paid for the book—why don't you send it?" He still could not rest; he traveled over to Los Angeles and haunted the dealers, and gained a wonderful bit of information—the shortage, or boycott, did not extend to brown wrapping paper—"kraft paper," as it was known to the trade. Nobody but Elbert Hubbard had ever printed a book on that! Upton thought of it, and came home and told me he had paid his last dollar for half a carload of kraft paper, and it was on its way to the printers in Indiana!

The happy result was a delighted lot of customers—it was an adventure to own a brown-paper book which had been sub-jected to a boycott because it "contained twenty criminal libels and a thousand civil suits." It was a bit hard on the eyes, to be sure, but Upton put in a brown paper circular explaining how and why it came to be, and after that it was an act of piety to read it, and something to show to everyone you knew, and get them to read.

Of course the real reason for this book was to tell the public the truth about their newspapers, and to urge the men who gathered the news to form unions and stand together for the right to tell the truth. This Upton wrote in the last chapter of *The Brass Check*. Thousands of newspapermen read it, and in time there came into being the American Newspaper Guild. A hundred and fifty-five thousand copies of the book were sold in America, and it was translated into many languages.

We had debts to pay, but I determined first to get a coat of one color on the former office. Paint and painters were expensive, but so was the strain on my nerves of people riding by in cars and coming back for a second look at our house of many colors.

The long one-story building the carpenters had put together under my instructions was simply a row of rooms with a bare, multicolored front. But I had had the foresight to order the buildings at each end set crossways, to break the monotony. I had had the upper floor of the one-and-a-half-story tailor shop taken out and it looked like the inside of a country church.

I chose a pale rose, my favorite color. I had always meant to put a full-length gallery on the house, with white columns along its ninety-foot length. When I told Upton my plans, he was pleased. He had never liked that "circus" we were living in, and was as color-conscious as anyone else, he said; but he had taught himself to be happy wherever he was, if only he was allowed to help make a less unhappy world.

"If I buy some pink rose-vines will you plant them?" I asked.

"A whole row, ninety feet long," he promised. "And then my *himmlische Engel* will have them in bowls all over the house— it will be just like Greenwood!"

"Will you learn to dance?" I asked. "That old tailor-shop with the high ceiling and big rafters would be a lovely small-size ballroom."

Kitty came in, and when I told her what I planned, she gave a sigh of relief. "I'm certainly glad," she said. "Now won't you let me—?"

"No," I answered. "I'm going to be an oil princess soon. What you will have to do is to write me a letter of protest about my 'unearned wealth.'"

Her advice was, "Salt it away, and don't let *him* get hold of it!"

When the pink and white house was completed, and the long row of roses planted and flourishing, Upton was rejoicing in the luxury of a spacious roofed gallery. Here he could work outdoors without risk of sudden invasions of his person by swarms of red ants—and best of all, where the sprinkler system never drove him to a new location. On it he had a small typewriter table with a drawer which he could leave outside overnight, instead of bringing it indoors for protection from unexpected rainstorms. The converted tailor-shop, with its high, vaulted ceiling stained a walnut-brown, the walls white and the floor yellow, made a study fit for a king. "I feel like a king," he said, when he had moved his things in.

There was room for everything—his typewriter, an indoor table for it, and a foot-rest (constructed and painted by himself); also a huge old walnut desk with enough drawers to serve as letter files, and a couch. There was also an ancient table, large enough for his big dictionary when spread open, and for his violin and stack of music. This latter was something he had not had the use of since he lived in tents in the woods. Now it was in a room at one end of a ninety-foot house, while my room was at the other end so I would not hear the strange noises he called music!

Someday I would find enough used bookcases to hold his books, in their many foreign editions, as well as his library of reference books. There was space now for all the things a prolific writer needed for his work. I had watched him through the years, working and writing wherever he could find a place for himself and his typewriter—sometimes cramped in a corner of our bedroom, sometimes on an old rug spread on the ground in a rocky "garden," and often in a tiny kitchen where the frying-pan was apt to get in the way of his manuscript as he piled page after page on the only table. He had worked while carpenters were hammering over his head, or sawing boards in the next room, talking as they worked. I had always meant to get him out of this misery. Now he was out!

Our apricot trees which I had nursed to maturity were in bloom, and soon the little fig trees—cuttings when planted—had grown tall and wide. Soon they would be bearing his favorite fruit. Fruit was the food he most enjoyed, and he could almost make a dinner of it if he could get enough. He would soon have enough, for the peaches, too, were in blossom, and three Japanese guavas, the only trees I had bought, had already delighted us with their small bird-of-paradise blossoms and their strange, tangy fruit.

My share of the luxury was that I had got him out of my way, that we had a living room which was not used for a dining room, and that at last I had my own bedroom where I could keep my clothes separate from his. This was all I needed, for I was so enraptured with the garden I was planting that I did not want to stay in a house. There were to be star jasmines, delicate white blossoms which would perfume the whole place and remind me of home, Chinese lilies, hyacinths, jonquils, violets and lilacs; a honeysuckle vine in honor of my always generous cousin, John Sharp Williams, whose favorite flower it was, and one red rosebush for Jerry and a Marechal Neil rose for Papa! All of them would remind me of the garden in Greenwood. Upton would pick fruit while I picked flowers. "Paradise enow," indeed.

The economy of the country had been geared to war production, and now suddenly all that stopped. The result was "hard times," growing constantly harder, in spite of all the cheer-up talk in the press. Hard times were good for selling a book like *The Brass Check,* but not so good for getting paid for it. Many of Upton's customers went bankrupt, and others couldn't pay except in promises.

The treasurer of Upton's printers wrote him a pained letter; it had just been brought to his attention that we had run up a seventeen-thousand-dollar account, and the treasurer hoped something could be done about it. He had been writing us fatherly letters, realizing that we were amateurs sailing a stormy sea. Now apparently he decided that we needed a talking-to, and came all the way from Hammond, Indiana, to give it. He looked like a hard-bitten skinflint, but he was most kind. When I told him I would put a mortgage on this pink-and-white-icing cake, he laughed and said that was not the way to do business. We had risked too much, but of course our books were important, and we had paid them thirty or forty thousand dollars so far, and they valued the account. In short, the verdict was, "Not guilty, but don't do it any more!"

During the years following this visit Upton had some three million books and pamphlets made and shipped out by that firm; there was one edition of a hundred thousand copies (*Letters to Judd,* whose hero was my old carpenter); and another of two hundred and twenty-five thousand (*The Flivver King*). He must have paid the firm a couple of hundred thousand dollars, and it is interesting to know that never once did they object to a line in any manuscript. If outside pressure was ever put upon them, we did not know it. That is something to be said for freedom in America, and this freedom is the reason why my husband felt sure he could win his victories without violence. He believed in our form of government so firmly he could never be seduced by any form of dictatorship, no matter how plausible its pretenses. He would take his chances in free America.

Upton now had a regular book-publishing business, with a couple of secretaries and several office girls, all in our hillside home. We had bought back the "perpendicular house" and made it the office. He had a cardfile of twenty or thirty thousand individual customers, and sent them a four-page circular every two or three months, quoting opinions of his recent books and telling about the new one he was writing. He had a large correspondence, and people would report personal experiences and suggest other things for him to write. He had become what Ed Murrow later called him—"the king of the muckrakers"— and it was frightening to know how much raking there still was to be done. It seemed that there was no aspect of our life where there were not forces trying to repress our country's precious freedoms.

The "hard times" hurt me in two ways. There was Upton's large new debt, and Papa had felt a severe jolt. There had been a succession of those "bad years" which beset all cotton planters, and about which he had always warned my extravagant mother and her equally extravagant children. "I must have a backlog," he would repeat, patiently. "The boll weevil comes and wipes out a whole year's crop. I not only have no income that year, but I have lost the cost of feeding, housing, and clothing all the fieldhands, and the mules and horses, and my supply of cottonseed. I must supply all this again in order to make a new crop. Then if an overflow comes, I lose the new crop! Can't you see, Mama, my bank account isn't a fair gauge of my finances?"

But Mama would reply, "You still have all these rich lands, all your bank stock and brick store-buildings in two towns. Sell something. What is money for if not to use?"

So the lavish life of the romantic Old South had gone merrily on, not only in my family, but in most of the other families of that empire of King Cotton. Of course there would be a sad reckoning someday, if not in Papa's, then in the days of his heirs. The lands our people were so sure of would fall into new hands, and the "old families" of the South would go out into the cold, cold North to earn a living as best they could. How could they do it, when so few of them received any training in anything but raising cotton?

When Upton argued for "plenty for all," I sometimes asked why make of the future a place for idle playboys and girls to gambol in? I had seen too many of such grown-up children. They didn't just play; they got bored, or they got jealous, or angry, and then they became ugly and dangerous. I could more easily excuse the children of the slums, who became criminals for lack of the necessities and the common decencies of life, and for lack of guidance. But the wealthy classes furnished a goodly share of delinquents, the difference being that the police and their parents kept their misbehavior from being publicized.

Wipe out poverty, Upton said, and it would be only a matter of time before the increasing resources of men would be used in wiping out sin, sickness and perhaps even death. Who could say what resources lay within the mind of man?

"What about a real study of that mind *now?*" I asked.

"Well, you do that," my husband answered. "My talents are of a lower order."

More and more I was coming to realize that what *I* wanted to do was to study the mind, beginning with my own. "If only we could get out of debt," I told him, "and I could get time, then I would search for the answer to 'sin, sickness and death.' "

"Don't you see?" he laughed. "If only *we* could get out of debt! Let's get all of humanity out of poverty first."

We came to a sort of working agreement; while he worked

to abolish poverty, I would study psychology. By the time he had got rid of poverty in the world, I would know all about the hidden powers of my mind—and his! Then he could write a book, and tell the world how to put these powers of the mind to work. New inventions would follow, science would leap forward with the speed of light, or perhaps with the still greater speed now hidden in the mind. It would discover a cure for cancer, arthritis, polio and other scourges. We would range the skies on wings, as comfortably as his people in *The Millennium.*

Upton still put his trust in economics while I was reading and thinking about psychic research. There were powers, only glimpsed by researchers in that field, which might revolutionize the whole of human life. What about levitation, telepathy, hypnotism? I couldn't rest without knowing whether they were real and usable. When I said that to my husband, he would answer, "Let us compete. You find these powers before I work myself to death getting poverty out of the way. Mind you," he would add, "I don't say your researchers may not do it. I know enough about psychic phenomena to believe in the hidden forces of the mind. But while you search for them, I may beat you to the goal; I may persuade men to accept the fact that science has already made it possible for us to produce enough material wealth for all men to have plenty. If I do this first, it will release many able scientists for your kind of research."

"It's a bargain," I said. "Now let's pay off our debts, and not pile up any more. Then we can do our work in comfort. I'm so tired of being uncomfortable, and seeing you at work in a state of worry about unpaid bills. Let's get rid of poverty for *us* first! Let other people publish your books for a while."

"If only they would!" said Upton.

The sun was bright, and my heart was brighter, for my father was coming to see us! How I had missed him all these years; how tragic it was that loved ones had to be separated as he and I had been! It was a long journey in those days to California and back to Mississippi, and with the financial reverses he had suffered during recent years, it had been necessary for him to stay close to his business. But now at last he was coming.

When we met his train, I was shocked by the change in his appearance. His erect, easy way of carrying himself was gone; he seemed to be literally carrying a load on his shoulders, and in his soft, dark eyes were the shadows of care and strain.

Papa said I had done a good job with the old houses on the hillside, and he hoped I would never mortgage our home. Everyone should have "his own vine and fig tree." My rocky soil was just right for both, for they had taken root and spread upward and outward so fast that we wondered what we could do with the big crop that was now coming on.

"There is no more wholesome food than figs," Papa said. "I've made many a meal on them, in those days after the Civil War when I was trying to get my start in a law office, and had only a few dollars in my pocket. I suspect they are more than a fruit—they are a substitute for meat, just as beans and peanuts are."

"I'll take your suggestion this summer," Upton told him. "It will be a bumper crop, and I'll reduce our living expenses by doing justice to it."

And when summer came Upton ate figs raw, and he ate them cooked, morning, noon, and evening. When I protested that he might be undermining his health by having no proteins, he looked up the food content of figs in a government bulletin and discovered that there was considerable protein in them and more fat than in other varieties of fruit. The only supplement was one shredded wheat biscuit at each meal.

Before he left, Papa told me he was happy about us; I had married a good man. Then he said to Upton, "I'm not so conservative as you imagine. I've always been a Jeffersonian Democrat, you know; and this recent depression has made me do some thinking." Also, when they talked about the Civil War, he said, "It is better that we did not win,"—a statement I had never expected to hear from any Mississippian!

Those were strenuous days for liberals; and they stretched into weeks and months and years. The little group of men who ran Los Angeles County, with the help of the great newspapers, were desperate because of the trouble *The Brass Check* was still making, and they were ready to do almost anything to stop it. American Legion members raided a Socialist bookshop in Los Angeles and carried off a hundred and fifty dollars' worth of books—some of them Upton's, of course; and at once the newspapers broke out with an eruption of hints and threats. They reported that a number of copies of *The Appeal to Reason,* containing articles by Upton Sinclair, had been confiscated and were "handed over to the district attorney." Next day the report was that "a magazine writer of national reputation" was to be indicted; then, "a writer of international reputation is to be called before the grand jury tomorrow." The *Times* had a scare headline:

DRIVE LEADS TO "PARLOR" REDS
"Action of Two Well-known Men Next in Limelight
Local Inquiry Will Center Upon Them Tomorrow."

It happened that Max Eastman, Upton's old tennis friend from the Croton days, was visiting Hollywood at the moment, and he and Upton and Rob Wagner wondered which of them would be the lucky one to escape. Max had once been indicted for "sedition," tried and acquitted. Rob had been investigated for having hung a card in a tree to let a Chinese peddler know when he wanted to buy some vegetables. Upton led with two jail records, one for having played tennis on Sunday and the other for having "behaved as a perfect gentleman" in front of the office of Mr. John D. Rockefeller, Jr. The three tried among themselves to make fun out of it, but there was no fun in it for me.

Upton accepted an invitation to address the convention of a group advocating the public ownership of water power. Surely that was a harmless idea; but the gathering was to be in Santa Barbara, and the local newspaper there became excited over the resemblance of the nationalization of water power in California to the fabled nationalization of women in the new Soviet Union. It was surely a Bolshevik conspiracy, thinly camouflaged; in a day or two the newspaper reported that the legionnaires intended to break up the assembly.

We couldn't back out, of course; and Mrs. Gartz, a pacifist who delighted in battle, asked to be allowed to take us in her car. I think she believed a limousine with a chauffeur would be some protection from a mob. We had a lovely drive, and when we arrived at the most expensive hotel in town—later destroyed by an earthquake—we all had a certain amount of heartquake. We saw an armed legionnaire hiding behind every tubbed rubber plant, and when we entered the lobby and saw a top-brass military man pacing up and down as if on guard duty, I did my best to persuade Upton to hide behind a pillar until I found out what his purpose was. He was a most menacing figure, grim and determined-looking, in a spick and span khaki uniform with a black leather Sam Browne belt and holster with a pistol—I am not sure of all his equipment, for my imagination may have supplied some of the armaments.

Nothing could stop Upton from going to the desk, and there, to our surprise, was a letter waiting for him. Not a search warrant, or notice to "go home" or anything like that, but something of even more menacing potentialities—a letter from a lady, in a dainty hand. Upton, always chivalrous, handed it to me unopened, and I opened it and read, "Dear Upton," and then the signature, "Lelia." "She's at this hotel," I said, and Upton took the letter and exclaimed, "For heaven's sake—my cousin, Lelia Montague!"

His childhood playmate, she had grown up to be a Baltimore beauty. She later married a wealthy landowner and political leader. Upton had visited her, and been so impressed by her loveliness that he had made her the heroine of his first novel. After being widowed, she had married Colonel George Barnett and accompanied him on a series of diplomatic missions, including a reception by the Empress of China. Her husband, now a general, had had supreme command of the United States Marine Corps during the war in France.

A sudden light dawned in Upton's mind and he told me, "*That's* the General!"

We sent up our names to Lelia and took her up to the suite

which Mrs. Gartz had reserved. We did not meet the general, and had no trouble in guessing why. "He has an important conference up in San Francisco this evening," Lelia told us, "but it will just have to wait." The general would continue to pace the lobby, and the military chauffeur would stand beside the long shiny car while Lelia and Upton exchanged reminiscences, and Mrs. Gartz tried to persuade Lelia that her general should stay and discipline those legionnaires!

Maybe there was a reporter from that Santa Barbara newspaper in the hotel waiting for us to arrive, who saw the wife of General Barnett kiss Upton, and call him, "My dear cousin"; or maybe he saw our limousine, and the pompous lady who descended from it. Or maybe the legionnaires had never had any idea of interfering with us! At any rate, we attended the convention without incident, and Upton explained that public ownership of water power was no more revolutionary than public ownership of the post office and the United States Army.

11. GIVE HIM THE THIRD DEGREE!

AFTER UPTON had finished his crusade against the "kept" press, it was the turn of "kept" education. In the wave of repressive terror which had swept over the country after the war, no group had suffered more than the educators. From the highest-salaried professor in the richest university down to the poorest-paid teacher in the smallest country school, all were under the control of governing boards made up of businessmen determined to see that no teacher should suggest any social change that might threaten profits. The study of economics must be confined to the wonders of big business. In *The Brass Check* Upton had called for a union of newspaper reporters; now he wished to support the American Association of University Professors and the Teachers' Union.

He proposed to write all the educators in his cardfile, and all whose troubles were on record, and ask them for advice and help. Then he would interview these persons and their friends. He would make careful notes, and come home and write another big book, to be called *The Goosestep*. The way the German recruits had been taught to march was the way American teachers were being taught to march and to teach their pupils to march.

He visited some twenty-five cities, going north to Seattle, across to New York and Boston, then south as far as Washington and home through the Middle West. In each city he found a group of men and women waiting eagerly, excited over the prospect of having a spokesman from a safe distance away.

Some of their experiences were comic and some were tragic. All were different, and yet all alike, having a common basis, the fear of big businessmen that somebody might speak a word that would threaten the foundations of their system. Often the trustees of colleges and members of school boards knew just enough to fear the power of ideas. Any teacher who made a speech in favor of regulation of power rates should be fired, and a group who asked for higher pay should be shipped off to the Soviets "where they belonged."

Upton's sessions with teachers would last for hours, sometimes for days. He would be loaded with literature, clippings, documents, all of which he would ship to me. Cartons would be filled with it and stowed in a closet; I would have been appalled, except that I knew his way of working. Every day or two I would get a note, always cheerful, always sure he was getting "the most marvelous" lot of material. In New York he found a research group had been collecting statistics as to the financial control of American universities, and it saved him months of work.

There was hardly a great university which did not have a group of discontented professors; some were fighting openly, and many more would talk in privacy. Upton and I have guarded their letters for thirty-five years, but by now most of these good and conscientious souls have left their earthly troubles behind, and so they can be named without harm to their jobs. Among several hundred names were many well known: John Dewey, Charles Beard, James McKean Cattell, Evans

Clark, Zachariah Chafee, G. Stanley Hall, Robert Herrick, David Starr Jordan, Robert Morse Lovett, Jacques Loeb, Alexander Meiklejohn, David Mussey, James Harvey Robinson, Harry Overstreet, Louis D. Brandeis, E. A. Ross, Vida D. Scudder, Ellen Hayes, Joel E. Spingarn, Harry F. Ward.

In Baltimore it was Elisabeth Gilman, daughter of Daniel Coit Gilman, founder of Johns Hopkins. As Upton wrote, "She sees her father's great university in process of being kidnapped, and now and then her distress breaks into pamphlet or leaflet form." She brought professors to talk with Upton, each separately and in strict secrecy, as if it were a criminal conspiracy.

Upton came back home and started another year's job. Hundreds of individuals were involved, and that meant as many possible libel suits. No use to think of any other publisher; he must do it himself. Dear and gifted Art Young made for him a delightful drawing of a "goosestepping" professor and a flock of his little goosestepping goslings for the jacket and cover of the book.

Next came the schools, public and private. Another year of writing, and then *The Goslings* was another book the author had to publish himself. There were many more schoolteachers than college professors, but not so many of them had time to read books. All those who were discontented did, of course, and the book sold as well as *The Goosestep*. So we were able to pay our debts—and write another book.

This was Upton's life, one big book a year, or maybe two small ones; and a part of my life was to keep guard over him, to see that self-seekers did not waste his time, and to fuss when he was overworking.

Mrs. Gartz's Sunday afternoon teas had become an institution. She called them her "Open Forum," and if a distinguished out-of-town guest showed up, the hostess singled him out and invited him to say a few words.

One such guest, Cornelius Vanderbilt, Jr., was important because he had made up his young mind to be something more than a rich man's son. His parents and grandparents had considered themselves American royalty. On his father's cup-win-

ning yacht the boy, Neil, had had to dress in a long ermine-
trimmed coat to hobnob with the great sovereigns of Europe
—Edward VII of England, Czar Nicholas of Russia and Kaiser
Wilhelm of Germany. He tripped over the coat, stumbled, and
almost fell overboard; the Kaiser saved his life.

In spite of all this worldly glory, he had run away at the
beginning of World War I and enlisted as a private. Wires
were pulled immediately in Washington to prevent his getting
to the front, and he found himself an army mule-driver in
South Carolina. He persuaded a fellow mule-driver, a Negro,
to smuggle him onto a transport bound for France, and on
shipboard was given the job of pants presser. He did so well in
this capacity that he was kept on over there, until he finally
got his chance to reach the front by demonstrating his ability
to drive a Rolls-Royce for an English general. He was pro-
moted to dispatch driver, which carried him into the battle
where he was severely gassed, and then sent back to his family.

Ill and horrified by what he had seen, he stood in the most
magnificent ballroom in America, that of the Vanderbilt mansion at Newport, and refused to take part in the festivities.
How could these splendidly-dressed young ladies and gentlemen laugh and whirl around the dance-floor while the youth
of the world was destroying itself, screaming in pain, dying in
every kind of agony on those battlefields he had just left?

He made up his mind to do something about it. He would
no longer be a self-centered aimless parasite, a playboy, spending his father's millions on frivolity! After cruel debates with
his grandmother and his parents, he wrote a book called *Farewell to Fifth Avenue,* and went forth on his own to start a chain
of truth-telling newspapers.

Here was another one like our friend Pryns Hopkins, like
Mrs. Gartz, like a dozen others we knew! Surely these rebels
were the salt of the earth, I thought, as I listened to this tall,
friendly young man tell of his desire to own and edit a truly
democratic newspaper in the city of Los Angeles. Mrs. Gartz
thought so, too, and when she heard that Neil Vanderbilt's
father had declared that his son's ambition was entirely imprac-
tical, for the simple reason that he knew nothing about running

a newspaper, she remarked to me, "He could learn, and that's all there is to it!"

Bertrand Russell was invited by Dr. Robert Millikan, head of the California Institute of Technology, to give a lecture there. We wrote inviting him to be our guest while in Pasadena. The arrangement was that we would pick him up after the lecture and bring him to our house, then take him to Mrs. Gartz's for luncheon.

Kitty and Doctor Millikan had been at war over the World War for years. He, an ardent patriot, and she, a belligerent pacifist, had exchanged blows in several letters. Now the war was over, but she would never rest until she had forced him to admit that "the war to end wars" had ended nothing but the lives of hundreds of thousands of innocent boys. She was going with us to Cal-Tech, as much interested in continuing the argument as to meet Bertrand Russell. He also was a pacifist, and would take her side in the coming battle, of course!

But alas, when we arrived on the campus in her blue limousine, there stood our British lion with Dr. Millikan, who was ready to carry him off to a luncheon with Pasadena's millionaire contributors to Cal-Tech. They had to know that their dollars were well spent, and what better way could there be than to show them what a distinguished lecturer Dr. Millikan was able to produce?

Upton and the chauffeur got out and Dr. Millikan with his guest left their group and walked toward us. Dr. Millikan said, "I'm sorry, but I have made arrangements for a luncheon at the Valley Hunt Club for—"

He got no further. Mrs. Gartz said firmly to Bertrand, "You get in back here with us—Mr. Sinclair will sit facing us."

"We are keeping our friends waiting," said Dr. Millikan. "I hope you will excuse us."

"Of course!" I said, "hop in, Upton—Mrs. Gartz's guests are waiting, too." And then, to Dr. Millikan, "We will be here again in two hours. Can you bring him back by then?"

The unhappy lion had been saved from being divided up, but when we were safely off the campus, Kitty exclaimed, "How perfectly outrageous! He didn't even invite Mr. Sinclair to join them! I'll never give Cal-Tech another dollar!"

I agreed that it was outrageous, but since Upton was used to snubs from people whose duty it was to bend the knee to rich donors, and since *she* hadn't been snubbed, everything was all right. She could go home and eat her good meal, and then come for tea with us.

"Who is going to make the tea?" she asked, dubiously.

"I am, of course," I replied.

"I'm going to make that tea," she said firmly. *"He* is an Englishman, and they are fussy about it."

When we finally picked up our lecturer, he was weary. He had to speak at the luncheon also, two lectures at the price of one. Now he had only one request, that we would take him to a shop where he could buy some socks—he had not had time for any shopping since he left England. Upton stopped at the first little store and our visitor went in and came out with some unwrapped socks in his hand. The moment he emerged, Kitty murmured to me in horror, *"Red* ones!"

"I took the first they showed me," remarked the philosopher, "and didn't wait for them to be wrapped."

"You might have been arrested for shoplifting," said Upton, "and then Mrs. Gartz would have had to bail you out. She bails everybody out!"

There was a strange conclusion to this Cal-Tech story: Years later, at the time when all America was debating whether or not we should go to the aid of England and France in World War II, Governor Phil LaFollette of Wisconsin was following in his father's footsteps and taking the pacifist side. Dr. Robert Millikan and most of Cal-Tech, like Upton, were ardently urging our entrance into the war. Phil's sponsor challenged Cal-Tech to produce an opponent to meet Phil in debate in the big auditorium of the Pasadena High School; and most surprisingly Cal-Tech called upon Upton Sinclair to serve as the champion. Would he accept this invitation? Upton hesitated; would Dr. Millikan approve of this? The answer was, Dr. Millikan's son (in khaki) would lead a contingent of Cal-Tech professors down the aisle to front seats in the auditorium!

Upton and I wrestled together with the revision of some of his books. This photograph is from the frontispiece of our book on telepathy, *Mental Radio*.

Our Italian-style villa in Monrovia where, we hoped, we could just disappear and live in peace.

Upton, who felt that the only way to end war was to end poverty, debated America's entry into World War II with Phil La Follette at the California Institute of Technology.

Cornelius Vanderbilt, Jr., and Upton in 1956, when Upton was seventy-eight.

"I am not as cross as I look. I'ts just that I'm 81. Sept. 20, 1959. Buckeye, Arizona. Upton Sinclair." Upton at his desert hideaway, Buckeye, Arizona, 1959.

Every visitor to California wanted to visit one of the Hollywood movie studios. Upton is shown (*above*) on a set with ex-Senator James Vardaman, who still wore his black hair long; my young brother, Hunter Kimbrough, and Charlie Chaplin, who wistfully told me he wanted to marry "an old-fashioned girl".

Upton shares a joke with "Doug" Fairbanks, Sr., of the silver screen.

George and Carrie Sterling are shown here with Jack London on San Francisco Bay. George came down to see us after the shock of Jack London's suicide.

One of our guests, the Hungarian Count Karolyi, escaped briefly from a fatiguing trip by snatching a few hours' sleep in our quiet—but cobwebby—storeroom.

I went with two of my nieces ahead of Upton and we seated
ourselves near the front. Just behind us was a group of Socialists who had come in order to boo Upton for being a "war
monger." Young Dr. Clark Millikan arrived with his contingent
and tramped down the aisle, simultaneously with the arrival
on the platform of the two gladiators. My nieces and I were
caught between volleys of cheers and boos. I turned and looked
back at the Socialists whom Upton loved and who loved him;
they stopped booing and several of them quietly rose and disappeared to the rear. After the debate, we picked up Phil La-
Follette and took him home with us for a reconciliation.

I do not know who won the debate—but I know who won
the war.

Our life was rich with a host of interesting friends.
Visitors came to see us from the world's four corners. Upton's
translators from North and South India, from Japan, South
America, and all of Europe. Johan Bojer, many of whose novels
had been translated and published in our country, came from
his native Norway. From England came S. K. Ratcliffe, journalist and lecturer, and one of Upton's best literary critics and
advisers. There came Ernst Toller, German poet and playwright
who later became a Communist.

Carl Eldh, the Swedish sculptor who had just made a bust
of the king of Sweden, wanted to make one of Upton; he did
it in a remarkably short time, because I had warned him that
Upton wouldn't sit still for long!

Albert Rhys Williams had written a number of articles about
his experiences in Russia, and now he wanted to make them
into a book. Pasadena was a good place in which to write, and
when he arrived we put him up and told him he might eat
with us when he felt like it. He grinned and asked, "What's
the use in saying that? You know you don't have anything."

"If you don't like our diet, there's the lunch counter over
on Fair Oaks Avenue," I reminded him.

He stayed for several months. He was lazy, he told us, miserably lazy, and he contemplated Upton's relentless day-by-day

drive with a mixture of amazement and shame. Would I please take charge of him and make *him* work, too?

So just as I scolded Upton when he overworked, I now scolded Albert when he didn't work at all. I would lay down the law to him: "Go to your room and let me hear your type-writer clicking. Bring me back three pages by noon, or you won't get any of my hot soup or Upton's stewed fruit." He would answer, "I don't want either!" But he would go and write the three pages. That is the way *Through the Russian Revolution* was written.

Nina Wilcox Putnam, the novelist, was another of our visitors. She was a vivid and eager person who had been a writer since the age of eleven. She and Upton chatted about the dancing of Isadora Duncan, and Nina gave an imitation of Pavlova. She asked me many questions and later wrote that when a friend had asked her what kind of person the second Mrs. Sinclair was, she answered, "A woman trying to do the impossible, and doing it."

The Spanish novelist Blasco-Ibañez came to visit Southern California. Everybody had read *Mare Nostrum* and *The Four Horsemen of the Apocalypse,* and everybody wanted to meet the author. He told the reporters there were two men *he* wanted to meet, Charlie Chaplin and Upton Sinclair.

Upton called on him at his hotel in Pasadena and invited him to our home. He was delightful company, full of humor and literary anecdotes. He was anti-Royalist, and had been ordered into a very pleasant exile on the French Riviera. He and Upton admired each other's many books, and so they got along well together. When our guest doubted the existence of a "millionaire Socialist," Upton offered to give a dinner party to which only these would be invited, and was able to produce half a dozen.

Then came tall and lanky, gracious and aristocratic Count Michael Karolyi from Hungary. He had read *The Jungle,* he told us, and had been converted by it to Socialism. He had given his estates, worth a hundred and twenty million dollars, to the government, and had become head of the state. Then he had been ousted by Bela Kun, the Communist, and of course was greatly saddened by the cruelty and disorder that had followed. Karolyi spoke at a banquet given in his honor in Los Angeles. The next day Upton called for him and drove him to our house. Karolyi said that he had almost no sleep at the hotel and was exhausted; could he have a room where he could have a long nap and not be disturbed? Upton explained that all four sides of the house had windows, and children played in the streets both front and back; but there was a storeroom with no windows, and a bed in it. Karolyi said that was what he wanted; so when I came in later I found the elegant nobleman was asleep in the storeroom, with all of our oldest clothes, broken-down pieces of furniture and other junk jammed around him and spiderwebs hanging from the ceiling.

When ex-Senator Vardaman came to California, he wanted what every visitor wanted: to be admitted to one of the studios. Upton was glad to oblige him in return for his help with the magazine.

"James K." was now in his sixties, erect and imposing as I had known him long ago. He still dressed in white and wore a big Texas hat. His hair was still black and he still wore it long—because, it was said, in his early days he had been shot in the back of the head. His manner was sedate, and he politely voiced approval of most of Upton's ideas; he pointed out that he had advocated the initiative and referendum from the beginning of his career, and in his weekly paper, the *Commonwealth,* had called for "the abolition of judicial injunctions used by plutocracy to crush and hold in check the robbed and restless toiler." We kept away from racial questions, of course, for on the "supremacy of the white man" he had based all his political campaigns, while we believed in equal rights for all men. Also we avoided the issue of the League of Nations, which he had ardently opposed, and we as ardently favored.

Upton took him to Hollywood to see two studios instead of one—those of Charlie Chaplin and "Doug" Fairbanks, and he was photographed with both these celebrities.

At that time Hollywood was a magic word. It was really the home of "the industry," not merely of the stars and directors, but of the powerful big men behind the scenes. They built fine homes in Beverly Hills. Rob Wagner and his gifted wife kept "open house" to distinguished visitors from near and far. When someone wanted to meet Chaplin, Rob would invite them to dine at his house, and Chaplin would be there. It was the same in the case of Upton—if some admirer of his books came to Southern California from overseas, we would sometimes get together at the Wagners'.

Fame was work; and Upton had more of both than one man could cope with. It was not the winning of fame that was so arduous; it was the fans. Fame and fans were inseparable, of course, and it was in this matter of fans that I became indispensable. I always had to remain alert to keep the dangerous ones and the wasters of time from gaining access to my husband.

Some of the visitors were obviously unbalanced; I was afraid of them, and the police told me I had reason to be. Now and then one would say that he had just been released from this or that psychopathic ward.

One evening there came a Swedish giant—he must have been seven feet tall, and wide in proportion—who entered our living-room and towered over my small husband, announcing in the most solemn voice his huge frame could produce, *"I have a message direct from God!"*

"Indeed?" said Upton, mildly. "What is the nature of it?"

"It is a manuscript."

"And do you wish me to read it?"

The reply came in a voice from Mt. Sinai. "No human eye has ever beheld it! No human eye ever WILL behold it! Neither yours nor any others'!"

"Then what can I do for you?" Upton asked, still mildly.

"Ah ha-a-a!" proclaimed the inspired one. "That's a secret, too!"

I had been sitting on the back porch and I now thought it was time to let our visitor know there was another man on the scene. I called, "Upton, the plumber is waiting for you to show him the job."

Upton is usually quick enough to get your meaning if you are talking about politics or economics, but he is completely dumb when it comes to a hint. "What plumber?" he asked, surprised.

So I had to become emphatic. "There is a leak, and the plumber is waiting for you. Hurry!"

Upton came and I whispered frantically, "Don't you know that man is a lunatic? Come with me," and I caught his arm and pulled him into the darkness of the garden. The giant prowled around the living room impatiently, peered out the back door, then the front, and finally hurried out and down the street.

Visitors came daily. Some wanted to buy a book; some brought a book to be autographed. Some, pathetically, just wanted to shake Upton's hand; if he was busy, mine would do. There was a lady who got out of a car in front of the garage where Upton was standing, rushed to him, flung her arms about him and started to kiss him. He managed to get loose, and hastened to tell me about it.

Here in California the I.W.W.—"Industrial Workers of the World"—were trying to organize the migratory fruit pickers and field workers, who lived most wretchedly. The I.W.W. boys were harried, beaten, jailed for long terms; when they came out from San Quentin they would make a four-hundred-mile pilgrimage to see Upton Sinclair. At first I was afraid of them, but one after another proved himself to be intelligent, trustworthy, and honest. Not once did I hear any talk of violence, such as the newspapers tried to pin on them. Now and then I would offer one of them some pocket change, knowing that their pockets were empty; but it would be refused.

The Russians had what we called the "Red Terror," while ever since the war there had been developing in America what its victims called the "White Terror," intimidation of labor union organizers by threats and brutality. It has been said that eternal vigilance is the price of liberty. It would soon be necessary for someone to call public attention to this growing threat to our freedom. In Southern California a group of reactionaries had formed the "Better America Federation," which forced members of the Merchants' and Manufacturers' Association to contribute five dollars for every employee they had; this fund was being used to pay spies on labor. Co-operating with them was the so-called police "Red Squad." (All radicals, including union organizers, were called "reds" then.) For any workingman to utter a sentiment in favor of labor unionism could mean being picked up and thrown into jail, held without bail—often without booking—and being "railroaded" to San Quentin for "criminal syndicalism."

This was a term recently created by reactionaries, and a law against it had been passed by the California legislature. But several thousand dockworkers at the harbor dared to go on strike. This harbor was a part of the city of Los Angeles although ten or fifteen miles to the south ; the harbor had been made by dredging at the mouth of the Los Angeles River, and harbor towns had grown up on both sides of it. The war had increased living costs and the workers struck for more pay; they had the temerity to walk up and down on the streets of the towns, singing their song about "Solidarity forever." An army of Los Angeles police surrounded them and escorted six hundred to jail. A woman came to our home and appealed to Upton. She declared that the men were packed in so tightly that no man could sit, to say nothing of lying down. They were groaning and screaming.

Upton heard the story, and said, "Craig, somebody has got to protest." I knew who that somebody was, and so I entered my protest first. "*You* must not be that somebody."

The woman said, "Mrs. Sinclair, a week or so ago down at that harbor, a hired mob raided a meeting of these wage slaves, beat some of them insensible with clubs, threw a little girl into a great receptacle of boiling coffee, scalding her almost to death, and dragged six men off into the woods and tarred and feathered them?"

Despite this report of violence I was not going to consent to another jail experience. Upton promised that he would not get arrested. He would take a deputation to protest to the mayor. I was ill and couldn't go; but my brother Hunter was visiting us—twenty-two now, and six-feet-two like Papa. He would go, he declared, "to protect Mr. Sinclair"! (He still called my husband "Mister.") Mrs. Gartz wanted to go, and took the precaution to pack her bag for jail—just in case. This was no small matter, for she had told me that when she packed her "overnight bag" she had to put in twenty-one articles.

Pryns Hopkins was one man who never flinched from a duty. He would go. My father had told me long ago, "When in doubt, employ a lawyer." I asked our lawyer to go. He would tell an ignorant mayor what rights were afforded citizens by the municipal and state statutes and the United States Constitution.

With so much protection it sounded safe enough. Only the newspaper publicity remained to be faced, and of course that was the only hope for the protest to succeed. To put the truth before "the bar of public opinion" was the blessed way of democracy, for which our Constitution was designed.

So the defenders of freedom of speech for striking workingmen set out. His Honor received them, and listened for an hour to what they had to say. Like the Governor of Colorado during the coal strike, he was a puppet put up by big business, too feeble to do anything but what he was told. But he admitted that conditions at the harbor were bad, and consented to the group's demand that they be permitted to go to the harbor, hold a meeting on private property and tell the strikers what their constitutional rights were. The mayor would phone the necessary orders to the chief of police, who was there, dealing with the strike.

So Upton thought it was settled, and the party of eight drove down to the harbor, arriving just after dusk. It was May 15, 1923. There was a vacant piece of land called Liberty Hill, where meetings had been held, and Upton found the owner and got written permission to hold a meeting on it. Then they went to the jail and interviewed the chief and several of his officers. There would be no meeting at the harbor, anywhere, any time! What the mayor said made no difference, said the chief, and if they were arrested, no bail would be allowed.

When the lawyers told him that the constitution of California forbade denial of bail, he replied, "Don't talk this Constitution stuff here!"

So there was the issue; either back down before a lawless brute, or else be arrested without bail. Upton had got a glimpse of that crowded "tank" with its shouting and groaning captives, and it moved him to fear, of course, but to greater indignation. He told the chief that he had the written permission of the owner, and was going to stand on that private property and read the Constitution of the United States. What the chief replied is not fit to print.

The little group went out and consulted. Then the men went up the hill, followed by Mrs. Gartz and her ladies-in-waiting. A crowd lined the way, held back by a cordon of policemen—there must have been a hundred, so Hunter reported, and every one of them had his gun in his hand. Perhaps that was to intimidate the ladies, or perhaps to intimidate anyone else who might be dreaming of martyrdom.

Upton took his stand, but it was dark and he could not see. Hunter said, "I brought a candle," and lighted and held it, while Upton read from the first Amendment to the Constitution of the United States: "Congress shall make no law abridging the freedom of speech or of the press; or the right of the people peaceably to assemble and to petition the government for the redress of grievances."

An officer told him he was under arrest. Hunter spoke next. "You have just heard the first Article of the Declaration of Independence." He realized that this was a slip, but had no way to correct it; he was under arrest. The elegant Pryns Hopkins came next. "We came here not to incite to violence—" and he was under arrest. The next speaker said something polite about the fine climate of California and was probably the only person in the history of the state to be arrested for that. Several officers marched off with the prisoners, but without Mrs. Gartz. She protested to the police against the arrests, but did not try to make a speech; she was held back by her ladies who just didn't want to go to jail. She told me afterward that the real thing that held her back was that when she had packed her bag she had forgotten her toothbrush!

At the foot of the hill was a great crowd, cheering wildly. Two police cars were waiting, and the prisoners were driven to the police station. They were being "booked" but the chief came in and stopped it; the law required it, but there was no law here. The four were taken out again, this time to one large car; it was rather crowded, and when my courtly brother attempted to step in, the chief pushed him aside. "You get out," he said. "There's no room."

"But I was arrested with the others," protested Hunter.

"Well, you're not arrested now. You're clear. Beat it—skidoo!"

They had an argument. Hunter said, "If you don't take me, I'll go right back and make a speech." And one of the officers said to the chief, "He held the candle."

"Oh, well," said the chief, "if you want to be a martyr—." So they let him ride, standing on the running board, holding on through an open window. A newspaper photographer tried to take a picture. Away they went; they asked where they were being taken, but no one would answer. It was a long ride with many turns; they guessed the purpose was to evade any newspaper pursuit. Hunter wrote an account of it for *The Appeal to Reason*. He said:

> "Finally we stopped. The officers pretended they were lost. They argued for a moment, then turned the car around. We were quite satisfied with our lot and talked about other matters. A discussion of psychoanalysis got under way. The officers listened at first, wondering what this unusual bunch of 'wobblies' (I.W.W.) was talking about. The discussion shifted to Coué; then to the jail system, Herbert Spencer, the Renaissance, the Ruhr situation, H. G. Wells, Ibañez, the Plumb Plan and so on."

And all this with my six-foot-two brother standing on the running board! He told me afterward that they had driven through the countryside for miles, and he hoped he wouldn't fall off and be left behind. He felt responsible for Mr. Sinclair!

They were finally taken to a small jail, they had no idea where. It was clean, and the officers were polite. Upton, of course, wanted to telephone me, and Pryns his wife; but they were told "No privileges." They did not want privileges, they wanted their rights—to communicate with a lawyer was one of these under the state constitution. All night long they protested, but "nothing doing." They were booked, and the charge was that blessed "criminal syndicalism," so dear to the hearts of those who wanted an excuse to get rid of friends of free speech for workingmen.

I sat up waiting, and at one o'clock a car came into our driveway. I jumped up, thinking it was our crusaders, but it was one of the lawyers.

He came in and told me of the arrests. "It was an ugly sight, that line of officers, guns in hand, on each side, as four of the most law-abiding men I ever knew were marched down that hill with three greatly shocked ladies following. I felt like a coward, not doing something about it!" He leaned forward, and put his head in his hands. "I'm yellow! I should have been arrested, too!"

"What good would that have done?" I asked. "And, besides, I need you to help get them out."

His voice was bitter as he said, "It's my country as well as theirs, and I'm an officer of the law myself; but look how they ignored both me and the law. I'll tell them in court what I think tomorrow!"

"Then go home and get some sleep, and be ready for them."

Of course I couldn't sleep—though I went to bed and tried. Upton had come out of jail safely in New York, so there was nothing to worry about except my long-suffering parents. This was the third jail episode to bow their heads, for of course they couldn't feel that going to jail was anything but a disgrace. That was how they had been brought up to feel and how everyone around them felt.

This time we had involved another member of the family. This time one of their young sons had become a "jailbird"! Would this have any harmful effect on the future of this boy, just entering the world as a responsible citizen? The seriousness of it could not be understood by Upton, for he was sure he was right. I asked him once if he did not think we were fanatics, and he answered, "Is the trained soldier, educated at West Point or Annapolis in the art of killing, a fanatic when he spends his life defending what he believes are his human rights, and those of his countrymen? I hate war as much as any man can—yet I do not believe the soldier is a fanatic. Freedom is something every man should defend."

I could only pray that Upton was right in taking the only peaceful way open to us, in this war attack against freedom. If going to jail was the only way to force the newspapers to tell the truth to the people, then someone must risk it. But was my young brother old enough in the ways of the world to know what he was doing?

The telephone rang, in that nerve-wracking way its bell sounds in the silence of three o'clock in the morning. I picked up the receiver and a man's voice asked, "Who is this?"

"Mrs. Sinclair."

"Have you heard from your husband and his friends?"

"No."

His voice became warm and kindly. "I hope you will take my word for what I am going to tell you. Your help is needed. Do not be too alarmed, please, but you must immediately notify every influential friend you have of the situation. I'm a newspaper reporter, and there are other reporters who are working for you—we can't find out *where* those men are! We've telephoned every jail in the county, and got the same answer, 'Not here.'" He paused a moment for this to impress itself in my mind.

I did not wait. "Can they be *dead?*" I cried.

"Oh, no!" he answered, emphatically. "Not possible. *But don't fail to act at once!* Ask every influential friend you have to put pressure on the authorities. Tell them it is very serious. Trust us to do our part—we have stories for the morning papers which will make these skunks open their eyes! Public opinion *can* make itself felt."

He hung up, and I ran to the kitchen and put on a pot of coffee. Then I started to work. My hands were trembling so that I could hardly hold the telephone. The first influential friend I called was Dr. John R. Haynes, physician, business-man, and more important yet, millionaire! Money was king in Los Angeles, and so I was sure this friend at court would know what to do. He did, but he needed reinforcements, he told me. "This is indeed serious," he declared. "I will act at once, and do my very best. But you must help. You should telephone everyone you can think of to go to work. Now don't worry, dear lady—just work!" He hung up.

I called a well-known clubwoman to whom I had often talked about our ideas. She answered at once that she would phone others whose help she could probably enlist. "We clubwomen are not helpless, you know. It was only last year that we brought the high prices of potatoes down by a boycott of potatoes."

I telephoned the city jail and was told emphatically the pris-oners were not there, and they had "no information" about them. Also, I was told that the police chief was out of town— no use trying to talk to him.

I began calling influential people, and when dawn came I telephoned Kitty. "You must take me to the city this morning," I told her. "I've telephoned everyone I know, but you may think of someone else."

"My lawyer," she answered. I agreed, for by now I wanted a whole legal battery behind us.

Upton's secretary, who lived on the place, came in early to make himself some coffee in our kitchen. I told him the situa-tion and asked him to get the morning papers. He came back pale and wide-eyed. "They drove them out into the country," it says here, "and that's the last anyone has seen of them. You and I must go out and beat every bush in the county and find them!" I couldn't summon the least smile at his panicky idea.

A man came hurrying into our place, and asked the secretary if he could see me. When I came, he said he must speak to me alone. I was willing to talk to anyone who might have news. He took a small folder from his breast pocket, opened it and showed me a card in it.

"Please be sure I don't show that carelessly," he said. "Do you know what it is?"

It was his credentials as an organizer of the Ku Klux Klan. It did not alarm me, for I was from the South. I told him so.

Then he explained that he had news of the prisoners; they were somewhere in a country jail, he was sure, because the police car in which they were taken last night had returned without them. Naturally this did alarm me, but I tried to speak calmly. I asked if this proved they were in a jail.

"That's why I'm here," he said. "There was a rumor last night that these men were to be taken to the country and kidnapped there by arrangement, and the blame put on the Ku Klux Klan. I want you to know that we had nothing to do with it. If it is a plot, it is not ours."

I am sure I had never felt such anguish as I did at that moment. Mrs. Gartz took me in to Los Angeles, and we waited in the offices of her lawyer all day. And all day our many friends tried to find out where the prisoners were. They were certainly "incommunicado," but it was clear that the authorities had no idea of paying any attention to the laws of the nation or of the state.

We read the newspapers, as many "extras" as there were, and the story was on the front pages of every one. I thanked God for the splendid way the reporters had taken up the fight! Maybe it was the first fruits of *The Brass Check,* or maybe it was because the situation was too dramatic—two millionaires and a famous author had disappeared all at once, arrested on a dark hill and carried off by police to no one knew where. And the "crime" had been reading aloud the Constitution of the United States on private property!

As we sat there, hour after hour, I could do nothing for the victims which was not now being done by our friends and lawyers. But I could pray, and I did, with all my heart. Then, at four-thirty, a man's voice on the telephone asked me if I would consent to meet him outside in the hall. I left the office and waited for him.

He was a stranger, young and frightened-looking. "You must hurry," he exclaimed; then his voice dropped low. "I'll lose my job if it is known that I have informed you. I'm a police reporter. Your husband and his friends are now in the city jail. They just arrived, and have been locked in for the night. To-night Mr. Sinclair will be given the third degree. He can't stand it—he's too frail. Hurry there with your attorneys—they should be prepared with bail money! The court closes at five. It is now four-thirty. Don't lose a moment!"

I rushed back to the room and told everyone what I had learned. They all leaped up and followed me to the elevator. On the street we looked for Mrs. Gartz's car, but it was not in sight, nor was there a cab. It was several blocks to the police court and we started to run. Mrs. Gartz was too stout to keep up. She turned back, and we left her to wait for her chauffeur. I ran as I had not run since my childhood. Two lawyers ran with me, one on each side, and held my arms in case I should faint.

The police court was in session and we went in. One lawyer notified the court clerk that he had a matter to put before the judge, and was told to sit down. He did so, and at five o'clock the judge announced that the court stood adjourned. Our law-yer rose, and pointed out very firmly that he had given notice that he had an urgent matter to put before the court, and he stood on his rights. The other lawyer joined in, and the two of them made it warm for the judge, reciting the series of viola-tions of law that had been committed in this case. They were flagrant, and the whole country knew about them. I doubt if they reminded the judge there were such things as disbarment proceedings, but they may have hinted at it; anyhow, they knew the law, and the police-court judge backed down.

Bail was set very high. I was asked to state the value of my real estate, but it was mortgaged. The lawyers offered their homes, and that was not enough. But in came a breathless Kitty—the value of her real estate would have bailed out every-body in the jail. She raised her right hand and took an oath and the papers were made out and handed to one of our lawyers.

We went to the jail, which was in the same building. All those bars and gratings, and the grim but matter-of-fact details horrified me. I imagined the horror of the third degree—was it too late to prevent that? Our papers were presented, and there was a clanging of steel doors deep within the jail. Pryns came to the bars ahead of the others, and happily put out his arm, to shake the hands of his friends. But this gentle convict was leaped at and shoved backward by a guard. The other prisoners came out, one by one, carefully decorous. It was late, and all of them had given up hope of getting out that night. They did not know why they had been detained so long, nor what danger they had been in.

Two of them went their separate ways, while Mrs. Gartz took Upton, Hunter and me to a tearoom for dinner. She wanted to hear everything that had happened to the prisoners, and Upton told us how, all day, they had demanded in vain to see a lawyer. At last, in the latter part of the afternoon, they were taken from their cells and put into a car, and driven just as on the previous night, around and around. It was observed that the police sergeant kept looking at his watch, and finally he said it was "time," and the car headed for the city.

In that dreadful old jail, "the Los Angeles louse-ranch," the four had been separated, each put into a cell with other prisoners. Upton was in a small cell with a Negro burglar and three white men; he stood in the middle of the floor, hoping to avoid the lice, and was prepared to spend the night upright if necessary. My young brother also drew one Negro and three whites as cellmates, one of these a notable character, a "wobbly" and striker who had determined to make a street-corner speech at the harbor, and had got himself a heavy chain and padlocked his ankle to a telegraph pole; it had taken the police some time to get a hammer and chisel, and in the meantime he had made his speech. No doubt he would be sent to San Quentin, but that was the way those strikers at the harbor felt about their rights.

I longed for nothing but to get home and rest for a week. Upton's answer was that rest would be all right for me, but *his* job had just begun. He had started something, and hoped I wouldn't ask him to stop before it was finished. My sense of indignation against his abductors was so great that I told him, "Anything that is within the law." His answer was, "I just want to go down to that harbor and make a speech on Liberty Hill —to anybody who cares to come and hear me."

"I'll go with you," I said.

The first thing we did was to rent a good-sized hall in the center of Los Angeles—by the week. Every night we had a meeting, and every meeting was packed to the doors. The provisions of the national and state constitutions, and the laws which bore upon freedom of speech and assemblage were read to the audiences, and first-hand witnesses told what had been done in violation thereof. Upton proposed to organize a branch of the American Civil Liberties Union, and lawyers and clergymen spoke in support. The minister of the Pilgrim Congregational Church of Los Angeles, Dr. Clinton J. Taft, decided to resign his pastorate and direct this work.

During the day we laid siege to the mayor. This time we sent clergymen and club ladies and lawyers—and always reporters. It was like a swarm of hornets after him, and they forced him, first to admit that the police had broken the laws, and then to agree that there should be free speech for all at the harbor. Yes, Upton Sinclair and his group would be allowed to speak on Liberty Hill, and to say what they pleased, provided they did not advocate violence—which assuredly Upton Sinclair had never done and would never do. Privately, the mayor agreed to see to it that the chief of police stayed in Los Angeles.

Just eight nights after the arrest, a mass meeting was held on Liberty Hill. One newspaper estimated there were five thousand people present. There were a few policemen on hand, but they had nothing to do but complete their education. A little stand had been erected, just large enough for one speaker; there was no light, except the half moon. Dr. Taft opened with a prayer; he raised his hands over thousands of bowed heads and spoke:

> "Our Father, we are made of one clay. We want to be brothers here. We want the liberties that our fathers conceived on these shores to be passed on to our children and our children's children undiminished. Amen."

Then Upton took the stand. I had never heard such a tumult of cheering. I had no assurance that the people of this town would have any realization of what his act meant to them, but I learned that night to trust the American people.

It was the first time I had seen my husband before a mass audience, and I discovered that he had mass appeal. He has an intense, almost mystical delight in such an audience, and somehow knows intuitively how to deal with it. He begins quietly, as if he were talking with two or three in our living room. Somehow his voice seemed to reach the farthest edges. He quoted the guarantees of freedom of speech and assemblage— he knew them all by heart. And he told the story of the past eight days, turning it into a hilarious farce, which I suppose it was if you never know fear. He ridiculed his captors, and got the crowd laughing so that he could hardly finish a sentence. He asked the crowd questions and they shouted their answers; all of them just had a grand time for an hour or so.

Then came Pryns Hopkins, gentle, dignified and earnest; no one could doubt the sincerity of his convictions. The newspapers had featured him, of course, and everybody knew he was a millionaire; it might be that these working people had never before listened to a millionaire.

Then came Hunter. He had shown his nerve that dark night when he had mentioned the Declaration of Independence, and had been arrested for it. He had had no fear of a police chief gone berserk, but he admitted to fear of five thousand people looking up at him standing on a speaker's platform. "I never made a speech in my life," he said as his opening sentence. Then suddenly he got stuck in the middle of the next sentence, groped around for a word, and then blurted out: "Mr. Sinclair told me that if Ah got *ner*vous, Ah was to tell you so. Well, Ah'm *ner*vous!" His Mississippi drawl made it funny; he couldn't say "*ner*vous" without dragging out the first syllable. The crowd roared; and after that he could blunder all he pleased, it was all in the family.

Again the story went out over the press wires, and we went on with the nightly meetings in the city, and the work of organizing the civil liberties group. I do not know how long Upton would have kept up this crusade, for he felt that he had the enemy in rout, and wanted to keep on his heels. But shortly afterwards came a telephone call, of very curious significance. I don't suppose General Grant was surprised by the surrender at Appomattox, or General Pershing by the surrender of Germany; but I was surely surprised when the telephone rang and Upton beckoned me to come and sit by him during the conversation. We made no record of it, but it is graven on our minds. It was from one of the top editors, I think the managing editor, of the Los Angeles *Examiner*. Upton had been in his office several times, and liked him personally. The conversation went something like this:

"Sinclair, how much longer are you going on with this show?"

"I don't know; I haven't figured it out."

"You're giving the town a bad black eye, you know."

"I didn't start it, you know."

"The question is, how to stop it. What do you want?"

"I want what the people want, the rights guaranteed them by the Constitution and the laws."

"Well, the strikers are having their meetings at the harbor, and you've been having yours in town. And you have your Civil Liberties Union, to see to the future. What else?"

"Don't forget that I am out on heavy bail, charged with suspicion of 'criminal syndicalism.'"

"You and your friends can forget that. We don't want any more fuss. We want to wipe the slate clean and start better. We hope that you will drop the civil suits for false arrest that you have threatened. They would cost you a lot, and you couldn't collect anything."

"I'm not looking for money, I'm looking for civic decency."

"All right, that's what I'm offering."

"Are you in a position to offer it?"

"The right people have come to me. They don't happen to know you and I do. I hope you will take my word."

"I will, if you give it."

"I am offering it. Is it a deal?"

I held before Upton's eyes a piece of paper on which I had

written: "The chief!" Upton said into the telephone, "One thing more. You have a ruffian as chief of police, and there'll never be any decency in this town while he runs it."

"He's on his way out. We just want to wait a few days, to let things blow over."

"You are sure your people won't change their minds?"

"Absolutely. They have talked it out and it's settled. But it's confidential. You'll have to promise that."

"You are sure they won't renege?"

"It'll be done within a month. You have my word."

"O.K. I'll go back to writing a book."

Soon after that it was announced in the newspapers that the Chief of Police of Los Angeles had been discharged, having been found in an automobile at night, while on duty, with a jug of liquor and a woman.

12. THE BOSTON TEA PARTY

KATE CRANE-GARTZ had become an ardent believer in the abolishing of the status quo. She set out on a letter-writing campaign to tell her reactionary friends what was wrong with them and with society. Presently she enlarged the scope of her campaign to include "public servants," as she called them. This was what they called themselves before election, and after election they should not be beyond the reach of those whose tax-money supported them.

Every day she would stop by with a letter she had just written and ask me to read and revise it. But one day she said, "I can't get any newspaper to publish anything I write them. Why do they publish silly letters from others and refuse mine?"

I pointed out to her, "Your letters are dangerous to special interests, and newspapers dare not offend these interests."

"Something happens every day to make me boil!" she declared. "What can I do about it?"

I could tell her honestly that she was accomplishing much. I read to her a letter I had just received from the editor of a labor publication: "I have the copy you sent me of Mrs. Gartz's letter to the district attorney of Los Angeles County. I will send you copies of our papers in which it will appear. It is an inspiration to know that we have so brave and powerful a friend right where we need one."

But of course that was not enough. A labor journal reached only a few persons, and she wanted to reach the general public. I thought it over and suggested to her, "Let me gather your letters together and publish them in a book."

The result was a book of collected letters which I called *The Parlor Provocateur,* with the subtitle, "From Salon to Soap-Box." In the introduction, I explained: "Mrs. Gartz does not approve the title of this book. She wants to call it 'Letters of Protest,' or something else which is dignified. So I have stolen the book and given it a title which I think will cause people to talk about it and read it." Year after year thereafter I compiled and edited her letters, seven volumes in all, and published them with my introductions. They were seldom reviewed or mentioned in the press, but they were sent to all her acquaintances, both conservative and liberal, and to many of ours. They brought her a large correspondence, both pro and con. And then she would bring me a check or a bond, and would say, "Don't let *him* get this. Hide it for your future." I no longer refused these, for I was really in her employ.

Henry L. Mencken wrote Upton that he was coming to California and wanted to see him. Tell reporters, Mencken directed, that "I am coming to play the part of Pontius Pilate in the new De Mille Biblical movie. I am to receive $6,000 a week." Mencken and Upton took delight in badgering each other. Mencken, for instance, found *The Brass Check* "a good job," with nothing exaggerated and "in many ways understated." For he thought that Upton had not gone sufficiently into "the relations between the newspapers and the warmakers," and the "newspapers' part in the extraordinary persecution of heretics that went on during the war." But "as it stands, the book is a valuable piece of work. You will be de-

nounced as anti-Christ, but you will open many an eye." Yet he
concluded, "Your case against the newspapers is perfect, but
your remedy makes me weep," for his general view was: "To
hell with Socialism. The longer I live the longer I am convinced that the common people are doomed to be diddled forever." This view he illustrated with the case of the returned
soldiers:

> "Most of them are true proletarians. They were conscripted,
> in the majority of cases, against their will, and forced to fight in
> a war that few of them could understand. While they were in
> France there was much tall talk of their determination to clean
> up the country on their return. Well, what did they actually do?
> They succumbed instantly to the most ridiculous blather and
> began raiding and beating up the very men who were trying to
> save them from another such war.
> "I by no means argue that the capitalistic cause is good. On
> the contrary, it is infinitely unsound. Capitalism in America is
> much worse than even you make it out to be, just as journalism
> is much worse. . . . But I am convinced that you will never do
> any execution upon it."

When his order for copies of *The Brass Check* was delayed,
Mencken suggested, "Perhaps the American Legion objects."
He asked for circulars on *The Goosestep,* promising to "see that
they get into the hands of learned and very sore men," and he
felt that "Every Episcopal bishop in the Republic ought to be
jailed until he can prove he has read *They Call me Carpenter.*"

Of course the editor of the newly-founded *American Mercury,* the darling of the intellectuals of that day, was an ardent
defender of "the old-fashioned American saloon" and of the use
of every kind of alcoholic liquor, upon which Upton was making bitter war. As I could see no chance for a happy meeting of
the two I asked Mrs. Gartz if she wanted to be present. She had
at least one point of agreement with Mencken—she was much
opposed to Prohibition. "Prohibition is an infringement of the
right of the individual to choose what he puts into his stomach," she would argue.

"It is an infringement of his right to choose his way of self-destruction," Upton would answer; "all forms of suicide are illegal."

Mencken was stocky, with a round red face. His eyes were china blue and round, and did not smile as Upton's did. Kitty thought he was dull, which of course he was not, though his brand of intellectualism bored me, also. He had called Upton a "tub-thumper," and I called *him* one. But apparently literary men enjoy disagreeing with each other.

What Mencken wanted was for Upton to write some articles for the *American Mercury*. Why not his recollections of the writers he had known? Jack London, for example; and Upton asked, how could he, when the central tragedy of Jack's life had been alcohol? When Mencken said he might write it without mentioning that subject, Upton said that it would be like the fabled project of playing Hamlet without any Hamlet.

In their arguments the gentleman from Baltimore was the more aggressive, and obviously was enjoying himself; his red face became even more flushed, and I wondered if he was carrying a hip-pocket flask. We had good food but only water to drink.

During luncheon our guest launched upon a wild tale of his adventures on the Southern Pacific Railroad. The general passenger agent had wired the news of his coming all along the line, and nowhere had he been able to get any rest; every time the train stopped there would come taps on the door of his compartment, and there would be the station agent with real Scotch, or a mint julep with tinkling ice, and in the larger towns a local deputation with brass bands playing "Hail to the Chief," also lovely maidens carrying flowers. It was all very funny, and I could guess that one-tenth of it was true. His humor was like that of Dickens, based upon wild exaggeration. When he was teasing Upton on the subject of public ownership, and was asked if he would care to get along without the services of a fire department, his answer was that fire departments were useless; the fires mostly burned themselves out.

Mencken was going to San Francisco to persuade George Sterling to do an article for him about Jack London. But I knew George well enough to be sure that he wouldn't tell the so-painful truth. George was drinking too much himself, and thought he was not the one to tell about any other man's alcohol.

It is a debatable question whether drink causes pessimism or whether it is the other way around—which comes first, the hen or the egg? All I knew was that George was becoming more and more depressed, and that I had failed to help him. Why did he drink? Was it, as some said, a "consolation"? Then the answer to my mind was: give up the poisonous consolation.

Both Upton and I loved him, and knew him as a man of amazing beauty of character. All his friends loved him as we did and most of them were bewildered by his "weakness" for alcohol. But of course drinking was a part of his life in San Francisco.

And in Carmel, what would an abalone party on the beach have been without liquor? Wherever he was, George was constantly a host, or a guest.

Mencken was one of his drinking friends, and George was expecting to entertain his guest with the usual celebration. I have a letter which George wrote to one of his cronies a month or so ahead, saying: "Menck is to be in Texas in October, and says he is coming on to the Coast to visit me for a week. Which will stop all this water-wagon nonsense." So George got off the wagon in advance, and by the time "Menck" was due, George was in such a condition that he was unable to meet his editor and friend.

The terrible news came to us as the news of Jack London had come—through newspaper headlines. George had been found dead in his room at the Bohemian Club, with the foam of cyanide of potassium on his lips.

Long ago he had written his own epitaph, and I had read it, in the poem which Jerry had read to me, "The Man I Might Have Been."

The more I thought about the heart-breaking cost of just a small reform in a world so in need of improvement, the more I longed for a magic carpet or a fountain of youth. At the rate we were going, we would be old and gray before we could see much more than the beginning of the social changes for which we were striving.

It was a temptation sometimes to say to Upton, "You'll have to go on without me. I'm tired, very tired. And as fast as one evil is brought under control, another appears."

But I couldn't say it—he was so buoyant, so "starry-eyed." And so far, something substantial had always been won. Here and there repression of the suffering masses had been checked and a new lift given to the idealists who were going our way. Public opinion had been aroused, and public opinion meant votes, and the politicians who were tools of "the interests" were forced to enact legislation more favorable to the working people.

But this was too slow! I was really growing old. Bernard Shaw had declared that we are too old and feeble before we acquire any sense, or have time to act on that sense. Was this true? My frayed nerves answered, Yes. But then I became defiant—nothing so dumb as a body should get me discouraged! I would ignore it. No matter how tired I felt in the morning, I could throw it off with good coffee.

But I knew there was something wrong, for Upton got out of bed every morning feeling like a lark, and went soaring off into the blue with not even a cup of tea. "It is hope that does it," he declared. "I *believe* in something! Without vision the people perish—and I too!" "If ye have faith as a grain of mustard seed, ye shall say unto this mountain, Remove." How did Upton get that faith? His grew, while mine was steadily waning.

A friend, one of the sweetest, gentlest souls I had ever known, told me that I was "ready for Christian Science."

Through the years I had searched for God, questioning Him for his aloofness, longing to understand Him. I could not accept Upton's answer to this age-old question. "How can finite mind understand the infinite?" To this he always added, "I truly believe I am doing His will. This is the source of my optimism."

But I wanted to hear with my bodily ears a human voice, and to touch His hand. I wanted to know why He had not given me some means of everyday contact with Him. I wanted Him on a human plane. With my reason I accepted the idea that God is spirit, but my reason was not enough. Spirit was a word—cold, impersonal, and aloof. Tennyson had said that He was "nearer than hands and feet." But how did the poet know this? Through the years I prayed for help and when help came, "faith" came with it, and gratitude. But earthly things, material things, always came between me and this faith, and left me groping again.

Upton said it was a spiritual universe. When the time came that some physical scientists announced that the old physics of materialism was supplanted by Einsteinian physics, and that this removed the stumbling block of materialism from between physics and religion, I could see that mathematics was metaphysics—but I couldn't understand mathematics! When the British mathematician and philosopher Sir Arthur Eddington wrote, "The stuff of the universe is some sort of mind-stuff," I rejoiced; this reinforced the idea that the universe is spiritual, and made a God who was spirit seem possible, and "nearer than hands and feet." But it was not easy for my reasoning mind to convince me that pain and grief were reasonable.

But now Christian Science gave me more faith, and a key to that magic book, the Bible. It made it reasonable for me to put myself into God's hands and relax my own helpless efforts. It gave me faith, and more charity than I had formerly felt toward human vanity and selfishness. But nothing stayed "put," I soon found out. I must work and work to hold what I had gained.

"Stand porter at the door of thought," Mrs. Eddy said, in her textbook. This was not easy to do. Through all the years of my life I had acquired the mental habit of believing that my body governed my thought. If it hurt, I thought that "I" hurt. This habit had been overcome for a while, but it was still a habit, a fixture in my mind. I must learn by practice to stand porter at the door of my thought, to keep out destructive thoughts; to hold the thought that I was God's perfect child. This meant that in God's perfect mind I was a perfect idea, and could not be perfect if I held imperfect thoughts. So I must keep myself as a perfect idea! "This is your work," my friend told me. "Christian Science is work."

I heard from home that Mama had a serious ailment. Her physician had said her trouble was incurable, and about this disease the Mayo clinic agreed with the small-town family doctor. So, I must rely on God, as Mama was doing. I must "work" for Mama, who could not be interested in the ideas of any denomination but her own.

I had neglected Christian Science because it took so much time, and I had so much to do. Besides, I wasn't sure about a lot of things in the textbook. It was not a simple religion, by any means; it was too exacting. "Pray without ceasing," Mrs. Eddy and her followers kept on saying. How could anyone do that in the modern world? Mama couldn't wait for that. I could get a Christian Science practitioner to work for her, giving her what they call "absent treatment"; but when I asked a practitioner about this, she told me that Mrs. Eddy did not allow Christian Scientists to treat anyone without the person's consent. Then, would it be wrong for *me* to treat Mama without her consent? Did I really believe that such "absent treatments" could have an effect?

To the average person it seemed nonsense. I was not sure. Christian Scientists explained that it was not the practitioner who did the healing, it was God. But I believed that it was the suggestion of health the practitioner put into the subconscious mind of the patient. An absent treatment would thus be by way of telepathy. So then the question would be: was there such a thing as telepathy?

In my reading I had run across cases of cures of organic diseases by suggestion under hypnosis, cures made by reputable physicians in England and other European countries and in India. To me, at that time, Christian Science seemed similar to the Coué cures by auto-suggestion, and I decided to find a trustworthy hypnotist, if I could, to give Mama the right suggestions. She would not consider this an infringement on religion, as did Mrs. Eddy.

We made inquiry of doctors and psychiatrists, but could find no reliable hypnotist. Then my search became less urgent when a letter from Mama arrived, telling me that God had answered her prayers. All symptoms of her disease were gone. She felt well.

Worldly affairs demanded my attention. Oil derricks were steadily moving nearer the two lots I owned on the edge of a nearby town. The lot-owners in the tract had awakened to the fact that they must organize and stand together—otherwise the oil companies could buy a few scattered lots and from these drain all the oil from under the adjoining lots. We met with the other lot-owners to discuss a proposed agreement for grouping the lots to make a drilling site.

At the first meeting controversy broke out. There were lots of various sizes and locations. Some had houses on them; some were vacant. What share of the oil royalties was each to receive? Who was to be paid, and how much, for the loss they had suffered in planting and beautifying the lots? Would corner lots have more value per square foot than inside lots? Back and forth the arguments raged, and tempers flared; men and women became suspicious of each other. Here were a score of "little people," suddenly seized by the vision of becoming "big people," driven half-crazy with a mixture of greed and fear.

We made half a dozen trips from Pasadena, thirty miles or so each way, and spent two or three hours each trip listening to these wrangles and trying to make peace among the shifting factions. I was willing, but I was surprised to see that Upton was willing to give the time to it, until I saw he had a notebook and a busy pencil. On the way home I said, "What's this—are you going to write about it?"

"Gosh!" he said—his favorite expletive. "Don't you see what we've got here? Human nature laid bare! Competition *in excelsis!* The whole oil industry—free, gratis, and for nothing! How could I pass it up?"

I knew what he meant, of course. I remembered the story of his Chicago stockyards experience when he was gathering material for *The Jungle.*

And now here was the oil industry of California, on a silver platter! Lawyers came and explained leases and the law. Oilmen came and told what they were willing to do, and how, and why, and when, and where—all the technicalities. Everybody in the room knew somebody else in the business. We were right in the center of an oil cyclone. And when we started home, all around us were the derricks, the thumping engines and the grinding drills. Presently there was a "gusher" and a road too slick with oil to drive on; and of course the newspapers, full of excitement.

One of the "big" oilmen wanted to buy our two lots, and asked us to come and look at a ranch he offered in exchange. So we let him drive us in a big fast car, breaking all the speed laws; what did it matter if he had to pay a fine, in exchange for his valuable time? Upton rode on the front seat with him, while I sat in back and listened. Upton was plying him with questions about the oil business, and the man was pleased to talk about it. All along the way was the wonderful scenery of Southern California: orange groves, mountains and deserts. Then in rolling back country that had more rocks than soil we turned into a rough dirt road with a little stream flowing beside it, and came to a three-room California-style house set in a background of eucalyptus trees. It was a goat ranch and the goats were all around, browsing on the hillsides. We got out and looked about us, and I didn't think much of it as a swap for an oil lot; but I saw eagerness in Upton's eyes. He rambled about, taking in everything; and later, when we had parted from the oil man and were back in our own car I asked him, "Would you like to own that?"

His answer was, "I own it already—every square foot of it!"

I understood such cryptic words; I was witnessing the birth of a novel. "It's writing itself!" he said. "That oil man is to be the father of my hero. The boy's name is Bunny Ross, and the father is Dad. The opening chapter is called 'The Ride,' and they are driving to a town where there has been a new oil discovery. All the way the boy is watching everything and learning from his father. The second chapter is 'The Lease,' and pictures all those lot-owners, crazy with greed, and fear, and hope, dickering with Dad and unable to make up their minds about anything. Wonderful scenes, all ready-made—not a thing needs to be changed!"

"And the goat ranch?" I asked.

"Dad is a wildcatter, and he buys that ranch and strikes oil; there'll be a chapter called 'The Gusher.' And on the ranch there's a boy who has lived all his life tending goats, and he becomes Bunny's friend. He works for Dad, and later he turns into a Socialist—"

"Oh, dear!" I said. "Another?" But nothing could stop Upton—he rushed on in a "gusher" of words, a whole book pouring from his mind.

"There's a chapter called 'The Strike,' and Paul Watkins— that's the friend's name—leads it. So you see, Bunny is torn between loyalty to his father and to his friend. That way he sees the whole of the class struggle."

"You don't have to explain *that* to me!" I hoped he would pause long enough to notice that we were at a bad place in the road and I was being jolted to pieces.

"And Paul has an older brother named Eli, who becomes a prophet, a hellfire-and-brimstone evangelist—he's going to be a male Aimée Semple McPherson. He reaps a fortune and builds a temple in Los Angeles, and then he runs away with a woman, and comes back with a wonderful tale about having been kidnapped and sets the whole town arguing over whether he really did or didn't."

"You're going to include Los Angeles, then?"

"The whole of Southern California, the new land of 'black gold.' When Dad becomes a millionaire, Bunny will go to Hollywood and meet a movie star—every time I think about it, it unreels like a ten-reel movie. It's a sure-fire one this time; it'll go all over the world!"

He thought that about every book he wrote. He hadn't had a real commercial success since *The Jungle,* twenty years earlier, yet his books had indeed gone all over the world. I had no right to dampen his enthusiasm. This was my determined attitude. I listened, and put my own imagination—so different from his—to work. It would be my task to give Bunny Ross a face, and to put "clothes" on Vee Tracy of Hollywood.

"How long will this writing job take?" I asked, and he answered, "Always a year, for a full-length novel. It's a long grind, but be sure it will pay for itself—financially as well. This time I *know!*"

It was a relief to me in one way—I had been feeling guilty about dragging him into business matters, which I knew were repugnant to his mind. But now, in nature's strange fashion, new life had come out of his pain. My "writing machine" was suddenly in love with one kind of business; he wanted to see everything and talk to everybody who had anything to do with oil. That was going to be the title of the book, just three letters, with an exclamation at the end to show how wonderful it was —*Oil!*

When Upton had got everything he needed for his new novel, it became a hardship for him to go with me to the meetings of the unhappy lot owners blinded by the prospect of sudden wealth. I, too, was tired of it, and decided to sell my two lots. I exchanged the lots for a five-room cottage and a garage with two rooms above it, and several thousand dollars in addition. The cottage was on the beach, and for the second time in my life, I could step out my front door in a bathing suit with no house between me and the ocean. On the other side, and separated only by a narrow strip of sand, was placid Alamitos Bay. Across it and fed from its waters were the canals which crisscross Venice, a subdivision of summer homes, silent in winter.

Upton collected all our books on psychic research and put them in our new beach house. At last I was going to make a real study of that mystery, the mind of man. My first concern continued to be to find out if telepathy was real, but I was going to find out everything I could on the problem of mind-body. The implications of it were so immense that I had always wondered why all the great minds of the world did not devote themselves to this subject. Throughout history, a few of them always had.

Among other books I now read one by Dr. Cannon of the Harvard Medical School, who had gone to Russia to study under Pavlov. Also I subscribed to a New Thought publication and read several books on yoga.

While I read and made notes for Upton on the margins, he would be strolling in the clear, clean sunshine along the water's edge, thinking up his next chapter. He had enjoyed the long, wide gallery on the front of our pink house in Pasadena. Now he was enjoying the lonely beach, with the incoming tide at his feet, and the white breakers farther out, and the feeling of awe and wonder which a great ocean arouses.

Our tranquility seemed assured. But a "bolt of lightning" had struck me when I was young—that day I came home to Greenwood from school in New York and found a strange young man who was fated to live in my mind forever. And now a second bolt struck. Jerry, my first sweetheart, was dead!

I kept saying to myself, "I did not know that you could die, Jerry. You *cannot* die!"

Here I was, in my California home; my beloved husband would come in presently from tennis, flushed and happy, his zest for his writing keen. He was truly my beloved, and his work was our life. I knew why I loved him, and I could never have explained why I had loved Jerry. Yet here it was—this awful grief; Jerry had gone out of the world!

He had been drinking heavily for years, so they said in letters from home, so no one there was surprised. He had often said he saw no sense in this earthly existence. But I could not think of his not being in it, somewhere, even though beyond sight, or sound, or the touch of a human hand.

Upton came home and called boisterously as he entered, "I've got another cup for you! I'm several times a champ!"

I looked up at him and tried to smile—then I knew that would be hypocrisy.

"What has happened, dearest?" he asked, soberly.

"Jerry is dead!" Then I put my head and arms on the table in front of me and began to sob.

Upton sat beside me and put his arms around me. "That is terrible," he said, as if he had known Jerry. "Oh, I'm so sorry, my dearest. Tell me, how did it happen?"

"Suicide—"

"My God! Poor fellow!" He wanted to comfort me, so he blundered on. "I can pity him," he said, "because I know what he lost!"

"Oh, don't say that!" I cried. "It was not because of me."

"What I mean is, if you had married him you might have saved him. But then I might have been the one who perished."

Upton would never have become an alcoholic, nor a suicide, but when I met him he had been eating his heart out with worry and want and loneliness, and now he was happy and useful. There was no way to know whether I could have saved Jerry. Nothing had saved George Sterling, or Jack London.

But one phrase continued to haunt me: "I did not know that you could die, Jerry!"

Upton and I heard of a young Polish "psychic," who was astounding physicians of Southern California. He could put himself into a deep trance during which his body became rigid and cold; two men put his head on one chair and his heels on another, and then stood in the middle of his body, as if he were a two-inch plank. International News Service made a motion-picture film, showing a 150-pound rock being broken with a sledgehammer on his abdomen while he lay in this trance. The vital faculties were so far suspended that he could be shut up in an air-tight coffin and buried underground for several hours; in Ventura, California, it was done in a ball park, and a game played over the grave. The film included one of these burials. The man, whom I here call Jan, was giving stage performances and demonstrations in the private homes of Hollywood. Among his friends was the popular comedienne, Fanny Brice, and Leopold Stokowski, the orchestra conductor. We arranged with him to come to Long Beach as our guest.

The first thing Jan did was try to get us to practice Hatha Yoga. But I had read enough to know that I did not want it. What I wanted was the knowledge which enabled him to control his body by the power of his mind. How did he control his circulation so that he could pierce his tongue with a nail without a flow of blood? How had he managed to stick corsage pins through his cheeks, his arms, his throat, night after night, as he did in his "demonstrations," without a drop of blood oozing from the wounds? How was he able to time himself exactly when he was in a deep trance? Before he went into a trance, he would ask the doctors, "How long before you want me to wake up?" And they would say thirty minutes, or sixty, and on one occasion, some rather reckless physicians said "two hours." This was a long time for anyone to risk leaving a man in a sealed box buried under earth. But Jan was willing to take the risk, and came out of his trance on the exact minute.

Had the doctors failed to get him out on time, he would have come out of his trance suffocated, he declared, for no conscious man could live in a coffin under the earth. On one occasion when the doctors had got him out a trifle late, he was bleeding from his ears and mouth.

We invited some of the doctors who had taken part in his burials to come to our home for experiments. They were interested in spite of themselves, for like most medical men, they had spent their lives ignoring the power of mind to affect the physical organism. They found it of great interest to watch him hypnotize the woman secretary of one doctor and then control, by suggestion, the flow of blood to her arm so that there would be no trace of blood during or after a puncture with a corsage pin. One thing the doctors refused, however, and we agreed with them; they would not trust Jan's assurance that the puncture could not become infected, no matter whose unsterilized pin was used. Iodine must be applied at once!

But neither they nor we could explain hypnosis or auto-hypnosis. Many students of the mind, including some of the finest psychiatrists, have tackled this mystery, but there is still no satisfactory explanation. It is some power, or state, in the subconscious. But what is the subconscious? Why are its powers greater than those of consciousness? Why do they hide? Why does it take hypnosis to reveal them?

Dr. William McDougall once remarked to me, "The mind does not like to think about itself. It can be persuaded to, but there is a limit to what it will reveal, except under hypnosis. Why is this?"

I wanted to convince myself that telepathy was real. If Mama's illness should return, this would help me to help her.

In order to verify telepathy, I began to experiment with it myself, with Jan. Once I wrote an account of what I had "seen" him doing on a trip to Santa Barbara. He was visibly agitated when I read this account to him, and admitted that it was true. Upton had read the account while Jan was away, and so I had really scored a success when Jan said he *had* escorted a young lady dressed in pale blue across a pavement during a rain storm into a hotel or public building. He had always led us to believe that he was not interested in girls—they interfered with the work to which his life was dedicated. We laughed at him, and his friend who had gone on the trip attested to the reality of my telepathy.

Our world was changing faster and faster, and the change was not alone in our way of life, but in our very minds. Not only were we growing old—we, who had almost taken it for granted that we were immortal here and now, and that everyone and everything we knew was immortal. Now we saw our friends and loved ones silently slipping out of the world. There had been George, and then Jerry. And now, Mama was gone.

This had been the one event I had never been able to face in my mind. I had foreseen it when I heard she had heart trouble, but time had passed and she had written me she was well again. She was going on with all her usual activities, including her work for the beloved "Lost Cause."

Then, suddenly, she had gone. Now I must face it—if I could.

For a long time I felt it simply was not possible that Mama was no longer there in the dear old home with all her busy, happy youngsters around her. I had thought, with sudden terror when Papa had come to see us in California, that he would go first; he had grown so old and tired and gray. But he was still there at home—and Mama had left him.

About the "certain success" called *Oil!* my optimist guessed right. Horace Liveright read the first half and was delighted with it, but his staff didn't like the second half. That never worried Upton; he took it for granted that every manuscript would be refused once or twice, or maybe six or eight times. A. and C. Boni were enthusiastic about *Oil!* Then the

Literary Guild accepted it and it went to the top of the best-seller lists and stayed there.

And now came a surprising development: the Boston police authorities banned the sale of the book, charging that it was "obscene." There was a "Watch and Ward Society," and a Catholic superintendent of police, and they were the judges of literature for the one-time capital of American culture. As Felix Frankfurter, then professor of law at Harvard University, wrote Upton, "We are suffering from a book censorship in this town that is as stupid as it is violative of all those traditions which we have treasured as typically American."

Upton, a warrior for his causes, wanted to take the next train to Boston; his publishers urged him to do this. I told him that Boston would say he had come just to advertise his book, and he answered that Boston had advertised it as obscene, and surely he had a right to advertise it as not obscene. So I said, "All right."

Daily bulletins and an occasional item in the newspaper came from Upton. He got a lot of publicity on arrival in New York, a city which didn't like Boston too much. When he found what the police objected to, he announced that he was going to prepare a "Fig-leaf Edition" of *Oil!* with the nine offending pages blacked out, and would sell that on the streets of Boston. He did so, and there was a lot of fun; the edition became a collector's item. He discussed the book at a mass meeting, and then went by appointment and sold a copy of the complete edition to the superintendent of police, and was placed under a temporary arrest. It was absurdly temporary, because when he appeared in court the judge wouldn't have him.

"We think, Mr. Sinclair, you have had publicity enough for your books"—declared His Honor. He said this off the bench, so Upton could argue with him, pointing out that it was Boston which had started the publicity.

Upton came home well content. *Oil!* was in its eighth printing, and was going around the world.

What pleased me most was a telegram from Senator Borah: "I read your book and did not find anything in it which shocked me. Now I must read it again as somebody has discovered something. There is one thing for which I am deeply grateful and that is that we did not have these censors in previous periods or we should have been deprived of some of the richest literature in all the world."

Oil! was translated and published in twenty-nine different languages and as usual with Upton's books it was pirated in others. The countries that we know of were Britain, France, Germany, Holland, Norway, Sweden, Denmark, Iceland, Spain, Poland, Czechoslovakia, Hungary, Russia, Latvia, Estonia, Lithuania, Finland, Jugoslavia, Rumania, Bulgaria, Syria, Japan, China, Brazil. Additional languages were Yiddish, Hebrew, Hindi, Gujurati, Bengali, Esperanto and Braille. To have watched such a work through conception, birth, and maturity is an experience which falls only to those fortunate women whose husbands are both scholars and humanitarians.

Another book grew out of that visit to Boston. Fred D. Moore, whom Upton had known for many years, was the defense attorney for Sacco and Vanzetti, the shoe worker and the fish peddler under sentence of death in the jail at Charlestown. Upton went off with Moore for a visit to Vanzetti, and talked for an hour or two.

Vanzetti was a self-educated man who still had traces of an Italian accent. Like Peter Kropotkin, he called himself a *philosophical* anarchist, and he was as gentle as the old Russian prince, radiating loving-kindness in every tone and word. In search of a cure for poverty he had read a number of the great moral philosophers and discussed their ideas. He did not say anything about his own case; he talked about the evil creeds which held the earth's disinherited in thrall, and Upton came away quite sure that he was a man who would not willingly have hurt a mouse.

Vanzetti's appeal was before the Governor of Massachusetts, who had appointed a committee of three, headed by President Lowell of Harvard, to study the case and advise him. Upton came home and followed developments in the press and in letters from friends in Boston. The case had become internationally famous, and when the Governor refused to intervene there was a tremendous clamor. On the night of the execution a huge crowd surrounded the prison and millions wept all over the world. Upton was deeply aroused, and decided that night that his next novel would be called *Boston,* and would center around the life and death of Bartolomeo Vanzetti. "So long as there is a man in jail for leading a strike, I am in jail," he declared.

This was his creed, and I knew it now by heart, and my heart was with it. The book meant another trip East, and at once. Upton had an infection on his heel, so that all the time he was traveling to Boston and in the city gathering his material, he was on crutches. But he met the relatives and friends of the two men, and met the lawyers and those members of the Boston élite who had interested themselves in the case. These few of the secure and affluent ones of the earth had hearts and consciences, like the few who had helped us in our California crusade. They wanted to do something about poverty and injustice, but did not know what to do; Upton did know, they felt sure, and they helped him by giving him entrée to the life and reactions of their class.

Before he left for Boston he had met in Pasadena a Mrs. Mary Burton, an elderly lady who had left her family home because of a quarrel. Upton, delighted, called her "the runaway grandmother," and decided to make her the heroine of this Boston novel. She was delighted in turn, and poured out local color to him.

He wanted to have a family quarrel follow the death of a patriarch; the novel would open with a behind-the-scenes view of a stately funeral. He read in the Boston *Transcript* that such a funeral was to take place at the estate of a wealthy manufacturer. Upton remembered vaguely having met this eminent Bostonian a quarter of a century earlier, when Upton had come to the city to gather material for his Civil War novel, *Manassas.* On that trip he had met Colonel Thomas Wentworth Higginson, Julia Ward Howe, Professor Barrett Wendell, the publisher Edwin Ginn and others. Now he rode on a trolley to the town where the great mills were situated, took a carriage to the mansion and went in with the other guests. Coming back on the trolley, he made some notes, but was interrupted by a reporter of the *Transcript* who had recognized and followed him. Upton's plan to write *Boston* was widely known, and the reporter shrewdly put two and two together. Upton wasn't in the least embarrassed and took delight in sending me the story which appeared in the next day's paper, describing his mysterious appearance at a "private" funeral. The reporter pictured him as "a mousy little man."

In New York was a monthly magazine, *The Bookman*, published by a rich man's son, Seward Collins, whom we had known in California. When Upton told him the story of the new novel he offered to purchase the serial rights, sight unseen, and publish it month by month as it was written. An old-time custom, going back to the days of Dickens and Thackeray! Upton came home to California and went to work on it the next day.

Boston was the longest of Upton's novels. The publishers were enthusiastic and prepared to bring it out in two handsome volumes. When they had the type set in pages their lawyers began to speak of possible libel suits, and Upton had to return to New York and sit down with the lawyers and make changes to calm their fears. It is quite an art to cut out a few words in a page of type and replace them with other words that occupy exactly the same number of type spaces. Upton has had to acquire perfection at it.

At this point I had been reading W. J. Dunne's *An Experiment With Time*. It is his thesis that dreams are frequently prophetic, and that you can prove it by his technique, which is to record all dreams in minute detail at once and then at intervals read the record over. You have to do the reading often, otherwise you will have forgotten the past dream, and so will not recognize the subsequent event if it occurs. I tried it for some time and became convinced that Dunne was correct.

Now I recorded that I dreamed of being in a magnificent room, with many splendidly dressed people; for some reason I knew they were there to honor me. Also I knew that it was on the second floor. Along one side of this room was a line of tables, and on these were flowers and fruit and dishes of food and bowls of punch. The walls of the room had shelves and these were full of books. I recorded especially the vivid detail in this dream, but nothing could have seemed less likely to happen to me. I was absorbed in my psychic studies, I was saddened about the world and the loss of my mother, and I wanted only to stay quietly in our little beach resort where no one knew me or spoke to me, and to have my husband busy and happy with a new writing job.

He was working as regularly as a clock: writing every morning, revising every afternoon, and in the evening walking up and down along our beach. There came a telegram, telling him that the publication date of *Boston* was set for a week or so ahead, and the publishers wanted to give a grand coming-out party to be called the "Boston Tea Party." All the critics and reviewers would be invited to attend and it would give a great boost to the book.

My impulse was to say No, a hundred times. I hated travel, I hated crowds, I had had all the parties I ever wanted to see in this world. But I knew that the most important thing in life to Upton was to get people to read his books and thus get their minds changed about the world's woes. We discussed the idea most of the night, and I changed my mind several times. In the end I said, "All right."

We had a comfortable trip, with no accidents, and at the station there were the publishers and the reporters they had invited. The "Boston Tea Party" was to be held in the ballroom of the Savoy-Plaza. We were put up at the Algonquin, where the literary lights gathered, and Mencken came to visit us, as well as George Jean Nathan, Fulton Oursler, W. E. Woodward, Max Eastman and Carl Van Doren—I can't remember them all. That night we went to the home of one of the publishers to meet some of his friends; and next morning one of these publishers, Charles Boni, said to me, very timidly, "Wouldn't you be able to persuade Upton to get a new suit of clothes?"

He was afraid of offending me, but I soon had him laughing

at my stories about Upton and his clothes. I said to the young
publisher, "I can't persuade Upton, but maybe I can trap him."

So that afternoon I invited him to take a walk. We strolled
up Broadway, and there was a men's furnishings store. I stopped
to look in the window, then said, "I see something I want."
Before Upton got his wits together I had him inside, and a clerk
came forward. I told him, "This gentleman has to make an important public appearance tonight, and he wants the sort of
suit the public will expect."

The young salesman said, "I think I know exactly the sort of
public appearance this gentleman has to make." He took from
his pocket a clipping from a morning paper, telling of Upton's
arrival and of the prospective "Boston Tea Party." Before
Upton could get over his surprise, the man said, "I think I have
exactly the suit you need."

Upton tried on a very dignified black suit, and it fitted him
magically. I had brought some money and Mr. Sinclair walked
out with a new suit, worthy of a famous man and his excellent
tailor! Again I remembered Papa and his admiration for the
Jews. If one needed help for an idealistic cause, they always
gave it; if one needed a tailor who could magically produce an
elegant ready-made suit for only twenty-five dollars—well, I had
found one!

Late in the afternoon we entered the Savoy-Plaza and went
up to the second floor in an elevator. As I stepped out and entered the ballroom I stopped in amazement. I had forgotten
my dream; but there it was before me, and it all came back in
a flash, overwhelming me. Every detail—the second floor, the
large and splendid room, the long line of tables against the far
wall, and all the flowers and food and bowls of punch. The
only things missing were the shelves of books; but the purpose
of this party was to sell a hundred thousand of them! I hadn't
read my record for some time, but I knew it was there at home,
scrawled with a pencil on some sheets of green copy paper. And
here were the guests coming to honor me; of course it wasn't
really for me, but Upton would have insisted that it was, and
the publishers would have gallantly agreed.

When I got home I looked up my dream record and read it.

There it was. I cannot tell what this seeming prevision means, but this I have read: the great German Kant, called the father of modern philosophy, told us a couple of hundred years ago that time and space are forms of our thinking. The greatest scientist of our day, Albert Einstein, told me the same thing, and modern physics is based upon his teachings. I am too ignorant to understand what the scientific words mean, but I do know what happened to me, and I record it as the truth.

The "Boston Tea Party" was a great success. Though there was no tea, there was fruit juice for Upton and champagne and punch for everybody else. All the critics and reviewers came, and said nice things about *Boston*. The two volumes, neatly boxed, were on all the bookstore counters that day, and it was pleasant to hear that they were disappearing rapidly. The reviewers praised it and *Boston* was another book that went around the world.

We stayed in the East for two weeks and saw some of our friends. At the home of W. E. Woodward we met Bill Seabrook, author of *Adventures in Arabia*, *The Magic Isle* and later *Asylum*, the story of his own struggle with John Barleycorn. Samuel Untermyer invited us to dine in his Park Avenue apartment, and weary as I was, I wanted to go. I had not forgotten his trust in us when he loaned Upton money for the publication of *The Brass Check* and gave his high-priced time to reading the book and giving us his legal opinion. He was a Wall Street lawyer for whose services we could never have paid. I was glad we had repaid his loan.

Dr. Morton Prince, an eminent Boston psychiatrist, had written a book, *Dissociation of a Personality*, a case record which Upton had read and never forgotten. Dr. Prince had expressed deep interest in what I had written him about Jan, and I arranged to bring Jan to Boston. A preliminary demonstration of telepathy convinced Dr. Prince of the genuineness of this medium, and he then told me he would invite some Harvard scientists to a demonstration of Jan's autohypnosis. Of that group I recall Professor Harlow Shapley and Dr. Walter B. Cannon.

Unfortunately, they put Jan in a rather frail antique chair to demonstrate autohypnosis, and during his deep trance this chair collapsed and he fell to the floor. I have never seen a man so frightened as Dr. Prince in those terrible minutes; Jan seemed to be dead and the psychiatrist knew the danger of such a shock to a psychic in deep trance. He told the company not to be afraid. He knew that Jan was a telepathist and therefore might receive the fear thoughts of the others, become frightened himself and go into a more profound state of shock, if not into death.

Our host was not *en rapport* with the psychic, and left me to try to bring him out of his trance. I sat by him—I had often had him near to hypnosis—and now I talked to him in a calm and soothing voice, telling him that he was all right, that no harm was done, and that he would come out of his trance at the precise moment he had set. The doctors had stop-watches, and were curious to know how he counted the time; at the exact moment he began to breathe deeply, opened his eyes and asked what had happened. That was the end of the demonstration, but not the end of Dr. Prince's concern. He wrote me afterward that I was "playing with dangerous forces."

Back in California, we planned to go on with psychic research; but the world continued to beckon us. A delegation of seventeen leading European journalists came to Los Angeles; somebody had had the idea of promoting international friendship by inviting them, expenses paid. They were given a banquet at the splendid Ambassador Hotel. Upton was always interested in meeting people who were informed about world affairs and persuaded me to go with him.

He had never had a dinner jacket and declined to be aware of "such nonsense." It was a summer night and he would be comfortable in a Palm Beach suit, and the rest of those present could call him an eccentric—as his colleague Rupert Hughes proceeded to do! We went, and in the lobby of the hotel I met someone I knew and stopped to chat. Upton strolled off, and ran into an old friend of the days in London, David Edstrom, Swedish-born sculptor, and good fellow with whom he had roamed Hampstead Heath, visiting the haunts of Keats and Shelley.

Edstrom's greeting was cordial, but he seemed nervous; he kept looking about him, and finally blurted out, "I'll be frank with you, old man; I'm afraid for this outfit to see me talking to you. You see, I'm expecting to get a commission to do a bust, and I need the job badly."

"Who's your victim?" asked Upton, amused.

"It's Harry Chandler himself—the publisher of the *Times.*"

"Gosh!" exclaimed Upton. "I would certainly ruin you! I'll make myself scarce." He did so, and presently saw his friend chatting with the all-powerful publisher.

We went into the crowded dining-room, which must have seated a couple of hundred persons. The seats had been reserved, and directly across the narrow table from Upton sat a gray-haired gentleman in correct evening dress. I did not know who he was until Upton told me after the dinner that it was Harry Chandler, whose newspaper had printed more untrue statements about my husband than any other paper in the state. It seemed impossible that this seating arrangement could have been an accident; some puckish person must have planned it.

Chandler listened attentively, and what he heard came from a stream of the honored European guests, who left their tables one by one and came to the chair of the unpretentious man in a Palm Beach suit. I do not know how many, but they came all through the meal, apparently willing to miss a part of their dinner. They wanted to stand and chat, and always to say that they had read the author's books, and especially the last one, which had told them so much about Southern California and prepared them to understand it. And across the table sat the most powerful man in the sprawling city, with not one of the visitors paying the least attention to him. He had nothing to do but munch his dinner and listen to praise of a book of which he had never even heard.

The time came when his curiosity got the better of him and he spoke. "What did you say was the name of that book?"

Upton hadn't said its name; it was the visitors who had said it. But he answered politely, "It is called *Oil!*"

"And what is it about?"

Again the answer was polite: "It deals with the oil industry in Southern California, and the struggle of labor against the control of the community by big business."

"And how many translations did you say?"

"I can't say positively. I have authorized about twenty-five."

And that was the end of the conversation.

13. NEW POWERS OF THE HUMAN MIND

DR. MORTON PRINCE'S WARNING about playing with dangerous forces did not alarm me. I was aware of the danger, but I was aware also of the danger of ignoring such an important aspect of life as the power of the mind. It could bring untold benefits—perhaps even "salvation from sin, sickness and death"—or it could bring destruction. As the apostle Paul said: "Be ye transformed by the renewing of your mind."

Upton was as conscious as I of the importance of what we were doing. He wrote: "If now it be a fact that there is a reality behind the notions of telepathy and clairvoyance, to which so many investigations are bearing testimony all over the world, who can set limits to what it may mean to the future? What new powers of the human mind, what ability to explore the past and future, the farthest deeps of space and those deeps of our own minds, no less vast and marvelous?"

When we were safe again from outside distractions in our cottage on the lonely Alamitos beach, we returned to our experiments. I undertook to be the recipient of messages from Upton's mind, and he to try sending them. Our technique was simple: I would relax on a couch and suggest to my subconscious mind that I would see what he was drawing in another room with the door closed. He would concentrate all his attention upon the drawing. When I thought I "saw" in my mind what the drawing was I would try to reproduce it or write a description of it.

At the end of several months of this kind of experiment and some spectacular tests with other persons—a total of 425 experiments—the results were so convincing that Upton said, "Enough is enough." We had proved to ourselves that telepathy happened.

Then Upton declared, "I am going to put it into a book." I was far from being willing for this to happen, for I did not want to talk about myself, and especially not in print. But I soon realized that having married a writing machine, I had to let it write. A restless author around the house all day, wanting to work and not allowed to, would make life unbearable. There were many experiments I could make without his help, while he wrote *Mental Radio*.

When the book was finished and in the hands of a publisher Upton sent a set of proofs to Professor William McDougall. I had been reading McDougall's books and admired him profoundly. He had been invited to Harvard from Oxford, where he held the chair of psychology. At Harvard he had become known as "the dean of American psychology." Upton was much pleased when he consented to write an introduction to our book. He praised our work beyond anything that I had hoped for; I knew we were in an unpopular field of research, and furthermore one in which we were laymen.

Praise from this authority gave me the courage to imagine that experiments so carefully planned and precisely reported would impress scientific minds, but it was not so. Only a few minds were open. Sir Arthur Conan Doyle thought I must be "a powerful latent medium." Mahatma Gandhi wrote: "Nobody in India would, I think, doubt the possibility of telepathy but would doubt the wisdom of its material use."

Albert Einstein wrote, as an introduction to the German edition:

"I have read the book of Upton Sinclair with great interest, and I am convinced that it deserves the most earnest attention, not only of the laity, but also of the specialists in psychology.

The results of the telepathy experiments which are carefully and plainly described in this book stand surely far beyond what an investigator of nature considers to be thinkable; but, on the other hand, it is not to be thought of that so conscientious an observer and writer as Upton Sinclair should attempt a deliberate deception of the reading world. His good faith and trustworthiness cannot be doubted, and if it should be that the facts set forth with great clearness do not rest upon telepathy, but upon some unknown hypnotic influence from person to person, that also would be of high psychological interest. In no case should the psychologically interested pass over this book without heed."

A detailed study of *Mental Radio* was made by Dr. Walter Franklin Prince, Research Officer of the Boston Society for Psychic Research, and published in their *Bulletin* XVI, dated April, 1932. Dr. Prince (not to be confused with Dr. Morton Prince, also of Boston) was a former Episcopal clergyman and a man of scrupulous rectitude and exactitude. He devoted 86 closely printed pages to the book and printed as an appendix an account I had written of my search for more knowledge. He wrote that, "The main points of what Mr. Sinclair tells us of the characteristics of his wife are to be discerned in this revealing manuscript," and quoted Upton: "She has nothing of the qualities of naïveté and credulity. She was raised in a family of lawyers and was given the training and skeptical point of view of a woman of the world. 'Trust every man, but watch him,' was old Judge Kimbrough's maxim, and following it too closely has almost made a pessimist of his daughter."

Upton had estimated our percentages of successes, partial successes and failures: in 290 experiments, successes, approximately 23 per cent; partial successes, 53 per cent; failures, 24 per cent. Dr. Prince wrote, "I personally think that certain examples which he did not publish are better than a few which he did, but have not yet found reason to quarrel with his general estimates."

Dr. Prince made a detailed and minute study of all our records, which we turned over to him (425 tests). Only 290 are discussed in *Mental Radio*. I cannot even summarize his work here but will mention one "series" dated February 15, 1929, containing 13 drawings "with only one absolute failure." Dr. Prince endeavors to figure the chances of such a series happening by guesswork and says: "The result, on what I think a moderate basis, is one chance in 16,777,216."

He proceeded to invite ten ladies of Boston who had no psychic gifts that they knew of to repeat the tests with the 13 drawings of this series reproduced exactly and sealed up in envelopes. He reported that in the 130 tests there was not a single success, only one partial success, seven suggestive and 116 failures. This against the Sinclair set of three successes, five partial successes, four suggestive and one failure in 13 tries instead of 130.

In July and August, 1930, Professor William McDougall came to see us half a dozen times, at Long Beach and Pasadena, and invited me to make some tests with him. I explained that my mother had just died, and I was in a continual struggle to keep myself from giving way to grief; when I tried to concentrate, I could see nothing but her image. But I reminded myself that he had done us a great honor, and we were in his debt, so I said I would do my best. He had prepared five postcards in sealed envelopes, and gave them to me one by one, and he and Upton watched while I lay on a couch and tried to divine what was in them. Altogether, during his visits, we made twenty-five tests, and McDougall preserved his drawings and mine, and sent them on request to Dr. Prince, whom he knew well. Prince reports of the results, "though inferior to many of the series of 1928 and 1929, yet show a ratio and quality of correspondence vastly beyond chance expectation." He sums up: "We have found 3 successes and 4 partial successes (not counting a possible 'anticipation,' and two instances of suggestive). He concludes that these results are "something for which chance is wholly unable to account."

Here are several of the more striking successes, reported in *Mental Radio*. In each case, the sketch with the number is what Upton drew and that with the letter *a* added is what I produced. The texts included are what I wrote on my drawing, always before Upton's sealed envelope was opened.

Upton's drawing was supposed to represent a bird's nest with eggs; I wrote: "Inside of rock well with vines climbing on outside." Figs. 4 and 4a.

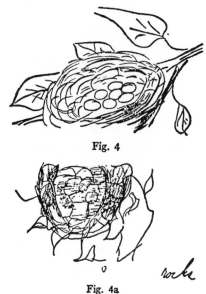

Fig. 4

Fig. 4a

Figs. 5 and 5a. Here I wrote: "Knight's helmet."

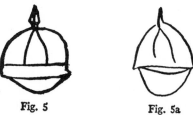

Fig. 5   Fig. 5a

Figs. 9 and 9a. This was supposed to be a puppy chasing a string. I wrote: "May be elephant's snout—but anyway it is some kind of a running animal. Long thing like rope flung out in front of him." On this Dr. Prince comments: "I should say that the addition of that 'rope' drawn out in front of the animal at that angle made chance of guessing of the combination at least ten times as unlikely, and on the basis of my hundreds of experiments in guessing, I should not *expect* in ten thousand such experiments on the basis of the same original drawing one reproduction as good as the summation of its correspondences."

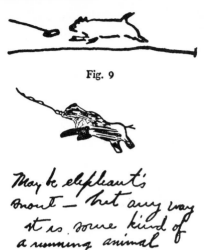

Fig. 9

May be elephant's
snout — but any way
it is some kind of
a running animal

Fig. 9a

Five of our early tests were made with my brother-in-law, a hard-headed young businessman, Bob Irwin, while I was at Alamitos Bay and he in Pasadena, thirty or forty miles away; and these were among the most striking successes. At an agreed hour he made a drawing and concentrated upon it, and I tried to get it. Thus, he drew a table fork, and I wrote the words: "July 13, 1928. See a table fork. Nothing else." Figs. 1 and 1a.

Fig. 1

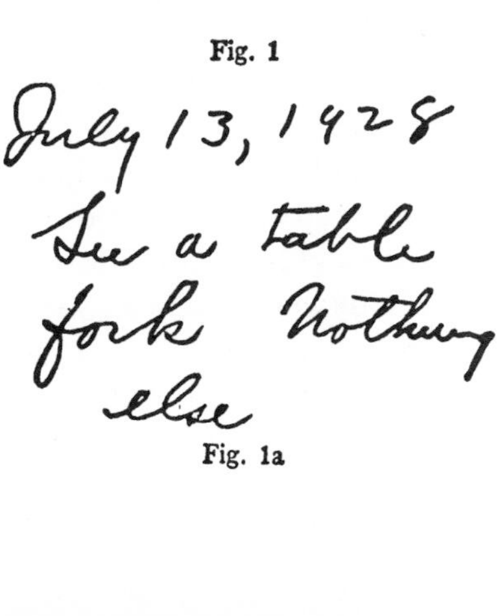

July 13, 1928
See a table
fork Nothing
else

Fig. 1a

Again, Bob drew a straight chair, and I drew one and wrote the words "See a straight chair." Then I drew a second straight chair, the difference between them being that in the first one the back supports ran horizontally, while in the second they ran vertically. The first drawing was in accord with Bob's—an unusual kind of chair; it developed that he, an invalid, was lying in bed and had been looking at the chair through the footboard of the bed, which had strips of wood running vertically. Figs. 16 and 16a.

Fig. 16   Fig. 16a

Dr. F. C. S. Schiller from Oxford came to lecture for a season at the University of Southern California. He was a friend of McDougall, also of dear Mary Wilshire. Dr. Schiller was surprised that no one at the university had ever met Upton Sinclair; he asked why, and Upton said, "The president of the university is an ultraconservative."

A few days later, there came a letter from our new friend, inviting us to dine with him at the University Club. When we went, we found ourselves in a private dining room with a group of the professors, also Dr. von Kleinsmid, the president of the university and his wife. He was seated next to me, and his wife next to Upton, and both were charming and cordial. We never knew whether it was because they valued their British philosopher, or whether they were not so ultraconservative after all. Maybe Upton and I had developed a "persecution complex."

Schiller, like McDougall, was one of the founders of the London Society for Psychical Research, during those days when his colleagues, Sir Oliver Lodge, the physicist, and William James, the American psychologist, helped to make respectable the study of the subconscious mind and its unknown powers. He was greatly interested in our experiments in telepathy, and sent us a number of his own writings on this subject.

Upton and I had lunch alone with Chaplin one day in a Los Angeles restaurant. It was a strange experience, for no one recognized either man. I thought it was pleasant to be able to eat our soup without having some stranger breathing down on it, and to finish a sentence without having it interrupted by "Isn't this Charlie Chaplin?"—or "Upton Sinclair?"

Charlie had to cultivate his "fans," so he did not comment, except with a smile. I thought his smile almost as fresh and as childlike as my husband's, and his interest in every subject we brought up was as keen as if it were something to which he had given serious thought.

I asked him to tell me what kind of girl he admired most. "An old-fashioned girl," he answered, promptly. "I want one who is interested in me and my work, not in a career of her own."

"Do you think there is apt to be one in Hollywood?"

"Where can I find her?" he countered.

"Surely not in a career colony."

"But this is where I live and work. I have to be here."

I had no interest in being a match-maker, but I promised him I would let him hear if I ran into one, and he thanked me as if he thought I really meant it. "I hope you will not forget," he said. There was something wistful in his look and voice when he talked about this, and I believed he really wanted to find an old-fashioned girl. After lunch, when we said goodbye, I told him I would not forget, and again he looked at me earnestly and said, "Please don't."

Not long afterwards we had supper in a studio dining room. Charlie and Paulette Goddard were there, and walked out to our car with us. I had never met Paulette before, but we had a friend who knew her well, and I was interested to find out if my friend's judgment of her was based on his admiration for all pretty women. This was one of my psychological questions— just why did men love only physical charm in women?

I asked her a few quick, impertinent questions, and she answered simply and naturally. We were walking ahead of Upton and Charlie, and when they caught up with us near the gates, I said, "Charlie, here's your old-fashioned girl." He asked me to repeat that, and I did. He beamed at me, and they walked away together, with his arm around her. Not long after that, they were married. I thought that marriage would last; but what does last in Hollywood?

The era of Prohibition had become an era of lawlessness. Bootleggers and hijackers had spread over the country, and drinking had become a social duty in many circles; people who had formerly been non-drinkers declared the law was an infringement of individual rights, so it was a duty to break the law! Hip-pocket flasks were the badge of sophistication in high-school circles, and men who ordinarily did not drink to excess now did so at parties because the precious stuff must not be wasted.

Upton, who had a long-standing grudge against John Barleycorn because of what had happened to his father and three of his uncles, decided the time had come to settle that grudge. He would write a novel, calling it *The Wet Parade*. He used as its setting the "family hotel" in New York in which he had spent a part of his childhood, a place kept by Virginians and patronized by people from anywhere in Dixie. It was in this hotel that he had helped nurse his father back to health after many a spree, and there he had watched Southern gentlemen slipping bit by bit to their doom. The theme was not a popular one with the élite of the literary world, where such fine minds as those of Jack London, George Sterling, Sinclair Lewis, Eugene O'Neill, and Scott Fitzgerald were being brought to ruin. So the novel was only fairly successful. But it brought him a contract from Metro-Goldwyn-Mayer, who bought the film rights for twenty thousand dollars.

I went with him to talk over the project with Irving Thalberg, who ran the production part of that huge enterprise. He was young, quiet in his manner and final in his decisions. He explained that he could not make a Prohibition picture, but gave his word that he would hold the balance fair and give both sides. He did this, and with excellent results. Robert Young, then beginning his long career, played the "juvenile lead," and Jimmy Durante, also beginning, played a comic prohibition agent. Lewis Stone played the drinking father. We went to the studio and watched the work, and since picture-making is mostly sitting around waiting, I met these friendly people and had frank talks with them about what their careers meant to them.

Not long after that, Upton's old friend, Edgar Selwyn, now a producer for MGM, proposed a writing job. After Noel Coward's prize-winning picture "Cavalcade," Edgar had the idea of "an American Cavalcade," and Upton was willing to try. There began a series of sessions with Thalberg, Edgar sitting in and me listening and putting in a word now and then. Upton offered to work out what ideas he could, and consult with Thalberg, until he was sure that he had given his best; then he would tell them so, and they would pay him ten thousand dollars and be free to use his material, all or none. Thalberg accepted.

We drove home, talking it over. We both knew that we were now inside the Cave of Aladdin. The chests of jewels were there, and we had only to dip our hands in and fill our pockets or suitcases. Upton could have a salary of a hundred thousand a year with no trouble at all; he had only to devote his trained imagination to producing the sort of material that the crown prince of the silver screen wanted. I saw it and knew that Upton saw it. Was he tempted? I asked myself. *I* was!

Here was another chance for me to influence the decision, but I did not. I silently watched a duel of wills conducted with the utmost courtesy, even kindliness. Ten thousand dollars was, of course, nothing for Thalberg to get excited about, or to regret; his only thought was to get a picture that would make

money for MGM. "The Wet Parade" cost $400,000 and didn't
bring in much more; how could you expect businessmen to be
interested in discussing any social problem on the screen? They
were not and they would not and they did not.

Thalberg had suggested a title: "The Star-Spangled Banner."
Pretty soon Upton came to me with a modification of that title
which would be still more wonderful, more striking, more brilliant: "The *Gold*-Spangled Banner"! I agreed that it was striking, beyond doubt; but how would it strike Thalberg?

Upton proceeded to work out a story, using the types of
American big-businessmen he had met in Wall Street, and the
stories he had got from Lincoln Steffens, and Samuel Untermyer, and Judge James B. Dill, who had been paid a million
dollars to show J. P. Morgan how to organize the steel trust
without tripping up over any law. There was all the wealth and
fashion in the story that even the gold-spangled M-G-M could
ask, and there was only one thing wrong with it: the wealth and
fashion somehow wasn't glamorous. It was sometimes ridiculous
and at other times deadly.

Upton mailed the synopsis to Thalberg, and we were invited
to another conference. We were told that there was a lot of interesting material in it, but unfortunately it didn't have quite
the right "slant." Upton had promised me that he wouldn't
argue too much, so he listened meekly while Thalberg explained the difference between what *could* be in a novel and
what *had* to be in a movie. "For example, Mr. Sinclair," he
said, "you have here an elderly man you tell us is a big Wall-
Street operator who has built himself a three-million-dollar
mansion in New York, and in the basement he has fixed himself
a place for pitching horseshoes!"

"But Mr. Thalberg!" exclaimed Upton, starting to argue.
"That place exists. I was told about it by Thomas Fortune
Ryan, perhaps the richest single operator in Wall Street. The
old man began as a farmboy and pitching horseshoes is what he
likes to do. He invites his friends, and he'll bet a thousand dollars on a throw. There are others—haven't you heard of 'Bet-a-
million' Gates?"

"I know, Mr. Sinclair, and I don't doubt it's true; but if you show it in a picture, the public won't take it—it's just out of line, and you can't put a statement on the screen that it really happened."

So that is how it went. It was a duel between the two titles. Upton would go away with new polite suggestions for "The Star-Spangled Banner," and would come back with a new version of "The Gold-Spangled Banner." I forget how many tries he made and how many conferences he attended, but in the end he said that he had done his best and was very sorry. He *had* done his best; he was incapable of writing without a serious purpose. The wellspring of his ideas just dried up. He and Thalberg parted friends, and Upton received his check for ten thousand dollars—and never saw that he hadn't really presented Mr. Thalberg with a wonderful scenario! He had got so thrilled over the idea of a story about our beautiful "Star-Spangled Banner" all spattered with Wall Street's gold!

Upton's old tennis friend and neighbor at Croton, Max Eastman, came to California after an adventure in the Soviet Union from which he escaped with a Russian bride. He had been a lecturer in philosophy at Columbia University and was now a poet of distinction and the author of various books on historical and critical themes. His philosophy seemed to be the opposite of George Sterling's; George feared life, thought it cruel and frustrating, while Max loved life and thought that everything he was doing was interesting at the time he was doing it. Being poets, both loved beauty; to George it was the supreme goddess, while Max, like Upton, found everything in human affairs a theme for a magazine article or a new book. Now Max played tennis with Upton and wrote books, while Eliena Eastman painted portraits.

Theodore Dreiser and Helen were on a visit to California and came for an evening of general chitchat. Once he had written Upton: "Don't forget that the brotherhood of man (this entirely apart from some of the cooperative phases of socialism) is mere moonshine to me. I see the individual—large or small, weak or strong—as predatory and nothing less." We discussed no problems at this visit. Both our guests were interested in psychic research.

Vachel Lindsay, whom we had not seen for many years, came to Pasadena, and during an evening visit the lovable poet of "boom-lay, boom-lay" read some of his poetry with dramatic gestures, walking back and forth on the porch. But he was distraught and ill-pleased with the world. We thought he should have chosen acting as his profession, but this was only while under the spell; for we knew that poetry lives and acting does not.

Upton had seen his old friend, Floyd Dell, on several occasions in New York, but I had not. Both of us were happy when we heard that he was coming to Los Angeles to collaborate with Paul Jordan-Smith on Sir Thomas Burton's *Anatomy of Melancholy*. This was a task for two scholars, and it meant to us a revival of old times together, as well as contact with a warm and lovable personality.

Floyd had not changed in appearance with the years, despite the fact that he was now a married man and father of two sons. There were no lines in his smiling face, no gray hairs on his paternal head! During the years since he and Max Eastman and Upton had played tennis on Margaret Mayo's court at Croton, Floyd had become the novelist of the young intellectuals' revolt, and had essays, poems and plays to his credit. In collaboration with Thomas Mitchell he had written "Little Accident," a play which had given delight to Broadway. More important to us, he had written a beautiful and sensitive biography of Upton, for which both of us were deeply grateful. While working on it, he wrote from Croton:

> Dear U: I went to see your mother the other day, and I really like her very much: a nice, hard-headed, conventional old reactionary—don't you tell her I said that! She is the very antithesis of you. If the world were made up exclusively of people like her, there would be no progress; if it were made up exclusively of people like you, it would prematurely explode! I like, as a matter of fact, both kinds of people, and I think it very amusing that you should be her son. Such people, too, are usually right about half the time.

Now there came the greatest blunder we ever made. Sergei Eisenstein, publicized as the great film director, inventor or master of "montage," came to Hollywood. He had made the Russian picture "Potemkin," described as a masterpiece. Upton was a believer in that mysterious thing called "Art." I say mysterious, because I had never yet been able to get from any artist a satisfactory definition of the term. However, Upton thought he knew what it meant.

Eisenstein came to the United States with a contract to make one of those multi-million-dollar films out of Dreiser's *An American Tragedy*. He failed, and his visa was about to expire when he sent an emissary, Berthold Viertel, to tell Upton that he had only three days more in the country. His proposal was to go to Mexico and make an "art" picture of the primitive Indians; it could be done for $25,000 and he would give the film outright to those who put up the money. This would save his having to go back to the Soviet Union a completely defeated man. We were told that Charlie Chaplin had suggested an appeal to Upton in the matter. When we thought about it later, we found it odd that a man who had seven million dollars should shift the problem to one who had only a few thousand.

But Upton had recently seen Eisenstein's, "Potemkin," and had been fascinated by it. He went to Hollywood to see the great director, and sent a score of telegrams to Washington to perform what Eisenstein had said would be "a miracle"—to extend his visa. A contract was signed, including provisos that the picture was to be nonpolitical, that it was to cost not more than $25,000, and that it was to be finished in three months—Eisenstein's own suggestions. The contract included the volunteer offer of the investors to pay Eisenstein ten per cent of any profits that might be earned. Mrs. Gartz put up the first five thousand dollars; and then we learned that one thousand had to be used to pay Eisenstein's debts in Hollywood. (Later, we found out he had had several thousand in the bank.)

Part of the agreement was that my brother, Hunter Kimbrough, an investment banker whose integrity was beyond question, should go along as business manager to handle the investors' funds. The expedition set out, and shortly afterwards, in Mexico City, the entire party was arrested.

Hunter was released immediately, with apologies, and the following day he was able to secure the release of the Russians. He pledged to the Mexican government that the picture was to be strictly nonpolitical and agreed to allow government inspection of every foot of film shot. He and the President of Mexico got along so well that Hunter left with a large autographed picture of the great man.

Then began a long process of delay. Eisenstein worked out an elaborate scenario, on a scale for a picture which would cost several hundred thousand dollars; whenever we resisted his demand for more money, the answer was: either put it up or the investors would have no picture. It was many months before we discovered what he was up to: carrying on negotiations to get a contract in India, in Australia, in the Argentine—any place in the world to keep from having to go back to the land of Stalin.

The entire ordeal lasted for almost three years, and came near costing Upton's life, for his health broke under the strain and he twice had to be taken to a hospital. He wrote hundreds of letters and succeeded in raising about thirty thousand dollars. The Soviet film organization in New York, Amkino, agreed to put in twenty-five thousand; but then came a cablegram from Stalin saying that Eisenstein's comrades considered him "a deserter." Amkino introduced Upton to a produce merchant in San Diego who agreed that if Upton would release Amkino from its promise, the merchant would put up the money when it was needed. Upton fell for this; but when he called for the money he was told that "hard times" had come and the merchant did not have it.

We could do no more, and ordered Hunter to wind up the expedition, and send Eisenstein straight to Russia; Bogdanov, then head of Amtorg in New York, had wired that Eisenstein had better get home as fast as he could. Eisenstein drove to New York in a car we purchased in Mexico and we never saw him again.

I had a vast sense of at last being free of an octopus. We still were guardians of the film which was the property of the investors, and Upton felt that although we had gone heavily into debt we must somehow get the picture cut and presented. This would cost us a lot more money which Upton would have to earn. This was his plain duty to the investors, he said. But just as he had grieved after his divorce for his broken marriage, now he felt sorry for the "great artist."

The head of the Soviet film industry came from Moscow to see us, and insisted that we should give the film to Russia; we had no right to the master's masterpiece. We explained that the film was the property of the investors. The Russian sat in our living room and heard our story from end to end; he was a highly cultivated man and spoke perfect English, and when he had heard the last word his verdict came with a shrug of the shoulders: "Well, he outsmarted you, that's all."

The proposition of Moscow was to take the film and have Eisenstein cut it, and send us a negative, keeping one for use in their territory. Accepting this offer, we sent the several hundred pounds of it, at considerable expense, to the Amtorg Trading Company in New York. The agreement was that the film would not be opened in New York but sent directly to Moscow, and that Eisenstein would go there at once. After a long silence on the part of Amtorg, we learned that Eisenstein was showing the film to his friends in New York. We repossessed the film and expressed it back to Hollywood; and so it was that Eisenstein lost his chance.

Our long, rambling house in Pasadena which I had made of five pieces of old houses and some pink paint, was really a dream place now. We had a wide lawn on the vacant lots, and the Italian cypress trees at the far end looked like stately green sentinels watching over the garden. Pink roses clambered over the high wire fence around the entire place, and the air was sweet with honeysuckle and star-jasmine.

Who could want a lovelier home? There was even a wide row of asparagus plants, interspersed with golden jonquils and creamy Chinese lilies. Kitty came often, and nibbled the raw young asparagus stalks, fresh from the ground, and carried home pails of luscious figs and olive-colored Japanese guavas.

One day someone came in a big car, with a chauffeur and a lawyer. He turned out to be William Fox, known to the world as the master of Fox Films.

I had a tall, red-haired youth from the mountains of Northern Oregon working for me at that time. He was a country boy, not used to the idea of masculine grandeur arriving in our poor neighborhood. He came to me quite awed. "What should I do with him?" he asked.

"You are sure he is the moving-picture Mr. Fox?"

"Yes ma'am—he says he is."

"Invite him into the living room, and tell Mr. Sinclair."

Soon he was back to report. "Mr. Fox *looked* at me—*hard*," he said, anxiously.

"He probably thought you were a bandit," I laughed. But I saw his worried face, and added, quickly. "What he really had in mind was that you might be a good motion-picture actor. What did you say to him?"

"I told him to rest his hat, and set."

I decided to go in and meet the caller. Not only was I curious about him, I wanted to make Upton accept anything he could get for one of his books, if Mr. Fox wanted to film it. I had realized long ago that propaganda was not popular with movie moguls. This, I knew, was one of the greatest of them; he had once bragged of the fact that "no second of those contained in the twenty-four hours ever passed but that the name of William Fox was on the screen, being exhibited in some theater in some part of the world."

I found that he was not thinking about a film. He had another purpose. He had been robbed, and wanted to expose his enemies, and perhaps force them to return to him the empire they had stolen. William Fox was the only man who could tell the shocking story, and he might as well tell it to a stenographer as to an author. But the author who would help would be paid twenty-five thousand dollars, and would have almost no work to do.

What he really wanted, it seemed, was the use of our office and Upton's name. We had a trustworthy secretary, while anyone he hired might take the secret to the enemy—"Wall Street," the proverbial enemy of all muckrakers. Would the arch-enemy of his enemy help *him?*

"I was never paid for fighting that enemy," Upton laughed. "There must be a catch in it."

"The catch is," said Fox, "your name is that of an absolutely honest man."

Upton seemed confused. It was a strange experience to be offered all this money for doing the very thing he had always spent his own money doing. He made a few joking remarks about this, during which Mr. Fox paced the floor, and lighted another cigar, as if the first one didn't taste right.

Finally the muckraker with the honest name said, "I think I must refuse, Mr. Fox. I'm sorry not to oblige you, but I can't see why you need me. I'll let you have my reliable secretary for the job, and help you find a publisher. I'm sure you can get one."

I knew that this was not bargaining—Upton knew nothing about driving a bargain. He had a book of his own in the making, and he would hate to drop it.

"Where can I get an office secretly?" argued Fox. "I'm a hunted man, Mr. Sinclair. I know too much, and I'm boiling mad, so they are afraid of me. They are gangsters, and won't let me go ahead if they find out what I'm doing. I'm too dangerous."

"But so am I," said Upton. "And no one has stopped me. They've boycotted me with their newspapers and their financial control of publishers, but I've been able to say my say just the same. That's the glory of this land of the free, and it's this freedom I'm trying to protect, more even than the voiceless, exploited masses. Your proposed book hasn't much to do with any of this, and my time is needed for my own work."

"Mr. Sinclair, do you mean that you are not interested in the rights of a rich man who has been exploited—is freedom of speech only for the poor?"

"You still have millions, Mr. Fox. You call that 'chicken feed'—"

William Fox tossed his cigar into the fire and turned to me. "What do you think of this man, Mrs. Sinclair? He is your hus-

band—" he waved his hand around the room as if to say, Look
at this shabby home you live in, and that shabby old car out
there under the porte-cochère. "You'll always have to live like
this, unless—"

I interrupted him. "You are right, Mr. Fox. I'm comfortable
enough in this old house, but I see no reason for Upton to refuse. It is exactly the kind of story he wants, and he does not
have to go traveling all over the United States to get his data."

The tormented face of our visitor brightened with a wide
smile. "Ah, here is a wise woman! Very often a woman has more
common sense than her husband. I listen to my wife, and I advise
you to listen to yours, Mr. Sinclair."

"Here is a proposition, Mr. Fox," I said. "I'll lend you this
room and furnish an honest stenographer. I'll guard your dictation day and night, until it's published, and I'll publish it
under the Sinclair imprint. All for twenty-five thousand dollars.
Upton can go and play tennis!"

Both men were staggered. Then Upton laughed, and said,
"OK, Mr. Fox! You win!"

William Fox's parents had brought him from Hungary
to America and at the age of ten he was peddling "lozengers" on
the streets of New York's East Side at one cent per package.
Soon he was a "contractor," putting other boys to work selling.
At thirteen he was foreman in charge of the cutting department
in a small sweatshop. He worked day and night and saved every
penny, and when he saw his first motion picture he recognized
his chance; he rented a small store and some machines, and set
up what was called a "nickelodeon," where you dropped a
nickel in the slot and peered in at a horse galloping or a railroad train coming at you.

Pretty soon he had a chain of such places all over the city.
And this evolved into a company called Fox Theaters. In 1914
this concern took in $272,401. Fifteen years later it took in $30,-
803,974. He started Fox Films, making the pictures the theaters
were to show, and this boomed in the same astounding way. Of
course all that money was not W.F.'s; he had stockholders and
paid them dividends, so they stayed with him and he could buy

more theaters and make more pictures, and merge other concerns with his own, both here and abroad. This meant borrowing huge sums of money, and a great investment concern, Hal-
sey, Stuart & Co., was planning to refinance his properties for
$93,000,000.

Then in October of 1929 came the worst of all panics in Wall
Street. It lasted a week or more, and every day for weeks thereafter brokers were jumping out of the windows of their offices
and hotels. (There was a saying that at one end of Wall Street
is Trinity Church and at the other end is the East River, so that
customers who jumped into the river could be buried in the
cemetery.) W. F. had been for weeks in a hospital after an automobile accident, and when he came back he discovered that his
enemies had combined to take his companies away from him.

He put up a tremendous, an agonizing fight; tears came into
his eyes as he told about it. He went everywhere trying to borrow money. He controlled properties worth about three hundred million dollars, and they were bringing in profits of between twenty and thirty million a year; all he needed was a little time. He appealed to President Hoover, whom he had
helped to elect. He appealed to everyone he knew—John D.
Rockefeller, Jr., Henry Ford, Bernard Baruch—all in vain. He
had committed again and again the unforgivable crime—he had
paid his profits to the stockholders instead of letting the big insiders loot it. His enemies got the properties for twenty million
—this was all they let him have, of his empire! And in less than
two years they had taken from Fox Films more than a hundred
million.

Upton had listened to many Wall Street men and heard
many melodramatic tales, but never one on so colossal a scale as
this which William Fox unfolded—four hours a day for weeks,
while he chewed up boxes of expensive cigars and drank orange
juice.

It took Fox about six weeks to tell his story and to answer
Upton's questions. Then he sent Upton a mass of documents, as
promised, and the long job of digesting this material was
begun. It took months, and Upton sent chapter after chapter
and got W. F.'s suggestions and corrections. Then, at long last,

the bulky manuscript was ready, and a complete copy was sent to Fox for approval.

Upton waited, and no word came. Upton waited a reasonable time. He wrote, and he telegraphed, and he got no reply. He had provided in his contract that he was to publish the book. When he has given his time to something he thinks is important, he wants it put before the public. Never would he allow his work to be suppressed. So finally he bundled up the manuscript and sent it by registered mail to his printers in Indiana.

The book, *Upton Sinclair Presents William Fox*, hit Wall Street and Hollywood like dynamite. We were told that on the Fox Film lot, which was no longer Fox's, a notice was posted on the bulletin board that anyone bringing a copy of the book onto the premises would be at once discharged; and who could ask for a better advertisement? The book sold fast, and another edition was published.

But maybe William Fox paid a high price for striking back at Wall Street, for later on he was indicted, tried and convicted of having attempted to bribe a federal judge. Of this case we know only what was in the newspapers. He served several years in prison. When he came out, he wrote that he wanted to make pictures from some of Upton's books. But soon after that he died.

Upton is not troubled about the facts in his Fox book, because Fox had furnished him with all the documents in the story of a poor little immigrant boy who rose to the pinnacle of wealth and was held up and robbed by Wall Street. Upton had studied them carefully. None of them has ever been denied, so far as we know.

While the story was being recorded I sat in my room darning socks and tennis togs, and thinking of the careers of the strange bedfellows whom Wall Street had drawn together in my living room.

Both Upton and William Fox had known fame, both had had all the worldly success anyone should want. Fox had had so many millions of dollars that he could say to me that twenty million was "chicken feed." Upton had spent several hundred thousand on his propaganda. Now was he going to spend the twenty-five thousand Mr. Fox had agreed to pay him? Was I going to let him?

I decided to "take an inventory." I had always been too busy to appraise my situation adequately. I had gone into each crusade voluntarily; but now I asked myself: What had we accomplished during these stressful years of our life together? How much of it was by his books, and how much had been won only by going to jail and making a big fuss in the newspapers?

I couldn't say that Upton hadn't made money; he had made a lot, but he had spent more. We were still young enough to believe that we could always earn a simple living. It was true, however, that if he had had the necessary money in the bank, he could have been spared the need of rushing through every book he wrote. He always spent more than he had, because he counted his chickens before they were hatched. He was eager, ardent and open-handed. I could always get the money as it came in and spend it before he did, but I would not. No matter how much help Upton said I was to him, I always felt that it was really his money, not mine.

But now I must at least consider taking a different attitude; I must protect both of us sooner or later from too much strain, too much worry, and someday, physical disability. Already I was dangerously near an illness of some sort. If I broke down and became a care to him—well, it would be foolish to risk that. Then what should I do about it?

Albert Einstein accepted a position at Cal-Tech. Upton had corresponded with him for some years, had sent him copies of his books and received cordial letters in reply. His coming to Pasadena was a great event, for he was a world celebrity, and to honor him was a proof of culture.

Upton wrote a note saying that he would be glad to come to see him when opportunity offered. My sister Dollie then came to me one day to say, "There is an odd-looking old man walking on the grounds and staring. He acts as if he wanted to come in."

I glanced out of the window and saw a rather frail-looking man with bushy gray hair, a black hat and a suit which had never been pressed. I said, "Go out and speak to him." Dollie came back and reported, "He says he's Professor Einstein, but I don't know whether to believe him."

Such was the beginning of our friendship. It lasted during that academic year, and later through another year of the same sort. From first to last the discoverer of relativity never refused a single request that we made of him. If it was a labor struggle, he would write a telegram of sympathy for the strikers, and Upton would give it to the press. If it was a meeting on behalf of free speech, he would sit on the platform, and make a few remarks when requested. If it was a demonstration of Jan's psychic powers, he would attend and manifest deep interest.

When I told him that some of our writer friends wanted very much to meet him, he agreed to come to a dinner party at the swanky Town House in Los Angeles. We came first, as was our duty to welcome the guests, and Einstein arrived a few minutes later; he came to the private dining room, wearing a humble black overcoat and the same much-worn hat. He looked about for a place to hang them. He took off his overcoat, folded it neatly, and laid it on the floor in a vacant corner and set the hat on top of it. Then he was ready to meet the literary élite of Southern California.

Elsa, his wife, was a dutiful German hausfrau, utterly devoted to him. I recall an evening at their home when I ventured to enter into a discussion of the most important of all subjects, the nature of God. The great physicist said that he believed in God, but not a personal God, and I questioned him about this. Surely the personality of God must include all other personalities! Afterwards, Frau Elsa said to me, very gently, something to the effect that I should not have disputed her husband's statement. "You know, my husband has the greatest mind in the world." I answered, "Yes, I know; but surely he doesn't know everything!"

14. MY HUSBAND FELL INTO THE TRAP

WHEN THE COLLAPSE of the Hoover administration's assurances forced Franklin D. Roosevelt's election, a major event was the new President's order closing every bank in the country. This was a startling experience for businessmen accustomed to drawing out what funds they needed. Many were caught with only what they had in their pockets. Upton, who had been predicting the collapse for years, had known when to draw out some money; and now he happened into the office of Sol Lesser, who was cutting the Mexican picture. Sol said, "I can't invite you to lunch because I haven't got the price." Upton asked, "Do you really need cash?" and when Sol replied he surely did, Upton took out a roll of bills and counted out ten twenties on the producer's desk. Sol never got tired of telling that story around Hollywood; and Upton never forgot that he had once loaned money to a Hollywood mogul!

In Mississippi the impact of this financial collapse was even more severe than in Southern California. The growing of cotton is a highly speculative activity at all times; a drought comes, or an overflow; the boll weevil comes and destroys a whole year's crop; or when a panic and a depression hit the outside world, the spinning mills shut down, the buyers go back to Liverpool or Boston, the planter has the cotton on his hands—and holding cotton is costly.

Upton wrote warnings of what was ahead; the cycle of "boom and bust" was to him the basic fact of the country's economy. The most arrogant of my brothers wrote me, earlier during the Depression, "Tell Upton he does not know how to see into the future. Between you and me, I have no belief in his prophetic visions; so I have just bought a splendid new plantation, and my wife invested more cautiously in another, less splendid one. I suppose her caution was due to your influence—you may recall that you actually persuaded her to eat raw cabbage!"

After Roosevelt closed the banks, another of my brothers wrote: "Conditions here are terrible. Papa has lost everything. The Negroes on the streets in town drop from exhaustion—they have nothing to eat."

As an officer and stockholder in two banks Papa was legally liable to the depositors for losses to the extent of his own stock holdings; and of course his "unlimited credit" in the big cities was gone, for these banks, too, were in trouble and there was no credit. Papa's creditors took everything, but they had such respect for him that they let him stay on in his homes at Greenwood and on the coast without letting him know that they were no longer his. He lived on cowpeas, turnip greens, tomatoes and the milk from his cow; at the coast there were figs and grapes, and the products of the sea.

As soon as we heard of his troubles, Upton and I sent him a check on our bank account. I knew how proud he was, and that only genuine want would cause him to cash this check. It was not cashed, nor did he write me anything about the situation for a long time. Finally he returned the check, faded and worn from long carrying in his pocket. He wrote: "My Dear Child: I am sure you know that I appreciate your thoughtfulness. You should know also that I would rather lose my right arm than accept help. I love you. Papa."

Later, after I had sent another check of smaller size, he did find it necessary to cash it. Realizing the meaning of this was a heart-breaking experience, and my husband was deeply touched. One of my sisters had told Upton that Papa's greatest trouble was having nothing to read; so, every week, Upton took it upon himself to bundle up all his magazines, American and British, and mail them to "the Judge."

All around us in California was suffering and tragedy resulting from no chickens in the pot and no car in the garage. People were walking hundreds of miles on tired feet in search of a job. Upton worried about it continuously, and finally there came his usual reaction to social misery: "Something must be done about it." He dashed off an account, for booklet publication, of how he had been enticed into the political arena and how the EPIC plan had grown from his efforts as candidate for governor to "End Poverty in California."

The EPIC booklet was completed and sent off to the printer and a few days later we set out for New York. "Thunder Over Mexico" was to open at the Rialto Theater, and it was necessary for us to be there, if only out of loyalty to the investors who had trusted us. Sol Lesser had worked hard to make something out of an almost impossible proposition and he was at the train to meet us with half a dozen reporters. After the usual interviewing and photographing, he told us that the Communists were picketing the theater with signs denouncing us. The news of Upton's having registered as a Democrat in California had leaked out, and so the Socialists were against us, too!

One who was for us was Otto Kahn, international banker and patron of all the arts, who had invested ten thousand dollars in the picture. He came to dine with us, and his first words to Upton were: "I tell my friends that if I, a capitalist, had money to invest where I was sure it would be conscientiously handled, I would entrust it to Upton Sinclair the Socialist."

The Communists were carrying on a frenzied campaign against the picture, charging that we had butchered "a great revolutionary masterpiece," sacrificing it to "capitalistic greed." They threw stink bombs into the theater and threatened Arthur Mayer, the theater manager. Upton undertook to meet all comers in the theater on a Sunday morning, and they packed the house and screamed at him for a couple of hours; one burly fellow in the lobby shook his fist in Upton's face.

The picture brought only trouble and loss. A silent picture about Mexican natives, no matter how beautiful the photography, had no charm for the great American public. "Thunder Over Mexico" had cost $90,000 and earned about $30,000. The balance we had to make up; it took most of what Upton had earned from *Oil!, Boston* and the motion-picture rights of *The Wet Parade*. We were poor again.

We went to a banquet celebrating a birthday of the League for Industrial Democracy, formerly the Intercollegiate Socialist Society, which was one of Upton's brain-children. I was seated

on one side and Upton on the other of the distinguished philosopher, John Dewey. I expressed the deep distrust we felt of the
Communists, and said they had adopted the formula that "the
end justifies the means." Dewey replied promptly, "The means
become the end." The more I thought about this remark the
more profound it seemed. "It contains the whole history of
Bolshevism," was Upton's comment. "It was worth coming all
the way from California to hear."

We went down to Washington and had tea with Mrs.
Roosevelt at the White House. We were inconsiderate of the
President's wife, in the usual way of callers; we took her the
book of a friend who had a plan for ending poverty—almost as
good as Upton's—asking her to endorse it. But of course she was
experienced in saying No. The wife of the President could not
endorse a "commercial product"—that is what she said. Upton
pointed out that our friend, Prestonia Mann Martin, author of
the book, was surely not a commercial person; she already had
much more money than she needed. "But," said Mrs. Roosevelt,
"what about the publisher?" But later she did praise the book
in her column.

Helen Hayes came in, and also "Sistie," Mrs. Roosevelt's small
granddaughter. Then came the man with the tea service, and
Sistie promptly spilled her cup of tea on the sofa beside me—
which temporarily put an end to my interest in prohibiting
poverty.

Upton's cousin, Lelia Barnett, took us to her house. Upton
wanted to talk about the present, but she wanted to talk about
ancestors and Sinclair heirlooms. She showed us the brass name
plate of the destroyer named for her and Upton's great-grandfather Commodore Sinclair, who founded what afterward became the United States Naval Academy at Annapolis. She had
christened *The Sinclair* by breaking the traditional bottle of
champagne, and still had the broken bottle in its wicker ham-
per and mahogany box. She also had the notebook of this mutual great-grandfather, in which he had recorded the events of
the battle of Lake Huron, where he had commanded the American squadron.

During 1934 Upton did nothing but speak, give interviews and write articles for the weekly *Epic News;* he described himself as a "portable talking machine." Except when radio required a typed script he always spoke "off the cuff."

Upton Sinclair - Candidate for Governor of California -

Upton's "Baltimore charmer" cousin, Lelia Montague Barnett, had helped to bring up a niece who would rock the British Throne: Wallis Warfield Simpson.

Upton with Harry Hopkins in 1934, when he went to Washington to confer with New Deal leaders in the hope of getting financial assistance for the California unemployed.

When Upton's novel about Henry Ford, *The Flivver King,* was published, the United Automobile Workers ordered an edition of 200,000; copies of the book were sold at the gates of Ford assembly plants all over the world.

She wanted to take us to the Army and Navy Club to dine. But "Can't you get him to wear better clothes, Craig?" she asked, and then added, with a gesture of despair, "Of course you can't —no one ever could!"

"He wore this suit to tea with Mrs. Roosevelt," I laughed; "but Mrs. Roosevelt is a real democrat while you are an unreconstructed aristocrat."

Lelia took us to meet her friend, the novelist Mary Roberts Rinehart, and I listened to some of the extraordinary psychic experiences which had befallen her. Of *Mental Radio,* Mrs. Rinehart wrote:

> "I am not on the fence, having decided the authenticity of cryptaesthesia (I am like Craig as to spelling sometimes, but that is nearly correct) long ago. . . . People are ready to accept telepathy because it is within the realm of their experience; but they quit there. They do not see the tremendous importance of its connotations. . . . What seems to me to matter is the tremendous influence of mind (thought) on all other minds.

EPIC was a people's movement. It had risen like a tidal wave, and in this ocean of human beings we struggled to keep our own bearings. There was no political machine of any sort behind us, nor did we have a half-dozen friends who knew anything about politics. A young and idealistic businessman, Richard Otto—inexperienced in politics, had come forward and offered his services. The day I met him, I said to Upton, "There is your campaign manager."

Upton leaned on him ceaselessly throughout the campaign, and so did I. When dissatisfied workers came to me with complaints, as so many of them did, I often had a feeling of suffocation by so many problems and troubles. But I would then remember that Dick was at the helm! I knew he was rigidly honest, and that was the greatest of essentials in this situation. I saw his patience and tirelessness, and his always smiling face. It wasn't the tailored smile of the campaigning politician; it was the warm, personal smile of one who felt real kindness, and meant to help and reassure.

I needed a lot of reassurance myself in those stormy days, and got it from this utterly inexperienced but extremely competent young man at headquarters. He was terribly overworked, yet always debonair, a remarkable combination.

There was no horror the biggest and supposedly most respectable newspapers did not commit in this campaign. One sent a spy into the EPIC headquarters and published a detailed article about the "fortune" the EPIC candidate was reaping from the movement. All the items were listed: pamphlets, books, collections—"to the tune of a quarter of a million dollars." The facts were that Upton gave the pamphlets to the movement and never got one penny from any of the EPIC activities and we came out of the adventure several thousand dollars in debt.

When we had found ourselves tied up indefinitely with "Thunder Over Mexico," having to go to Hollywood every weekday and under the pressure of earning money so that Upton did some writing for a studio in Culver City, we looked for a house to rent in Hollywood. A friend pointed out to us that half the houses in Beverly Hills were for sale and you needn't have a dollar of cash; you had only to assume the mortgage. Then a retired stockbroker friend discovered for us "the greatest bargain in Beverly Hills."

That house in Beverly Hills was almost a mansion. Now the Los Angeles *Times* called it a mansion, to prove that we had moved out of a mansion into a cottage for the period of the campaign, in order to deceive the poor into believing we were one of them. The exact opposite was true—we had moved to the "mansion" from a cottage. The "poor" thought we still lived in Pasadena in our old home, for we occupied it a portion of the time, and it was there they came to see us, to bring us gifts of food and drink, and serenade us with EPIC choruses.

The visitors who came to the mansion were millionaires and business executives and high-ranking politicians. Some of these were alarmed by Upton's program, others were hopeful of deals, still others wanted only to see what kind of person this strange traitor to his class was like.

Among these callers was George A. Hormel, Sr., packer of Hormel's meat products. Like our old friend, King C. Gillette, he had great respect for Upton, but for a different reason. He knew him as the young man who had stood the meat-packing industry on its head and reformed it. Like the razor-king he also had a plan, and submitted it to Upton as superior to Epic. The only difference was that Gillette's plan was the same as Upton's, only Gillette did not know it, while Hormel's was different from Upton's and he thought it was the same. Hormel's plan was to share the wealth, but to leave this process to the fair play and common sense of the big businessmen! Couldn't Upton agree with that?

The great meat-packer wrote out this plan in a clear, orderly statement—and brought it for Upton to study. It took fourteen typewritten pages to say the same thing over and over: The big industrialist was to raise wages, and reduce the hours of labor *increasingly* as the advances of technology and business management made necessary—all this to one end: keeping the buying power of labor high. This would maintain permanent prosperity for everyone. I've forgotten whether he stated what should, or would happen when technology provided machines that would practically supplant labor.

Mr. Hormel put it this way:

"We have a man-made depression, a businessman's panic, created by the leading business minds at the head of our American industries.

"Then and there our industrial minds made their most serious blunder in the history of business and created the most hellish situation our country ever experienced. Laying off men and cutting their pay reduced buying power and started business down the toboggan, and it will continue going down until buying power is re-established by employing the jobless with a normal pay check.

"The industrial machine is the golden chariot, capable of great speed, which carries along those who are aboard—the owners—at a terrific rate, with destination unknown. The tragic part is that the human souls helping to create the machine and provide for it in every way are left alone by the wayside, helpless and bewildered, begging for a ride."

Upton and the great meat packer never got any closer than that; but that struck me as being very close, and I am sure that at that time Mr. Hormel's plan would have been as indignantly repudiated by other big business men as Mr. Gillette's plan had been.

The active campaign for EPIC occupied exactly one year, from November of 1933; during that year Upton did nothing but speak, give interviews and write articles for the weekly *EPIC News*. He described himself as a portable talking machine.

In the primary campaign there were eight candidates for the Democratic party nomination for Governor, and seven of them devoted their time to trying to save the party from being "captured by an interloper."

Upton's way of making a speech was quiet, but somehow electrifying. He always spoke "off the cuff," except when radio required a typed script. Occasionally he gave a little chuckle which seemed to be contagious, for an audience chuckle followed. Now and then he would say something in a suddenly quickened tone and point his finger at the audience and ask, "Do you want that? All who do say yes." There would be a delighted cry in unison, "Yes," or "No," never a combination of both. Once he suddenly asked, "All who want to starve say Yes." There was a roar of "Yes." Then he asked, "All who want to eat, say No." Everyone roared "No." And then there was pandemonium.

The other seven Democratic candidates could not agree upon policies, and as it turned out, agreement would have done them no good, for the EPIC candidate polled more votes than all the other seven put together. That result caused an immense sensation throughout the country, and especially in New York and Washington. All the national magazines hastened to get stories about EPIC, and the politicians who wanted to get elected hastened to pick up bits of EPIC timber and build them into their political platforms.

The primary election was at the end of August, and from then on the EPICs were the legal masters of the Democratic Party of California. A convention was held, under the provisions of the state law; a platform was adopted and a party chairman and committee selected. Upton left immediately afterward for New York and Washington, to do what he could to influence the national party in the direction of "Production for Use." Everywhere he went the reporters swarmed after him and radio stations welcomed him, which meant just one thing to him: a chance to teach the American people how to End Poverty in California, and maybe in "civilization."

He went up to Hyde Park by appointment and spent two hours with President Roosevelt, making sure that the father of the New Deal knew exactly what the "interloper" was trying to do. I heard from insiders that the President was deeply impressed. The first thing he told his visitor was that they were old friends—or enemies—because as a very young lawyer, looking forward to a political career, his mother had read him passages from *The Jungle* every morning at breakfast.

There has recently been published an elaborate biography of F.D.R. in which the writer takes it for granted that he made it a practice to tell convenient falsehoods. The writer cites this as one of the cases, calling it "the improbable story." Upton wrote to Mrs. Roosevelt, asking her opinion, and she replied, with permission to quote: "It was not a falsehood that my husband's mother read passages from *The Jungle*."

One who was not agreeably impressed by Upton's visit to Hyde Park was Raymond Moley, one of the first "brain-trusters" of the New Deal—and one of the first to desert it. In his book, *After Seven Years*, Moley wrote:

> "Sinclair came East, talked to Roosevelt at Hyde Park and emerged happily. His mood suggested that the New Deal and his own EPIC plan were wholly consistent. He had a friendly talk with Jim Farley in New York. In Washington, after consulting with Ickes and others, he stated that he was pleased to be a Democrat. Hopkins expressed the hope that Sinclair would be elected. 'He's on our side, isn't he?' asked Harry. Back again in California, Sinclair published in his 'EPIC News' a letter from Jim Farley urging Democrats to give their full support to

the ticket, including Sinclair . . . Greatly disturbed by this seeming endorsement, I pleaded with F.D.R. in September, to dissociate his administration from Sinclair. He answered that Merriam, Sinclair's Republican opponent, was accepting the support of the Townsend-plan advocates and that the Townsend heresy was no smaller than the EPIC heresy. 'Besides,' he said, 'they tell me Sinclair is sure to be elected.' . . . Sinclair, whose direct endorsement by Roosevelt had been avoided by inches, was repudiated via George Creel and Jim Farley."

But as Mary Roberts Rinehart wrote Upton,

"Here the President is coming out with your ideas and what are we old Conservatives and Standpatters to do about it!"

In Washington Upton went from one to another of the New Deal Cabinet members, the men from whom he hoped to get funds and assistance in putting the California unemployed at labor for their own support. That included Morgenthau, Secretary of the Treasury, and Ickes, Secretary of the Interior. He spent an evening at the home of Rexford Tugwell, with Harry Hopkins and Jerome Frank. Also, he was invited to address the National Press Club at their weekly luncheon. The Washington newspaper correspondents plied the candidate with questions. Upton was told afterward that they were surprised by his readiness in answering the questions they asked. He had been traveling all over the State of California answering questions for ten months, and there was no question he had not answered a dozen times to his audiences.

Back in California, the remaining seven weeks of the campaign were like living in a cyclone. There was no rest for either of us, day or night, and the fury of the attack was beyond imagining. The EPIC candidate was denounced as atheist, anarchist, Bolshevist, Puritan, Social Fascist,—none of which he had ever been. Words were invented and put into his mouth, and fantastic stories about him were told. Billboards on the highways all over the state blazoned warnings of the horrors to come if he was elected. Motion pictures were shown with Hollywood actors, made up as ruffians, representing EPIC supporters coming into the state to find easy pickings when their hero Sinclair was elected.

A woman friend wrote me that friends in her drawing room had got into an argument over EPIC so furious that they had thrown sofa pillows at one another. A businessman of Beverly Hills told Upton of an experience his high school daughter had had; she was invited to dine at the home of a schoolmate, and during the meal the head of the house denounced Upton Sinclair. The girl remarked, "I heard him speak, and I thought he sounded quite reasonable." The host flushed with anger and replied, "No one can talk that way in my house. Get up and get out!" He drove her from his home.

Of course there were some humorous episodes during that terrific affair. There were threats against Upton's life, and I had no way to protect him except to go with him, and this I did when none of the busy EPIC friends were available. When he was making radio addresses in Los Angeles, I never let him drive to the radio station without me. When we reached the place there would be a group of men, all strangers to me, waiting on the sidewalk to go in with him; they were usually strangers to him also, wanting him to sign something, or to look at something, or to accept something from them. I insisted on any proffered gifts being taken to the EPIC headquarters, where more experienced persons than I could examine them and decide whether or not to turn them over to the police. There had been cakes, pies, wines and once a pitiful bunch of carrots, but so far, no bombs.

I would walk close behind Upton until we reached the door of the studio, to keep anyone from entering this room with him. After a few such trips, I discovered that there was a pale-faced fat man who came each time and tried to crowd in just behind my husband. From the moment we arrived on the sidewalk he was there, and always walked as close as he could to us, trying to nudge me aside. Finally, I turned and looked at him sternly and asked why he did this. He replied, so that all who followed us could hear, "I'm his bodyguard."

I told him my husband had no bodyguard, and asked who had appointed him. "Crane Gartz," he replied.

"I'm sure Mr. Gartz would have told us if he had employed a bodyguard," I said; and to that he answered, pleadingly, "What harm am I doing?"

"Why do you always have to keep your hands in your pockets?" I countered.

"To keep them out of my way."

"I wish you would keep them out of your pockets," I said.

We had almost reached the door, and I told him I did not want him to come in. "Please let me come!" he pleaded. "I would feel so bad if anything happened to him."

He seemed so hurt that I gave way; I said, "You may come, provided you will keep your hands on the top of the piano."

The studio announcer signaled us to enter and the man exclaimed, "I will! I promise!"

He stood there, first on one foot and then on the other, with his hands on the piano through a half-hour radio speech that Upton was making. I took a good look at him now; he was pudgy, and I'm sure I could have pushed him over in a struggle.

When I saw Crane Gartz again I asked if he had employed that man. He said he had not; the fellow had come up to him at a meeting and asked if Crane "minded" if he acted as the bodyguard of the candidate. Crane had laughed and told him he didn't mind, but feared it would be hard for any stout man to move around as fast as Mr. Sinclair did.

Such things seem funny to me now as I look back on them, but nothing was funny at the time; I thought only of a hundred dangers. And the police agreed with me.

We had locked up our Pasadena house and were staying in Beverly Hills; but now and then we would spend a night in the old home. On one of these occasions a friend drove us there in his car, and when we reached Upton's old office, next door to the house, Upton said he wanted to stop for some papers. He went in, and I said to the friend, "I want to get out here—you detain him a few moments while I run ahead to see if there are any dangerous characters on our gallery. Do not leave him until I give a signal. If it's a bad signal, use the telephone here to notify the police." Then I raced away.

I ran down half the length of our long gallery to the front
door of our kitchen, my heels giving resounding notice to all
assassins that someone was after them! There were heavy curtains separating the gallery, and as I reached to get the key
which I kept over the kitchen door, I stumbled and fell into
the curtains. I had stumbled against a human body!

I was shocked, of course; but I kept my self-possession. "I beg
your pardon," I managed to say, just as if I had been accustomed to human bodies concealed behind curtains. I suppose I
wanted to make whoever he was think I was not alarmed.

He stepped out between the curtains and turned a flashlight
on me.

"Who are you?" I asked, calmly.

"Who are *you*?" he countered.

"I am the owner of the house."

"Can you prove it?" he demanded.

I told him where the key was, hidden above the door frame.
"That's not the only door opening onto this gallery," I said.
"As you have probably discovered by now, there are three on
this side of the curtain and two on the other side. Is it likely I
would know which one has a key over it? Reach up and get
the key."

Of course I was terribly frightened, and trying to think how
to tell the friend who was waiting for a signal to call the police.
But the man with the torch reached up and got the key, and
then said to his buddy who was still behind the curtain, "Come
on out, Joe. This lady is all right."

The other man was in police uniform, and so I was safe. I
laughed with relief, and said, "Now turn your torch on yourself
and let the officer see what *you* look like."

I called loudly, "Come on," to the friend in the car, and
when he and Upton arrived, I invited the policemen in. But
they wanted to stay where they were. They would be there
until morning. "We've been guarding this house for a week.
Now we must guard Mr. Sinclair."

Upton and I went in and our friend drove away in his car.
A few minutes later the doorbell rang, and I ran to the front
door and opened it, and there stood the plainclothes man with

his torch on the face of a stranger, asking who he was. The new-comer was pale, and obviously as alarmed as I had been. I re-membered suddenly that I had told a news reporter he could meet us there for a brief interview with my husband. With my help, he managed to escape the clutches of the law.

"It serves you right," I told him, "for being a reporter for the 'Brass Check' press!"

As for myself I was mentally torn in half. The dishonest and treacherous tactics of our enemies would make me hot with indignation, and I would then want to win as much as Upton did; I would want to lick those rascals, and I would write a "pep-up" piece for the *EPIC News*. But in the midst of it I would check myself; did I really want to win? Of course I didn't; I knew that a few months of it would kill my frail hus-band. Already he was on the verge of a breakdown and imagine him Governor of California! It was a literal fact—we had talked it over and agreed—we did not know a single man in the State of California who had executive experience and who also be-lieved in the EPIC program! We knew a number of fine, de-voted sympathizers, but they had had no such experience, and we knew some men of experience, but they didn't believe in EPIC.

There was never a moment that I was not "on edge" about the physical safety of what the "boys" in headquarters called their "fearless leader." Upton was driving a six-year-old car that had never been very good. It had had several breakdowns, and twice he was forced to "hitchhike." Once, delayed for repairs, he was speeding to get to a speaking date and a motorcycle officer stopped him. The man must have been an EPIC sympathizer, for instead of giving him a ticket he said, "All right, Mr. Sin-clair, I'll ride ahead, and if I'm going too fast, blow your horn." So he took the candidate many miles and the audience was not disappointed.

Another day Upton was driving to a series of dates in the North, and in the car with him were three of his young helpers, one of them just out of the University of Southern California. Paul Kiepe had heard Upton talk about my psychic experiences and had been too polite to say what he thought—which was that we were fooling ourselves, because such things just couldn't happen. Some miles above Santa Barbara the coast highway turned into the interior—or did in those days—and wound around the sides of hills. On one such curve the pavement was slippery, and the car skidded and slammed into one of the white-painted posts which protected the highway.

When the four men got out, the left front wheel of the car hung over a declivity of a couple of hundred feet; the other front wheel was almost over, and the car hung precariously over a post that was bent almost horizontal. One of the men hitchhiked to the nearest town and a towcar pulled Upton's car back; the four drove on, with nothing worse than a bent bumper. They reached San Francisco, and in the morning there was a special delivery from me to Upton. He read: "Darling, do be careful about your driving. Yesterday I woke up from a nap and had a terrifying vision of your car, hanging over the side of a precipice. I won't have a moment's peace until you wire or phone me."

Upton turned to Paul Kiepe and handed him the letter. Paul read it, and when he looked at Upton again it was with startled eyes. "My God!" he half-whispered. "It's *real!*"

Upton did not tell about this narrow escape. Instead he wrote me:

Blessed Angel:
    All well and having nice time. Spoke to Voters' Council last night, seemed to like it. Going to see Mooney this aft. and then debate Moore in the evg. Am kept in cotton wool and watched all the time. Expect to see George Creel, maybe Gertrude Atherton. Lunched with Oswald Garrison Villard yesterday. He's coming to L.A. Good Headquarters here, devoted people. You'll be Governess willy nilly. Love x x x x (kisses)
                                                    Uppie

Fear is a dreadful thing, and it had come to reside with me for a year. One night, for example, I received a special-delivery letter from the Reverend "Bob" Shuler, a Methodist preacher who was immensely popular in Los Angeles and who had strong political inclinations. He urged me to have Upton withdraw from this campaign; Upton had too many enemies, his life was in real danger. My reply was an invitation from me to speak out in behalf of this campaign in the name of Jesus: "For I was an hungered, and ye gave me no meat." But I went up to my lonely bedroom in the Beverly Hills mansion and wept.

Upton came back from San Francisco, and toward the end of the campaign the EPIC headquarters hired the Philharmonic Auditorium of Los Angeles for a series of noon-day meetings. Every day, in addition to an evening mass meeting, Upton drove in to address two or three thousand men and women who had given up their lunch hour to hear him. The great hall is right in the center of business, and not far from the *Times* building, where Harry Chandler was publishing daily pictures of bums riding the freight trains into Los Angeles in anticipation of an EPIC victory. Upton said to that audience, "I am told that just half a century ago Harry Chandler came into the city of Los Angeles, riding on just such a freight car. He married the boss's daughter; and now I say to him, 'Harry, give the other bums a chance!' "

Aline Barnsdall, another restless, tormented oil princess in search of a way to help others, came to our house in Pasadena one day toward the end of the campaign.

"Upton," she began in a businesslike tone, "what are you going to do about Tom Mooney?" The famous labor leader was then serving a life sentence in San Quentin.

"How can you ask?" was the reply. "He is innocent. Fremont Older says so, and he knows the case from beginning to end. Older is honorable, just and wise. The whole history of the case has shown that Mooney was framed; even the judge who tried him has become convinced of it and has said so publicly. If I am elected, my first act will be to free him."

"Then I am going to put ten thousand dollars into your campaign," said Aline. "All I ask is that you will let me hand Mooney his pardon. I've already put a lot of money into that case. Some of it was mishandled by the so-called Mooney Committee. But I know you will do what you promise."

"Take your contribution to headquarters, and specify what

you want done with it," Upton replied. "Craig and I have not handled one penny of campaign money; on the contrary, we have paid our own expenses. Everything we own has been mortgaged."

"You need more chances to be heard on the radio," insisted Aline. "You are a wonderful speaker, and I want this money spent only on radio time."

"Fine," answered Upton. "Go buy the time yourself!"

I hoped then that Upton, who was near exhaustion, would be able to talk to the people without traveling incessantly. But broadcasts seemed only to have increased the demand of the people to see him in person.

For one meeting the prize-fight stadium in Los Angeles was engaged, with four loudspeakers installed in the ring. The huge crowd was seated below, and as Upton spoke, he had to move from one loudspeaker to the next so as to face everyone part of the time. It required good acting, but he was always at ease on the platform, graceful with the elasticity which made him a champion tennis player.

Sheridan Downey, candidate for lieutenant-governor, was speaking to another mass-meeting in San Francisco, and Upton explained to the audience that the San Francisco audience was hearing Upton, and that they, in Los Angeles, would hear his running mate later. When the eloquent voice of Downey came over the radio, there was thunderous applause.

After Sheridan's speech Upton resumed his own, and when he finished, he told the audience that Aline Barnsdall of Barnsdall Oil was seated just below him, and that she had paid for both the broadcasts. "Come up here, Aline," he called, "and take a bow."

Aline was shy, but she climbed into the prize-ring and the audience loved her.

Two or three weeks before the election, Upton had made up his mind that the misrepresentations of his enemies were succeeding and that he was going to be defeated. I warned him that he must not let this idea be known, and this he promised. By the night before election day he had become fully convinced, but I had not, and shall never forget the anguish of that long night. I could not sleep; I lay for hours, imagining the horrors that were about to fall upon us—the responsibilities, many times heavier than those current ones which had brought my husband to the verge of breakdown. I was sure he would never live to take office; and if he did, who would help him, who would know how? I saw myself having to move into that dreadful old wooden mansion in Sacramento which had once been the home of the boy Lincoln Steffens and was now the official residence of the Governor of California.

Upton did his best to assure me that there was not the slightest chance of our victory; but so often I had had to disagree with him—and so often I had been right! What an odd whim of fate, that now I longed to be wrong, and couldn't believe that I was—couldn't sleep because I couldn't believe it! I had to pretend to, because I knew my husband was exhausted, and ought to be allowed to rest. I lay by his side, making no sound, but envisioning the scene in the radio station where he had agreed to come on the following night to say whatever he might care to say to his supporters.

Upton later was told by a woman writer in Hollywood whom he knew and respected that a businessman of her acquaintance had arranged his affairs, made his will and told his family of his purpose; he went to the studio where Upton was scheduled to speak that night, with a gun in his pocket and the firm resolve that if Upton were elected, he would shoot him.

On election night some of our friends came to our Beverly Hills home to listen to the returns on the radio. Very early it appeared that the Republican candidate was leading; and when the radio voice declared that the EPIC defeat was certain, I lost my self-control; I think it was the first time in my life that I ever lost it publicly. I sank down to the floor and burst into tears, crying, "Oh, thank God! Thank God!" I remember that our friend Lewis Browne, the author, came to me, and said, "We understand, Craig. We were all hoping he wouldn't win."

Our friends drove with us to the studio, where Upton spoke to the EPIC people of the state. He was deeply moved, because he knew how grieved they were; his feelings were apparent in his voice. What he told them was that they were not to give up; what they had learned could not be taken from them. It was a lesson in democracy, and if they kept on being active in politics, their demands would be granted in the end.

One of Upton's finest lieutenants came to see me the next day. He bowed his head in his hands and almost broke down as he talked of the defeat and the terrible disappointment of all those people. I who had worked as hard for victory as he, because I thought it was my duty, was thankful for the defeat and told him so. I reminded him that we had done an educational job of the greatest importance. What more could we have expected? Like the old Socialist Party, we were schoolteachers; that old party had done its job, and so had we. He raised his head, smiled brightly, and said, "The people have learned something about self-government. They needed the lesson."

Aline Barnsdall came, greatly excited. "He must run *again!*" she insisted. "He must *win!* Otherwise it is his swansong." I answered, "There are forty-eight states; and how many governors can you name?" Except California, she couldn't name one. I said, "How does a governor compare with an author whose books are read in every country of the world, and whose name is not forgotten as soon as he goes out of office? Let the political swan die so that the literary swan can go on."

A few days later came a letter from Albert Einstein:

Princeton, N.J.
November 23, 1934

Dear Upton Sinclair:

My son, when he was about five years old, attempted to split wood with my razor. You can be sure that it was less bad for the wood than the razor.

I remembered that story when I heard from you that you had got yourself into this rude business. As I read that this cup had passed from you, I rejoiced even though it had not gone exactly according to your wish.

In economic affairs the logic of facts will work itself out somewhat slowly. You have contributed more than any other person. The direct action you can with good conscience turn over to men with tougher hands and nerves.

To you and your wife, the hearty greetings of your

A. Einstein

15. FOUNDATION BRICKS AND MOUNDS OF ASHES

I HAD THE IDEA that the defeat would set us free; that our duty was done; it must be done, for we were exhausted in every way—mentally, physically, financially—and we could do no more. But I soon discovered that as usual it was *not* the end. There was that great organization; there was a weekly paper; and there was the Democratic Party of the State of California, all having to be managed. There were still the unemployed— the New Deal took a long time to get going, and it didn't always work.

Upton had to go to headquarters the day after the election and meet the leaders. He had polled 879,000 votes, and all those people would be looking to him for guidance, for hope. We had made such a dent in California thinking that the Republican candidate who had won the election felt obliged to adopt Upton's platform and promise that he would "put the unemployed at work producing for themselves." Of course we knew he wouldn't; now it was up to the EPICs to take him at his word and keep the pressure on.

The telephone rang and a man's voice said it was Cornelius Vanderbilt, Jr. speaking from Phoenix, Arizona. Neil had a message from his life-long friend F.D.R. to deliver to Upton: to offer him a most important diplomatic post. Could he come out to our house?

From that moment, I was on the warpath. When Neil arrived, he found me firmly set against anything the President had to offer my husband. "Upton is out of politics," I said, "and he will go back in over my dead body."

I have a vivid picture in my mind of this tall, broad-shouldered young man standing, hat in hand, after a long visit with us in which he had listened patiently while I poured out on his innocent head all the sufferings we had endured during the

EPIC campaign. I was out of politics, and had dragged Upton out, both of us nearer dead than alive. Upton was a writer who reached millions of people with his books, and that was the best way he could serve the people. I had married him because he was a writer, and though I had gone with him, perhaps foolishly, into all his other crusades, I would never do it again. Furthermore I would never let him do it again. Upton assured the President's emissary that I was right. Thus ended Upton's political career. It did not, however, end the efforts of the people to keep him in politics.

I did not love those people who were willing for him to die in a vain attempt to win the world for them. I had argued with some of them and said, "Do you know that he would die long before he could bring about the realization of the EPIC Plan?" Some of them had said to me, "Every hour that he stays with us his voice is going all over the world. A partial victory would be far better than nothing."

Three days after the election was over Upton settled down to write the story of the campaign. He knew that EPIC people all over America would want to hear from him. He prepared a circular, offering the serial rights to newspapers at a very low price, one dollar per thousand of their circulation. He sent out a couple of thousand circulars, and took in about fifteen hundred dollars, not enough to pay his debts but enough to keep us going while he wrote, and to pay for the printing. He had the facts at his finger tips, or in his files or the memories of his friends, and he wrote the booklet in a month or so. The first EPIC book had been called *I, Governor of California, and How I Ended Poverty*. He called the new one, *I, Candidate for Governor, and How I Got Licked*. He told the story quietly and carefully for the record; the facts spoke for themselves, and nothing could ever change them.

When that book was done, he wrote another, called *National EPIC*, for the many people who hoped to carry the movement forward on a nation-wide scale. He wanted to sustain his ideas in the Democratic Party, where he had put them. The New Deal at that time consisted mostly of relief and doles, based upon a fantastic increase in the national debt, and to Upton this was simply disguised inflation. It left the profit-takers in full possession of the instruments and means of production, and so, of course, in command of prices. To him the hoped-for "prosperity" would be just one more boom; he had watched several during his lifetime, and the next depression would follow as night follows day—unless, of course, war came.

With these books out of the way he must earn some money to pay our debts. The surest way for him was by a lecture trip; also, this would enable him to talk again to the people, or at least to many of them. He made arrangements with a lecture bureau; but making a schedule of dates took time, and meanwhile there was a novel haunting his mind. For more than a year he had been meeting the unemployed of the state, literally thousands of them, talking over their problems and hearing their stories. They had been forming what they called "self-help" cooperatives, getting the use of some old warehouse, bringing to it such tools and materials as they possessed, combining all their skills, and sending out scouts to search the town for odd jobs, for anything they could do or make for anybody. If that "anybody" had no money to pay, maybe he had some tool or material or skill that could be got by a "deal." Everybody had something, but nobody had money.

These enterprises spread and grew amazingly, until by the time of the EPIC campaign there were two hundred and fifty of them, keeping hundreds of thousands of people alive and happily at work. To Upton it was the most hopeful development of our time. It was not merely an economic but a moral phenomenon; cooperation was brotherhood, cooperation was order, cooperation was peace! This was being demonstrated, proved. It was in every way the opposite of competition, a blind, animal, anti-human relic of a cruel and evil past. He went up to Santa Barbara, where the first "self-help" had been started by Hjalmar Rutzebeck, a Norwegian giant who had written a book called *Alaska Man's Luck* which Upton admired. It took him a week or so to fill a notebook with all the details of that one venture in cooperation—stories as strange as any fiction writer could invent.

Upton compared the growth of a co-op to that of a river;

it starts very small, and as it flows, other small streams flow into it, until it becomes immense. He built his novel, *Co-op,* on that same pattern. The story starts with three men living in a sewer pipe, which may sound unlikely but was a fact of the time. The city of Oakland had been putting in an outfall sewer, and had a great number of six-foot concrete pipes lined up by a road; the money had run out and the work had to be postponed. The wandering unemployed discovered this free shelter, and it became "Pipe City." It was there that three men—all of whom Upton knew—had dreamed up the idea of "self-help," and had got the use of an abandoned building for the labor of cleaning it up.

So there was a center, a place not merely of shelter but of vision and hope. It was a stream for the other streams to flow into. Men came, women came, whole families came. Each chapter of *Co-op* starts with a new person, or group—always a real story of the people Upton had met. By some chance or other they land at the co-op, and are put to work doing whatever they can. There is tragedy, there is humor, and above all hope in their lives. As usual, Upton wrote this story in a state of prolonged mild ecstasy; as always, it was the most wonderful thing he had ever written, and I had learned not to dampen his enthusiasm.

By now he had worked out an arrangement with his publishers, by which they had their edition to be sold to the trade, and he had his, to be sold to his customers. So *Co-op* went out to the world, and as happened so often, Upton's kind of people loved it, and the rest of the world cared for it not at all or only mildly. The philosopher, John Dewey, wrote: "I began reading *Co-op* Friday p.m. and hardly laid it down till I finished it Saturday. It is one of the finest things you have done— or anyone else on the American scene has done." And Rob Wagner, editor of *Script,* wrote, "Every word is priceless. It's a GRAND JOB, Uppie, and I will sing its song . . . Your *Co-op* is a thrilling tale, beautifully done."

Needless to say, that is what Upton thought.

The Klan movement was spreading its poison all over the world, and agents of vicious fanatics came to Greenwood to incite anti-Semitism. Dollie wrote me what happened. Their meeting was well advertised and a large crowd gathered, including our brother Orman, now a lawyer in Papa's office. He was outraged by what he heard, and leaped to his feet and hurried to the platform to denounce the agitators. They tried to shut him up; they shouted, "Kill him. Kill him!" He told them that this was his town, and the town of the Jews whose cooperation and brains had helped to make it. He told the strangers they were not welcome here, and he asked them to remove themselves and their obnoxious propaganda without delay. He carried the meeting, of course, and the Klansmen left Greenwood.

Not long after this, Orman wrote me the only "scare" letter I ever had from him. He reminded me that this was the first.

Dear Sister:
    You have often feared that Upton was in danger of assassination. I've never thought so until now. Last night I heard a broadcast by Goebbels from Germany in which he warned Upton Sinclair of the fate he was earning for himself by his public attacks on the Nazis. I think Upton is in grave danger.

A lecture tour was as dangerous as anything Upton could have thought of, but he had never been afraid since he was a small boy. He had learned on the streets of New York that a " 'fraid cat" was a "sissy," and a "sissy" was such a contemptible thing that any risk was preferable. There he had learned to show the other street urchins that he was no "chappie," as they had called him for a while. He hated violence too much, however, to want to swagger and be a "he-man," as the poor waterfront boy, Jack London, had done.

My father had been firm in the idea that early discipline by playmates was something every boy should have, and this Upton had surely had. But I hadn't had anything of the sort, and it was not always easy for me to live with a fearless man in a world so full of his deliberately-made enemies.

Now Upton proposed to set off alone on a tour of the whole country in our Ford! I informed him that if he went, I would go along. During the campaign, when so many threats had been made against his life, one of my friends had brought us a beautiful police dog named Duchess, to guard our home; so now I packed a traveling bag and stowed some cans of dogfood in the car, and the three of us set off through the wilds of our native land.

We drove first up the Pacific Coast highway, and suddenly we found ourselves entering a place of magic, the groves of giant redwoods, some of them big enough for a car to drive through a hole in the trunk—there was one through which we actually did drive. We parked, and Upton went wandering off, gazing up at the high canopy above and the deep carpet of lovely green ferns beneath. He came back, pouring out his wonder and delight; it was a place for fairies, for elves, for all the creatures of primitive fantasy.

He talked about it through a good part of that day, and I watched the mind of the poet he had wanted to be. He would turn this beauty into a tale for children, he told me. He imagined two little gnomes living in that forest, and they drove with us. The story became "The Gnomobile."

We had a lecture in Portland, where we were welcomed by a young journalist named Dick Neuberger, later to become a U. S. Senator. The meeting was in a baseball park, and it was raining, but a good crowd came.

Next was Seattle, where we knew nobody; but for some reason beyond understanding the governor of the state or the mayor of the city had ordered out a detachment of the militia; no one knew whether it was to protect the speaker or to prevent his speaking. Naturally, I had a good deal of trepidation—was I in for another San Pedro? Of course Upton would speak, regardless. The militia made a fine advertisement for a lecture, and a huge crowd laughed at Upton's humorous comments on the authorities.

At Tacoma I was amused to watch my husband dealing with a heckler. A man got up in the audience and challenged some idea he had expressed. Upton discussed it with him, and the man persisted. The audience grew angry, and there were cries, "Put him out!" But Upton said, "We don't want to put anybody out, we want to settle this the American way." Addressing the man, "My friend, you believe in democracy, do you not?"

The man said, "Yes," and Upton explained, "These people have paid to hear a lecture by me. Of course, if they prefer to hear one by you, that is their privilege. Will you agree to leave it to them?" The man couldn't say no to that, and Upton said, "All who want to hear this gentleman, please raise their hands." One hand went up, the man's own. "And now all who want to hear me?" All the other hands went up, and the man sat down amid general laughter.

I suppose it is hard to believe that there was ever a lonely highway in our country. But a generation has been born and grown to adulthood since the time we set out on that lecture trip. We drove on many lonely roads, and on some of them the filling stations were far apart. So were the towns, and motels were practically unknown. Upton's lecture bureau had routed us with many a zigzag, so that we almost doubled on our own tracks several times, and often, in an effort to get somewhere on time, we drove on unpaved roads. We couldn't afford to get lost, because at each place where he was to speak the posters were out, the auditorium engaged and tickets sold.

Once, on a country road, we stopped to walk the dog. Duchess, city-bred, saw a rabbit, tore off into a field of high weeds and did not return. We called and waited, and finally Upton, who loved the high-spirited police dog, said, "We must find her."

After quite a tramp, we heard a feeble whimpering. We found Duchess in an open cement hole, a deep, round basin through which underground irrigation water swirled furiously to some far-off field of grain or alfalfa. At least, that was the best guess we could make as to its function. Our dog was almost exhausted, but still paddling hard to keep her head above the water. By lying flat on the ground Upton could barely reach her.

I couldn't be sure which was the heavier, my tired, campaign-thin husband, or a large, water-soaked German shepherd. I sat on Upton's legs while he reached down and caught the front paws of the struggling dog. Somehow he lifted her out, and while she dried herself by shaking the water from her coat onto us, Upton lay still to get his breath.

On a long drive across high plains we hoped in vain to find an inn where we could stop for the night. At last we saw two one-room shacks side by side, on the edge of the road. It was late, and a cold rain was falling. We decided to ask for lodging until daylight.

One hut was dark. We knocked on the other where there was a light showing under the door. Three rough-looking, unshaven men occupied that room. One came to our car to look us over, before agreeing to give us a place to sleep. He did not seem to be afraid of Duchess, but spoke to her kindly while we quieted her. Then he said he had no place for travelers, but there was a bed in the other shack in which we might sleep. He brought a kerosene lamp, and let us in, said good night and went back to his own shack. There was only one blanket, an awful-smelling horse blanket, covered with horsehairs, with a few prickly burrs added. But we went to sleep—this time in God's hands, I said, not trusting to Upton's charmed life.

At dawn our host knocked on the door and Upton opened it and asked, "How much?" The man hesitated, then said, "Twenty-five cents ain't too much, I hope. I'd like to say nothin', but times is hard." We thought a dollar wouldn't be too much.

Eastward from there, two thousand miles of mountains and forests lay before us.

At Butte, Upton's lecture was part of a rodeo and the cowboys all saluted him. In St. Louis the lecturer was introduced by a distinguished astronomer who got him mixed up with the author of *Main Street* and *Babbitt,* to the vast glee of a large audience.

At Chautauqua, in upper New York State, Upton was scheduled to debate with Congressman Hamilton Fish, Jr. This was the third of a series of debates with this ultraconservative Republican whose congressional district, up the Hudson River from New York City was the one in which President Roosevelt lived.

Upton had known Ham's uncle, Stuyvesant Fish, the Wall Street banker, and had crossed swords with the nephew more

than a decade earlier, when Ham had been chairman of a congressional committee which had come out to Los Angeles to
investigate labor troubles. Upton appeared to testify as to
events at San Pedro and the Congressman browbeat him merci-
lessly. "Six hundred men thrown into jail? How do you know
the number? Did you count them?" When the author said it
had been reported in all the newspapers, the answer was, "I
thought you didn't believe what you read in the newspapers."

"I believe it when it is something they don't like to admit,"
Upton replied.

Now the four EPIC debates with Mr. Fish were conducted
with great courtesy, and at the end of the Chautauqua affair
something happened which seemed to me extraordinary. I sat
in our little Ford sedan in the park near the open-air assembly
place. When the debate was over, crowds walked by and after
they had thinned out, there came Congressman Fish with a
friend; they strolled past without so much as a glance at the
dusty "flivver." Fish was speaking, and I am not sure of his
exact words, but they were to the effect that Upton had got the
better of him.

From that debate we set out for home, with several lectures on the way.

One was in Rochester, and as we were leaving that city we
collided with a grocery truck. Our car was demolished, and we
had to buy a new one in Rochester in order to make our next
lecture date.

The last date was in Salt Lake City, where the Mormons
were kind to us. From there we started homeward after dark;
but near Provo our engine blew out a gasket and we had to be
towed into town and put up at a hotel. It was eleven in the
morning before repairs were made and then we started on what
proved to be a record-breaking job of driving for one man. We
both craved to be at home, and Upton drove without rest; I
couldn't relieve him because I know nothing about cars.

I remember gray deserts and pink mountains, and weird for-
mations of multicolored rock. Crossing into California it was
night, but suffocatingly hot—Death Valley was only a few miles

away. But Pasadena was cooler and we yearned to get there; Upton insisted he could stand it, and we drove on. When we came through El Cajon Pass it was one o'clock in the morning and I urged that we go to a hotel in San Bernardino so he could rest; but he said, "It's only another fifty miles, and how wonderful to be in our own pink house!" We drove on and arrived at half-past two; our speedometer showed seven hundred and twenty-four miles and our watches showed a time of fifteen and a half hours. It was a stunt I hope he will never repeat.

One of the darkest days of my life came now. A telegram from home told me that Papa was gone. I sank down where I was when I read it, and wept, while Upton tried to persuade me not to stay there on a hard stone floor. He tried to lift me, and I begged him to leave me alone.

"You can't help me," I sobbed. "I thank God that I still have you. But you are not enough—"

Then I thought this might hurt him. So I let him help me to my feet, and we sat together on a sofa, while I cried with my head on his shoulder.

"What is wrong with this terrible universe?" I kept asking, and of course he had no answer that I could accept. No one did. I kept asking questions about God and His purposes. Surely He must have a purpose—but why must it require such losses, and such cruel suffering?

The days passed, and in time I was able to see that my grief was not fair to the one of my three dearest people who was still with me. Now I must put my mind on a renewed search for God. Only He could give me understanding, and I knew that only by searching would this come to me.

The wise woman of Christian Science had written that "man's extremity is God's opportunity." But Christian Science did not give me all the understanding I needed for the search. It had saved me once from despair, and it had saved Upton's life; I was certain of this, and so was he. But our prayers are not always answered in the way that we think best. More often than not the way we think best is not God's way.

I felt sure now that I could never believe it was best for me, or for them, for God to take my father and mother. I must try to find out the meaning of that—for I did believe there was a Creator, and that there was meaning in His universe.

We still had debts to pay, and a second lecture tour had been arranged. At Topeka, Kansas, Upton was introduced to the audience by the Episcopal bishop of the state. At Fort Wayne, Indiana, he debated "Production for Use" with a Republican Congressman who jeered at him because he was charging two hundred dollars for the debate. Upton's reply was to ask if there was anyone in the audience who thought fifty cents was too high a price for what he was getting; if so, his money would be cheerfully refunded at the box office. There were no takers.

Snow fell early that November, and Upton drove over icy roads to a lecture date at Stamford, Connecticut. On that trip he took his son David and the German writer Emil Ludwig. Upton was surprised to find how sympathetic this popular writer was to his own views. Ludwig offered to introduce him at the lecture, and did so in a speech that warmed Upton's heart.

On another date he took his son to Princeton. There, in the afternoon, they paid a call on the beloved Albert Einstein, in the Gothic-style office which the ultra-modern Institute for Advanced Studies had provided for him. This kindest of great men said he was coming to the lecture, but doubted if the rest of Princeton would. He asked permission to tell Princeton what he thought of Upton, and so once more there was a brief speech to make a muckraker's heart beat faster.

Upton drove to Philadelphia for a debate with Norman Thomas. The great auditorium was packed, and mostly with Socialists, who took the side of their presidential candidate. Norman had from the first hour of the campaign taken a vehement stand against the EPIC program, describing it as a "tin-can economy." They had debated earlier in Los Angeles, appropriately in the fight arena, and Upton described Norman Thomas as by all odds the toughest debater he had ever met. But they have remained good friends for half a century, each respecting the other's right to be wrong.

After the last lecture, we were free to go home for that long-awaited rest. I had a stubborn cough which worried Upton, and he suggested a few days of complete rest in Florida. "We can be there in a day and a half," he said.

We set out from chilly New York early in December, drove through Washington in a cold drizzle at night and on and on without a stop except to eat and sleep. The east coast of Florida seemed as cold as New York and we turned inland toward the Gulf of Mexico. I had a longing for the sight of those waters which Papa had so loved. The Gulf of Mexico belonged to me and my family and I remembered it as always warm, peaceful and safe. That was what I craved—safety! The safety of my old home in the South—a yearning for it would be in my heart forever.

At St. Petersburg we found the sunshine we had been seeking, and there we rented a poor little place, almost out over a lagoon. Upton hauled the steamer rug from our car and lay down on a patch of lawn and announced that this was paradise!

I did not join him, for we had stopped at a market and bought a pail of shrimp, fresh out of the water. I told him I wanted to play "make-believe"—this was Ashton Hall and the Negroes, Adam and George, had just pulled the seine and I was going to have some hot boiled shrimp! We could bring them out in the sun to eat them. Duchess would devour all the skins, for she hadn't had a bone since we left California.

Upton came in, and before long decided there must be fleas in this cabin. Pink welts were coming out all over him, and they itched terribly. "Let me see," I told him. Then I laughed. "Redbugs—chiggers!"

The next morning, he started writing a book. "We don't know a soul in this place," he said. "In California we will be at the mercy of everyone who wants me to make a speech, or to run for the United States Senate. I want to say here!"

But I knew we had to get back to the unfinished duties of that crusade. A week later we left Florida for our long pink house in the West.

When we reached the Mississippi coast, I was not sure that I should pause there for even a day. My emotional nature was going to find it hard to be traveling again on that old shell road along the beach from Biloxi to Ashton Hall.

I sat in the back seat of the car, and tried to think of the tired yet always buoyant man in front of me. The once wavy blond hair had become straight and was fast turning gray. I must not grieve about the past, but keep my mind on our life together. He was the same gallant crusader who had won my heart with his determination to keep democracy a living force in America, and make it possible for every man to live in peace on the fruits of his own labor. "They shall not build and another inhabit; they shall not plant and another eat." Thus spoke the prophet Isaiah, and Upton had quoted him in two-score cities on this trip.

Past Beauvoir, I kept my eyes on the horizon and the dim outlines of Ship Island to the south, where the Confederates had a fort used as a prison for Yankee soldiers during the Civil War. During my girlhood, when we chartered a schooner and crew to take our guests to see the old fort, the ladies would declare they must go inside to search for their family silver—the tea sets and coffee-urns and spoons which the Yankees had stolen as they marched through the state during the last days of the war.

The car stopped and Upton announced cheerfully, "Here we are!" A moment later he exclaimed, in consternation, "Why, it's all grown up with underbrush—and where's the house?"

We got out, and Duchess jumped out and began to race around where the children's dog Dink used to run with my small brothers and Jimmie.

The house was gone, and nothing was left to mark the place but foundation bricks and mounds of ashes. I went closer, and saw some broken pieces of Mama's blue willow ware. The rains must have washed the ashes away from them.

I sank to the ground, sobbing. Upton stood in silence for a while, then stooped and took my hands. "Come, beloved. We must go home."

When we got there, we had motored more than twenty thousand miles in about seven months.

Soon after our return to Pasadena, Upton considered it his duty to make a radio address to the EPIC people. An incredible movement called "Ham and Eggs" had been recruited among the EPICs, and was growing rapidly. Because one of the leaders of this foolish and inflationary thing had been an EPIC candidate, the people assumed that he had Upton's approval.

Upton exposed the futility of this "Ham and Eggs Plan," and it cost him many good but stupid admirers. It cost me something, too. After much searching I had found an excellent laundress; but the day after Upton's talk, my laundry was returned with a note:

"Dear Mrs. Sinclair: I can't do your washing any more. The reason is, Mr. Sinclair doesn't want us to have our ham and eggs."

"Mother" Tipton was an old lady who worked hard for a living; she helped run the Socialist local, and at her house gave "bean suppers" at which the members paid twenty-five cents each to sit down at a long plank table in her small backyard and eat a plate of cold beans served on wilted lettuce leaves with salt and vinegar poured over them. She told with pride how each plate cost only a few cents, leaving a good profit for the local.

Now this faithful crusader for the poor and oppressed of the world was beginning to despair because of the slow progress of Socialism. She saw in Communism a fast-moving working-class army, worthy of at least a "new look." It had not tempted her yet, beyond an occasional thought; she said to me that she was "just wondering."

The humble home of the Tiptons had always been open to any working-class visitor who wanted a night's lodging, or an introduction to one of the party leaders in the area. Upton was someone whom many visitors wanted to meet, and one day Mrs. Tipton telephoned to ask if she might bring Earl Browder up to call. "He seems so gentle and harmless," she said, "and he wants so much to meet Upton." He was leaving town the next day, so I told her to come with him that afternoon.

I was curious to have a look at this Communist Party head,

and I thought Upton would be, too. I knew it was a risk, for we had learned by now that all they usually wanted from my husband was a chance to journey on to the home of Mrs. Gartz, and say to her secretary, "I just came from Upton Sinclair, and have a matter which he wants me to put before her." Thus he might succeed in getting into her presence and leaving with a substantial check in his pocket.

Browder was a melancholy-looking young man, far from brisk and brash. As Mrs. Tipton had said, he was gentle. Upton stopped in the living room for a while, and then left me to entertain this sad Communist. The large, stout Mrs. Tipton sat nervously on a sofa, looking as if she had introduced a bomb into our house and left it for me to dismantle.

I had meant to be cold and severe, and instead I felt compassionate. Here was an educated, mild young American, not filled with revolutionary ardor, nor with the self-assured aggressiveness of a fanatic, determined to save you or else wring your neck.

But of course this might be a pose to impress me—and later, Mrs. Gartz, to whom he was sure to ask for an introduction. So I proceeded with my intended lecture, but in a more friendly manner and tone of voice. He sat perfectly still, never interrupting me, listening as patiently as had Neil Vanderbilt when I lectured the politicians over his shoulder.

I reminded Earl Browder of all the evil things I had discovered in the Communists I had met—mostly renegade Socialists, weary of the long, hard road to a fair deal for the workingman. I told how they practiced deceit, treachery, flattery and even religion to gain friends and converts; how they called all Social-Democrats, including my husband, "Social-Fascists." I told how they had denounced Upton's EPIC plan in their press as "one more rotten egg from the Blue Buzzard's nest," and had called him "a vain old peacock." I ended by asking, kindly, "Now Mr. Browder, you don't impress me as being that kind of rascal. Don't you think it would be better if Communists would be honest?"

"I *do*, Mrs. Sinclair," the then leader of the American Communists replied, gently.

Mrs. Tipton drew a deep breath of relief, sufficiently audible to reach Mr. Browder's ears. He did not ask for an introduction to anyone, but rose to go when Mrs. Tipton got up and stood over me to murmur, "You have been so kind!"

Later, when Earl Browder found himself in the Party's disfavor, I realized that he had never been the type to remain with them permanently. He was just another discouraged idealist, seeking a religion, a purpose in life.

Now there broke upon the world the greatest of international sensations—the possibility that a lady from Baltimore might become the Queen of England. Upton, a novelist, was instantly alert to the fact that here was "copy." And it was *his* copy for the special reason that this lady from Baltimore was none other than little Wallis Warfield, a member of the Virginia clan to which Upton belonged. She was a Montague, niece of Upton's lovely cousin, Lelia Montague Barnett. Little Wallis was a half-orphan whose mother was another widow of the South's "Lost Cause." Lelia had helped to train Wallis as a charmer.

We were more than ordinarily intrigued by the terrible thing which had befallen the great British Commonwealth. Worse than having a twice-divorced lady chosen by King Edward VIII would have been the idea that the American muckraker Upton Sinclair might become even remotely connected with the Throne. But it was true that Wallis' great-uncle Powhatan Montague had also been Upton's "Uncle Pow" and this, in the South at least, made them cousins. "Pow, you devil!" was the term Upton's mother had used when addressing the jovial Virginia gentleman who had married her husband's sister.

Now an "old devil" got into Upton's mind. The Throne was rocking, and he would give it another nudge. Had not his ancestor Edward III sat on that throne? How impudent of them not to welcome little Wallis Warfield! So he wrote a playlet called "Wally for Queen." Also he wrote for the Hearst newspapers a story which made the front page of them all. We never knew whether it hurt "Wally's" chances, but it caused a sensation among the doctors in a Washington hospital where Lelia

lay recuperating from an operation. Early in the morning the
doctors came in to inspect their patient. On her bed lay a copy
of the city's Hearst newspaper, nearly all its front page taken up
with two feature stories, one with a large photograph of Wallis
and the other a large photograph of Upton. Lelia, amused, held
it up before the doctors, saying, "One of these persons is my
niece and the other is my first cousin!"

Recently published have been the memoirs of Wallis Montague Warfield, now Duchess of Windsor, and the Cornelius
Vanderbilt, Jr.'s story of his mother, who was Grace Wilson of
Tennessee. Both these ladies carried off the great marital prizes
of their times, for both as Southerners had been trained in the
subtle art of "charm." And yet, there is nothing subtle about
it! It is all stated in one simple sentence: "Talk about *him*, not
about yourself." That is what Wallis did. She was the first
woman to express interest in "his" work.

Bernard Shaw and his wife, Charlotte, were taking a
world cruise, and their ship was docked at the Los Angeles harbor. We drove over in the evening to pay them a visit, taking
with us Judge Ben Lindsey, famed as the founder in Denver
of the first children's court in this country.

In 1931, when a 19-man committee recommended Upton for
the Nobel Prize, Shaw had written: "Mr. Upton Sinclair is not
a Henry James; he is rather a Daniel Defoe and though Daniel
still lives in his works after 200 years, his contemporaries put
him where several respectable Americans would like to put Mr.
Sinclair—in the pillory."

But we had not seen Shaw then. Now we were shocked to
find him a weary-looking old man, instead of the lively and
buoyant one to whom we had talked beside a meadow in Germany. Mrs. Shaw, stout and blonde, looked as if she would live
longer than her husband. But Shaw's smile was as sweet as ever,
his skin pink and free of the blemishes of age. The impression
he always gave was of shining cleanliness.

It was a long visit. Our host and hostess gave no sign of
being tired of their callers, but I was sure they must be, because I knew they had left the steamer at San Francisco and

had motored to Los Angeles, stopping off at San Simeon to visit William Randolph Hearst. They had had a long drive that day.

Ben Lindsey had a story of persecution and hardly paused once in the telling. As the enemy of all those who preyed upon juvenile weakness he had offended the politicians of Denver, and finally they had hounded him out of the city. Ever since then his indignation had grown until it occupied his whole mind. Now, he took almost all the time of our visit for the telling of his story; no one was willing to interrupt him, for he was a good man and a pioneer in a most important field.

But to burden the distinguished visitors with all the details was surely an imposition. Finally, though I knew there were many things Upton and Shaw wanted to talk about, I rose and said we must go. Poor, tormented Judge Lindsey didn't budge, and went on talking. Fortunately, he was our guest—we had brought him in our car—so I said, firmly, "We simply *must* go," and shook hands with the Shaws. I went out the door of their stateroom, and Upton arose and said goodbye. Mrs. Shaw joined me, and with her arm around me, we started walking down the passage of the ship.

"Thank you, dear!" she said, with fervor. "We are *so* tired! And we had heard all that long story before. Poor Judge Lindsey!"

As soon as we were in our car, Lindsey started scolding me for dragging him away.

We had long since discovered that we did not have to go away from home to see the world; it came to Hollywood and to us. Now came a man we had long known through his letters and books, Dr. J. B. Rhine, who had succeeded McDougall as head of Duke University's Parapsychology Laboratory.

We discussed our telepathy experiments, and he asked what had caused me to become so seriously interested in the subject. I told him at some length of my search for God and for a purpose in the universe, and I knew that the place to find Him was in the mind. Rhine remarked that this had been his own motivation. Upton told at length of his interest in the subject of

psychic research, dating from his youth, and how long he had
waited for a chance to witness some proof of the reality of such
phenomena. At last it had come about by accident—he had discovered it in his own home!

Dr. Rhine's work at Duke University and his books on the
subject of his scientific demonstrations there are unique and
have made him famous; but he is one of those consecrated men
of science who have no interest in personal fame. What he
wants is understanding, and the power to give it to others. This
has made a close bond of friendship between him and my husband, who shares this attitude toward both understanding and
fame.

Dr. Rhine wrote me that McDougall had said to him, "Upton
Sinclair has perhaps the best mind in America." I have an old
letter from McDougall in which he made the same statement.
Dr. Rhine's own estimate was: "The amazing thing to me, dis-
tinguishing you from most artists, is what I would call strength
of character. This," he said, "gives consistency to your major
purposes throughout, and a conscientiousness and determination to your crusading that, as far as I am able to judge, puts
you at the top of the constructive propagandists. You seem to
have had a weak acquisitive propensity. . . ."

I once wrote Dr. Rhine that I thought his research was the
most important work in the world. But probably there can be
two "most important works." Certainly no one can live without his daily bread, not even a psychic researcher.

Labor had come a long way toward recognition since
The Jungle. But now, in the vast domain of the Flivver King
at Dearborn, Michigan, the Ford plant had become an armed
fortress guarded by thirty-six hundred lawless private police,
and every worker therein was aware that a labor organizer was
in danger of his life anywhere near this preserve. There was
such intimidation that Frank Murphy, mayor of the adjoining
city of Detroit, had stated publicly, "Henry Ford employs some
of the worst gangsters in our city." This was what a billion dollars had done to the one-time mechanic, Henry Ford. The English Lord Acton had written, "All power tends to corrupt, and

absolute power corrupts absolutely." Sixteen years ago Ford had paid his workers more than any other factory in the country, and Henry had said publicly that his workers were free to organize. Now he paid less than others, and his workers were fired instantly for joining a union.

This struck Upton as a sort of personal affront. Had he not brought the Flivver King together with the gentle and justice-loving Razor King, hoping that the latter's spirit would soften the heart of the owner of a billion dollars? Had he not argued with the Flivver King on those long walks in the mountains above Pasadena? Had this served only to harden a billion-dollar heart?

Walter Reuther, while a student at Wayne, had organized a chapter of the Intercollegiate Socialist Society, now the League for Industrial Democracy. He later became an organizer of the United Automobile Workers of America. Upton resolved to help him educate the workers in their right to organize, and explain their problem to the American public, by telling the story of Henry Ford. So he went to work on a new book, *The Flivver King.*"

When the book was done, the United Automobile Workers ordered an edition of two hundred thousand copies, and it was sold at the gates of the Ford plants and of the assembly plants all over the world. This netted about forty thousand dollars for the workers. Four years later the billion-dollar heart melted. The Flivver King went the whole way, agreeing to recognize the union and signing a contract with them.

This was the way for Upton to lend a hand to labor, without killing himself and me with political campaigns. This was the way he had told me about before I married him. This was the path he would follow in future, if it lay in my power to keep him on it. No matter how attractive he was as a platform speaker, he reached more people with the printed page.

I had proof that the lesson had been learned.

16. YOU HAVE MADE HISTORY

UPTON HAD ALWAYS FELT that the only way to end war was to end poverty. He had hoped to prevent World War I, and had failed. Now he saw World War II on the horizon, black and terrible, and he went back in his mind to his earlier struggle "for a Clean Peace and the Internation." He had failed; now he began a long novel called *World's End*.

Peace settled upon my soul when I saw him launched upon a task which would keep him at home and out of mischief. Every morning, if the weather was fair, he took his typewriter out into the garden; and there, with our adoring Duchess at his feet, he would stay until lunchtime. Now and then, just to get his head clear, he would get up, and then up would jump Duchess. He would pat her head, then walk up and down on the garden path, while she raced around joyously and barked at birds in the fig trees. As soon as he sat down, and gave her another friendly pat or two, she would again take her place beside him, and silently maintain her vigil. Somehow she knew that she must not interrupt that typewriter. I was too busy to read the manuscript, and could not judge whether Upton had a basis for his excitement about it.

When completed, the bulky script, seven or eight hundred pages, went off to a publisher friend, and soon came back with a report that it was found "dull." Upton was staggered for an hour or two; then he recovered and sent it off again. So many times it had happened in his life! I won't name the four publishers who declined *World's End*. Then by happy chance Upton thought of an old friend, B. W. Huebsch, of the Viking Press. Ben had been a Civil Liberties Union man from early days, and would understand what Upton was driving at. Ben told us afterward that he got the manuscript one afternoon, took it home and started reading that evening. By the next evening he knew they would publish it.

So the first Lanny Budd book went out to the world in May, 1940. The Literary Guild took it, and that meant a large first edition. It went at once to the best-seller lists and stayed there for months; it was translated into sixteen languages. And meantime Upton was already hard at work upon a sequel, *Between Two Worlds.*

One of Europe's greatest men of letters, Dr. Thomas Mann, had left Germany when Hitler rose to power. He brought his family and his furniture to America, first to Princeton, New Jersey, then to Southern California. Soon after he arrived he and his wife came to see us, and I thought that he, like his books, lacked that greatest of qualities—humanity. His face was narrow and austere, and his chilly gray-blue eyes seemed wholly absorbed in something inside himself.

But Upton, whose outflowing of interest in his fellow man was his chief characteristic, did not seem to miss this quality in Thomas Mann. More important to Upton at this time was the fact that Mann was another gifted man of letters driven from his German home by the Nazi regime, so he must be welcomed to our land of freedom with the warmth which the German author himself probably did not feel for the country to which he had come. He had much to tell Upton about Europe and its tragic fate, and Upton stowed it away in his mental treasury. They talked about their methods of work, and Mann stated that a page and a half of manuscript was a good day's product. Upton felt rebuked—for he was, alas, too fluent. There is precise and carefully-chiseled prose; and there is that which flows out like a mountain spring, day and night. Later, I was grateful to Dr. Mann for his praise of the "Lanny Budd" books.

There are high-brow literary gentlemen in our own country who look down upon novels which are too popular, but the greatest of modern German novelists took the trouble to read the Lanny Budd books as they appeared and to write Upton, "Someday the whole cycle will certainly be recognized as the best-founded and the best-informed description of the political life of the epoch." About *Dragon's Teeth,* which received the Pulitzer Prize, Thomas Mann wrote:

"It is painful reading-matter, especially for a German, but the pain is turned into pleasure by the art of the presentation—a pleasure, of course, mingled with rage and shame. Whoever knows Nazi Germany will admit that not a word in your book is exaggerated.

"While I read it, my principal feeling was one of satisfaction that all this has been written down and preserved for the future. Naturally, one is inclined to ask whether those to come will believe all these unbelievable things which even our contemporaries never quite could or wanted to believe. Those to come, however, will have less interest in not believing it than our contemporaries, and therefore I count on them."

Like the rest of our country, we on the West Coast were stunned by the news of Pearl Harbor. But almost overnight, on the vulnerable shore of the Pacific came a frenzy of activity. People were doing the most absurd things in the way of home defense. There was a ruling that, to be prepared for incendiary bombs, every householder must keep a pail of sand and a shovel at all four corners of the house, with a ladder close by, and be ready the moment a bomb fell on the house to race up to the roof with sand and shovel to smother it. This would have been an impossible feat for two people as frail as Upton and I. Our house was over ninety feet long, and we could not have even carried a tall-enough ladder from one corner to the other, to say nothing of climbing up with shovel and sand and putting out a fire. But we managed to get a ladder, and the necessary sand and shovel. This was a feat in itself, for there was strict rationing of gasoline, and delivery of sand and a ladder were things competed for.

The next crazy thing was the order to darken every window we had so that not one tiny gleam of light could be seen from the outside; this was to prevent the Japanese planes from knowing where there was a town or city to drop bombs on. Then we were told to paint all windows black, as there was not enough heavy cloth to go around. Fortunately for us, since we had thirty-two windows, we could not get any black paint. It had all been bought up hastily—just as had the cloth. Great factories painted their windows, and almost immediately most of the factory windows in Southern California split; the black paint on the glass heated in the hot sun and that finished the glass panes.

The likelihood of being bombed was severe on everyone's nerves. No matter what materials were available, or not available, something must be found with which to darken our thirty-two windows—unless we were willing to go to bed with the chickens. Upton would have much preferred to be struck with a bomb. We found some old rugs and quilts in one of my favorite secondhand stores, and Upton had to stop writing long enough to nail them over the windows. Everyone had immediately been called into service of some sort while the young men were being mobilized for war.

We still had in our employ a young man who did garden work and he now helped us to prepare our "home defense." He was kept busy shopping for food, which was rationed. I had told him that we felt it would be necessary to move away from Pasadena to some country place as soon as possible, where we would not have to conform to impossible restrictions. Being a generous soul, he assured me that whenever there was an alert he would come at once to help us. I asked what he was going to do to protect himself. His face brightened with pride as he answered, "Oh, I'm already fixed up, and I've been practicing. The minute there's an alert I dive under a mattress that I've put in my closet, and I shut the door. No flying glass will hit me there!"

Pasadena was no longer the quiet residential city we had loved. It was growing fast and the streets were crowded with traffic. Even before our entrance into the war, we were shipping mountains of war goods to Britain and France; small factories were being set up in Pasadena, and that was fine for the realtors and merchants, but not for us. Our neighborhood had been quiet but now was filling up with strangers, and there was a problem for which a new phrase had to be found—"juvenile delinquency." Young rascals raided our orchard, and were not content to take the fruit, but broke down the branches. One of my grown-up nieces ordered them away; instead of running one of them replied, "I'll cut you open with a knife."

Also, we had no freedom from visitors, many unwanted; ever since EPIC everyone had our address, or could get it. There were old friends whom we wished quietly to discard, because they had gone over to the Bolsheviks, or were repeating phrases which the Bolsheviks had put into their heads; but they would not take hints, and I disliked having to hurt them.

I was now looking about for a place farther from the center of industry, traffic and smoke. (The word "smog" had not yet been invented, but the substance was apparent to my eyes and nose.) Also, I had in mind a fireproof house, for we had accumulated a mass of papers and books and I had to keep them safe.

I saw an advertisement of a two-story concrete residence for sale on the edge of the town of Monrovia. We went to look at it, and met an elderly contractor and banker who had built it for himself and family; now he was alone, and wanted to move into a small place.

I examined the house carefully. It was Italian-villa style, and looked much larger than it was because of the great thickness of the double-tile walls. In after years we met plumbers, masons and others who had taken part in building the place, and they agreed that the elderly man had spent money "like crazy." Walls, floors and roof were webs of steel reinforcing; all floors were plastone, easy to clean. All this was to the good; but such things as fancy hand-made friezes and a bronze grill front door that cost six hundred dollars, and an interior wall finish which cost a thousand dollars a room, of course meant nothing to us. The place comprised three lots; we later counted twenty-two varieties of fruit trees; we would have something to eat, free of charge, every week of the year.

All of this was offered at a bargain price, and Upton, always quick on the trigger, said, "Buy it!" But I had to have a night to think it over. Then I telephoned, and we met the old man at the bank where he was a director, and in a few minutes we had a new home. I laid down the law to Upton: he was not to give our address to a living soul; our mail would come to the post office, and we would just disappear from Pasadena. He would sit in the shelter of shrubbery and revise proofs of volume three of the Lanny books, *Dragon's Teeth,* and I would have a shut-off put on the telephone, and lie down in an upstairs bedroom and have peace, blessed peace.

It was a balmy summer evening. Standing at the window, we listened to an owl hooting in the trees and a coyote barking in the hills. In the morning when Upton went out, there was a deer under one of the orange trees.

One day the telephone rang and a voice introduced itself as the editor of the town's local paper. "Mr. Sinclair, have you heard that the Pulitzer Prize has been awarded to *Dragon's Teeth?*" Upton was as happy as if he had inherited enough money to buy the world and make it over according to his lifelong dream. He had been recommended for the Nobel Prize for Literature, the petition being signed by 770 professors of colleges and universities in fifty-five different countries; but more dear to Upton's heart than any prize are the millions of readers in those fifty-five countries. His collection of foreign translations includes more than seven hundred and fifty separate editions scattered among those countries. He doubts if there is another writer in the world who can show the equal of it.

The eleven Lanny Budd books have by now been translated into a score of languages and published with success. Thousands of letters have come from people in these countries, and they marvel that a man could write about their lands, customs and events, and make no errors. The answer lies in his knowledge of French and German, and of the literatures of Europe, and the pains he took to have every chapter checked by experts in the matters concerned. Albert Einstein checked the scenes having to do with atomic affairs, and so did Dr. Samuel Goudsmit, head of the Brookhaven National Laboratory. Half a score of men who served at the Paris Peace Conference checked scenes in *World's End.* Dr. Rudolf Engelsberg, former deputy finance minister of Austria, a refugee in America, checked scenes having to do with German lands. Martin Birnbaum, art expert and

Upton's former classmate, supplied the data having to do with his field and figures in the books as Zoltan Kerteszi.

Cornelius Vanderbilt, Jr., gladly gave Upton information about President Roosevelt. He had been a friend of F.D.R. from his infancy—quite literally, for F.D.R. had attended his christening. Neil suggested *Presidential Agent* as a title for one of the series, and Upton accepted that as a valuable gift.

Upton did not ask permission to use such men as Roosevelt and Churchill, because they were in the public domain. He asked permission in the case of many other persons, and only one refused, on the ground that his role had been confidential. In every case, unless there was a written record, each person checked his own story. So, when you read these books, you are reading history as well as fiction. Bernard Shaw wrote Upton, "When people ask me what has happened in my long lifetime, I do not refer them to the newspaper files and to the authorities, but to your novels."

Among the distinguished Europeans who had been driven out of Germany by the Hitler terror was the novelist and playwright, Franz Werfel, author of *The Song of Bernadette,* a best-seller which was being filmed in Hollywood. Ben Huebsch, Werfel's publisher as well as Upton's, came to Hollywood, and wrote us offering to bring Werfel to see us. Mrs. Werfel came with them, but as she was very deaf, she only looked lovely and smiled sweetly. But Werfel himself had much to tell us.

A handsome man, with large dark eyes and dark hair, he tried to explain in words the "terror" as he had experienced it. He was nonpolitical, an "ivory-tower" artist. He wrote books and gave lectures on literary subjects in a strictly objective way. But neither the Nazis nor the "Commies" would allow this—he must be strictly partisan. Everyone must be. Unfortunate for him in this situation was the fact that he was a Jew. He tried to stay on his ivory tower, where he had always been and where he felt at home. But this availed him nothing. He was accused by the Nazis of being a "Red," and by the Communists of being pro-Nazi.

Finally it became clear that if he stayed in Austria any longer he might be "liquidated." He found it hard to leave—he had been successful and happy as a novelist, playwright and lecturer. But the day came when there could be no more hesitation. As he told this tragic story, his beautiful brown eyes were like those of a bewildered and hurt child. His blonde wife, who had shared these tragic times, nodded her head in agreement, for it was not necessary for his words to be heard—the eloquent face of the narrator underlined what he was talking about.

He escaped to France, and spent his time at Lourdes, gathering material for *The Song of Bernadette*. Then the Nazis conquered France, and with some companions he and his wife fled on foot over the Pyrénées into Spain. He was a stout man, and was now suffering physically as well as mentally from the effects of these trials. The next time Ben Huebsch came to see us, he told us that Franz Werfel had a serious heart condition. I now had the same thing, and I was sure that stress and worry had been at least a contributory cause of my trouble.

Upton was writing another "Lanny Budd" book now, and this glimpse of a gentle and sensitive literary man's ordeal added to his zeal to help in wiping out once and forever dictatorship all over the world.

There came a dreadful day when the radio brought us the news of Franklin Roosevelt's sudden death. Like everyone else who had watched with admiration this great man's work for human welfare, we were stunned and grief-stricken. We thought that a calamity beyond repair had befallen the world. Upton doubted if there was any man in the country who could take his place. I watched Upton's distress as he paced the room, trying to think what the effect of the loss would be. This first shock must have engraved itself upon his mind, for later he wrote it into the novel, *O Shepherd, Speak!* as the feelings of his hero. In the story, Lanny Budd was in the President's house at Warm Springs when the stroke occurred.

"Lanny had done his praying for Roosevelt over a long period; now he confronted the fear that his prayers were vain. This must be death.

"A cruel, a terrible thing, a fact of the universe which man
confronts with dismay, and for which he makes up whatever
explanations and excuses he can find. For a great and good man
like this it seemed something monstrous, intolerable."

The brutality and hypocrisy of the Stalin regime had
kept Upton in such a state of indignation and horror that he
had gone off upon another crusade—though this time I had seen
to it that it was carried on at home. He had written articles denouncing Communism for his translators in Tokyo, Hong
Kong and Calcutta; and these were translated and published.
They were broadcast over Radio Japan. He wrote frequently
for the Voice of America, the Central Intelligence Agency,
Radio Free Europe, and various American Anti-Communist
committees against Bolshevism; he made tape recordings, copies
of which I have put away in a storeroom.

The Voice of America sent a recording team to our home,
and Upton made speeches in both English and his somewhat-
rusty German. There was no country in the world in which he
did not have readers; he had been told by Norman Thomas and
others that the Communists were proclaiming that the conditions portrayed in *The Jungle* still prevailed in our country.
Upton repudiated this false use of his books and told his listen-
ers that the workers in America now had strong unions and
negotiated on equal terms with the great corporations. In every
way at his command he used his voice to point out to the
peoples of the world who had read his books since the turn
of the century that they must not fall under the spell of Communist propaganda and false promises.

He had thought that he had rounded out the Lanny Budd
saga in ten large volumes, but under the urgency of this situation he wrote one more, *The Return of Lanny Budd,* pictur-
ing this "cold war" in all its complications along the border
between the free world and the slave world in Europe. This
book, like the other ten "Lanny Budd" books, was published
not only in America, but in countries as far apart as Britain,
India and Japan.

He was one of the first to support the Atlantic Pact, which he did through newspaper releases to the Associated Press and United Press. These were widely published in this country and elsewhere in the world, and immediately brought down upon his head violent and complete repudiation by Radio Moscow and *Pravda*. The Russians charged that he was a "lackey of Wall Street" and "a friend of Henry Ford and William Randolph Hearst." Arthur Koestler wrote Upton comparing bookburning in Germany in 1933 by Goebbels and in 1953 by Pieck, with the top books on each pyre his own and Upton's.

During the Cold War Communists in Southern California took advantage of Mrs. Gartz's "open house" to lay siege to her, pretending to be pacifists like herself. They filtered into her weekly afternoon teas and became familiar faces. They reminded her that she had often called herself a Communist, in the days before she had any idea of what the word meant. Now she claimed agreement with them in the same spirit which moved the aged Bernard Shaw to do the same. Yes, she said, she remembered; and being by nature a loyal person who always stood by a friend, she now began to believe that she had actually been a Communist.

I protested and argued; but of course no one could protest successfully to a mind that was going into second childhood. Finally, when I saw that this was the case, I decided that the only kind thing I could do was to avoid this dear old friend, who had been almost a mother to both of us. Her gatherings had once been useful as an open forum for legitimate discussion of differing opinion; but to attend now would be a sort of recognition of the Communists as merely people who held a different opinion from ours. I could not make Mrs. Gartz see that their different opinion was that no one should have any opinion at all, unless it was approved by the Cominform.

So we saw less and less of her. She complained like a petulant child that we never came to see her. I knew that her present "constant" friends kept reminding her how she had defended us when we were attacked; and now, how could we expect her not to defend the rights of "Commies" to their opinions?

The end of the long and precious friendship came when she

telephoned and argued with me, "Here is my guest, the 'Red Dean' of Canterbury Cathedral, high prelate in the Church of England," who wanted to meet us. Surely here was a man with whom there could be no argument! Surely *he* knew the truth! We must come at once to her house to meet him.

When I told her that here was a man who either did not know the truth, or liked truth less than an opportunity to make himself conspicuous, she was plaintive, but no less sure that we must obey her summons. Everyone must!

The next day, looking from a window, I saw her car at our locked gates. There she sat, an invalid who could not get out of her car, and beside her a figure in black, with flowing white locks. I knew him from his pictures. I did not open the gates; and after she had driven away there was only one thing I could do—wipe·the tears from my eyes.

The ephemeral joy of our Monrovia home proved to me that the old idea of a permanent abode was obsolete; to plant trees and shrubs and improve a house to fit one's need was wasted time and money. The machine age had changed all this. Just as the unexpected "smog" of industry had destroyed the beauty of our mountains and valleys and even our great, calm ocean with its charming bays and peninsulas, some new and unexpected atrocity would turn up tomorrow to make a home untenable.

Neil Vanderbilt had long been a victim of "the wanderlust." He had told me the first time I had a talk with him, that he couldn't be still. And now that contagion of wanderlust had spread all over America—and not merely to the leisure class. Workingmen piled their families into cars and went seeking better jobs and higher pay; airplane passenger service lured all Americans to cross seas and continents as casually as our parents went from winter to summer homes.

One day after World War II Neil came to tell us that he had a wonderful new gadget—a huge trailer, designed by himself. Why not carry your home around with you wherever you go? His house on wheels, like his car, was a luxury affair, and even had a bathtub in it! All you had to do when night came was to find a "trailer park," drive in, and the owner of this utopian piece of real estate came running to park you, connect your electric lights and water hose and you were at home.

Neil painted this life in glowing pictures. We asked him a dozen questions; then we were converts. No more gardens without even a schoolboy to help rake the leaves, mow the lawns, spray the fruit trees, hold the hose on famishing plants during the long dry season! Not even the bother of remembering to pay the taxes on your ground! The park owner paid them, then you paid him. He did the remembering, not you.

We wanted no more property! No more roofs to be repaired, no more plumbing to replace, no more painting of outside walls to preserve them from splitting and warping and going to pieces. No more termites, threatening to eat the floors from under our feet; no more chasing vandals away, and putting up fences to keep bores and red deans from wasting the time of two hard-working people; no more private telephone numbers for Communists to steal by various devices—making it necessary for you to keep your phone turned off so that not even your friends, or the telegraph company, could reach you. We bought a trailer.

Of course Neil's trailer was a Vanderbilt—that is, it was custom-built, the finest and most expensive ever made. We had trouble in finding any kind of trailer, for there was a severe housing shortage at that time, also a shortage of mechanics and materials. The few trailers made were spoken for in advance. We wanted one of aluminum, which would be fireproof, and that was the hardest to find.

But we persuaded a dealer to let us have his sample of a small trailer—if we would not haggle over the price and could pay cash. We were able to do that, for we were going to sell all we had of "things," and be footloose. We rushed the deal through, and tried to persuade the dealer to hitch it up to our car then and there—we were afraid to leave it over night on his lot. We talked so fast about the reasons for our haste that he had no chance to explain why he was holding back. Finally he got it across to us that we had no "ball" on the back of our car to hitch it to. We left it in his care with the promise that he would shut up shop at once and go get us the license we had to have before we would be allowed to haul it around on streets and highways.

We went to a welder, who was so busy he could not promise to put the necessary knob on the back of our car for several days. But with some sort of magic which Upton had developed over the years for getting the impossible done, the welder agreed to stay overtime and do the job on our badly worn old car.

We had made up our minds now—at all costs, we were going to get rid of "things"! I wanted to get rid of even the "thing" called a body, with its endless demands, its pains, its temptations. But I saw no hope of doing it yet, without losing also the consciousness which I called "reality." Bernard Shaw's *Back to Methuselah* suggested an alternative: to achieve perfect mental control over the body. Once we do this, he implied, we will know how to keep our minds, and shed our bodies as a crab sheds its shell, or a snake its skin. But is that what we really want? To be aware of the loved one's presence might not require a body; but would we not miss the touch of a hand, the look in the eyes of a dear one, telling us we were loved?

And so the search for understanding, that is, for God, was the only true goal of mankind. To this our efforts should be devoted. But our bodies and their needs were still with us, and so our concern now was to put an end to at least some of these so-called needs. A velvety green lawn was a beautiful sight, but what a sight it made of my husband when he was pushing a lawnmower over it on a hot summer day, while he longed to be doing almost anything else! We would live on a small piece of asphalt-covered ground in a trailer camp, from which we could depart on a moment's notice to some other town where we might find a more desirable restaurant or a better climate. And above all other blessings, we could get away from the smog!

As usual, Upton was as delighted as a child with his new toy. He wanted to put his typewriter and a couple of camp chairs into the car trunk, and set out at once for Lake Elsinore, a beauty spot we had passed a couple of years before. The lake was like a bowl of sapphires under a turquoise sky, and its shores were not overrun by noisy mobs of pleasure seekers. It was eighty miles from the Los Angeles area, and surely there would be clean air for us to breathe.

Upton's delight in his home on wheels was marred at the outset by his inability to disentangle it from the guava hedge in our garden. He backed the trailer into it, very much against his own wishes, and the perverse thing insisted on going where it shouldn't. We persuaded our garageman to leave his shop and come up to save our hedge from further ravages.

On the way to Elsinore, our new aluminum home heated up like a furnace. It was fireproof, but not heatproof; on the contrary, it was a perfect solarium. We stopped in Riverside for gas, and some books we wanted from the public library. Then we got lost trying to find the road to Elsinore. We found something else, however, which fascinated Upton. It was a barren country of rolling hills, on which large flocks of sheep were herded.

"I'll have a novel started, if we don't get out of here," my husband declared. "It is just like Palestine, I'm sure."

We watched the shepherding of the flock by the trained dogs, and marveled at the intelligence which had been bred into these speechless creatures. Had they been taught, or had they taught themselves through love for their masters? It was a question we had often discussed. What was instinct? Just a word men had adopted to explain something they could not explain! Was it "God in us," in all His creatures? Now we saw that the shepherd, a Basque instead of a Hebrew, was moving his flock. The dogs were helping, and it was such a charming sight that we left the highway and found ourselves on a dusty bumpy side-road. Soon we had to stop, for the road stopped. Ahead and on all sides were rolling fields of barley stubble, plentifully scattered with large and small boulders.

Upton gazed thoughtfully at the landscape, then got out to stroll around—for he always walked when he was thinking profoundly. Was he writing a chapter about sheep, and Palestine, that land of torment and the cradle of Christianity as well as of the Hebrew people? Was he thinking of the carpenter of Nazareth who said, "Feed my sheep"? Perhaps he was planning

a book about the wolves who always lie in wait for the gentle
and kindly of this world.

I, too, was aware of the charm of this lonely wasteland, which
seemed inhabited only by rabbits. Suddenly I remembered that
this was exactly the kind of place "where the rattlesnakes play."
"Get back in this car!" I called. "There may be rattlesnakes
out there!"

"Damn the rattlesnakes!" was the reply. "We are stuck here.
I can't back this trailer all the way out to the highway, and I
can't turn around on account of the boulders!"

Of course the only thing we could do was to detach the trailer
and maneuver the car so that we could drive in search of help.
I was afraid of the Basque, who suddenly looked like a villain
in a melodrama. We found a couple of men repairing a telephone pole who helped us out of our trouble. After three or
four such misadventures, I decided that i preferred a stationary
home after all.

One of the telephone linemen who helped us to get out
of the rocky sheep range had called our trailer "a pesky thing."
He assured us there was no smog up in these hills, and told
us of a group of cottages not far away. One of them was for sale,
and we had a look at it. So it came about that we bought a small
hollow-tile cottage in the rolling hills far above Riverside, and
a few pieces of shabby furniture from a second-hand store
which agreed to deliver them. No furniture vans were obtain-
able, for the war shortages continued, and everything in America seemed to have started moving.

Then a real estate boom started nearby in a most unexpected
fashion. There was a shortage of homes, due to the long period
of building inactivity during the war, and the need of homes
for returning veterans. The Army began to sell the barracks
from a nearby Army camp, and these shoddy buildings were
sawed into sections and sold at very low prices to be moved
and converted into residences. A tract of land adjoining our
property was being cut into lots for this project.

After a few months, another thing came up to spoil our hideaway. My heart began to behave strangely. I wondered if the

altitude we now lived in was not too great. We came and went
to Monrovia about once a week, as Upton's secretary still
attended to his mail and did his typing there. I decided to stay
there for a week or two and see if the unpleasant symptoms
would disappear. In a couple of weeks I felt normal again.

When Upton's elderly secretary became incapable of handling his affairs, we both had memories of those conscientious
people, the Seventh Day Adventists, whom we had met at the
Battle Creek Sanitarium long ago. I suggested that we make in-
quiries for a secretary at their college in La Sierra. That was
a small place, and we paid a visit to it. Nobody there knew
us or cared anything about us, and there appeared to be no
smog. We came upon a quiet little cottage, and also an excellent
stenographer, so we decided to go into hiding once more.

Here Upton was meeting a new sort of people. Put him anywhere, and right away he begins to watch and listen—or I do,
and tell him about them—and presently a story begins taking
shape in his mind. Here we met people who were as poor as
the proverbial church mice, sober, hard-working, devout; some
of them brought him their tracts—just as he himself in his early
days had passed around Socialist "literature" to the people on
the farms near Princeton. Our laundry was done by a lean,
tired woman who lived in a shack that seemed to be made of
tar paper held on with old scraps of boxes. Yet not for all the
wealth of Wall Street would she have been persuaded to iron
one of Upton's shirts between sundown on Friday and sundown
on Saturday. "The seventh day is the Sabbath of the Lord thy
God: in it thou shalt not do any work, thou, nor thy son, nor
thy daughter, thy manservant, nor thy maidservant, nor thy
cattle, nor thy stranger that is within thy gates."

Upton's imagination worked all seven days of the week, and
in the nights also. Presently it was working on this rigidly upright washerwoman, prototype of the pioneer mothers who had
crossed the continent in covered wagons. She had a daughter—
one of the blooming girls we saw at the college. What fun to
hire this girl out to one of those multimillionaire ladies we had
come to know so well during our years in Pasadena! This great
lady would have a son, one of those gilded youths we had known

who brought their movie mistresses to their mother's house; and when this youth met the daughter of the Seventh Day Adventist—what would happen?

Upton knew he had a story there; and his memory leaped back to his early days, when he had read the first great English novel. It was the same story—a tried and true theme—and Upton knew that he had a title, also. *Another Pamela!* It was written quickly, and published quickly, and went into many lands, as all his books did. It pleased even me, his most severe critic. But nothing would satisfy him but another Lanny Budd. He had lived with Lanny so long that Lanny was a real person to him, and he was lonely when Lanny was not around.

Before our marriage, Upton had quoted to me a ballad of Sir Walter Scott:

> Maiden! a nameless life I lead,
> A nameless death I'll die;
> The fiend whose lantern lights the mead
> Were better mate than I.

I had smiled at his frankness, and also at his awesome and romantic imaginations about himself. He knew quite well that I was aware of his life purpose and sympathized with it. What I was not aware of, alas, was how long it would take to accomplish such a purpose. I had shared to some extent his childlike faith in human nature, and his ignorance of how many kinds of human nature there were. Both of us had thought that the average person was fundamentally good, and would act accordingly when shown the right way—which, of course, was *our* way! Neither of us knew of the innate egotism of all human beings, or of the power this characteristic had to move for good or for evil, depending on circumstances or on whim. It was the hunger for power, that all-corrupting growth. It motivated dictators, and it drove silly women to use their power over men for purposes of self-glorification and for parasitism.

These were only some of the impediments in the way of changes Upton wanted in the social status quo. He wanted poverty abolished tomorrow, and with it all injustice in the affairs of men. He wanted war made an impossibility by the ending of poverty, and by international organization; this was the passionate purpose of his always young heart, and I shared it.

Now, as he approached that milestone, "three-score and ten," he knew he had been utopian in his dream, even childish, he sometimes said. But I knew he didn't really believe this latter, any more than I did, for though I had often cried out in protest against the speed with which he moved to his goals, I knew that he had spread sound knowledge of social evils far and wide across the world. He had helped to spread the ideal of democracy, which meant in essence "the brotherhood of man."

And now science was inventing such deadly weapons that brotherhood was a necessity!

While the cold war was changing many things, political, military and social, the swift advances of science were increasing the tempo. The average person seemed to take it all as a matter of course—everything, even the marvelous new appliances and gadgets which made life so much easier for the housewife. Almost everyone had a new house, a good car, new furniture and brighter-colored clothes for both adults and children. There were new homes for every size pocketbook, new cars, new playgrounds, swimming pools, baseball diamonds, football and basketball fields, and new schoolhouses that resembled luxury hostelries—all designed to keep the youngsters healthy, happy and out of the way of their parents.

David came on a vacation from his physics job. We had thought of him as being young, and couldn't realize that he was in his mid-fifties. He was happy with a lovely second wife. He belonged to the new world, which needed physicists badly. He published papers in scientific journals and sent them to his father, and the father was glad if he could understand the first two or three sentences. What is an aerosol? Do you know, without a dictionary?

"What is smog?" I asked David, and he smiled and shrugged.

"All right," I said, "I'll tell *you!* It is fifty per cent poison and sixty per cent politics."

David smiled and said, "Very good mathematics!"

The people were so busy obeying the glamorous appeals of advertisers, that they had no time to ask what was happening to the world. They paid the politicians to attend to that, they said. Besides, what could they do about atom bombs, to say nothing about H-bombs and jets, and trips to the moon, and spaceships in the vast unknown above the earth? This was their excuse.

The mansions of the rich were being abandoned, for there was the increasing servant problem; who wanted to be a menial when there were factories to give them jobs with higher pay, and the advantages of daily companionship with other workers? More and more people began to "take off" in airplanes for Europe, Hawaii, islands in the Caribbean, where new luxury-hotels, cabarets, restaurants and night clubs with highly-paid entertainers were springing up overnight. The middle and working classes had merged so completely that it was difficult to distinguish between them.

The world was changing fast and Upton watched it, fascinated. I was more concerned with what was happening to us, for we were changing, too; suddenly we were old! And I was finding out that old age was certainly something to escape from —if you could. Medical science was now trying to discover if it was a necessary disease; they had a name for the new branch of knowledge, gerontology. Looking at the affliction from a religious point of view, I kept asking, was it God's will? I could not believe it was. I remembered the words of the apostle Paul: "The last enemy to be destroyed is death."

Old age was never expected; it was never even realized until enfeeblement of the body became painful in one way or another. Those few of our old friends who were left on earth shared my feeling that it was not a pleasant matter. When I had mentioned that Upton and I were old now, the spontaneous comment of several had been: "I am, too, and I don't like it! I try not to think of it."

But whenever I mentioned it to the man at my side—whose hair was thin and silvery white, and whose body, once so straight and swift in his perpetual haste, was now bent—he would smile the same youthful smile and answer, "Darling, we have spent our lives trying to relieve some of the suffering of the world; and we have not failed entirely. We have lived long enough to see an era of marvelous discoveries. It is one of those leaps of evolution by which man has progressed through millions of years. In a few years we may see the cure for all our diseases." I was tempted to say, "In a few years it may be too late." For this earth which had been our home for so long was being deserted, just as were the homes of the rich!

"Do you realize, Upton," I asked one day, "that nearly all our old friends are dead? The world is populated by a new generation, by two new generations—the children of our friends and the grandchildren. I'm lonely!"

"We have new friends," was Upton's cheerful reply.

Of the old ones, Max Eastman and Eliena were at Pacific Palisades. Max was now a roving *Reader's Digest* editor. He was my age, but felt much younger than I and declared that he was as much in love with life as ever. "The world picture looks ominous," he said, "but not hopeless. Yes, I want to stay, no matter what happens." And Upton agreed.

Love of life is a deep-rooted thing in the human consciousness. Surely we are meant to stay, and perhaps the time will come when men will develop the power to do so if they wish. This was Shaw's theme in *Back to Methuselah,* which is, in my opinion, his masterpiece. But Shaw himself had not wanted to stay and said so. I wondered if I would ever be willing to go. I didn't want to leave Upton here without me! I knew he needed me and yet I didn't want him to go first. I couldn't stay without him.

There had been so many defeats, disappointments, and personal sorrows; so many times of almost unbearable frustation and worry. I would ask myself why Upton seldom reacted as I so often did, with grief, anger, or despair. Was he heartless in the presence of personal grief? Was his failure to brood over disappointments—or, to phrase it differently, his continuing hope—due to egotism? Did he never ask himself if he mightn't be on the wrong track?

His answer was, "Grief in any form is destructive. Hope is creative. I do not want to destroy or be destroyed. I want to *use*

the life the Creator has given me. I think He means for me to
use it. As for the 'wrong track,' I use the best judgment I have.
Human beings are endowed with consciences, and I think the
Creator speaks through them. We have only to listen."

World War II was over, but "Preparedness for defense"
was going on at the rate of thirty-five billions of dollars a year.
There were more and more industrial plants, there was more
and more gray smog. We were forced to the decision that beautiful Southern California was no longer a desirable residential
area. It was for the great god Industry, who cared nothing for
people.

We studied our maps, and read about climate in the different states—for the next move was going to be the last, we assured
ourselves. There were hurricanes in some states, mosquitoes in
some, ice and snow, or humid heat, in others. The ideal place
seemed to be right next door, over the high Sierras in Arizona.
That state had every kind of climate and there was no real-
estate boom anywhere then, and very little big industry to make
"prosperity." In the Salt River Valley I would have no altitude
to trouble my ailing heart, and no harsh winter cold. It was the
land of permanent sunshine, and by now it was possible to get
a "desert cooler" to temper the heat.

We traveled there in our car on a summer day, and nearly
perished of 118-degree heat in the rich Imperial Valley of California, as well as the Salt River Valley beyond Yuma. But we
saw sturdy and cheerful ranchers and their families who lived
in that dry heat, and they assured us we would soon get used
to it. Besides, we could do our work indoors. But there was still
a shortage of houses, and it was two years before we came upon
a couple of small concrete-block cottages in the little town of
Buckeye, 30 miles from Phoenix. We moved.

Upton still believed in most of the things he had accepted as facts early in life. He was sure that ignorance was the
source of more human misery than any other one thing. The
evil qualities—selfishness, greed, vanity, cruelty—would disappear when men knew the better things of life. He wanted to

persuade them that neither poverty nor war was necessary, that through knowledge the human creature could advance to higher planes of happiness and kindness.

I loved Upton for this optimism—this love of life, this ability to see beauty wherever we were, whatever the circumstances.

"You really like it here?" I asked him.

"Oh, my!" he exclaimed. "I think it is marvelous. Just look at those white clouds overhead." He was aging, but still lively; just before we left Monrovia he had sawed large limbs from old apricot trees and cut them up to be burned. He pushed wheelbarrow-loads of earth from one part of the grounds to another and seemed to enjoy it and lifted any piece of furniture I wanted moved. We settled down happily to enjoy our blessings.

Then one night I couldn't get my breath. I had worked very hard packing before we left California and worked overtime after we arrived in Arizona, trying to fit our things into too small a space. I hadn't felt ill, although I had consumed many cups of coffee to give me the necessary energy. Upton had worked steadily at heavier tasks and needed rest, so I sat miserably on the side of the bed, hoping for the passing of this strange inability to breathe whenever I lay down.

But it didn't pass, and after a time I became exhausted. I cried out to Upton—it was a terrifying thing to be suffocating, unable to get a breath of air. Upton thought I was dying, and I thought so, too. He went down on his knees beside me and began to pray aloud. "Oh, God, make her well! Dear God, make her well!"

He continued this prayer most of the night, and as I listened I prayed God to let me stay on earth with him.

When the doctor in Phoenix told me I could leave the hospital, he warned that I could never again take prolonged exercise. "Take it easy," was his command. So, from this most recent of our experiences, Upton has learned to be an excellent lady's maid, and I have learned how to enslave a husband. As a wicked woman friend said to me half a century ago, "Just be helpless!"

But Upton chose his own enslavement. Since the hour of that "congestive heart attack" when I came so near to leaving him forever, he has refused to leave my side for more than an hour at a time.

Upton had written *The Wet Parade,* his contribution to the crusade against the demon rum. But the poison had continued to flow more and more freely. Without the restraint of Prohibition, the youth of the world was drowning itself in alcohol. Teen-age boys and girls now carried it in their cars, in hip-pocket flasks, in beauty-kits. They went off together in groups to mountains or beaches to indulge in orgies of drunkenness and sexuality. The highways were turning into slaughterhouses, with tipsy drivers destroying not only themselves, but the innocent who dared to travel.

Upton's mind ran true to form. He must write another book against the poisonous "John Barleycorn." Sobriety was essential in the era of the H-bomb. This time it would not be fiction, like *The Wet Parade.* He said, "I think that a book telling the sufferings of the victims I have personally known will make the tragedy of alcoholism real to the reader. Only the alcoholic knows the agony which comes to him. Some of them are brave enough to tell the world about it, hoping to save others from falling into this pit. Some, like Bill Seabrook, had themselves committed to asylums. Jack London told me he voted for Prohibition; but soon after that, John Barleycorn drove him to suicide."

"One more crusade!" I said. "This one will not be pleasant, I assure you, my dear Upton."

He gave me figures on the increase in the consumption of alcohol—more per capita than ever before in our history. The Yale University studies of drinking in college showed 74 per cent of college students drank alcoholic beverages. I said, "Edison said he never gave advice to youth, because youth never took advice."

Upton answered, "When I was a youth, I took the advice of a clergyman friend, and I thank God for it."

The Cup of Fury was declined by a dozen New York publishers; one and all agreed that the public would not take it. Upton had the happy thought to send a copy to Dr. Daniel Poling, editor of the *Christian Century,* who accepted it and turned it over to the Channel Press. In the first year it sold 70,000 copies. I am most grateful to these publishers for permission to quote freely from this book.

The day he was seventy years old we were in Monrovia. Upton asked, meekly, "Have I made you too unhappy?"

I looked out the window of this lovely home and saw the fig trees bearing the ripening fruit he never grew tired of. I answered, "I'm not sure. I'll have to think it over."

"You always have to think things over!" he protested.

"And you are always in a hurry," I said.

And this is what Count Keyserling meant when he came to America and told us: "Marriage is tension."

"But tell me," Upton insisted, "have I made you too unhappy?"

"No," I answered, "but you have kept me too busy. You are in too great a hurry. I have never found time for my own crusade."

"For psychic research, you mean?"

"We have proved telepathy, but we have never gone as far as I want to in finding out what can be done with hypnotism."

I often felt that Upton's absorption in ending the evils of poverty was a mistake, because his mind, one of the best, might better have been devoted to a study of the stuff of which it and all other minds are made. All these so-called intellectuals who had peopled our lives, including physicists as well as poets and novelists—if they had combined their efforts toward the end of making discoveries in regard to the source of the intellect which they were using but ignoring, they might by now have found a gift for the world's welfare more spectacular and useful than atomic fission. "Seek first the kingdom of heaven," and surely it is the mind in which to find it.

One day a most cordial letter from Dr. Carl Jung favored us with several pages of analysis of Upton's book, *A Personal Jesus*. We turned our day into a discussion of Dr. Jung's writings. I had pored over them diligently with more or less understanding, and to me the highlight of his letter was the sentence "I have such a devilish time getting people to understand what I write."

That of course is true of every written or spoken effort of any learned person to make his ideas clear to a semi-ignorant audience. And the general ignorance of the mind and its profound mysteries had been astonishing me ever since I had first begun a study of the subject. I had never forgotten McDougall's saying, "The mind does not like to think about itself." I had found this to be correct of most of the people I knew. Too many of our friends were dogmatically materialistic. I remembered telling a woman writer of a demonstration of levitation which we had once witnessed in our own home, where we had complete control of the medium, the house, the table which was levitated, and where all the participants were our personal friends, highly literate and earnest. This writer had inquired, "But what in the world is the use of proving that a material object can be lifted by mind force, when all you have to do is to pick the table up and move it with muscle force?" No wonder Dr. Jung had "a devilish time" trying to explain to materialistic man the mythologies which hide in the dim, deep caverns of the unconscious.

One of our blessings was that we could look back over the years and tell ourselves we had not lived uselessly. We had not merely tried to alleviate the world's troubles, we had sometimes succeeded.

There had always been, among the Socialists, those who called themselves Fabians. "The inevitability of gradualism" was one of their formulas, and we believed in gradualism as necessary for education. Neither of us had ever been Marxists, and I had not even read Marx. In 1933 we had borrowed a plank from old Fabian platforms and inserted it into the platform of the Democratic Party of California. This plank was old-age pensions; and even the Marxists should have rejoiced to hear Upton and his running mate, Sheridan Downey, demanding 50 dollars per month for old people in their campaign speeches up and down the length of the state. They should have rejoiced later when EPIC-elected legislators helped to put this program into law. It was a minimum old-age security, but it was the best that could be got at that time.

During that campaign the idea had become sufficiently popular to stir the Republican politicians who saw the crowds of old people holding meetings of their own and rallying to the EPIC banner. So they took up the plan of a Republican, Dr. Townsend, who promised much more. Thus "Socialism" crept into the Republican Party. I wonder if the Republicans know that the old-age security they have given to more and more groups took its first creeping steps out in California under the EPIC banner?

Such was one of the achievements we could look back upon in our sunset years. Someone has said that "The business of people with ideas is to have them stolen," and we can thankfully say that in this business we have succeeded.

But, as my old Greenwich Village friends would have said, what about Art? During World War I Sherwood Anderson wrote to Upton, "There is something terrible to me in the thought of the art of writing being bent and twisted to serve the end of propaganda." And he asked, "As writers, can't we leave politics and economics to the more lusty-throated ones and run away, one by one, into the streets, the offices and the houses, looking at things, trying to write them down?" But Upton never ran away, and of his kind of art Albert Einstein wrote: "I am convinced that you are doing very valuable and important work in giving to the American public an insight into the psychological and economical background of the tragedy evolving in our generation. Only a real artist can accomplish this."

The Art vs. Propaganda objection was most elegantly put by Van Wyck Brooks: "You use fiction for ulterior purposes and that is the cause of the great quarrel between you and the critics." But Mr. Brooks was kind enough to add, "You are obviously something on a large scale that literature has to include, though you don't fit into any of the usual categories." And when a note announced Mr. Brooks' arrival in California, Upton said, "I like him so much better than he likes me that I'm going to spend an evening converting him."

Mr. Brooks and his wife came before dark and Upton, by way of "converting," showed them his collection of foreign editions and original manuscripts. They were among the last to inspect these literary treasures before everything was packed up—eight tons of papers—and transported to a permanent home, in the library of Indiana University.

From an upstairs window I saw in the patio a man who looked as if he had just stepped out from an old painting and might at any moment go back into the frame on a wall, for he belonged to a more gracious era than that of the muckrakers; and surely Upton would never have been able to persuade him to come down into the streets with the mob and "soil his wings."

But both men were truly great in understanding that all was not well in the world in which they had lived as contemporaries. Mr. Brooks, who seemed in both his writing and his social presence wholly without bitterness of any sort, certainly did not approve of the sordid things which had stirred Upton's indignant protest. He had done his writing in a gentle and tolerant manner; Upton had written with the flaming pen of a crusader. And maybe this was for the best; each of them had been sufficiently successful in his own field.

In our living room I watched them, while Gladys and I exchanged the confidences usual between the wives of authors. I saw that they liked each other; and when the next book of the gentle critic came, it was autographed, "With affection."

In the art of crusading there must be failures; as Shaw said, even Jesus had failed, meaning that a whole Christianity had never been tried. But there are always gains, as Shaw at 93 wrote Upton, "We are in the same boat on the same tack. What we have to say has been said again and again for at least 8,000 years, apparently without producing the slightest effect; still, there are little groups of Shavians and Sinclairites everywhere, whose influence, though imperceptible, counts for something."

Upton's invincible optimism has never taken account of temporary failures. But when once in some verses he mentioned a search for hope in the universe, I exclaimed, "Uppie dearest, you have not failed, even slightly. Before I leave this planet I want to testify to what I know: by your lifelong effort you have changed the nature of human relations; you have made history in the realm of human brotherhood! Remember what

John D. Rockefeller, Jr. said about the Colorado coal strike: it had brought him 'a conception of the kinship of humanity.' That is what your books have done for millions of people all over the world."

But I reminded him of what our doctor had said when I had jokingly asked him how the world could get along without Upton. "You should be wondering," the doctor replied, "how heaven could get along *with* him."

S O N N E T S

By Mary Craig Sinclair

MIDNIGHT: 1917

I drink my blood in secret grief, I weep,
  I cry for truce, I dare not think for long
  Of that which has befallen men. The wrong
Is too immense. I babble in my sleep
  Of it. I try to think, to understand,
And am engulfed in wild bewilderment,
And every frenzied thought is impotent
  Against the awful thought of No-Man's Land!

And yet I do not die. I eat and drink,
  I walk the earth, I wear a gown, I see
A rose; it is the same old world, I think.
  But oh, it was not known before to me
How Love and Pity vanish as a breath
When Hate has loosed its hounds of Hell and Death!

PEACE: 1919

The jonquils bloom again upon the hill
  And call me through the window-pane, "Come out!
  Rest you! The Beast of war has fled in rout,
And there is sunshine on the valley still.
  Long you had thought the sun itself was dead,
Or quenched in human blood and could not shine.
But Peace has come! The yellow jasmine vine
  Is blooming, too, and noon is overhead!"

But they will never rest, the frenzied men!
  The worlds are toppling here, and crashing there,
And calls to arms, to arms, resound again!
  The maddened peoples grapple everywhere,
To snatch what they have dreamed, or lost, or won—
And tears are gathering to drown the Sun.

UPON THE WINDS OF SPRING: 1919

I feel the terror in the world tonight—
  Unbridled lust of power, and bridled lust
More cold but no less merciless. The dust
Of perished legions drifts upon the bright
  And tender winds of spring, a seal, blood-red,
Upon man's last insanity. Surcease
Of war? Ah, so they thought! To purchase peace
  For aye, with their young blood! Ah, so they said!

But peace is not upon the winds of spring.
  The nostrils of new wars flare wide, and sniff
The dust of heroes greedily, and fling
  An evil breath upon the world—and if
I chance to laugh because the spring is here,
Pain stabs my heart and binds the wound with fear!

WAR FOR DEMOCRACY

You did not mention patience yesterday,
  But called for men of might to fling the Hun
Into Eternity! The deed was done—
But not till men had learned to hate and slay.
  No sweet and patient word had power to move
The Hun to reason, who knew naught but Might.
No sacred thing had meaning in his sight—
  And so, death to him! Waste no breath on love!

But now, you masters, hard and blind as those
  Whom you called Huns, are full of harsh surprise
That we who call you Huns should dare propose
  A war of your own kind. Well, we advise
No further patience with a heedless foe—
Get off our backs, or else to Hell you go!

LAUGHTER

The Autumn sun is shining, round and gay,
  Above my garden, and I hear the low
  Sweet laughter of the flowering things. "Yo ho!"
They cry. "The world is beautiful today!"
  Rose-hedges circle all the smiling space
Of suave, green lawns, and gaudy flower-beds.
"The world is beautiful" . . . They toss their heads,
  And fling their perfumed beauty in my face.

But there are people at my garden gate
  Upon whose foreheads are the jagged fears
Which have companioned them; and sullen hate
  Plays on their lips, and smoulders where the tears
Long since have drowned the laughter in their eyes.
"Yo ho!" they say. "Your laughing garden lies!"

DAILY BREAD

I match my will to live against the will
  Of the entire community of men—
  For every man conspires against me when
He must compete with me for bread. The swill
  Is none the cleaner for its shallow crust
Of evolution's pastry, nor can be
Until the mind of every man is free.
  Who trusts his loaf to swine shall feed on dust.

Cannot the bread be set apart from shame—
  A sacred, true communion beyond trade?
Toss all the other things into the game—
  Compete for fame, for love, for gems, for jade—
But leave each man enough of bread to live,
So that at last his soul may dare to give!

TO A RICH YOUNG MAN

You wear a silken undervest and hose
  And all your garments are immaculate.
  No care disturbs your leisurely estate
When you are cushion d softly for repose
  In a fair chamber kept by her deft hand,
Which, you assume, God made to cleanse your room—
The hand of servitude, of mop and broom,
  Of consecration to a boy's demand!

You have no purpose but to find some way
To entertain an idle mind all day
  At golf or with the decorated few.
  And yet, you are a man, to outward view!
A man—while women labor everywhere,
And you do naught for life but blink and stare!

YOUTH

The baby's fancy leaps to clasp the flame;
  Negation has no meaning to Desire,
  But questing hands must touch the searing fire
To comprehend the meaning of a name.
  The morning lays its freshness in a smile,
And open covenants are in a face
Which knows not pain, but only that strange grace
  Of ignorance, called babyhood, a while.

Is there no memory from vanished minds?
  Must every hand clasp fire to know its sting?
Oh, harsh and pitiless the law that binds
  To instinct, seeking self, that stubborn thing
Called man, who must begin anew at birth
With every infant born upon the earth!

INVOCATION

Oh great mechanic with a steady hand
   Upon the wheel, with brain and nerve alert,
   Of knowledge sure, stand by! Oh thou expert
In Clarity and Truth, yours to command
   That Reason shall make harmony of strife.
Man's soul, aspiring to high heaven's lap
Is heavy with the ancient handicap
   Of Nature vomiting chaotic life.

For she remains a wanton in her age,
   Hard-driven by a vast fecundity,
As heedless of a whole world's heritage
   As who may sire a countless progeny.
Oh, spirit who once met and loved this whore,
Stand by the mongrel whelp the union bore!

CALIFORNIA

Like honey flowing from a golden jar
   The days of Autumn pour upon the hills
   Whose peaks are purple while the sunlight fills
The vistas where the valley winds afar.
   I share the drunken lethargy of bees
When they have sucked their fill of flower-lips,
For I am drunken, too, and Duty slips
   A wanton way from me upon the breeze.

Oh, there are white wild-roses on the ledge
   Above the trail that leads to a dim crest;
   And gleaming on the trout-stream's bouldered edge
   Are violets, within a green fern nest.
Beat it, Duty! I am done with you—
That is, for just a shining hour or two!

CIRCE

With all my woman's charms I set the snare,
   And then, lest these should fail, I searched you through
   For whims and cherished dreams to pander to.
I followed you at work, at play—oh, there
   Was naught of you too small for my design!
   For well I knew, if I would make you mine,
That I must draw the image fair and whole
And flattering—the image of your soul!

Into myself I subtly wove each part,
   Component of your being, and as well
      Those things which you in dreams had thought to be.
Oh, rose and sesame of Circe's art!
   Then was it strange that when in love you fell
      With that reflected self, you worshipped me?

SISTERHOOD

Last night I woke, and in my tranquil bed
   I lay, and thanked my God with fervent prayer
   That I had food and warmth, a cosy chair
Beside a jolly fire, and roses red
   To give my room a touch of light and grace.
   And I thanked God, oh thanked Him! that my face
Was beautiful, that it was fair to men.
I thought awhile, then thanked my God again.

For yesterday, on Broadway I had walked.
   And I had stopped to watch them as they stalked
Their prey; and I was glad I had no sons
To look with me upon those woeful ones—
   Paint on their lips, and from a corpse their hair,
   And eyes of simulated lust, astare.

BEAUTY

How can you smile when pain is everywhere;
  How flaunt complacently your vulgar wealth?
  "It is my duty to be gay. My health
And calm delight the eye and banish care—
  It would be sad indeed if none were free
To sanction Beauty and embody Joy.
Enough of you, who would with gloom destroy
  My grace. I do my share of Charity!"

Your share of charity! Who tipped the scales
  To Sophistry and weighed a fancy gown
Against a street rat's need of bread? The nails
  Of Calvary, the cross, the thorned crown,
The face of sorrow that He wore, reply:
"Forgive them, God, they know not when they lie!"

TO KATE CRANE GARTZ

"Have mercy, God, upon the poor to-night!"
  And shuddering, she drew the blind and crept
  To where her softly nestled babies slept.
"Thank God that mine are safe!" She laid the bright
And down-filled covers close. The youngest sighed,
  His cosy dream disturbed. She soothed with touch
  And murmurings: "The wind is ice! How much
The poor are suffering! Some must have died!"

With pity that is swift and short they pray—
  And leave the poor to God. In selfish peace,
Oh, hear the mothers of the sheltered say:
  "What can we do?" But you! Maternal ease
Has not sufficed for you! Oh, wide and free
Your pity flows, a world-maternity!

CHALLENGE: 1914

The bugles call and flame-lipped cannon roar,
  And England's hosts are marching in the dawn—
A nation's beardless youth, and dotards hoar,
With hearts athirst, like England's heart, for gore!
Oh, heart of England, rotting to the core!—
    That offers up your sons for sordid Gain!
  Oh, beardless youth and dotards, hapless spawn
    Of England's lust for Power and wide Domain!

Now mighty Germans tramp your foggy isle
  To set it straight, its squalor, pride and vice;
And German ways, methodical and nice,
    Make order in your filthy styes! Forsooth,
  A people given up to Sloth and Guile,
    Arise through Germany to Light and Truth!

WAR

The sharpened steel whips round, the black guns blaze.
  Waste are the harvests, mute the songs of birds.
  Out there in ice and mud the lowly herds
Of peasant-folk in pitiful amaze
Take their dire portion of the grief and want
  Of this red cataclysm that has come
  Upon the world. Colossal is the sum
Of bodies in that field the buzzards haunt.

So, all forgot is Reason's high estate!
  Where Man once climbed and visioned Love and God
He grovels now in primal Night. Aye, men
Of mind are but as mindless brutes again:
  The clod, through evolution, to the clod
Has traveled back—to feed, to breed, to hate!

BAL MASQUE: 1915

The sabres sing, the deep-bass guns resound,
And Death is host, and Flesh is meeting-ground
    For shot and shell and bayonet and sword.
A horde of allied men, a German horde,
With salutations loud, join in the rout;
The Serbs engage the Austrians in a bout;
    The Prussians with the Russians dance a "glide";
    And black-skinned men, with nostrils flat and wide,
Dance "grizzly bear," or maybe "Hottentot."
The French and English waltz, the Turkeys "trot";
The scouting Birdmen do a minuet
    Among the Angels guarding heaven's dome.
"Salute your partners! Give the bayonet!"
    Till up from Hell a Voice commands: *"Come home!"*

THE GODS THAT REIGN: 1916

The battle-music streams across the plain,
    And you are marching blithely to the call!
    Oh flame of ruddy life, oh soul in thrall
To Patriotism's Lie! The gods that reign
    Are Greed, and Vanity, and savage Hate,
That care not for the cost in human pain,
    But send you forth in circumstance and state,
A-junketing with Death to martial strain!

The blood-sick sun has dropped into the West,
And you lie still, a stain upon your breast.
    At peace! . . . Or do you, from some far-off place,
Gaze wistfully to earth, a spirit shamed,
    And seeing that pale mold with upturned face,
Revile the gods your carnal mind acclaimed?

FINIS

Oh, not for me emotion sublimated;
  I like my mutton bloody, raw and red;
Warmed over biscuits have no charms related
  To biscuits in the young impulse of bread!
No poetry for me, but seeing, sounding,
  And touching for myself the thrilling things;
No rehash of the poet's senses bounding
  At second-hand to me on worded wings.
I want the touch, the sight, the sudden feeling
  Of things that live for me to feel them live!
I want no violin, no organ reeling,
  To tell me what the living things will give.
Go poets, artists, music-makers, all ye!
  Go otherwhere to tell what you have felt—
I want red life! Your recitations pall me!
  Avaunt! Begone to Hades! Vanish Melt!!

TO MY DEAR MOTHER

(Who is too busy to follow dreams)

A thousand thoughts of solid things—
A bill to pay, a key to find,
A hat, a coat, some curtain rings . . . .
A thousand things to fill the mind.

And what! Just things; just sticks and stones,
The wingéd mind a pig-skin sack
Of old tin cans, and bricks and bones;
The mind of man—a peddler's pack.

But now and then in dreams it flies,
Scorning nature's "solid" plan.
Now and then in dream-lit skies
It wings its way—the Soul of Man.

Mary Craig Sinclair

INDEX